D0805413

Black Americans in Congress

Black Americans in Congress

Maurine Christopher

REVISED AND EXPANDED EDITION

Thomas Y. Crowell Company   New York
Established 1834

This book was formerly titled
America's Black Congressmen.

Copyright © 1976, 1971 by Maurine Christopher

All rights reserved. Except for use in a review, the reproduction or utiliza-
tion of this work in any form or by any electronic, mechanical, or other
means, now known or hereafter invented, including xerography, photocopy-
ing, and recording, and in any information storage and retrieval system is
forbidden without the written permission of the publisher. Published simultaneously in Canada by Fitzhenry & Whiteside Limited, Toronto.

Designed by Virginia Smith

Manufactured in the United States of America

Library of Congress Cataloging in Publication Data

Christopher, Maurine.
  Black Americans in Congress.

  Published in 1971 under title: America's Black
congressmen.
  Bibliography: p.
  Includes index.
  1. Afro-Americans—Biography. 2. Legislators—United
States—Biography. I. Title.
E185.96.C5   1976   328.73′092′2 [B]   76-8943
ISBN 0-690-01102-4

1 2 3 4 5 6 7 8 9 10

To Milbourne Christopher

Sources and Acknowledgments

Few men in United States history have been more neglected than the blacks who went into government after the Civil War—as soon as they were allowed to compete for public office. A search to find out more about those political pioneers was the genesis of *America's Black Congressmen*.

These sketches are based on government documents, contemporary newspapers and magazines, unpublished materials, researches of students, professors, and earlier authors, and the writing of some of the congressmen themselves.

I am indebted to Ernest Kaiser and the entire staff at the Schomburg Collection of the New York Public Library, where the early black newspaper and magazine files, letters, scrapbooks, diaries, and other memorabilia were invaluable. Gracious assistance came from Dr. Lawrence C. Bryant, South Carolina State College, Orangeburg, an expert on the early legislators of his state; Clarence M. Mitchell, Jr., director of the Washington Bureau, National Association for the Advancement of Colored People, and M. A. Harris, president of Negro History Associates.

The Library of Congress, Washington, provided federal and state records and worthwhile guidance. Robert H. Land, chief of the reference department of the general reference and bibliography division, was particularly helpful. The New York Public Library, where I was assisted by scores of people, was my research headquarters, but the quest for special data took me to several states, to the Caribbean islands, and to Great Britain.

Librarians and archivists who aided me include J. V. Nielsen, Jr., *Charleston News & Courier*, Charleston, South Carolina; Edward W. Chabot, *Raleigh News and Observer*, Raleigh, North Carolina; David Mendenhall, *Chicago Tribune*, Chicago, Illinois; Virginia Brazington, NAACP, New York; Jacqueline K. Haring, Knox College, Galesburg,

Illinois; Mrs. J. E. McDonald, *Macon Telegraph*, Macon, Georgia; Elizabeth Middlebrooks, Washington Memorial Library, Macon, Georgia; E. L. Inabinett, University of South Carolina, Columbia; Mary Skiffington, Bermuda Library, Hamilton, Bermuda; Betty M. Ragsdale, Beaufort County Library, South Carolina; Patrick Strong, Eton College, Windsor, England; Ruth Braun, *Detroit News*, Detroit, Michigan.

Equally cooperative were Charles Martin, *Philadelphia Bulletin*, Pennsylvania; Rochelle Neal, *Philadelphia Tribune*, Philadelphia; Basil Phillips, *Ebony*, Chicago, Illinois; Kimball C. Elkins, Harvard University, Cambridge, Massachusetts; Anita L. Lowe, *Denver Post*, Denver, Colorado; James P. Johnson, Howard University, Washington, D.C.; William Sannwald, *Chicago Sun-Times*, Chicago, Illinois; Lilla M. Hawes, Georgia Historical Society, Savannah, Georgia; Alexia E. Jones, South Carolina Department of Archives and History, Columbia, South Carolina; W. E. Biggleston, Oberlin College, Oberlin, Ohio; Margaret L. Chapman, Florida Historical Society, Tampa, Florida; Milo B. Howard, Jr., Alabama Department of Archives and History, Montgomery, Alabama; C. F. W. Coker, North Carolina Department of Archives and History, Raleigh, North Carolina; Samuel Boone, University of North Carolina Photo Service, Chapel Hill, North Carolina; and Mark Eckhoff, National Archives and Records Service, Washington, D.C.

Thanks are also due to John D. Brooks; John W. Maund, grandson of Jefferson F. Long; Thomas Feagans, great-grandson of Thomas E. Miller; Congressman William Fitts Ryan; Dr. Herbert Aptheker; Dr. E. Merton Coulter; Martin Litvin; Jack Greenberg; L. C. Battle; Paul A. Henningsen; Norma O. Williams; Doraine J. Price; Juanita E. Barbee; Michael C. McPherson; Henry R. Williams; Arthur Kinoy; Haig Ellian; Melinda Smith; William Littman, Jr.; John Apperson; Robert Alcock; Beverly A. King; Mark Stout; Francis Canavan; Robert Johnson; Thomas Offenburger; George A. Dalley; Howard Gleckman; and Nell McDaniel.

My appreciation goes to all the subjects of this book, whose careers should serve as an inspiration for generations to come. Of the contemporaries, I am especially grateful to representatives Ronald V. Dellums, Ralph H. Metcalfe, Yvonne Brathwaite Burke, Cardiss Collins, Augustus F. Hawkins, William L. Clay, Louis Stokes, Charles B. Rangel, and Senator Edward W. Brooke.

Introduction

The political tradition started more than a century ago by the first black congressmen—Senator Hiram R. Revels of Mississippi and Representative Joseph H. Rainey of South Carolina—is being perpetuated by 3,500 black elected officials thoughout America.

Black representation in Congress totals eighteen members, with seventeen from eleven states and the District of Columbia serving in the House of Representatives, and one, Edward W. Brooke of Massachusetts, in the Senate. Although an all-time high, this is proportionately a modest number for the country's largest minority of nearly 23,000,000 citizens.

For generations Negroes were systematically ignored or depreciated in most accounts of American history. Careful research shows that black men, once they were emancipated and allowed to compete, moved into public office promptly, confidently, and enthusiastically. Evidencing an amazing lack of bitterness despite 250 years of forced labor, they began working with white men to heal the wounds of the Civil War. For women, white and black, political participation was still more than half a century off.

Blacks substantially helped to quash the Confederate rebellion—a role with which they are not always credited. Negroes had sailed across the Atlantic with Christopher Columbus "to discover America" and had been making contributions to the nation's agriculture, industry, and culture ever since. They fought in the Revolutionary War for their country's independence from England and in all the conflicts that followed. Their casualty rate in America's most recent war, in Vietnam, was higher than for whites because of their disproportionate representation in the front line infantry units.

After the Civil War ended in 1865, blacks filled prominent positions in the Reconstruction governments of several Southern states and assisted in rewriting state constitutions to provide wider public education, more equitable taxation, and improved judicial systems.

Hiram R. Revels, a Mississippi minister-teacher, broke the color line in the Senate on February 25, 1870, following three days of vituperative debate; within a year the House of Representatives without drama seated Joseph H. Rainey, a former South Carolina slave who had taught himself to read, and Jefferson F. Long, a Georgia tailor. By 1875 there were eight blacks in Congress, and they joined with the white Radical Republicans to grant amnesty to most of the Confederates who had fought against the Union, and to pass an omnibus civil rights bill to ban discrimination in transportation, inns, theaters, and other public amusement places.

The pioneer black congressmen were exceptional individuals by any definition. Many had been born free; the majority had begun life as slaves; several had fought for the Union army or navy; many more would have, had they been allowed to enlist. Nearly half of the twenty-two early congressmen had attended college and five were graduates; others had educated themselves, sometimes at great peril.

Before entering politics they were ministers, teachers, lawyers, barbers, farmers, bricklayers, editors, photographers, labor organizers. Some had white mothers or fathers, and it is likely that most were of mixed ancestry, though tracing their lineage is difficult. One probably was a white man passing as a Negro. All considered themselves Negroes, were so regarded by others—black and white—and made it their business to speak out for the rights of the black community. Several were generations ahead of their time on vital issues, particularly in their support for women's rights and for fair treatment of the original Americans, the Indians.

Had the momentum of the nineteenth-century civil rights movement continued, a truly integrated society might have evolved in the United States. However, the 1875 Civil Rights Law—weakened before enactment by the deletion of a clause opening all schools to all children—was declared unconstitutional by the Supreme Court, while the Fourteenth Amendment to the Constitution, passed to force the states to recognize the citizenship rights of blacks, and the Fifteenth, reconfirming the right of Negro men to vote, were widely flouted.

Radical Republicans lost out to conservative Republicans; the national Republican party deserted its new Southern wing. Democrats, often led by former Confederate officers, regained control of Southern statehouses. Legal stratagems, harassment, and murder were used to turn blacks out of office and prevent them from going to the polls. By 1902, America's black citizens no longer had a vote in the national legislature.

Introduction

Nearly three decades passed before a wave of migration to the North brought about the Negroes' return to Congress. In 1928, Oscar DePriest won election to the House of Representatives from Chicago's First Congressional District. This seat has been filled by blacks ever since, with William L. Dawson holding it from 1943 until his death in 1970. New York's Adam Clayton Powell, Jr., elected in 1944, and Dawson were the first blacks to serve long enough to rise through the congressional seniority system to committee chairmanships that enabled them to shape a substantial amount of legislation. A particularly effective chairman who later was unconstitutionally disciplined by his colleagues, Powell battled his way through the Supreme Court to prove he had been illegally barred from the House in 1967.

While the number of black representatives gradually increased, the sex barrier against black women was shattered by Shirley Chisholm of New York. Six newcomers—the largest freshmen group since Reconstruction—entered the House in 1971. By 1973 the deep South once more was sending blacks to Congress. Soon the whole country would watch television in fascination as Barbara Jordan of Texas presented her arguments in the Presidential impeachment hearings.

This book covers all the blacks who have gone to Congress since the Senate was desegregated in 1870, and one man, P. B. S. Pinchback, who was elected to both houses and should have been seated but wasn't. Profiles are included for forty-one male and four female legislators, all but three of whom served in the House of Representatives.

The purpose is to tell their stories—who they were, how they got to Congress, what they accomplished in public life. The action begins with Sentor-elect Revels, waiting to see if the Senate will admit him.

Contents

xiii

Contents

Illustrations

Illustrations

Hiram R. Revels/Mississippi

Sitting patiently on a sofa in the Senate chamber, a forty-eight-year-old clergyman heard Vice-President Schuyler Colfax announce on February 23, 1870, that the President had just signed a bill readmitting Mississippi to the Union. Outwardly the minister showed no signs of excitement, though any moment now debate would begin on his qualifications to serve in the United States Senate.

For more than three weeks Hiram Rhoades Revels, son of a black Baptist preacher and a Scottish mother, had been in Washington, waiting to present his credentials. The senator-elect had traveled a circuitous route from Fayetteville, North Carolina, where he was born on September 27, 1822, to reach this climactic moment.

Although Revels and his family had always been free, his early years were full of "sorrow and grief" because of the suffering of other enslaved blacks. Free Negroes in North Carolina had been able to vote, discuss politics, attend church, and enjoy some educational advantages until a thirty-year-old slave who heard voices led a revolt in Virginia in August 1831. Before Nat Turner was captured, more than fifty-five whites had been killed in Southampton County.

Fearful the spark of rebellion would spread, North Carolina and other Southern States passed repressive laws to keep slaves more closely under control, and free blacks were summarily deprived of many of their rights. Hiram Revels was then ten.

Revels finished the education available to him in Fayetteville and began teaching the younger children. He was ordained a minister in the African Methodist Episcopal church in Baltimore in 1845, but he had been preaching since his teens. Wanting "something more than a mere business education," he traveled to Indiana—a free state—and enrolled in a Union County Quaker seminary as the only Negro student. Later he attended a black seminary in Darke County, continued his theological studies in Oxford, and married Phoeba Bass of Zanes-

1

ville, Ohio. His last formal education was as a scholarship student at Knox Academy in Galesburg, Illinois, in 1856–57.

Interspliced with his years of study was his work as an educator and pastor in the free states of Indiana, Illinois, Kansas, and Ohio and in the slave states of Kentucky, Tennessee, and Missouri. It was a hazardous life, particularly in those states where schooling for blacks was discouraged or forbidden by law.

"At times, I met with a great deal of opposition," Revels said in the sketchy autobiography he dictated late in life to his eldest daughter. "I was imprisoned in Missouri in 1854 for preaching the gospel to Negroes, though I never was subjected to violence. According to the slave code no free Negroes had even any right to remain in that state because their presence, tended to arouse discontent among the slaves but in large towns and cities, this was seldom enforced.

"I sedulously refrained from doing anything that would incite the slaves to run away from their masters. It being understood that my object was to preach the gospel to them, and improve their moral and spiritual condition, even slaveholders were tolerant toward me. But when in free states I always assisted the fugitive slave to make his escape."

The itinerant preacher returned to Baltimore in the spring of 1858 as copastor, and later pastor, of a downtown church. His brother, Willis, was also a minister in Baltimore. After the Southerners fired on Fort Sumter, South Carolina, on April 12, 1861, and the Civil War began, Revels helped to organize the first two black Maryland regiments for the United States Army. During the four years of fighting he taught school, helped the Freedmen's Bureau set up schools in Mississippi, and assisted the provost marshal in Vicksburg.

With the return of peace in 1865 he went back to church work. The Methodist Episcopal church assigned him to pastorates in Leavenworth, Kansas, and New Orleans before transferring him to Natchez, Mississippi, as a presiding elder. He became a Natchez alderman in 1868.

Mississippi, an almost 60 percent black state, was still under military rule with General Adelbert Ames as provisional governor. Exslaves were moving into politics as members of the Republican party, and they demanded some of the top offices. All black males of the age of twenty-one could vote under the congressional reconstruction plan, while some whites were disqualified because of their wartime activities.

An election was set for the fall of 1869 to select state and federal officers and to ratify the new state constitution. Revels was the compromise candidate, who broke a two-day stalemate, when the Adams

2

County Republicans deadlocked on their nominee for the state senate. His principal backer was John R. Lynch, a Negro party leader.
The Natchez alderman and minister was an easy victor in the election in November winning by a majority of more than fifteen hundred
votes.

Revels was one of forty blacks at the opening of the newly elected,
one-hundred-and-forty–man state legislature in January. The legislature ratified the Fourteenth and Fifteenth Amendments, which reaffirmed the citizenship rights of freedmen and forbade racial discrimination at the polls. The legislature also wiped the black codes off the
state statute books. A top order of business was to fill three vacancies
in the United States Senate—two for unexpired terms left open when
the state seceded, and one for a regular term to start later. James
Lynch, one of the most capable members of the black group, was a
favorite for one of the posts, but he had already been named secretary of state and chose to stay in that position.

The legislature elected Caucasians to the longer Senate terms—the
full term going to former Confederate General James L. Alcorn, a
Whig turned Republican, and the next longest to erstwhile Union
General Adelbert Ames. This left the blacks with the thirteen-month
term. It took three days and seven ballots to come up with a winner.
Revels, again a compromise candidate who did not seek the job, was
nominated between the third and the fourth ballot. On the final tally
on January 20, 1870, Revels won with eighty-one votes against fifteen
for Abel Alderson, his nearest rival. Oddly enough, none of the candidates voted for himself.

Revels later offered his version of the contest: "An opportunity of
electing a Republican to the United States Senate, to fill an unexpired
term occurred, and the colored members after consulting together on
the subject, agreed to give their influence and votes for one of their
own race for that position, as it would in their judgment be a weakening blow against color line prejudice, and they unanimously
elected me for their nominee. Some of the Democracy favored it because they thought it would seriously damage the Republican party.
When the election was held everything connected with it was quiet
and peaceable and I [was] elected by a large majority."

Only one Republican, State Senator William Hancock, a lawyer,
voted against Revels—on "constitutional grounds," he said—because
he thought a Negro could not meet the nine-year citizenship requirement.

Now thirty-four days later in Washington, Senator-elect Revels, the
black Republican state senator and clergyman from Natchez, and
Senator-elect Ames, the slender, erect former officer from the North,

sat awaiting their fate. Mississippi had been without a voice in the Senate since 1861. The strategy of the Republican leaders would be to present the two Mississippi senators separately, with Revels, the more controversial figure, coming up first.

Soon after Vice-President Colfax announced that the state of Mississippi had been readmitted to the Union, Senator Henry Wilson, a Republican from Massachusetts who had been chosen to lead his party's fight for Revels, formally began: "I present the credentials of Honorable H. R. Revels, Senator-elect from Mississippi, and I ask that they be read and he be sworn in."

The secretary then read the credentials from Provisional Governor Ames and James Lynch, Secretary of State of Mississippi, attesting to the legality of Revels' election. A transcript of the proceedings of the legislature also went into the record.

The documents were immediately challenged by Willard Saulsbury of Delaware, who termed "this man's" credentials invalid because they had been certified by a provisional military governor. Saulsbury was not going to employ the customary flowery terms of senatorial courtesy when referring to the black member-elect. The Delaware senator candidly confessed that he was against Revels because he was a Negro; he made heavy-handed jokes about the obviousness of the Mississippian's African descent.

Democrats Saulsbury, Garrett Davis of Kentucky, and John Stockton of New Jersey questioned whether the provisional governor was really the governor, the legality of the results of a senatorial election in a rebel state before it had been readmitted to the Union, and the form of the credentials themselves. These transparent quibbles might have been surprising had they not come from men such as Davis, a rabid white supremacist who four years earlier, just before the passage of the 1866 Civil Rights Act, had warned: "I am henceforth the enemy of your government and will devote the feeble remnants of my life in efforts to overthrow it."

Revels' supporters pointed out that provisional governors had signed certificates for senators from Virginia, that representatives from other reconstructed states and from states formed from territories, elected before those states or territories were formally in the Union, had been seated, and that some members had been sworn in without any credentials whatsoever when these had been misplaced. After hours of haggling, Revels' credentials were accepted by a voice vote. The senators then took up the more serious business of challenging the validity of his citizenship qualifications.

Round Two began with Stockton questioning whether Revels could meet the constitutional requirement of nine years of United States citizenship. It was a neat ploy since Negroes—even free men like the senator-elect and his father before him—generally had no clearly defined legal status as citizens in either the North or the South until the passage of the Civil Rights Act of 1866.

Stockton tried unsuccessfully to complicate the issue by bringing the Ames question back into the discussion. Debate on Stockton's resolution to refer Revels' credentials to the Judiciary Committee for study dragged on for two days during which racial stereotypes were rehashed. Davis drew titters from the audience with "I believe your man here is of mixed blood"—a not very subtle reference to Revels' parentage. Frankly admitting his intent to resist "at every step," Davis was determined that the color line should not be broken in the Senate before it was in the House—and not by the will of the people of Mississippi but by that of a "military dictator. . . . I do not know why the law of the universe permitted that race to be brought here; and above all, I do not know why the Yankees were made their instruments to bring them here, unless it was to curse and to create another devil for the white man! . . . I say that Revels is not a citizen under your legislation."

James Nye of Nevada, a Republican, chided Davis about racial prejudice, asking good-naturedly if he feared competition from blacks. Nye said he regarded the "mountain of prejudice" arising from his colleague whenever the word Negro was spoken as an infirmity which he was inclined to treat kindly. "I have a warm sympathy for the honorable Senator from Kentucky," Nye continued. "This is his last battlefield. It is the last opportunity he will have to make this fight. . . . It seems to me this is the day long looked for, when we put into practical effect the theory that has existed as old as man. We say that men are brothers; whatever their color, all are subject to the same law, and all are eligible to fill any place within the gift of the people." Charging that whatever the pretext, the real objection to Revels was his color, he asserted: "I had hoped that that prejudice was over. Color never made a man; color never unmade a man. . . ."

Nye also saw significance in the fact that Revels had been sent to replace a man who left to lead the rebellion against the United States government—as did other senators during the debate. "In 1861 from this Hall departed two Senators who were representing here the State of Mississippi; one of them who went defiantly was Jefferson Davis. He went out to establish a government whose cornerstone should be oppression and the perpetual enslavement of a race because their skin differed in color from his. Sir, what a magnificent spectacle of retributive justice is witnessed here today! In the place of that proud, defiant man, who marched out to trample under foot the Constitution and the laws of the country he had sworn to support, comes back one of that humble race whom he would have enslaved forever to take and occupy his seat upon this floor."

George Vickers of Maryland, a Democrat, cited several precedents of senators-elect who had been rejected because of their failure to meet the nine-year citizenship requirement. Davis gave examples of challenged senators whose qualifications were turned over to the Judiciary Committee for study. Nye, noting that most of these cases were men who were challenged because of their activities for the Confederacy, asked angrily: "Now, what does the honorable Senator mean by giving us those cases as a guide for our action upon this? Here is a man as to whom the honorable Senator cannot say, for I know how just he is, that his [Revels'] hands were ever stained with the rebellion. On the contrary, in his lowly position he had been the advocate of the flag of his country, while these men [Davis' examples] were willing to see it torn down."

Senator Henry Wilson, who had originally presented the Mississippian's credentials, pointed out that Revels had voted as a citizen of Ohio more than twenty years earlier. The Ohio citizenship of Revels was also confirmed by Ohio Senator John Sherman, who explained how the senator-elect had qualified. He said the state court—an all-Democratic court, as he put it—which had interpreted the Ohio constitution, had defined white citizens as not only those who were wholly white but also racially mixed people who were "nearer white than black." One had but to look at Revels as he sat watching the proceedings to see that he qualified under that definition.

Wilson warned the Democratic party that eight hundred thousand Negro voters would remember its line of unbroken opposition to every effort to give blacks the rights of citizenship. Responding to repeated taunts that the Republicans were in power because of the military, Frederick A. Sawyer of South Carolina reminded the Democrats that it was their party which had tried to destroy the Union.

"I am tired," he said, "of this dreary detail of dead and defunct dogmas on the question of the rights of man. . . . The country expects . . . us to admit Mr. Revels to a seat . . . not because he is a black man or mulatto, but because he is a man and a citizen, having the same qualifications which the law requires of any Senator, and because he has been sent here by the State of Mississippi. . . ."

Throughout the debate Charles Sumner of Massachusetts had remained silent, although the issues were of paramount concern to him. Finally late on the afternoon of February 25, 1870, the dedicated antislavery leader, who had never quite regained his health since suffering a brutal beating from a Southern congressman while sitting at his desk in the Senate in 1856, rose to speak. This was a clue that discussion would soon cease, and the crucial voting begin.

"Mr. President," he said, "the time has passed for argument. Nothing more need be said. I doubt if anything more can be said in the way of argument. For a long time it has been clear that colored persons must be Senators, and I have often so declared." All men must be equal before the law, regardless of color, he continued, reminding his colleagues that no one had yet refuted the evidence he had presented to the Senate several years before to show that at the time of the adoption of the Federal Constitution, blacks were citizens according to the terms of most of the state constitutions.

Stockton still had one last shot to fire, charging Revels' backers with discrimination in reverse. Radical Republicans supported Revels "not because he is the choice of Mississippi, but because he is a black man," the New Jersey senator told his opponents.

After three days of debate the Senate had had enough. Several members of the House of Representatives hearing that a vote was imminent came to the Senate chamber. They knew that the outcome would influence the House when its new Negro members-elect came up for consideration. In the galleries even the standing room was filled. The chamber bristled with excitement as Vice-President Colfax called for a vote on the Stockton motion to shuttle the Revels' problem to committee to study his citizenship qualifications. Gallery observers rose and listened with rapt attention as the senators' names were called and their votes recorded. The visitors stirred as the measure was defeated forty-eight to eight on party lines.

Colfax was about to administer the oath of office to Revels when someone objected even to that, necessitating another round of voting. Before the second roll call started, the bearded, gray-haired Vice-President warned visitors to refrain from expressions of approval or disapproval, with a gentle suggestion that otherwise the galleries might have to be cleared. The roll was called again, and the tally was exactly the same. Mississippi's black senator—after three days of pros and cons and three votes—was accepted.

Dressed in a clerical black suit with a long coat and waistcoat, and holding black gloves and a brown walking stick, Revels had sat impassively as he heard himself and his race belittled. Now he arose at a signal and began moving with confidence and dignity down the aisle. Realizing that there was no senior senator from Mississippi to pay Revels the customary honor of escorting him to be sworn in as a member of the United States Senate, Senator Wilson quickly stepped forward to accompany him and to stand by as the Vice-President administered the oath of office.

In his home state, Revels' election had been hailed by the *Natchez Democrat* as a "good omen" for the future of Mississippi after four years under the rule of the Radical Republicans: "That it is a triumph of the moderate wing of the legislature cannot be questioned."

In Georgia the *Savannah News* "hoped he was as black as the ace of spades and would get a seat next to Sumner." The *New York Herald* deprecated Mississippi's choice, noting that he "would hardly have an opportunity to shine very brilliantly among his distinguished confreres unless it is by his glossy complexion."

The *New York World* thought Revels was a generous man who could not be ignored or snubbed "either on grounds of color, or being a carpetbagger or for intellectual inferiority. . . . The Negro Senator is being lionized to an extent that promises to eclipse all our attentions to Prince Arthur." (Queen Victoria's son Arthur, then on a visit to the United States from England, was the toast of American society.)

Revels was sworn in and settled into the Senate without any outward sign of being embittered by the ordeal of hearing himself in particular and Negroes in general demeaned. His wife and daughters remained in Mississippi during his brief tenure. He wrote home often, sending money for household expenses and for the children. Invariably he asked his wife to pray for him.

Those who met him were impressed by his pleasant voice and dignified manner. The Washington correspondent of the *Boston Commonwealth* described him as a "remarkably intelligent-looking Negro mulatto, not much darker, if any, than Senator [Hannibal] Hamlin [of Maine], though of a yellower tinge. He is, to my sight, a much more wholesome-looking person than Senator Garrett Davis of Kentucky, who had strenuously opposed his admission to the Senate. I had much rather room with him at a hotel than with Davis."

Revels made his first speech on the Senate floor earlier than was usual for a junior member, and sooner than he would have, had he been elected to a full term. As the only black there, he felt compelled to speak out on March 17, 1870, when recalcitrant Confederates appeared about to retake Georgia through the passage of a bill to reconstruct the state for the second time since the Civil War. If the former rebels were successful, the legally elected government of Georgia would be disbanded, and Negroes would be deprived of their right to hold office.

White Georgians in 1868 had expelled the black legislators and declared that persons having one eighth or more of Negro blood were ineligible for public office. In 1869 Congress restored the blacks to their seats and ousted some white members who were ineligible to serve under the terms of the Fourteenth Amendment. The reconvened state legislature, including the blacks, was now petitioning Congress to reopen its doors to Georgia. It was this bill to which the rider was attached that would have the effect of again throwing out the Negroes; and once the federal troops had been withdrawn from the state, it was feared the blacks would be out permanently.

Revels apologized for speaking so soon, but explained he must appeal for federal protection for loyal citizens throughout the South. The Negroes, he said, had no animosities toward the whites and were not, the record would show, striving for domination at any price. Pointing out that many blacks had flocked to the colors in the Civil War when the United States of America, its armies thinned by death and disaster, needed their aid, Revels continued: "Many of my race, the representatives of these men in the field of battle, sleep today in the countless graves of the South. If those quiet resting places of our honored dead could speak today . . . I think that this question of immediate and ample protection for the loyal people of Georgia would lose its legal technicalities, and we would cease to hesitate in our provisions for their instant relief. . . .

"We are told that at no distant day a great uprising of the American people will demand that the reconstruction acts of Congress be undone and blotted forever from the annals of legislative enactment. I inquire, sir, if this delay in affording protection to the loyalists of the State of Georgia does not lend an uncomfortable significancy to this boasting sneer with which we so often meet?"

His speech was praised by newspapers and fellow Republicans, but it had no effect on the course of events. The bill allowing Georgia back in Congress was enacted on July 15 with the sense of the amendment Revels was fighting left intact, and political life in that state became as exclusively white as it had been before the war. Ousted from office before they had a chance to serve their full terms and gain some community power, the black leaders lost their influence in civic affairs.

Revels' maiden speech, however, had an impact on lecture bookers. Offers poured in for him to speak in Northern cities. He drew large crowds in New England, and was entertained by state officials. On one occasion the popular orator Wendell Phillips dramatically introduced him as the "Fifteenth Amendment in flesh and blood." There were also less happy occurrences. A scheduled appearance at the Philadelphia Academy of Music was canceled when the directors decided they did not want to hear a Negro speak.

Late in March Revels introduced a bill to grant lands and right of way to aid the New Orleans and Northeastern Railroad. His first effort at originating major legislation, the measure failed to pass.

In the spring of 1870 Congress was considering restoring full citizenship rights to the former Confederates whom the Fourteenth Amendment made ineligible for public office. In this controversy Revels erred on the side of forgiveness for pre-Civil War officials who had broken their oaths to uphold the Federal Constitution by fighting for or supporting the South during the rebellion:

"I am in favor of removing the disabilities of those upon whom they are imposed in the South just as fast as they give evidence of having become loyal . . . ," he said, explaining that the Mississippi state legislature had instructed him to support complete restoration for all Mississippians. "If you can find one man in the South who gives evidence that he is a loyal man . . . [who] has ceased to denounce the laws of Congress as unconstitutional [and] has ceased to oppose them . . . I am in favor of removing his disabilities; and if you can find one hundred men that the same is true of I am in favor of removing their disabilities. If you can find a whole state that that is true of, I am in favor of removing the disabilities of all its people."

Revels introduced individual petitions for the restoration of voting and office-holding privileges for numerous Mississippians and other Southerners. He asked that the federal government pay his constituents claims due them for the use of their property by the United States during the war. Two years later, Congress passed the Amnesty Act of 1872, covering everyone except five hundred Confederate leaders.

Not long afterward, the whites of Mississippi, for whom Revels had spoken so forcefully and forgivingly, were again "systematically depriving" their fellow black citizens of their constitutional rights—in the words of a Senate investigating committee. To compound the irony, Mississippians in 1890 would set the precedent for the Southern strategy of Negro disfranchisement by ratifying a new constitution requiring people to read or interpret it as a prerequisite to voting.

During this session of the Senate, Revels recommended a young Negro for admission to West Point. Having been approved, his candidate then failed the military academy's entrance examination. Whether he was frightened by the circumstances and not up to his best, whether he lacked the academic background, or whether he was kept out on a pretext is not clear. Revels, who had gone home to Mississippi in June to visit his sick wife, was criticized in the press for having embarrassed the young man and his family by placing the son in an awkward position.

The senator had returned to Mississippi during the summer recess by way of Ohio and Kansas where he made a number of speeches and visited friends. He submitted another ambitious bill when the Senate resumed that winter; it would have provided federal funds to repair and construct levees along the Mississippi River. The measure did not pass.

Revels, who served on the Education and Labor Committee and the Committee for the District of Columbia, succeeded in putting a token number of Negroes on the employment rolls of the navy yard after a delegation from Baltimore asked him to intercede. He threw his support behind a bill to desegregate the schools of the national capital in February 1871. While making a plea for schools open to all, he argued against the harmful effects of spreading Jim Crowism in all aspects of American life.

He might have been talking about the 1970's when he spoke of the growth of racial prejudice. This February eighth speech began by answering those who insisted that Washington Negroes did not want their children in mixed schools:

"In regard to the wishes of the colored people of this city I will simply say that the trustees of colored schools and some of the most intelligent colored men of this place have said to me that they would have before asked for a bill abolishing the separate colored schools . . . if they had thought they could obtain it. They feared they could not; and this is the only reason why they did not ask for it before."

Joshua Hill of Georgia, who introduced an amendment to retain segregated schools, intimated that Congress was trying to legislate social equality among the races. He said black children would not be comfortable with whites, that they would be overcome with memories of the past and "mortified" in the presence of those who used to be the master race.

Revels told him that Negro children had already shown they could be quite comfortable in schoolrooms with whites. "The white race need not be harmed in order to build up the colored race," he continued. "Let me ask, will establishing such schools as I am now advocating in this District harm our white friends? . . . By some it is contended that if we establish mixed schools here a great insult will be given to the white citizens, and that the white schools will be seriously damaged. All that I ask those who assume this position to do is to go with me to Massachusetts, to go with me to some other New England states where they have mixed schools. . . . They will find between the white and colored citizens friendship, peace, and harmony."

On the general question of prejudice, he was pessimistic: "I find that the prejudice in this country to color is very great, and I sometimes fear that it is on the increase. . . . It matters not how well they behave themselves, how well they deport themselves, how intelligent they may be, how refined they may be—for there are some colored persons who are persons of refinement; this must be admitted—the prejudice against them is equally as great as it is against the most low and degraded colored man you can find in the streets of this city or any other place. . . .

"And is this prejudice right? Have the colored people done anything to justify the prejudice against them that does exist in the hearts of so many white persons, and generally of one great political party in this country? . . . No, sir. Can any reason be given why this prejudice should be fostered in so many hearts against them, simply because they are not white? I make these remarks in all kindness and from no bitterness of feeling at all."

Revels called it the duty of the federal government to move promptly to discourage this "wicked prejudice." He sought to reassure the opponents of the bill that blacks would move with restraint once the barriers were down. Apparently convinced that there was more good than bad in the average man, he held that it was not the white people themselves who were fostering racial discrimination but "school boards, school trustees, railroad companies, and steamboat companies."

Senator Charles Sumner also argued strongly for this bill. He said he was tired of seeing civil rights measures knocked down as impractical or untimely while there was general agreement that they were right in principle. It was another losing battle: Washington's schools were not desegregated until the mid-1950's.

Revels' mini-term in the Senate ended March 3, 1871. President Ulysses S. Grant reportedly considered giving him a Washington assignment to keep him from "falling from obscurity," but Revels chose to return to Mississippi to head a new Negro college—Alcorn—to be opened at Lorman in buildings once used by an all-white college. This black institution—now called Alcorn A & M—was opened to stave off the threat of integration at the University of Mississippi. The lower house of the Mississippi legislature objected to the move, but Revels succeeded in pushing through a measure appropriating fifty thousand dollars in the spring of 1871.

Revels obviously believed in desegregated schools and was willing to fight for them in Washington, where the support of Sumner and others had given him some hope of success. In Mississippi the Radical Republicans were fast losing power. The veteran teacher, who knew compromise was necessary to get along in life, felt he was making a contribution by obtaining the only possible college education facilities for blacks. Classes began in February 1872 with the former senator as president and philosophy professor. He left briefly in 1873 to be secretary of state for Mississippi.

Governor James Alcorn's appointees became vulnerable in the fall of 1873 when Adelbert Ames recaptured the governorship. In accordance with American tradition, Ames staffed his administration with his loyal friends and sympathizers. Revels was among those fired in 1874. Sixty students and some faculty members walked out in protest. He went back to the ministry, preaching in Holly Springs. In the bitter, bloody election of 1875 he campaigned for a congressional candidate who ran with Democratic support, and wrote a letter to President Grant explaining why he had turned on the party that had given him one of the most coveted offices in the land:

"Since reconstruction, the masses of my people have been, as it were, enslaved in mind by unprincipled adventurers, who, caring nothing for country, were willing to stoop to anything no matter how infamous, to secure power to themselves, and perpetuate it. My people are naturally Republicans, and always will be, but as they grow older in freedom, so do they in wisdom."

Revels wrote Grant that he did not recognize most of the men who had been in power in Mississippi for the past couple of years as Republicans. He charged that Negroes had been told that for the sake of the party they must vote for "notoriously corrupt and dishonest men." Ames, who had given Revels an early assist in politics, was a hardpressed governor with party feuds at the top level and accusations by his enemies that he was too close to the "worst kind of Negro Republicans."

Later this much publicized Revels letter went into the record when a Senate committee headed by George S. Boutwell of Massachusetts traveled to Mississippi to investigate the murder and intimidation of voters by Democratic clubs. Part of the responsibility for the terror of the Mississippi election rests with Grant, who had refused to send troops to maintain order when Ames requested them. Later the President reportedly said that he had not done so for fear the Republicans would thereby lose Ohio.

After listening to 162 witnesses the Boutwell committee decided there had been so much systematic terror that the state legislature elected in 1875 was not a valid body. The legislators retained their seats nonetheless since nothing was done to implement the committee report. Revels was about the only prominent black who did not testify against the methods used by the Democrats to win. Sounding a bit confused—he did not answer the first question as to how long he had lived in Mississippi correctly—he said that he had no personal knowledge of fraud, terror, or intimidation. He minimized his own part in the campaign, stating that he had been active to a degree for the Democratic-backed congressional candidate from his district.

How can Revels' testimony before the Senate committee and his letter to Grant be explained? His motives, doubtless, were mixed. He was disappointed with the Republicans personally and generally. His party's state administration had fired him from Alcorn despite student protests. A pious, rigidly honest man, he had been offended by corruption in high places, and the Ames administration, despite the governor's personal integrity, was touched with irregularities and extravagances. A moderate, he had chosen to live out his days in Mississippi, getting along as best he could with his state's establishment. Though some black leaders in the state, notably Clay County legislator J. W. Caradine, were literally forced to make speeches for the Democrats, there is no evidence this was a factor in the Revels case. And as it turned out, he obviously wanted his former post at the college back, and this was in the power of the Democrats to bestow.

Revels' accommodating posture paid off, and he was renamed president of Alcorn College. By early 1882 there were rumors he was on his way out. Not waiting to be dismissed again, he resigned in July and went home to Holly Springs. His last years were spent as presiding elder of his church there.

The seventy-eight-year-old preacher died on January 16, 1901, a few hours after collapsing at the Upper Mississippi Conference of the African Methodist Episcopal Church in Aberdeen, where he was to have delivered a report. Just before he was overcome by a paralyzing stroke, Revels whispered to a friend that he was ill and asked him to read his remarks. The former senator left little for his family besides the nine-room home at Holly Springs. He never had much money, and the bad debts of friends had further drained his resources. There were less than two thousand dollars to be parceled out to his three surviving daughters and grandchild. The widow, already weakened by a lingering illness, died within a month of her husband.

Hiram R. Revels had buffeted a barrage of prejudice to become the first black in Congress. He made the way easier for those who came after him.

Blanche K. Bruce/Mississippi

Blanche K. Bruce was the first Negro to serve a full six-year term in the United States Senate, the first to preside over that upper house of Congress, and the first to sign his name on the country's currency.

In 1875, four days after his thirty-fourth birthday, Bruce took his seat in the highest legislative body in America as one of Mississippi's two senators. Unlike his black predecessor, Hiram R. Revels, he had deliberately set out to get the position and worked hard to gain it.

One of eleven children, Blanche Kelso Bruce had been born into slavery on a Farmville, Virginia, plantation on March 1, 1841. His mother, Polly, the house slave of a wealthy planter named Pettus Perkinson, had eleven children. His father's name is unknown. Bruce's ancestry was more white than black; he was said to have been from three fourths to seven eighths Caucasian.

On a plantation in the South the master's son was frequently presented with a servant of about his own age. This was probably young Blanche's lot, although he seems to have been less of a servant than a playmate. Blanche and William Perkinson shared a tutor, and tradition has it that the Negro pupil was the more adept at learning.

Perkinson was a widower, and Blanche's mother took care of William, as well as her own brood. As they grew older, Blanche and his brothers earned money by raising their own tobacco. They were given more freedom than many other slaves, and later newspaper accounts of Bruce's life said that he might "have escaped slavery whenever he chose."

A few years before the Civil War, Pettus Perkinson moved his family and slaves to Missouri. When the war broke out, William joined the Confederate Army. Blanche and two of his brothers went to Hannibal, apparently with the hope of joining the Union forces, but blacks were not yet accepted by the army.

15

Instead Bruce, who later wrote that he had emancipated himself after the attack on Fort Sumter, spent the war years teaching school in Hannibal and Lawrence, Kansas, where he founded that state's first Negro elementary school. He also worked as a printer. About 1867 he became a porter on the steamer *Columbia,* sailing out of St. Louis. He traveled to Arkansas and Tennessee before moving to Floreyville, Mississippi. Though he had only seventy-five cents in his pocket when he arrived there, the personable, energetic, and shrewd Bruce had little difficulty in establishing himself as a successful planter.

The newcomer was immediately attracted to politics and soon became a familiar figure in Republican party circles. His first public job was to conduct elections for Tallahatchie County. He attended the inaugural festivities in Jackson for the new Republican governor and legislature in January 1870. Bruce was named sergeant at arms of the state senate.

The next step up for this astute politician was the combined post of sheriff and tax collector of Bolivar County, one of the richest counties in the state. He easily raised the amount required for the substantial sheriff's bond with the assistance of white neighbors. He also served as a member of the Mississippi River levee board and as school superintendent. *The Floreyville Star,* a weekly newspaper, helped establish his name with the public by crusading for the election of a capable Negro as senator. He built his own home, bought several lots, and a 650-acre plantation during this period.

In 1873 the Radical Republicans asked the Bolivar County leader to be their candidate for lieutenant governor on the ticket headed by Adelbert Ames. Bruce, his heart set on the United States Senate, declined to run for the state office. Had he taken the job, Ames was believed to have been prepared to resign his position with the idea of returning to the Senate and leaving the governorship to Bruce. Another Negro, A. K. Davis, ran with Ames to attract the black vote to the Republican ticket, and Bruce supported them.

Bruce's work for the Republicans was rewarded the following year. With the support of Governor Ames, he received the Republican nomination for the Senate on the second ballot, getting fifty-two out of eighty-eight votes cast at the caucus. Several blacks wanted the post. Whites made an effort to split the Negro legislators into factions before the election on February 3, 1874, but most held firm for Bruce, and he was named to the Senate, with the help of some Democratic votes, over a Democratic opponent.

With a year to wait until his term began, the erect, broad-shouldered senator-elect was inundated with advice from the newspapers.

The *Daily News & Courier* of Natchez cautioned him not to jeopardize his political career by marrying. The paper thought that the Senate was holding up the credentials of another black, P. B. S. Pinchback, former lieutenant governor of Louisiana, partly because the senatorial wives did not wish to associate with Mrs. Pinchback, a strikingly beautiful woman. (Whatever the reason, Bruce was to remain a bachelor for three more years.) The *Vicksburg Times* had words of encouragement for him: "One newly-elected Senator, although colored and formerly a steamboat porter, is a man of liberal and comprehensive views . . . , he fully realizes the necessity for adoption by his race and by the white Republicans of an honest and liberal policy."

Bruce's senatorial career began on March 5, 1875, during a special session held to decide what should be done about civil disorders and a challenged state government in Louisiana. This time there was no singling out the new black member for derision before he was admitted. Vice-President Henry Wilson, in routine fashion, read off the list of freshmen members and asked them to come forward when their names were called. Wilson as a Massachusetts senator, had expertly piloted Revels past a roadblock of racist objections into the Senate.

As Bruce rose to go to the rostrum to take the oath of office, he was surprised to see his fellow Mississippi senator, James L. Alcorn, hiding behind a newspaper, in order to avoid paying him the usual courtesy of escorting a new member. Bruce started to walk alone—then, within a matter of seconds, he was joined by another senator who whispered a greeting while they moved forward together. This was the beginning of a lifelong friendship with Roscoe Conklin, a Republican from New York. Conklin steered him through the procedural maze and saw to it that he drew some good committee assignments. Bruce later named his only child for the New Yorker.

Alcorn's bad manners that day were probably the result, not of color prejudice, but of intraparty squabbling between the more conservative Alcorn wing of the Mississippi Republicans and the liberal Ames faction. These two ex-generals, who had fought on opposite sides during the Civil War, were not comfortable sharing the state party leadership. Neither could make up his mind whether he'd rather be governor or senator, and there were times when both wanted the same job at the same time. Alcorn was in no mood to play the chivalrous Southerner now that Bruce, a member of the Ames faction, was joining him in the Senate.

Bruce, a portly, bearded man, drew more attention from the floor and gallery than most of the other new senators, except former President Andrew Johnson who was now back at his old desk.

P. B. S. Pinchback was still waiting for the Senate to make up its mind about him. Had the Louisiana senator-elect's credentials been accepted, he, not Bruce, would have been the first black to serve a full term, starting on March 4, 1873. Bruce was distressed over the Senate's continuing refusal to seat Pinchback because of alleged election irregularities. During the short special session the freshman senator from Mississippi chose to work behind the scenes and to say nothing on the floor, though privately it was clear he was annoyed by the failure of his party and a Republican President, Ulysses S. Grant, to support a black Republican whom Bruce and many others considered honestly elected and fully qualified. When the Senate reconvened in December, Bruce's was one of four desks decorated with flowers from friends. Having learned the routine during the special session, Bruce could look forward to service on three committees: Pensions, Manufactures, and Education and Labor. He introduced a bill to pay bounties to black servicemen and their heirs, but after an adverse committee report, it was tabled. He also submitted the first of a number of petitions calling for prohibition of the sale of liquor.

The controversy over seating Pinchback continued into the regular session. On March 3, 1876, Bruce, speaking for the first time on the subject in the Senate, refuted the argument that the Louisiana legislature, which had elected Pinchback, was not a legal government by pointing out that for three years it had been recognized and dealt with as such by both the President and Congress.

"I believe," he continued, "whatever seeming informalities may attach to the manner in which the will of the people was ascertained, that Mr. Pinchback is the representative of a majority of the legal voters and entitled to a seat." Louisiana, he reminded the Senate, did have a "colored majority" of 45,695.

Of even more worry to Bruce was the furor over the 1875 election in his own state. Arguing for a Senate investigation, Bruce asked by what "miraculous or extraordinary" means the Democrats had gained more than fifty thousand votes within a span of two years. Neither the issues nor the caliber of Democratic campaigning could account for such an "overwhelming revolution in the sentiments of the colored voters." As a clue to what really happened, he cited the case of Yazoo County where the Republicans had a majority of two thousand votes in 1873 and only seven votes in 1875, after the county had been "cursed by riot and bloodshed." Some of those votes, he said, were "cast in derision by the Democrats, who declared that Republicans must have some votes in the county."

To demonstrate the atmosphere in Mississippi during the campaign, he quoted from the *Yazoo City Democrat:* "Carry the election peacefully if we can, forcibly if we must." The paper bragged that no Republicans were canvassing for votes because "they dare not press their claims." If Republicans elsewhere were bold enough to show their faces, the paper advised: "Try the rope on such characters. It acts finely on such characters here."

In Yazoo City on September 1, scores of blacks had been killed by white rioters after the white Republican sheriff, A. T. Morgan, was hounded out of office. In the next four days, thirty-five to fifty Negro and white leaders had been murdered in Clinton.

In this Senate speech, Bruce explained why the Mississippi Republicans had not been able to maintain order, even with support from the majority of Mississippi voters. "If," he suggested, "the Honorable Senators ask why such flagrant wrongs were allowed to go unpunished by a Republican State government, and unresented by a race claiming 20,000 majority of voters, the answer is at hand." Bruce explained that local officials had been unable to control the mobs and had called on the governor for help. The governor, who had to depend on a poorly organized and armed militia, was enjoined by the courts from using even the limited funds available, and appealed to the President for assistance. The President refused lest he be accused of undue interference in state matters, the senator continued.

Bruce said blacks, who had shown "in blood their courage" in all the country's wars, wanted to live in racial harmony with the whites. He denied that Negroes had generally proved to be incompetent government officials. He reminded the Senate they were political novitiates in states drained and demoralized by war. He said they had been forced by expediency to accept "vicious leadership" in some cases, because these men were the only whites who would work with blacks.

The senator emphasized that the new state constitutions written by legislatures having "colored majorities" were great improvements over their predecessors. He warned there would be disaster for both races if the White League's shotgun policy prevailed, "for they would first become aggressively turbulent, and we, as a class, would become servile, unreliable and worthless." He said Negroes in Mississippi asked nothing special, only the protection of life, liberty, and property as guaranteed under the Constitution. "We do not ask the enactment of new laws," he said, "but only the enforcement of those that already exist."

Investigation of the 1875 election in Mississippi by a senatorial committee was authorized on March 31, 1876—the very day of this Bruce speech. His charges were amply documented in the report of the Boutwell committee, which called this election "one of the darkest chapters in American history." Declaring that the Republicans would have won both houses of the state legislature if the election had been a fair one, the committee held that the Mississippi government was not entitled to recognition by the United States. No action was taken on the report, and all those elected in that "dark chapter" kept their offices.

In the next Congress, which began with a special Senate session, Mississippi's black senator was named chairman of a select Mississippi River committee. This committee recommended the establishment of a permanent Mississippi River commission to guard against floods and erosion and to make improvements in the channel.

A strong party man, Bruce split with the Republicans in March 1877 by voting for the admission of Democrat Lucius Q. C. Lamar to the Senate, in spite of allegations against his election methods. This black and white senatorial team showed mutual respect for each other during their time together in Washington, notwithstanding their differences on virtually every major issue. In other contested elections involving whites, the Negro Mississippian voted against accepting a challenged Democratic senator from South Carolina and in favor of a Republican one from Louisiana. Arguing that mixed crews in the navy had proved that blacks and whites could function well together in the military, he fought futilely for integrated army units.

Not the sort to bear a grudge silently, Bruce was straightforward in his relations with other senators. When Lewis Bogy of Missouri asked him to support a bill of local interest to Missouri, Bruce listened quietly to the request. He then told his colleague about an experience he had had as a porter on a St. Louis steamer. A traveler had brusquely ordered him to hurry with his heavy luggage. Bruce got the baggage and his customer to the ship on time, but he had not been paid a single cent for his effort. The Mississippian said he had never forgotten the incident and wondered if Bogy, the nonpaying traveler, remembered. The matter off his mind, he voted for Bogy's bill, and they were friends thereafter.

Bruce lost his bachelor status on June 24, 1878, when he married Josephine Wilson. She was a tall, pretty schoolteacher, the daughter of a Cleveland dentist, whose ancestry also was well mixed. After the wedding they left for a leisurely tour of Europe. Secretary of State William M. Evarts wrote ahead to the various American embassies to pave the way for VIP treatment for the Bruces in England, France, Belgium, Holland, Germany, and Switzerland. Unaccustomed to seeing many American Negroes, Europeans were attracted by the manners and charm of the newlyweds.

When they returned to Washington, the Bruces lived first on N Street, then moved to a five-story brownstone on R Street. Mrs. Bruce entertained the Senate wives. Their neighbors included James G. Blaine of Maine and other solons. They maintained a full social and working schedule.

In the Forty-fifth Congress Bruce sought a hundred thousand dollars for four hundred of his constituents who wanted to migrate to Liberia, although personally he did not approve of such emigration-colonization schemes. In the *Cincinnati Commercial* of February 9, 1878, Bruce, who favored a liberal western land-grant policy and other government measures to aid financially depressed Negroes, expressed his opposition to proposals to solve the country's dilemma by shipping illiterate poor blacks to Liberia: "The Negro of America is not African but American—in his physical qualities and aptitudes, in his mental development and biases, in his religious beliefs and hopes, in his political concepts and convictions, he is an American. He is not a parasite, but a branch, drawing life from the great American civilization and adapting himself to the genius of its institutions."

Bruce presided over the Senate in the absence of Vice-President William A. Wheeler on February 14, 1879, as the senators wrestled with the issue of Chinese immigration to America. Arguing in favor of a motion to exclude Chinese, one senator said the nation could not absorb more than two races. The United States, he asserted, should be kept "black and white." As a man who had once been bereft of the privileges of citizenship himself strictly because of color, Bruce entered into the debate and voted against the bill—attesting to his faith in the assimilative powers of the American people.

"Senator Bruce occupied the chair yesterday during a portion of the debate on the Chinese bill," the *New York Tribune* wrote. "This is the first time a colored man ever sat in the seat of the Vice-President of the United States. Senator Bruce is universally respected by his fellow senators and is qualified both in manners and character to preside over the deliberations of the most august body of men in the land."

Bruce's primary goal during this period was to hammer out a bill improving navigation on the Mississippi River and get it through Congress. His bill passed in the Senate, but died in the House. The Forty-fifth Congress, embroiled in a fight over the use of federal troops to keep peace at the polls, ended on March 3, 1879, without having acted on appropriation measures to run the government or the military.

As a result Bruce and other holdovers had almost no rest. On March 18, Rutherford B. Hayes summoned the Forty-sixth Congress to Washington. In control of both Houses, the Democrats put through a bill specifying that "no money be used for the army to act as a police force to keep peace at the polls" and the Republican President, true to his no-interference pact with the Southerners, signed it. As James G. Blaine wrote in *Twenty Years of Congress*, this was the beginning of the end of meaningful participation in government by black Southerners.

When the new Senate was organized, Bruce, being now a member of the minority party, lost the Mississippi River Committee chairmanship to his Democratic colleague, Lamar, but when Bruce proposed a probe of the bankruptcy of the government-backed Freedmen's Savings and Trust Company, the Senate named him to head the six-man group. Thousands of black depositors in more than thirty cities lost their meager savings after the collapse of three big New York investment houses started a run on deposits which forced the banks to close. The committee held hearings during the summer recess of 1879 and into the following spring. As a result of its work the depositors got back some of their money.

By this time the Bruces, who knew there was no future for them or for any Republicans in the state of Mississippi, had decided to live permanently in Washington. In the fall the Democrats, with federal troops no longer around to protect Negroes from intimidation at the polls, took the state legislature by a margin of 4 to 1. The legislators in January 1880 named James George to Bruce's seat, with only four members voting for the incumbent. He was a lame duck, but he still had about a year to try to work his will in the Senate.

During this period Bruce advocated, among other things, full citizenship rights for the Indians. In the debate on April 7, he flayed this country's dealings with the redskins as "inspired and controlled by a stern selfishness" designed to get the Indian lands for the whites through broken treaties, wars, bounties, and beads. He charged the government with pushing the Indians toward extinction.

On April 9, 1880, a few days after Johnson Whittaker, a black cadet, had been found unconscious in his room at West Point, with his head bleeding and his feet tied to the bedstead, Bruce and other senators called on the secretary of war to provide the Senate with the facts in the case. Whittaker, after he recovered enough to talk, had told officers at the academy that three masked men, whom he believed to be cadets, had cut off part of his left ear and slit his right one; they had then tied him up, warning him not to shout for help. He did cry out as loudly as he dared after they left; but no one came until the next morning when the duty officer arrived on his rounds as usual. Neither Bruce nor John A. Logan of Illinois, who had been the senator to introduce the resolution calling for information, believed the West Point superintendent's suggestion that Whittaker's wounds might have been self-inflicted.

"We have for several days been engaged . . . in an attempt to pass a bill which will more effectively Christianize the Indians," Bruce stated. "I think the Senate would do well if it would devote a little time to the civilization of West Point. . . ." He said that for such an outrage to occur there must have been laxity at a high level and demanded that "the criminals" responsible be hunted down and punished.

No action was taken on the resolution after some senators asked for a delay until a West Point court of inquiry could make its report. On the basis of conflicting expert testimony that Whittaker had written a threatening note to himself, that court had found by the end of May that the South Carolina cadet was guilty of self-mutilation. He was dismissed not for this, however, but for flunking natural philosophy for the second time.

The only Negro then in Congress presided over the Senate again on May 4, 1880. In the summer he served as temporary presiding officer during the Republican national convention in Chicago. Several delegates were vying for the floor, and Bruce gave the nod to James Garfield, an Ohio senator-elect who favored liberal reconstruction measures.

Garfield, a dark horse, captured the presidential nomination on the thirty-sixth ballot. Bruce received eight votes for Vice-President. Bruce worked down to the wire in Congress, offering bills or resolutions on education, railroad construction in Mississippi, aid to the Indians, and court-redistricting in his state. None of these proposals was enacted. When his term ended on March 3, 1881, Mississippians in the capital presented him with a gold-headed cane as a memento of his years in the Senate.

There was speculation about a Cabinet post for the ex-senator. A surprising, no doubt tongue-in-cheek, boost came from a Democratic paper, the *Charleston News and Courier:* "Why should not ex-Senator Bruce receive a cabinet appointment? He is equal in ability to the average cabinet officer of these times, and bears a higher character personally and officially than nine out of ten of the prominent candidates for public position." Bruce refused an appointment as minister to Brazil because that South American country still had slavery. The cabinet post was not offered, but on May 18, 1881, President Garfield named him Register of the Treasury. It was another first as his signature went on all the country's paper currency.

The former solon was in charge of the Negro exhibit at the World's Cotton Exposition in New Orleans from November 1884 to May 1885.

The extensive display included contributions by black Americans to art and industry. His engaging personality made him popular on the lecture circuit, where he earned as much as a hundred dollars a night. He was in demand to write magazine articles as one of the favorite "race experts" of his day. A delegate to the GOP convention again in 1888, he was influential enough to garner eleven votes for Vice-President on the Benjamin Harrison ticket. From 1891–93 he was Recorder of Deeds in Washington. Reputedly one of the wealthiest Negroes in the country, he still owned a valuable plantation in Mississippi and real estate in Washington.

In 1896 he campaigned for his party's presidential hopeful, William McKinley. The talk of a Cabinet post was revived. When McKinley went to the White House, Bruce was remembered, not with a Cabinet assignment, but with reappointment as Register of the Treasury. He remained in this position until his death from diabetes on March 17, 1898, at the age of fifty-seven.

Washington turned out in force for the funeral, where diplomats mingled with party leaders, professional men, scholars, and clergymen. Bruce's eighteen-year-old son, Roscoe, came home from Phillips Exeter Academy in New Hampshire to attend the service. The black-draped casket with silver bars and nameplate was borne by congressmen.

Blanche K. Bruce, a committee chairman during his Senate term, had enjoyed more acceptance and influence in Congress than his black contemporaries in the House. Leading government figures of the period, who wrote about their lives in Washington afterward, assessed him as one of the most able men to have served on Capitol Hill.

Joseph H. Rainey/South Carolina and Jefferson F. Long/Georgia

Joseph H. Rainey was the Hiram R. Revels of the United States House of Representatives. The first of his race to sit in the lower body, the thirty-eight-year-old, olive-complexioned South Carolinian began his congressional career ten months after the Mississippian had broken the color line in the Senate. The metaphor, however, relates only to the timing of their entry into Congress. The forceful, aggressive, demanding Rainey was a direct contrast to the gentle, trusting Revels.

The House admitted the former state senator from South Carolina without drama or debate on December 12, 1870, a few days after the third session of the Forty-first Congress got under way. He had been named to fill the seat made vacant by the House's refusal to accept the credentials of B. Franklin Whittemore, a white man who was disqualified because he had been elected before the state had completed the requirements for readmission to the Union.

Rainey was eased into his niche in history because of Congress' refusal to seat a fellow black. Two years before, J. Willis Menard of New Orleans had been elected to represent Louisiana's Second District in the Fortieth Congress. His election had been duly certified by the Louisiana governor, but Caleb S. Hunt, his white opponent, contested its validity. When Menard, a college graduate and poet, arrived with his credentials, he was allowed to present his case, but the House was unable to make up its mind between the two contestants. The disputed seat remained empty for the rest of the term. In spite of the fact that the weight of the evidence was in favor of Menard's claim, the conservative element of the Republican House cautioned that it was too early to accept a Negro member, and this view carried the day.

25

Joseph Hayne Rainey had been born on June 21, 1832, in George-town, South Carolina, to mulatto parents, Edward and Gracia Rainey. His father was a successful barber, who purchased freedom for himself and his large family. He also secured as much schooling for his children as was possible in a slave state.

By 1846 the Raineys had moved to Charleston, and Joseph had taken up his father's vocation. When he was in Philadelphia in 1859, he married and returned South with Susan, his part-French bride. He got into trouble with the authorities for unauthorized travel to a free state, but friends managed to settle this problem. The Raineys, father and son, were working as barbers in Charleston when the Civil War started. Joseph was conscripted as a steward on a Confederate block-ade runner. When the rebels drafted him to work on the defenses of Charleston harbor, he began plotting ways to escape. Eventually he and his wife managed to get passage on a ship to Bermuda. He opened a barber shop near the waterfront in St. George's, and his wife set up a dressmaking shop. Both did a thriving business.

Rainey spent his free time educating himself. The customers who came to the shop helped him in correcting his exercises and gave him tips on the best books to read. The islanders were proud enough of him to name the street on which his shop was located, "Barber's Alley." The street and the significance of its name are pointed out today in Bermuda guidebooks.

Bermuda was attractive, but South Carolina was home, and Rainey heard encouraging reports after the Civil War ended that life there was being transformed for the newly freed black men, who were moving into public life and planning to compete for elective office. The lure was enough to bring him back to Georgetown, South Carolina, in 1866. Politics attracted him. In 1867, while earning his living as a merchant, he served as a member of the central committee of the newly formed state Republican party. The next year he was a delegate to the state constitutional convention and made enough impact to run successfully shortly thereafter for the state senate. While in that body he headed its Finance Committee. In July 1870, during the summer recess of Congress, the Republicans nominated him to fill a vacancy in the House of Representatives. He won the election over C. W. Dudley by nearly nine thousand votes and resigned from the state senate to move to the national scene.

By the time Rainey arrived in Washington, only a few months remained until the close of the Forty-first Congress. He spent most of the first weeks studiously watching what was going on around him. A confident, attractive, outgoing man, with polished manners and regular features, he performed what was to become a routine chore for Southern Reconstruction congressmen—the presentation of individual petitions from former members of the Confederacy for the removal of political disabilities. He also entered a petition on behalf of the National Colored Labor Convention, and he was named to the Freedmen's Affairs Committee. In January 1871 he had the pleasure of welcoming to the House its second black member, Jefferson F. Long of Macon, Georgia.

Congress had taken so long to work out the compromise under which Georgia finally was to be reseated after having been barred for flagrantly violating the conditions under which the state had reentered the Union in 1868 that Jefferson Long's abbreviated term was almost up before the House cleared him for admission.

More significantly, the concessions made to end the controversy had dashed the political hopes of blacks in Georgia. The provisions for the readmission of the state to Congress in July 1870 had the effect of ending the terms of legally elected Negro state legislators, who had already been thrown out of office once by Georgia whites, before the biracial state government had a chance to start functioning in an organized, unobstructed way. Further, the former rebels candidly ad‧mitted that they intended to see that all in public office were as lily white as they had been before the Civil War, once the federal government turned its back and Georgia was left alone. To Georgia blacks, the "compromise" seemed more like "surrender."

Jefferson Franklin Long had been born a slave of mixed parentage near Knoxville, Georgia, on March 3, 1836. He was self-educated and had a going business as a tailor in Macon by the end of the Civil War. Becoming active in politics, he worked his way up in the Republican party, and was nominated in 1869 to represent the Fourth Congressional District. He fought a hard campaign, speaking out against lynching and other violence, winding up with a rally in Macon on the eve of the election. "If you will stand by me, we will take the polls tomorrow and we will hold them," he told the cheering crowd. He made a forceful appeal to the newly enfranchised blacks to vote for the party that had improved their lot. His followers marched with him to the Macon courthouse on December 20. There they were attacked by a mob of whites, and several people were killed. Yet Long was elected by nine hundred votes over a Caucasian Democrat, notwithstanding the racial flareups that occurred during this bizarre three-day election. He—and three other members from Georgia, all white—were seated on January 16, 1871.

Long was warmly received by many in the House of Representatives. Within a week he was so well accepted that he was chosen to present the credentials of William W. Paine, one of the three remaining members elected from his state to Congress.

Long had a strong profile; he wore his black hair close-cut and had a moustache attached to cheek sideburns. Editor-publisher Frederick Douglass, who had been touted as a congressional possibility himself, covered the news of "another colored member in the House" with two paragraphs on the editorial page of Washington's *New National Era.* Douglass described the Georgia congressman as having a "light brown complexion with manly, independent carriage . . . [he] gives the impression of a man activated by a high sense of duty and of the position he occupies."

Although Long's congressional career was too fleeting for him to demonstrate either ability or the lack of it, he did become the first black member to address the House on February 1, 1871. At issue was a move for general restoration of officeholding rights to former Confederates through the revision of the test-oath. Since 1862, every paid public official in the United States, except the President, had been required to swear he had never voluntarily borne arms against the country or aided those who did. The Fourteenth Amendment provided a formula for the restitution of political rights to prewar Southern officials; if Congress, after consideration of a specific case, agreed by a two-thirds vote to lift a man's disabilities, he could serve again merely by swearing to defend the Constitution in the future. Now Congress, over the objections of the Radical Republicans, also proposed to exempt from the so-called iron-clad oath, in one action, all former rebels who had not previously been officeholders, regardless of their behavior since the war. Long categorically opposed the bill, which, as he said, in his state would benefit the midnight riders of the Ku Klux Klan. Instead he favored consideration on an individual basis for those who demonstrated their loyalty to the federal government.

Long said the former Confederates were bold and candid about their intentions to seize control as soon as their political disabilities were removed. He charged that in Georgia where it was not safe to carry the Stars and Stripes more than "500 loyal men [had been] shot down by the disloyal men there, and not one of those who took part in committing those outrages has ever been brought to justice. . . . When we take the men who commit these outrages before judges and juries we find that they are in the hands of the very Kuklux themselves, who protect them." Just that day he had received word from a postmaster, a man loyal to the federal government, who had been beaten in the streets a few days before. Long added that law-abiding citizens were continually losing their jobs because of their political beliefs. This bill, clearing the way for most ex-Confederates to qualify for public office without first establishing their allegiance to the Union, passed in a few days and become law without the signature of President Grant.

The Forty-first Congress, the first in history to accept blacks, ended its work on March 3, 1871, and Long, together with Mississippi's Senator Hiram R. Revels, went home. Despite his affinity for politics, Long was realistic enough to know that there was no point in running again in Georgia, for the local whites, now in full control of all the forces of government, had made it clear that Negroes would be kept out of public office by whatever means necessary. He therefore returned to his tailoring business and to his wife, Lucinda, and their six children.

Reelected, Rainey stayed on in Washington with the Forty-second Congress as one of the four representatives from South Carolina, three of whom were black. He clashed with an Alabama congressman who argued that Northern whites could move South with their families and become Republican without fear of personal harm. This was not true in the state he represented, Rainey maintained. He recalled South Carolina Congressman Robert Elliott's stories of Winchester rifles being shipped into Charleston to arm ragged whites, who were then turned loose to force Republicans into inaction and silence through threats and murder. Rainey said that South Carolina was in a near state of war and Congress would be justified in taking whatever action necessary to maintain order.

His first major speech, delivered on April 1, 1871, was in support of a bill to crack down on individuals and groups terrorizing Negroes and white Republicans in the former slave states. Designed to enforce the citizenship rights set forth in the Fourteenth Amendment of the Constitution and the 1866 Civil Rights Act, this so-called KKK Act made it a federal crime for two or more persons to conspire through force, intimidation, or threats to keep any person from accepting or discharging a public office, from functioning in court without hindrance, or from voting or otherwise participating in political campaigns—on penalty of a five hundred to five thousand dollar fine and six months to six years in jail.

Rainey said the crimes constantly being perpetuated against Americans in the South were unparalleled in the nation's history. "The prevailing spirit of the [unreconstructed] South is either to rule or ruin," he charged. "Voters must perforce succumb to their wishes or else risk life itself in an attempt to maintain a simple right of common manhood." Whites, as well as blacks, were in need of protection by the federal government, he said, citing a newspaper account of the case of Dr. J. Winsmith, a seventy-year-old white physician, who had been called out of his house in the middle of the night and severely wounded by the Ku Klux Klan for "no greater offense" than his decision to join the Republican party in 1870.

As for the argument that all was tranquil in South Carolina from 1865 until the enactment of the reconstruction laws, he said that in the early postwar years the Southern whites were constrained because they felt that as former rebels they would certainly be punished. Once treated with clemency and kindness in a plan designed to return them to political life, they changed their tactics and again began to fight the federal government—this time through the Ku Klux Klan and other terrorist groups. "If the country there is impoverished it has certainly not been caused by . . . those who love the Union, but it is simply the result of a disastrous war madly waged against the best Government known to the world . . . ," he charged. "I pity the man or party . . . who would seek to ride into power over the dead body of a legitimate opponent."

Pointing out that he and his colleagues from South Carolina did not know when they returned to their home state whether the killers would strike them in the dead of night, he asked Congress and the country to remember, if such a fate befell them, that they had been loyal even though "bloody treason flourish'd over us." The bill for which he spoke was enacted into law on April 20, 1871, but the bloody terror in South Carolina was far from over.

In March 1872 he spoke in favor of appropriations for the federal courts set up under the KKK Act. In answer to a congressman from Virginia, who charged that federal moneys were being used to harass law-abiding citizens in his state where the Ku Klux Klan was not a force to be reckoned with, Rainey said the facts showed that Virginia voters were being intimidated and generally abused. In Norfolk, for example, he said the state legislature passed a law giving one Democratic councilman two votes when there was a deadlock of six Democrats against six Republicans in the Norfolk City Council.

He favored the appropriation of every dollar necessary to carry on the court prosecutions "until every man in the southern states shall know that this government has a strong arm"; and anyone—black or white—who did not willingly obey the law would be forced to comply at the point of a bayonet if necessary.

During this debate, while Rainey was in a conference, Congressman Samuel Cox of New York flayed the "disgracefully corrupt . . . state government of South Carolina, both black and white—and especially the black."

Informed of this intemperate assault, when he returned to the debate, Rainey politely skewered his opponent. He was surprised, he said, by Cox's attack. He considered Cox a man of talent, and he had not realized his respect was not reciprocated. If the Negroes could have enjoyed the same advantages of wealth and education as the New Yorker, "they would have shown to this nation that their color was no obstacle to their holding positions of trust, political or otherwise." Even without benefit of such advantages, they stood ready to be useful, intelligent citizens if allowed to exercise their rights. Rainey regretted he did not have time to defend the South Carolina government, but he noted that in that state where blacks had a nearly 2 to 1 majority, they had promulgated a liberal constitution designed for the good of all and had never once sought to use their majority to deprive the white minority of anything.

Rainey's dignified performance during this exchange was applauded by the press. The *New York Herald* said that this fine-looking, almost handsome, man, who would not have been allowed in the chamber ten years ago except as a servant, had the rapt attention of the members and galleries as he met the aspersions made against his race with well-chosen words and able arguments that evoked sympathy from both sides of the House. Warmly congratulated at the finish, he accepted the compliments "modestly while his face wore a pleased expression."

In this session Rainey indicated he favored political amnesty for former Confederates only if combined with a strong civil rights policy. His record was so pleasing to his district that he had the happy experience of running without opposition in the fall of 1872 and in this no-contest race, nearly twenty thousand of his supporters turned out to send him back to Washington.

No bill was of greater concern to him in the Forty-third Congress than the civil rights measure to afford equal treatment to all in public transportation, hotels, amusement places, and schools. Discussing the proposal, toward the end of 1873, he said blacks would certainly not ask Congress to pass legislation for themselves as a class if they could be guaranteed their full rights as citizens as a matter of course.

To those who were unwilling to give the black man his political rights if this would have a tendency to make him feel his manhood and elevate him above the "ordinary way of life," Rainey stated: "Just so long as you will let Kentucky and the other Southern States . . . mete out to us what they think we ought to have, and we receive it without objection, we are good, clever fellows; but just as soon as we begin to assert our manhood and demand our rights we are looked upon as men not worthy to be recognized, we become objectionable,

we become obnoxious, and we hear this howl about social
equality. . . ."

He said "the gentleman from Kentucky" knew they were not talking about intermarriage. "I am contented to be what I am so long as
I have my rights," Rainey asserted. "I am contented to marry one of
my own complexion. . . ." What he wanted, Rainey continued, was to
be able to go into a restaurant or hotel without being insulted and to
be treated like "our white colleagues on this floor." Black citizens, he
reminded the House, had been given their rights step by step in the
last three amendments to the Constitution, and now all that was
being asked was for the government to use its power to enforce laws
already on the books. He was the last person to speak before Congress went home for Christmas.

The next year the civil rights bill was still being batted back and
forth, with the Senate favoring a comprehensive measure and the
House trying to weaken it. The *Pittsburgh Evening Leader* caught
Rainey for an interview on June 8, 1874, just after Benjamin Butler of
Massachusetts had failed to shake the proposal loose for action in the
House through suspension of the rules.

Rainey, leaning his medium tall, rather stout frame against the
wall, told the reporter he had resigned all hope for passage of a
stronger bill that would cover education when it became clear that
there was not the two-thirds vote necessary to get it off the Speaker's
table. The reporter hinted that perhaps Butler was not really trying,
that he might not be as friendly to the bill as he pretended.

The South Carolina congressman answered that he personally believed Butler to be absolutely sincere. "We colored men will be content to wait if our friends think it unwise to push this measure at the
present," Rainey added resignedly. "We have been retiring in our position in this House, and no man can say we have been importunate
in our demands. We have been content to wait patiently in the background to see if justice will be done us, but we are tired of this dilly-
dallying. We want to know one thing or another. We want to know
what we can expect and to be kept no longer in mortifying suspense
as to our rights."

Rainey called it nonsense to contend that the blacks, if they chose,
should not block legislation, a strategy other members constantly
used. Negro members had deferred so far in an attempt to get things
done, but if pushed to the wall and given no consideration, they
would retaliate, he warned.

The manner of the smooth-shaven South Carolinian became even
more earnest as he asked: "Do you think it is right that when I go
forth from this capital as an honored member of Congress that I

should be subjected to insults from the lowest fellow in the street if he should happen to feel so inclined?"

The reporter wanted to know if Rainey was not fairly well treated in Washington. Pretty well, Rainey judged, but he said the black congressmen had to "live about" as best they could and pay higher expenses than the whites. He could not say how the city's hotels might treat him since he had never tried one. He had been openly insulted in Washington only once—at Ralf's, opposite the Post Office Building. He had ordered a glass of beer. When the waiter brought it, he told him the price was fifty cents. Knowing that five cents was more like the going rate, Rainey asked if he had not been overcharged because he was "a colored man." The waiter said yes. "I went away at this much mortified," the congressman told the reporter.

Rainey spoke of traveling from Charleston to Savannah first class by rail, only to be denied his first-class return accommodations. "Now how can it be that I am all right one way and a social leper the other?" Men sent to Washington to conduct the nation's business "should not have to go out in fear and trembling that we may be openly insulted when we are seeking only common necessities of life," he asserted.

When traveling first class by boat from Washington to Norfolk, he was forced to wait for the second table and eat with the servants, even though he had paid full fare. "I'd starve first," Rainey said. He always carried his own lunch on such a trip.

The reporter reminded Rainey that he was said to favor mixed schools, which was generally regarded as the most "obnoxious" provision of the bill. "Perhaps it is, but you must admit that it is our right," Rainey replied. "Do you suppose I want my two children hindered in the enjoyment of educational opportunities in this country merely on account of their color when we are taxed to support those schools?" If the civil rights bill failed, he said he would send his two children to school in Europe or Canada, even if he had to sell all he owned to pay for their education.

As a member of the Indian Affairs Committee, Rainey was called on to preside over the House early in May 1874, during the absence of the Speaker, when a proposal to improve conditions on the reservations was under discussion. He was the first black ever to do so. Soon afterward it was election time again, and he faced competition from Samuel Lee, a Negro who ran as an independent. Rainey won by eight hundred votes after a hard campaign, and returned to Washington for the second session of the Forty-third Congress.

Repeatedly the first black congressmen were called upon to explain why Negroes did not sue if they felt they had been mistreated or improperly served in public places. Rainey on February 3, 1875, still pressing for the civil rights bill, which was then moving toward the crucial vote, said he had once started to sue for having been thrown off a Richmond streetcar, but was prevailed upon to withdraw the suit so as not to cause greater dissension among the races.

He said rather wearily that every time a Negro took another step toward political participation—voting, jury service, whatever—the criers with alarm were there to protest that the change would only cause more trouble. He warned the other members of Congress that regardless of discouragements blacks had no intention of giving up the fight: "We do not intend to be driven to the frontier as you have driven the Indian. Our purpose is to remain in your midst an integral part of the body-politic. We are training our children to take our places when we are gone. We desire this bill that we may train them intelligently and respectably. . . ." At long last, on February 5, 1875, the House approved the civil rights bill, and Senate passage came a few weeks later.

Rainey's right to his seat in the Forty-fourth Congress, which convened on December 6, 1875, was challenged by Lee. Sometimes these election contests dragged on interminably, but Rainey's right to represent the First District was upheld by a Democratic House on May 24, 1876. Rainey was assigned to a special centennial committee, as well as to two regular committees—Invalid Pensions and Freedmen's Bank.

The major order of business for the second session of the Forty-fourth Congress was to verify the election of a President in time for the beginning of his scheduled term on March 4. The electoral count showed Rutherford B. Hayes, the Republican, the winner over Samuel J. Tilden, the Democrat, by a single vote; but for three of the states—Florida, South Carolina, and Louisiana—two different sets of electoral votes had been presented, and there were challenges to individual electors in a number of other states. A tripartite Electoral Commission, comprised of senators, representatives, and members of the Supreme Court, upheld the Republican slate in each of the challenged states.

The question before the House on February 28, 1877, was whether it would join the Senate in accepting the commission's decision to certify South Carolina's Republican electors. A Virginia Democrat argued that the members of no state should be included in the roll call when the House and Senate sat in joint session to count the votes for President and Vice-President if, like South Carolina, the election in that state had been carried at gunpoint, with the military acting as judges at the polls.

Rainey said the army had been called only because South Carolina was near anarchy. He advised the gentlemen on the other side to bear in mind that the voting constituency of his state was not the same as before the war. "It is for that reason," Rainey said, "that I stand here to speak, not in defense of any one man, not in defense of any set of men, but . . . of an enfranchised people, one and all, white and colored." He clearly disliked having the names of John C. Calhoun and other famous South Carolinians from the past thrown in his face and resented the gall of one member who said in his presence that South Carolina no longer had a voice in the House:

"She has not the voice of a former slaveholder and oppressor, but she has the voice of one of the oppressed race who stands here to vindicate the rights of his people whenever an opportunity is accorded him," Rainey retorted.

The Democratic House voted against accepting the Electoral Commission's decision on South Carolina, but as the Republican Senate voted to accept it, the commission's ruling held, as it did in all the other disputes over presidential electors, for the rules under which the matter was handled held that the Electoral Commission's findings would be accepted unless both houses of Congress voted against them.

The next two days were perhaps the most frenetic period in congressional history. The Senate and the House, separately or jointly, met almost around the clock trying to get the country a President in time to take office. Frantically the Democrats scrounged for the one elector who would change his mind. State Senator William Beverly Nash, a Negro South Carolina elector, was reportedly offered a hundred thousand dollars to switch his vote to Samuel J. Tilden. At one point the Senate left to consider a mysterious unopened package allegedly containing another set of electoral votes for Vermont. The president of the Senate refused to accept them, ruling they had arrived too late.

At 5:04 A.M., on March 2, just two days before the date of the inauguration, the votes from Wisconsin—then the last state alphabetically—were counted for the Hayes-Wheeler ticket, and the presiding officer declared that the Republican candidate, having received the majority of votes by a count of 185 to 184 "is duly elected President for four years commencing March 4, 1877." If the election had been decided on the basis of the popular vote, Tilden would have won; he outpolled Hayes by more than a quarter of a million votes.

This was the onstage action. Backstage the Republicans and Hayes had mollified the Democrats with the promise that the remaining federal troops would be pulled out of the South. This deal doomed the Republican party there and left the whites free to deprive blacks of their citizenship rights.

Though reelected to a fifth term in 1876, Rainey did not know from one day to the next if he would be serving in the Forty-fifth Congress since his seat was contested by a white Democrat, John Richardson, who claimed that he had been certified as the winner by the governor. Rainey maintained that the secretary of state, not the governor, had the legal authority in South Carolina to issue election certificates and that he had been certified by the same board of state canvassers that had validated the other Democratic and Republican representatives from South Carolina. The House voted to seat him, 175 to 108, on October 16, 1877, the second day of the session, after a congressman suggested that if Rainey were subject to such summary dismissal, all might be. However, the House Elections Committee decided to continue its investigation into the affair.

In midterm, the committee recommended that Rainey be ousted. A majority of the committee had found the charges and countercharges of corruption and intimidation so overwhelming that it recommended that the disputed seat be declared vacant. Although the House never got around to acting on the committee's report, the uncertainty cast a pall over Rainey and served to limit whatever influence he might have otherwise had. It also was not much of an inspiration for the battle he had to face at the polls in the fall of 1878 for election to the Forty-sixth Congress. That summer Rainey worked for the party in Michigan. In the fall he campaigned harder for a fellow Negro, South Carolina Representative Robert Smalls, than for himself. Both men were defeated, Rainey losing by more than eight thousand votes.

The early black Congressman who served longest in the House— by a few months over Robert Smalls—again defended the record of the Republican government of which he had been a part in South Carolina. He did not deny that there had been some "pecuniary corruption" among the Republicans, but he charged the Democrats had been shameless in their bribery. He added: "The destruction of the free ballot by the Democrats is an evil of greater magnitude than the extravagance of the Republicans."

Out of Congress for the first time in nearly nine years, Rainey had some party support for appointment as clerk of the House. When the Forty-sixth Congress convened in March 1879, however, the Democrats were in control. He joined the Internal Revenue Service as an agent in South Carolina and kept the position until July 15, 1881, when he resigned. After the Republicans regained control of the lower chamber in 1881, Rainey checked in at the Willard Hotel in

Washington and began to campaign for the House clerkship, which had seemed nearly within his grasp two years earlier.

His old friends encouraged him to his face, but when the vote came, the job again went to somebody else. He was willing to serve on the clerk's staff to get back in the political picture, but no position was forthcoming.

He entered the banking and brokerage business in Washington but was not successful. In 1886, his health impaired and his money depleted, he went home to Georgetown, South Carolina, where his wife opened a millinery shop. He died the next year at the age of fifty-five. According to the press, his "residency in Washington had ruined his health." In its obituary, the *Charleston News and Courier,* no friend of his when he was active in public life, termed him, next to Robert Elliott, the most intelligent of the South Carolina reconstruction politicians, and thought that if he had been less honest, he probably would have obtained even greater distinction.

Rainey's colleague from his initial year in Congress, Jefferson Long, had a few more years to live. After he left Washington in 1871, politics in Georgia became even more dangerous for blacks. In the fall of 1872, *The New York Times* reported, Long was accused by some newspapers of inciting a riot by advising Georgia blacks to go armed to the polls in order to protect themselves. Long denied the charge at a public meeting and urged the people to trust the federal government to maintain order.

Long said that he and other Negroes intended to leave the state and go where they could be secure in their rights as citizens. He recommended the organization of colonies to migrate west. Although his letter to the state's black population calling a June 1, 1872, meeting in Macon to organize emigration societies was printed twice—once on the front page—in Washington's *New National Era,* nothing ever came of the project.

Long occasionally attended Republican party gatherings such as regional or national conventions. His political career, his daughter later told a reporter, had lost her father some business temporarily, but J. F. Long and Son appears to have, nevertheless, fared well financially. He had an excellent library and spent his spare time reading. The prosperous tailor and ex-congressman died on February 5, 1900, at the age of sixty-four, at his home in the city of Macon. His passing was mourned by whites as well as Negroes.

The House trailblazers, Joseph Rainey and Jefferson Long, were both courageous battlers. They typify the black leaders who might have taken hold in the South if the national Republican party had not deserted them.

Robert Smalls/South Carolina

The *Planter's* eight Negro crewmen could scarcely mask their excitement as they watched the white officers of the dispatch vessel leave to go ashore to spend the night in Charleston. The 140-foot-long steamer, which had been plying between the South Carolina port and the outer islands transporting military supplies for the Confederate army, was in their hands until the commander returned. The *Planter* was loaded with guns and ammunition intended for Fort Riley and Fort Sumter.

The crew was headed by twenty-three-year-old Robert Smalls, whom the rebels had conscripted as a pilot. Ever since he learned that nearby Union forces under General David Hunter were welcoming blacks into their lines, Smalls had been waiting for an opportunity to steal the ship and turn her over to the federal commanders. It was bound to be hazardous, getting the side-wheeler past the guns of the Confederate harbor forts and guard ships, but the crew was willing to try. Now was his chance.

There was a flurry of activity as wood was taken aboard for fuel and steam was raised. On shore Small's wife and children made preparations to come aboard. At about three o'clock on the morning of May 13, 1862, the *Planter* slipped away from the dock and moved toward the Atlantic wharf to pick up the passengers who were waiting hidden on the *Etowan*.

In the boarding party, along with Mrs. Robert Smalls and her two small children, were her sister-in-law, Mrs. John Smalls, wife of the ship's engineer, three other women, a man, and another child. Smalls dropped anchor near the *Etowan* and sent a rowboat to pick up his family and the others. A half hour later, the ship, which could carry fourteen hundred bales of cotton or one thousand soldiers, was steaming across the harbor with its little band of patriots.

As she passed Fort Jackson, Smalls blew the usual whistle salute and continued on his way. The greatest danger came as they drew within range of Fort Sumter's guns. Wearing the Confederate captain's familiar floppy straw hat and gold-trimmed jacket, Smalls stood in the pilothouse, leaning on the window sill with his arms folded across his chest—as the white captain so often had. His trim figure was very much like that of the ship's commanding officer.

An answering signal to proceed came from Fort Sumter. The ship began to gather speed as it headed toward Morris Island, then in the hands of Union forces. The vessel had passed beyond the range of Sumter's fire before the guards on duty—finally alerted when the *Planter* quickened pace—suspected that something was amiss. By the time Sumter had signaled the *Planter* to stop, it was too late for counteraction from the Confederates.

Having outwitted the rebels, Smalls now faced the Union fleet blockading the harbor. He instructed a sailor to lift higher the white sheet that had been hoisted as soon as they were out of reach of the Confederate batteries. The pilot's main concern was the ship *Onward,* the vessel nearest the *Planter.* Could they see the white banner? Would the *Onward* lookouts think it was a ruse by the *Planter* to get in close enough to ram her?

Still the *Planter* pressed on, and the *Onward* held her fire. As soon as the two ships were within hailing distance, Smalls shouted that he and his compatriots were bringing the Southern craft to turn her over to the Union. The *Onward* captain, J. F. Nickels, boarded the *Planter,* and Smalls surrendered command of his vessel.

This bold deed made Smalls a celebrity overnight. His fame spread further when the Confederates offered the enticing sum of four thousand dollars for his capture. Everyone talked of how the black sailors had outsmarted their "white masters." Not only had the crew delivered a valuable, seaworthy ship into the hands of the Union fleet— literally under the noses of the Confederates—but they had deliberately waited until she was loaded with war supplies before making their move. Besides the *Planter*'s own armaments, there were cannon slated for transport the morning of the escape.

The man responsible for this exploit had been proving what could be accomplished through drive and daring ever since he was a child. At the age of twelve, Robert, the cheerful ingratiating son of Lydia Smalls, a house slave, and a white man, had been taken from the small town of Beaufort, South Carolina, to Charleston, where his master, Henry McKee, hired him out. His mother had been responsible for talking McKee into sending her boy away. Robert, who had been born in Beaufort on April 5, 1839, did not have the temperament of a slave, and she feared he would get into trouble if put to work on a plantation. Already he had balked at obeying such restrictions as the curfew bell. Robert was the fourth American generation of his mother's family, which came from the coast of Guinea.

Robert went to live in the home of Mrs. McKee's sister, working first as a lamplighter for four dollars a month and then as a horse driver on the Charleston wharves. At fifteen he became foreman of a crew of stevedores loading cotton for shipment north. He picked up the basics of sailmaking and rigging on the docks, and learned how to pilot steamships before his sixteenth birthday. Most of his wages were turned over to the McKees.

Though busy earning every extra penny he could, Robert was not too busy to fall in love with Hannah Jones, a hotel maid with black shining hair and sparkling eyes. While her regular earnings as a slave went to her owner, after hours she took in laundry to make money for herself. Robert, short, broad-shouldered, and slim-waisted, was nearly eighteen when he took Hannah home to Henry McKee's in Beaufort to marry her. The day after the birth of their daughter, Elizabeth Lydia, on February 12, 1858, the young father contracted to pay eight hundred dollars for the freedom of his wife and baby.

After the nation's split over the slavery issue reached the fighting stage, Robert was put to work on the Confederate-chartered *Planter*, first as a deckhand and then as a pilot. As a Negro, he was usually called wheelsman instead of pilot and fifteen dollars out of his monthly salary of sixteen dollars went to McKee. When the North took Beaufort early in the war, his mother, Lydia, was among the thousands of blacks who stayed behind after many of the whites fled. She remained in the McKee home to cook and keep house for the occupying Northern forces.

After the *Planter* became federal property, the Union made good use of Smalls's skill as a pilot, assigning him to various ships throughout the war. His familiarity with the South Carolina coastline and his knowledge of fortifications proved to be extremely helpful to his commanders as he assisted in pointing out and destroying the mines he had helped to plant. His up-to-date information on onshore gun placements was also invaluable.

Samuel F. DuPont, flag officer, wrote to Secretary of the Navy Gideon Welles recommending that the *Planter's* crew be rewarded for their large contribution to the war effort. "This man, Robert Smalls," he wrote, "is superior to any [of the Negroes] who has yet come into the lines, intelligent as many of them have been. His information has been most interesting, and portions of it of utmost importance. . . . I do not know, whether in the view of the Government, the vessel will be considered a prize; but, if so, [I] respectfully submit to the Department the claims of this man Robert and his associates."

Despite this appeal, the navy was far from generous with its prize money. For nearly a year the award was delayed, and Smalls was paid no salary for his work on the Union's ships. The value of the *Planter* and its cargo was set at only nine thousand dollars, of which the crew received 50 percent. Smalls, as leader, was awarded one third, or fifteen hundred dollars, of the crew's share. Later a congressional committee criticized the navy's evaluation, saying that the property was actually worth sixty to seventy thousand dollars and that Smalls and the other crew members should have received proportionately higher awards.

Smalls was sent to Port Royal, South Carolina, to join the *Crusader* as pilot. In June 1862 the *Crusader* and the *Planter* steamed to Simmon's Bluff, where they engaged Confederate artillery and infantry forces on shore before troops from the *Planter* landed and captured the supplies left by the fleeing rebels.

Smalls proved of great service to the Department of the South in obtaining Washington's approval for the use of Negro troops, some of whom General Hunter had already organized without authorization. The commander of the Department of the South hoped that by sending the witty, self-possessed Smalls to Washington as an example of the kind of courageous men he wanted to put into the military, he would convince President Abraham Lincoln and Secretary of War Edwin Stanton that black men should be given the chance to fight for their country.

Smalls talked first with Stanton and then conferred with Lincoln several times before he was given a message to take back to South Carolina in answer to Hunter's letter. In it Stanton authorized the general to accept up to five thousand volunteers of African descent, their pay and rations to be the same as those of white volunteers. The *Planter*'s pilot also made some speeches in New York before he returned to his ship for a strike against the bridges of the Charleston-Savannah railroad.

Finally in the spring of 1863 the military clarified Smalls's status somewhat by placing him on the army payroll as a pilot at fifty dollars a month. He was dispatched to work for the navy, with his first assignment on one of the new ironclads, the *Keokuk*. This ship was hit ninety-six times during an attack on Fort Sumter on April 7. The *Keokuk* managed to limp away but sank the next morning, with Smalls, whose eyesight had been impaired in the fight, and other survivors jumping off in time to be picked up by the *Ironsides*.

Smalls was back on the *Planter* when she encountered heavy fire from Southern guns at Secessionville while on patrol in Folly Island Creek, South Carolina. When the *Planter's* commander abandoned his station and shut himself up in the coal bunker, Smalls hurried to the pilot house, took command, and steered the ship out of danger. In recognition of his courage and initiative, the twenty-four-year-old pilot was promoted to the rank of captain. Not long afterward he became a father for the third time; he and Hannah named the baby Sarah. Their son, Robert, Jr., had died of smallpox, but their daughter Elizabeth survived. For the rest of the war, Smalls served as captain of the ship he had filched from the South. He was paid $150 a month —one of the highest salaries earned by a Negro serviceman during the Civil War.

During the final stretch of the war, the *Planter*—after time out for repairs in Philadelphia—was used as a troop transport. Taking advantage of the layoff in Philadelphia, Smalls, who had never had an opportunity to go to school, hired a couple of tutors to teach him to read and write.

The *Planter's* last big wartime assignment was to help ferry General William Tecumseh Sherman's men into South Carolina. She also transported ex-slaves to the farmlands being distributed to them by order of General Sherman. After Charleston was captured on February 18, 1865, Smalls piloted the *Planter* back to her home city. Vanguard units into Charleston were the Twenty-first United States Volunteers and the Fifty-fourth Massachusetts Regiment, both Negro. He worked with the Union commanders, setting up public meetings with the blacks and introducing those in charge to whites as well.

Smalls piloted the *Planter*, carrying more than two thousand passengers, to the gala victory celebration at Fort Sumter. In the fall of 1866, his life with the beloved ship drew to a close. With Captain Smalls in command for the last time, she sailed to Baltimore, where she was put out of commission and sold.

Smalls settled in Beaufort and bought for seven hundred dollars, at a tax-sale auction, the McKee property on Prince Street where he and his mother had lived in slavery. For a while he ran a store. The McKee family had lost everything in the war, and the ex-slave gave his former owners a home and some tillable land where they lived out their days. This gift was to repay the "many kindnesses shown him and his mother," according to the notes made by his son William.

In Beaufort, he hired a teacher—a Northerner who had come South to teach in the public schools—to come to his house and give him private instruction, taking up where he had left off in Philadelphia. Always a man of action, he charted for himself a concentrated course of learning. For three months he arose every day at five in the morning and studied until seven to prepare for his two or three hours of instruction. This was the extent of his formal education. The rest came from studying along with his children and from reading the newspapers.

Smalls found the black population of South Carolina eager to take advantage of the new rights and privileges granted by the government. More than 80,000 Negroes and 46,882 whites signed up during voter registration in October 1867. Caucasians in the state were greatly outnumbered by blacks, and some whites were still disqualified as voters because of their wartime activities. Nonwhites were in the majority in twenty-one of the state's thirty-one counties; in Beaufort county, the ratio was 7 to 1.

The state Republican party was formally organized at a meeting held in Columbia on July 24, 1867. When the South Carolina constitutional convention was held in that city six months later, Smalls and five others, who later became congressmen, were among the 76 Negro delegates attending in a total of 124. This convention produced a constitution far ahead of its time in terms of social and civic reforms. Smalls introduced a resolution calling for compulsory free education for children, but the opposition amended it to stave off mandatory attendance. He was elected to the lower house of the state legislature in 1868, and finished a term there before graduating to the state senate.

Smalls was active on many fronts during this period. He was a delegate in 1872 to the Republican national convention in Philadelphia. As a brigadier general in the state militia, he helped maintain order. After traveling throughout the United States to raise money for a school in his county, he bought a site and deeded it to the Negro children of Beaufort. There are now two schools in Beaufort named after him—Robert Smalls high and elementary.

A hard worker for the Republicans, he reaped his political reward in the fall of 1874 with his election to represent the Third District in Congress by a comfortable majority over J. P. M. Epping for the term starting December 6, 1875. Since his wife preferred to remain in Beaufort, his companion in the capital was his elder daughter, Elizabeth, who left school in Boston to act as her father's secretary and hostess.

Appointed to the Agriculture Committee, he supported a bill to extend time for redemption of lands held for direct taxes and introduced his own measure to make improvements in Port Royal harbor. He did what he could to get positions in Washington for the son and daughter of his former mistress, Mrs. Henry McKee. In June 1876 the freshman representative vainly attempted to tack an antidiscrimination amendment to an army reorganization bill. His amendment would have specified: "Hereafter in the enlistment of men in the Army, or the merging of enlisted men into other organizations, no distinction whatever shall be made on account of race or color."

Unable to get the floor for any length of time, Smalls nonetheless managed to make his point succinctly in an exchange with Congressman Henry Banning of Ohio, who argued that no special mention of race was required to assure Negroes of equal treatment by pointing out that "the gentleman [from South Carolina] has the same right to enlist in the army that he had to run for Congress." Smalls came back with: "I know, sir, that no colored man could have enlisted in the Army if Congress had not passed a special act authorizing such enlistment, and I feel if matters go on just as they are going on now, and if we should have one or two more Democratic Houses of Representatives, I shall not be allowed to come here; and no change in the law will be made either."

The House was asked to authorize troops to protect the Texas frontier from the Mexicans. In July, Smalls wanted Congress to show equal concern over the need for protection in South Carolina, where Negroes were being terrorized by heavily armed whites. He proposed that the Texas bill be amended to specify "that no troops for the purposes named in this section shall be drawn from the State of South Carolina so long as the militia of that State peacefully assembled are assaulted, disarmed, and taken prisoners, and then massacred in cold blood by lawless bands of men invading that State from the State of Georgia."

Again pressed for time on the floor, having been allotted only five minutes, Smalls sent a newspaper clipping of an "eyewitness account of the massacre at Hamburg" to the clerk to be read. The news story was a letter to Smalls describing in detail the torture and murder of black militia and police officers by a white mob, led by a former Confederate General Matthew C. Butler.

Two congressmen pressed Smalls to reveal the identity of the eyewitness. Smalls said that he was responsible for the name and would vouch for the writer. When the question was reiterated, he shot back: "I will say to the gentleman if he is desirous that the name shall be given in order to have another Negro killed, he will not get it from me."

White harassment of political figures was by no means limited to Negroes. The campaign of 1876 was a particularly harrowing one for South Carolina Republicans. Smalls not only covered his district for himself but toured the state with Governor David H. Chamberlain working for the reelection of the governor and for the Hayes-Wheeler presidential ticket.

One sultry Saturday afternoon in August the people of Edgefield gathered in a grove to hear stirring band music and listen to speeches made by Governor Chamberlain and Congressman Smalls. The mood was carefree and relaxed until the sounds of galloping horses and rebel yells filled the air. In a flash the temper changed to apprehension as the Democratic leader, General Butler, and his pistol-packing, rifle-carrying Red Shirts rode through the crowd, got off their horses, and ringed the speakers' platform. They demanded that Butler and some of his supporters be allowed to address the throng, saying they wanted equal time with the Republicans. Anxious to avoid injury to the unarmed men, women, and children gathered for what they expected to be a peaceful political meeting, the Republicans agreed. Chamberlain began to outline his plans for a reform government, but the troublemakers, who pressed in against the platform and climbed into the branches of nearby trees, harangued him with shouts and gibes.

Butler, who during the Civil War had ridden into battle carrying a silver-mounted riding crop and fought on despite the loss of his right foot at Brandy Station, took the stand surrounded by his armed guard. The handsome, dashing Democrat taunted Smalls and Chamberlain to prove their charge that he was a leader of the Ku Klux Klan or "to stand as self-confessed liars." There was no opportunity for either man to reply. No sooner were the words out of Butler's mouth than the overloaded platform collapsed from the weight of his men. Even on the trip back to the railroad station Smalls and Chamberlain were accompanied by the Red Shirts who warned them to stay out of Edgefield.

Later that month Smalls broke off personal compaigning in his district when the governor ordered him to take a militia company to quell disturbances in the rice fields by the Combahee River. The Negro workers had chosen harvest time to strike for a 50 percent raise and payment made in checks good somewhere else than at the planters' stores. They were threatening the strikebreakers sent in to gather the crops and had shut some of them up in outhouses.

Smalls elected to go alone without the troops. Strike leaders had been arrested by the sheriff, but freed on the way to jail by a band of workers who had overpowered the lawmen. The trouble was escalating toward a confrontation between the sheriff's special posse—to be comprised mainly of Red Shirts, no doubt—and the determined but unarmed strikers.

The congressman defused the situation by listening to the grievances of the rice workers and promising to support them if they followed his advice. He persuaded the strike leaders to submit to arrest at the Beaufort courthouse before the posse arrived; he then succeeded in having the charges against them dropped after they spent a single night in jail.

Smalls informed the newspapers about the workers' complaints and managed to convince some of the planters they should pay their employees in cash and raise their wages. The strike continued, however, in other parts of Beaufort County where the workers were less fortunate. Within a matter of days he was back again to act as a buffer between the planters and the irate workers. The angry strikers had massed outside a company store in which several planters had locked themselves for protection.

This time the workers would not follow his counsel. They refused to disperse when he asked them to. He warned them that if one of the white men inside were the slightest bit wounded or roughed up all their lives would be in danger. The crowd's mood was surly. One man threatened him, and others shouted angrily that he had sold out his own race to the whites. Still, Smalls stood his ground on the steps of the store, facing the tense, wrought-up crowd and talking for hours, until the danger dissipated and the strikers drifted away.

The next stop for Smalls in that long hot summer was Columbia where he chaired the Republican state convention through a five-day session. Governor Chamberlain was renominated, and the party's national ticket for President was endorsed. It was a dangerous time on the hustings with armed bands roaming the state, threatening Republican voters. Twenty-five Negroes and two whites were killed in Ellentown. The President ordered the "rifle clubs" disbanded, but the Red Shirts simply regrouped under innocuous names such as Mother's Little Helpers and the Allendale Mounted Baseball Club—a ruse that fooled no one.

Despite the hazards and his wife's pleas that he not expose himself unnecessarily, Smalls felt compelled to return to Edgefield before the campaign ended. He believed he must respond to the insults hurled by the Butler crowd—as a show of courage to inspire blacks to go out and vote despite threats.

Federal marshals and an election commissioner made the trip to Edgefield with him; United States soldiers were on hand to meet him at the station. He spoke to the Republican faithful, and although his military guard was outnumbered by white civilians on horseback with their pistols in full view, and insults were hurled at him, there was no violence at the meeting.

When this nerve-wracking campaign was over and the votes were counted, Smalls had held off the challenge of his opponent, George Tillman, by more than a thousand votes. Two men claimed the governor's office; both parties were trying to organize the state legislature; and there was a dispute over who was entitled to South Carolina's presidential electoral votes.

The Republicans did not hold South Carolina, though their challenged electoral vote helped to put a Republican in the White House by the margin of a single vote. Little more than a month later—in April 1877—the United States Army detachment was withdrawn from the South Carolina statehouse, where the two rival governments had been struggling for control, and returned to quarters. Many South Carolina Republicans—white and black alike—soon left the state. The reform administration of Chamberlain collapsed when the governor, powerless without federal help to maintain order against armed dissidents, was forced to turn over the office to Wade Hampton, the Democrat. The state board of canvassers ruled that Hampton had won in the election of 1876 by a slight majority, but they took no cognizance of the fact that the Red Shirts had barred Negroes from the polls and stuffed the ballot boxes. The Republicans charged fraud and fought to hold the governorship until the army left, after which Chamberlain moved to New York where he practiced law.

Reelected despite voter intimidation, Smalls was confronted with a contested election, but the House of Representatives upheld the count giving him the seat. He had little time to function in the Forty-fifth Congress, however, as he now faced the gravest challenge of his political career. As soon as the Democrats recaptured the South Carolina statehouse in 1877, they launched an investigation of the Republican reconstruction legislatures, tracking down reports of mishandling of public funds and other corruption. Though justified by the irregularities they uncovered, this study helped to divert public attention from the violent methods the Democrats had used to gain office.

Smalls was indicted on the charge of accepting a five thousand dollar bribe from the Republican Printing Company. Several other Republicans were also accused of having been suborned by this same firm. Smalls maintained his innocence in the face of what he called a politically inspired charge. The only witness against him was Josephus Woodruff, white clerk of the state senate and head of the Republican Printing Company, which had made Woodruff rich. He confessed that he had robbed the state of $250,000 and then testified that he had given Smalls a check for $5,000; but the cancelled check was never presented.

Smalls was convicted by a jury of seven Negroes and five whites, and sentenced to three years at hard labor, a sentence that was upheld by the South Carolina Supreme Court. In a week he was released on bail to return to Congress, while awaiting an appeal of his case to the United States Supreme Court. To Smalls's complete surprise, he received formal notification from the governor that he had been pardoned. The surprise turned to dismay, however, when he heard reports of a state-federal deal whereby the state would quash charges against reconstruction legislators in exchange for the federal government's dropping its suits against white South Carolinians charged with violating the federal election laws.

Hoping for vindication by the Supreme Court, Smalls tried to reach his lawyers in time to head off South Carolina's attorney general, but he lost the race and his case was dropped from the Supreme Court calendar. Aware that he would have to live with this shadow for the rest of his life, the congressman did not waste time in brooding but directly took his fight to the voters of his district. The Red Shirts—those armed whites with blood-colored garments who had intimidated Negroes and other Republicans at the polls in 1876—were active in Smalls's district, and this time their work paid off. A white Democrat, George Tillman, won South Carolina's Third Congressional seat in the election of 1878.

When election time again came, Smalls decided to try to regain his old position. He still had great influence with the mass of the people, though some of the Republican leaders refused to support him because of the printing scandal. Years later, the *Charleston News and Courier,* which had given him anything but aid when he needed it, said he had been convicted on insufficient evidence in an unfair trial. Smalls mounted a forceful campaign, and protected by armed guards from the terrorists who regularly disrupted Republican meetings, he traveled throughout his district to tell Negro and white voters he was innocent of the charges made against him.

After the canvassing was over and the votes were in, an official state count gave the election to Tillman by more than eight thousand votes. Charging intimidation at the polls, Smalls appealed for a recount, to Congress, which did not take up his challenge until July 18, 1882. The Elections Committee report was presented by Representative John T. Wait of Connecticut, who cited the case of Edgefield to demonstrate how Smalls supporters had been kept away from the polls. There the Red Shirts firing guns had ridden through the streets to intimidate the blacks. The balloting took place in an upstairs room in the courthouse with a door that opened just eighteen inches and a Democratic guard standing in back of it. The Red Shirts also lined up in front of the courthouse, brandishing their firearms. Still 2,000 to 2,500 black voters were brave enough to walk past the guns to cast their ballot. Yet when the votes were counted at Edgefield, the Negro candidate had only 11, against 763 for Tillman, the House committee found.

Wait said that the committee believed Smalls was entitled to the seat by at least 1,500 votes, though the governor of South Carolina had declared Tillman the winner with 23,325 votes, against 15,287 for Smalls. After protracted debate, Smalls was seated the following day by a vote of 141 to 1 to serve the remaining months of his third term in Congress. Always alert for his district's interest, he guided an amendment through to authorize an appropriation for harbor improvements at Port Royal.

By the time of the election of the Forty-eighth Congress, South Carolina had been gerrymandered so that a black candidate would have a chance in only one district, the Seventh. Smalls planned to stand for that seat, but encountered opposition in the Republican convention from Samuel Lee, a Negro, and E. W. M. Mackey, a white, whose wife was a mulatto. To break a week's deadlock, Smalls pulled out of the race and threw his support to Mackey. The Democrats passed up the contest. Lee entered as an independent, but lost to the regular Republican Mackey. Following Mackey's death on January 28, 1884, Smalls was elected, without opposition, to fill the vacancy in Congress.

Smalls, throughout his congressional career, represented the interests of all his constituents—not just the blacks. Many of his numerous bills for individuals were on behalf of whites. He invariably favored the liberal approach in easing the tax burden of his state. In Beaufort, where every house had been commandeered by the Union army for hospitals during the Civil War, he wanted federal help for Southerners who had lost their property for nonpayment of wartime taxes. "It's true," he explained, "that many persons who lost their property are now dead and gone, but their children (minor children in large part) should not suffer on account of their actions."

Like other early black congressmen, Smalls sought to shore up ignored or court-weakened laws with enforceable statutes. In February 1885 he tried to attach a rider to a District of Columbia bill requiring operators of all eating places in the capital to serve everyone regardless of color. A procedural dodge kept this amendment from even getting before the House. When a West Virginia representative assured Smalls that the District of Columbia already had such a law, Smalls came back with: "That law I do not think exists in the District. If so, it is constantly violated."

Both Smalls and his West Virginia colleague were right to an extent. There was an 1872 District of Columbia law—supported by an

49

1873 enforcement act—which forbade discrimination in eating places, barber shops and ice-cream parlors, but they were dead statutes, not only in Smalls's day, but until 1953 when John R. Thompson asked the United States Court of Appeals to make the District implement them.

Some observers thought Smalls might lose the Republicans' support for reelection to a fifth term. The *Washington Bee,* a black weekly, on August 30, 1884, took editorial note of the considerable opposition to his renomination by people "who charged him with doing things he ought not to have done and not doing things he ought to have." While admitting that he was like other men and not Simon pure, the paper said that paid emissaries were going through his district spreading falsehoods about him. The *Bee* did not want to raise the "color line," but it suggested that a district with thirty thousand voters and only six thousand of them white should not go to a white man. Such a thing would not happen, the paper said, "if the colors were reversed the other way around."

Smalls succeeded in getting his party's nomination and defeated William Elliott, a Democrat and former Confederate in the election by four thousand votes. Smalls's victory was sweetened by the honor of receiving three votes in the state legislature for the office of United States Senator.

By now, Robert Smalls was a familiar figure in Washington; he was a short man who had grown heavier with the years and who favored Prince Albert suits, top hats, and high button shoes. His wife had died in July 1883. His companion at capital functions was his younger daughter, Sarah. His other daughter, Elizabeth, had married and was running her own home. In 1891 he married Annie Wigg, a teacher, much nearer his daughters' age than his own. Two years later she bore him his last child, William Robert.

In 1886 the veteran congressional campaigner took his case to the people for the last time, again running against Elliott. Democrats in the state received help from the national party in this all-out effort to rid South Carolina of its only remaining Republican congressman. The Republicans did little to assist Smalls in fighting back. The local organization was split, and the national party showed faint interest in the contest. By this time, keeping Negroes away from the polls had become a routine procedure—and one no longer of any real concern to Congress, which was inclined to allow the unreconstructed elements in the South to have their way. Elliott won, and the Republicans lost this "safe black district." Smalls challenged the count and went to Washington to speak to the House on his own behalf. Eight hundred pages of testimony documenting how thousands of voters had been forced away from the polls and thousands of other votes had been thrown out was not enough to convince a Congress already weary of hearing about "the Negro problem." He lost by a vote of 127 to 142 on February 13, 1889.

By then the forty-nine-year-old politician, whose whiskers were now quite white, had already been prevailed upon to step aside to allow a younger man, Thomas E. Miller, a lawyer, a chance at the congressional seat, which Miller succeeded in recapturing for the party in 1888. In 1892 Smalls lost in a four-way race for the Republican nomination.

South Carolina's elder statesman kept his hand in politics as a delegate to the Republican party's national conventions. In 1895 he was a member of the state's constitutional convention. Smalls feared that this group would erase the civil rights advances gained in the precedent-setting constitutional convention of 1868, but he was determined to make a fight of it. He battled hardest to preserve voting rights for the blacks.

The ex-congressman charged that 53,000 people—mostly blacks— had been killed in the South since Reconstruction times and "not more than three white men have been convicted and hung for those crimes." He pointed out that as of 1890 the Negroes of South Carolina were already paying taxes on $12,500,000 worth of property. On behalf of the 600,000 blacks, 132,000 of them voters, he demanded a "fair and honest election law."

While declaring that blacks would be willing to accept literacy or other qualifications if these restrictions were applied to all, Smalls argued against a proposal requiring a voter to be able to read the constitution himself or interpret it when read to him. "You dare not disfranchise them [the whites]; and you know that the man who proposes it will never be elected to another office in the State of South Carolina. . . ." Ordinary men, he said, could not be expected to understand every section of the constitution and explain it in a way to correspond with the interpretation of an election manager. He noted that in a recent state supreme court decision, two of the justices put one construction on a section of the constitution while a third had an entirely different interpretation. "To embody such a provision in the election law would be to mean that every white man would interpret it aright and every Negro would interpret it wrong," he declared.

Smalls pleaded with the delegates not to enact laws that would drive out the Negroes, who were so vital to South Carolina's cotton and mining industries. He said the unrest in the state was bad for business, that foreign investors were unwilling to risk their capital on its timber. And, as was typical of his easy-going style, he used humor to answer the racial slurs of an old adversary, Senator Ben Tillman, who had returned home from Washington expressly to ram through the suffrage revision: "The other day . . . I heard him make a very eloquent speech . . . but before he got through he had acted like the good Jersey cow, which gave her two gallons of milk, and, though she did not put her foot in it before she was through, she had shaken so much dirt from her tail into the pail that we could not accept the milk."

But neither good-natured jokes, logic, nor eloquence could move the majority of that convention. Smalls's suffrage plan, calling for retention of the right of suffrage for all males of the age of twenty-one was not even put to a vote. The chairman, in violation of the existing constitution, which allowed two members to ask for a roll-call vote, ruled that ten were required; and that, as Smalls pointed out, was four more than were available in his "dark corner."

The constitutional interpretation requirement was adopted as a not very subtle subterfuge to keep blacks from voting, and it worked just as effectively in South Carolina as it did in Mississippi.

The veteran politician was at his scathing best in introducing an amendment to the new state constitution's proposed ban on intermarriage between the races. The section, as proposed and passed, and since declared unconstitutional by the United States Supreme Court, read: "The marriage of a white person with a Negro or a mulatto, or a person who shall have one-eighth or more of Negro blood, shall be unlawful and void." Smalls proposed this addition: "and any white person who lives and cohabits with a Negro, mulatto, or person who shall have one-eighth or more of Negro blood, shall be disqualified from holding any office of emolument or trust in this State, and the offspring of any such living or cohabiting shall bear the name of the father, and shall be entitled to inherit and acquire property the same as if they were legitimate."

Though obviously of partially white ancestry himself, Smalls said he personally did not favor racial intermarriage. But if there was to be mixing, he preferred legal to illicit relationships. The last census, he noted, put the number of African Americans of mixed blood at 1,132,060, out of a total of 7,470,035 Negroes. Most of this miscegenation—two thirds—had taken place in the South.

"A careful perusal of the census, also history, shows that more than three-fourths of the mothers of this large number of mixed blood whom you seek to legislate against, are colored women. If so, who could have been their fathers?" he asked. "So you see, gentlemen, you are responsible for the wrongs that have been done; let us in the name of God, and in behalf of virtue, try and put a stop to this cohabitation."

Smalls agreed with an earlier speaker's assessment of the quality and chastity of South Carolina womanhood, but he said that black women, as pure as any on this earth, must be included. Perhaps, he suggested, women should be given the vote so they could enact laws to "make you as pure as they are." On the other hand, he continued: "If your women are as pure as you stated, and I have reason to believe that they are, they can be trusted; then why the necessity of this being placed in the Constitution? Can you not trust yourselves?"

Smalls charged that wrongs were still perpetrated against South Carolina womanhood but by white, not black, men: "If a Negro should improperly approach a white woman, his body would be hanging on the nearest tree filled with air holes before daylight the next morning—and perhaps properly so. If the same rule were applied on the other side, and white men who insulted or debauched Negro women were treated likewise, this Convention would have to be adjourned . . . for lack of a quorum."

This speech prompted the *New York Press* of October 5, 1895, to say: "It's not the Negro ignorance, but the Negro intelligence that is feared." Though burdened with grief over the unexpected death of his young wife and depressed by the handwriting on the wall for his people, the dedicated public servant stayed through the long meeting.

Smalls refused to put his name on the revised constitution, which he felt had succeeded in its purpose of "legalizing the frauds perpetrated upon the elective franchise in this state since 1876"; as a result he was denied the expense money that was legitimately his as a delegate.

After Smalls was named customs collector for Beaufort in 1897, he and his son frequently visited Washington, where the former congressman sat in on House debates and sometimes met with the President William McKinley. Once in the capital both Smalls and his son enjoyed themselves, but the trip in an uncomfortable, stuffy Jim Crow railroad car was depressing. He was among the few blacks permitted to vote in Beaufort.

The Civil War veteran turned down an offer to become the colonel of a Negro regiment during the Spanish-American War. He also declined the post of minister to Liberia, probably because his health was not up to such an assignment. In his last years he suffered from diabetes. In 1900 he took to the campaign trail again, touring the Midwest to work for McKinley's reelection. The ever loyal Republican lost his last federal job in 1912 when a Republican Congress did not confirm him as customs collector.

His final test as a community leader came in the spring of 1913. Two Negroes, suspected of murdering a white man, were threatened by a lynch mob marching on Beaufort. Smalls quickly dispatched blacks to key points throughout the city and spread the word that the torch would be set to Beaufort if the sheriff did not protect his prisoners. The message got through. The sheriff posted special guards at strategic places and the white lynching mob was turned back. Two years later, on February 22, Robert Smalls, a resilient man who had fought fiercely and effectively for his convictions in war and peace, died quietly in his sleep at the age of seventy-six in the home where he and his mother had once worked as slaves.

John R. Lynch/Mississippi

John R. Lynch, the son of a white father and a black slave mother, was an adroit political leader before he was old enough to vote, and he remained a power in Mississippi until the last spark of the Republican reconstruction party flickered out in the South.

His father, Patrick Lynch, a rich man, had left instructions that Catherine Lynch and their children were to be freed should anything happen to him. After he died unexpectedly, his wishes were not carried out. Instead, mother and children were sold and shipped from Louisiana to Mississippi as the property of one Alfred Davis.

John Roy, who had been born in Vidalia, Louisiana, on September 10, 1847, managed to learn to read and write. In Natchez, Mississippi, he worked as a photographer. He went to night school for four months after the federal troops took Natchez in the Civil War.

As an enthusiastic member of the Natchez Republican Club, he attended political meetings whenever possible and spoke when called upon. Though still a minor, he campaigned hard in 1867 to get the vote out for ratification of the new state constitution. He attributed the defeat of that document, by a margin of about 8,000 votes out of a total of 120,000 cast, to a combination of intimidation of black voters and general opposition to a clause disfranchising a great many of the state's former officeholders.

One of the first acts of the Forty-first Congress, after the 1868 elections, authorized President Grant to resubmit the rejected Mississippi constitution to the electorate on a clause-by-clause basis. Until the election machinery approved by Congress could begin working, a number of offices were to be filled on an appointive basis by the military governor, Adelbert Ames. Aware of this, the Natchez Republican club held a meeting to assemble a list of recommendations of people to fill the various political positions. The committee designated Lynch to present the club's choices to Ames.

Taking a leave of absence from his Natchez photography shop, Lynch made the week's trip to Jackson where he saw Governor Ames without difficulty. Lynch outlined the qualifications of the people on the list to the provisional executive, who indicated that his selections would be made within a few weeks. When the official appointments were announced, it turned out that few of the Natchez candidates had been selected, but much to his amazement, Lynch's own name appeared as justice of the peace. This unsought honor brought on his first political crisis.

The Reverend H. P. Jacobs, who had the Natchez club's endorsement for justice of the peace, was certain that Lynch had double-crossed him. A black Baptist minister, Jacobs had been a delegate to the Mississippi constitutional convention. Lynch assured Jacobs and his associates he had made no pitch for himself, and fearful of destroying party unity, considered refusing the post. Friends, however, urged him to accept the offer, and he finally decided, "despite my youth and inexperience," to take the position. The appointment gave his club some recognition, and he did not want to offend the governor, with whom he had established a comfortable rapport.

The twenty-one-year-old appointee now faced the dilemma of raising the required bond of two thousand dollars. There were no Negro bondsmen, and few blacks owned real estate. He finally found two blacks who could and did sign a note for a thousand dollars each. Lynch took the oath of office in April 1869. The news was greeted with sarcasm by the local Democratic paper: "We are now reaping the ravishing fruits of reconstruction."

It was this dispute over Lynch's appointment, a relatively minor political plum, that split the Republicans into two factions in Adams County and brought on the intraparty fight that gave compromise candidate Hiram Revels the choicest prize the Natchez Republicans had to offer—their nomination for the state senate. More than any other person, Revels credited his friend Lynch with helping him to become a state senator.

Once the battle over the state senate seat ended, the warring factions united and agreed on a three-man slate for the legislature, which included one white man and two rival black leaders—Jacobs and Lynch. All were elected without difficulty in November. Lynch resigned in December as justice of the peace to assume his duties in the Mississippi house of representatives.

In Jackson, Lynch rapidly developed into an adept parliamentarian and a leader to be reckoned with. In the early postwar period many white Republicans worked harmoniously with their black colleagues.

There was little overt racial discrimination within the ranks of a party built primarily on Negro votes.

During his years in the legislature, Mississippi was reorganized on a top-to-bottom basis—the judiciary, the school system, the prisons. Before the Civil War there were few schools in the state except in the larger towns. Lynch was particularly proud of the public school system established while he was in state office. The blacks took what they could get at the time—separate schools for whites and blacks— but Lynch put through an amendment requiring any district with only one school to open its doors to all eligible children. He called the schools a "creditable monument to the first Republican state administration." He also thought the penal reforms worthy of praise.

In 1872 the regular Republican caucus backed Lynch for Speaker. The Republicans had a comfortable majority in the legislature, but only about a third of the membership there was Negro. On the floor vote five white Republicans broke away from the leadership to vote for an independent Republican. Two independents and one regular Republican and one Democrat ran against Lynch. He received fifty-five votes—just one short of the number required for election.

The Democrats would have swung to either of the white Republicans to organize the house, but neither man would give way to his rival. The deadlock continued for days. Fearful lest the Democrats capture the speakership, Mississippi's two United States senators, James Alcorn and Adelbert Ames, returned from Washington to try to get the balky Republicans in line. The presence of Alcorn, who had resigned from the governorship to take the Senate post, was crucial; most of the bolters took their cues from him.

As Lynch recounted the story in his book, *The Facts of Reconstruction,* Alcorn told the holdouts that representatives who had been elected as Republicans were honor-bound to support the caucus nominee for Speaker or else they should resign and allow their constituents to elect someone who would. He said that a Republican-organized legislature would be an endorsement of his administration as governor.

Two Carroll county legislators confessed they were dubious as to how their constituents might react if they supported a "colored man" for Speaker. "But," said Alcorn, as quoted by Lynch, "could you have been elected without the votes of colored men? If you now vote against a colored man . . . simply because he is a colored man, would you expect those men to support you in the future? Can you then afford to offend the great mass of colored men that supported you in order to please an insignificantly small number of narrow-minded whites?"

After Alcorn's lecture, the Republicans came up with sixty-three votes for Lynch and organized the house with him in the Speaker's chair. The newspapers thought his natural ability and expertise as a parliamentary tactician made him an obvious choice for the spot.

The light-brown, curly-haired speaker was named a trustee of Alcorn College, the new Negro institution headed by his protégé, former Senator Revels. At the close of the legislative session in the spring of 1873, Lynch indicated that the speakership had been a very rewarding and fruitful assignment for him. Now he was set to move up to a larger arena, having won the seat from the Sixth Congressional District in the fall of 1872, besting Democrat Hiram Cassidy by six thousand votes.

The Mississippi House met on Saturday, April 24, 1873, to give its speaker a rousing sendoff. The orators were lavish, warm, and sincere-sounding in their praise of the young man who would soon be leaving them for Washington. As the son of a former Speaker presented the retiring Speaker with a gold, stem-winder watch with a chain a yard long—a farewell gift from Democrats and Republicans alike—one of the legislators said if the house's sentiments could be put into a phrase, it would be "God bless John R. Lynch. He is an honest and fair man."

The *Jackson Clarion* enthused: "His bearing in office had been so proper and his rulings in such marked contrast to the partisan conduct of the ignoble whites of his party who have aspired to be the leaders of the blacks that the conservatives cheerfully joined in the testimonial."

At twenty-six, Mississippi's first black representative was the second youngest man ever to sit in the House. (The youngest was William Charles Cole Claiborne, of Sullivan County, Tennessee, who was only twenty-two when he went to Congress in 1797.) Lynch was as aggressive in Washington as he had been in his home state. In December 1873 as a very junior member, he urged a compromise on the move to repeal a twenty-five hundred dollar raise in pay, which Congress had voted for itself, bringing the salary up to seventy-five hundred dollars annually. No Congress, he argued, should be allowed to tamper with its own pay; any salary increase or decrease should not apply until after the next election. He recommended a figure of six thousand dollars plus travel expenses for one trip home. Public clamor for a cutback was effective, and the salary was rolled back. During his first session he also put through two bills of significance to his state— one involving judicial revisions, the other a year's postponement for a Mississippi election.

Lynch, who looked younger than his years, participated in the protracted debate on the 1875 Civil Rights Bill. Asking the lawmakers to "know no race, color, religion or nationality," he insisted that not all Southern whites were opposed to the measure, which after all did not confer on blacks any rights they were not already entitled to under the federal and state constitutions.

He used sarcasm on February 3, 1875, to answer those who said the bill would legislate social equality: "I can then assure that portion of my Democratic friends on the other side of the House whom I regard as my social inferiors that if at any time I should meet any one of you at a hotel and occupy a seat at the same table with you, or the same seat in a [railroad] car with you, do not think that I have thereby accepted you as my social equal." He also appealed to the chivalry of the "gentlemen of the House," asking them to imagine how they would feel if their mothers, wives, daughters, were constantly being insulted in public places.

Addressing himself to an earlier speaker, who rather sardonically had noted that even in bondage blacks excelled in song, dance, and eloquence while lagging behind in other respects, Lynch said: "The answer is an easy one: You could not prevent them from dancing unless you kept them continually tied; you could not prevent them from singing unless you kept them continually gagged; you could not prevent them from being eloquent unless you deprived them of the power of speech."

Driving home the point further, Lynch continued: "But you could and did prevent them from becoming educated for fear that they would equal you in every other respect; for no educated people can be held in bondage."

Undoubtedly already aware that Benjamin Butler had decided to push the civil rights measure through without the school clause as the best he could hope for, Lynch made it clear that while he favored schools open to all, he was willing to accept the bill without that provision. He voted yes on the amendment covering schools and yes on the main measure.

The bill, the last contribution of the Massachusetts senator and antislavery fighter, Charles Sumner, passed the House in diluted form on February 5, 1875, and became law. But it was soon nullified by a Supreme Court ruling in 1883 and again in 1913.

Lynch hurried back to Mississippi to plunge into a rough fight for reelection. Democratic clubs in the state had been converted to military companies, designed to keep blacks from voting their own choices. Lynch canvassed the district with the help of Senator Blanche Bruce and other Republican leaders. He was the lone Republican congressman to survive the Democratic sweep of the state in

1875—and he did it by a mere two hundred votes. His right to a seat in the Forty-fourth Congress was contested, but the Elections Committee reported unanimously in his favor, and the House confirmed the report by a voice vote. This was the year Mississippi's governor appealed in vain for federal help to keep order at the polls.

Returning to the capital, the reelected congressman made an appointment with President Grant to ask him why he had not sent troops when mobs were taking over in Mississippi. Grant told him federal interference in Mississippi would have lost Ohio for the Republicans, and he saw no reason to give up Ohio for Mississippi which was bound to be lost to the party in any event.

Lynch charged the Democrats with having stolen the Mississippi state offices in the election of 1875. Speaking from his own bitter experience, he said the Democrats were determined to resist the reconstruction plans of Congress and to deny Southern Negroes their newly won political rights. He described "the colored people" in the South, if not in the whole nation, as being on the brink of political and personal ruin with the Democrats trying to overwhelm them, prejudice them, and crush them. Even some of their allies, he said, were growing tired of their problems.

"Some of you may say the colored man having been invested with the same political rights that are enjoyed by the whites he ought to be able to take care of himself. Plausible argument," he said in a floor speech. "To this we would have no objection if we were allowed to exercise and enjoy the rights and privileges thus conferred. But in some localities we are not. The Democratic party has an armed military organization in several Southern States today called the White League . . . for the sole and exclusive purpose of accomplishing with the bullet that which cannot be accomplished with the ballot."

Lynch never missed an opportunity to defend the Republican administrations of Alcorn and Ames in Mississippi when broad sweeping charges of corruption in Southern state governments were made in the House. He was particularly annoyed—though undoubtedly not surprised—when those charges came from a Mississippi Democrat. Asserting that the Republican administrations had been efficient and honest, he said he did not defend all Republicans; that "no honest man would attempt to defend all the members of the party with which he may be identified." And no one knew better than his "honorable colleague" that not all the bad men in Mississippi were Republican.

He taunted the Democrats with being quite willing to accept carpetbaggers when they decided to join that party. He said government was bound to be unsettled in the South as long as the Democrats sought to gain control over Republican counties through the terror of the White League. He asked for an end to mobocracy and the beginning of a two-party appeal to Negro voters, warning that "otherwise you will lay the foundation for the dissolution of this republic."

In the fall of 1876 Lynch was defeated for reelection by James Chalmers, former Confederate general. The Republicans also failed to carry the state of Mississippi for Rutherford B. Hayes, their candidate for President. When Lynch returned as a lame duck to Washington for the second session of the Forty-fourth Congress in December 1876, he charged that the Democrats had stolen Mississippi's electoral votes.

Lynch opposed the appointment by Congress of an electoral commission to resolve the quarrel over the electoral count in South Carolina, Florida, and Louisiana. He thought the plan violated the spirit of the separation of powers provided in the Constitution. He said that Congress, however, did have the authority to look into the validity of the election in states where the electors had been chosen in a manner contravening the Fifteenth Amendment, and this, he charged, an investigation would show to have been the case in Mississippi, where blacks had been kept away from the polls by force and intimidation.

Lynch took the position that Hayes had been elected and should be installed, even if President Grant had to call out troops to do so, without the new President's being bound by any preinauguration deals.

The question of election irregularities, this time in Louisiana, was still being discussed in the House later that spring. This brought a reminder from Lynch that nothing had been done about the documented evidence of election crimes in his own state: "If elections such as the one held in Mississippi in November last are to be accepted by the people of this country as a legal and valid expression of the will of the people of a State, then indeed our elective system will have come to be a convenient medium for giving legal effect to the most outrageous frauds that were ever committed in the conduct of elections." He foresaw the decay of the South unless there was meaningful reform to encourage the better elements of the white population to protect Negro voters from intimidation, up to and including murder.

His growing pessimism notwithstanding, Lynch continued to move affirmatively to try to rebuild the party structure in the South. He recommended ex-Senator James Alcorn for the post of postmaster general, but though a Republican, President Hayes chose an ex-Democratic senator from Tennessee instead. The aristocratic conservative Mississippian thought it would have been better for the Southern wing of the party had the Republicans let the presidential election go to Tilden and built for another day. "What inducement can a southern white man now have for becoming a Republican?" Lynch quoted Alcorn as saying. "Under the present state of things he will be hated at home, and despised abroad."

Lynch found other Cabinet appointments equally indicative of Hayes's lack of support for the hard-pressed reconstruction elements in the South. The Hayes administration soon made it official that federal troops would not be used to sustain legal governments in the South. "In other words," Lynch wrote, "it was a public announcement of the fact that if there should be an armed revolt in a State against the lawful State Government which would be strong enough to seize . . . that government, the National Government would refuse to interfere, even though a request for assistance should be made by the Chief Executive of the State in the manner and form prescribed by the Constitution."

The former congressman thought how fortunate it would have been had Hayes evolved into a strong man like Napoleon or "even an Andrew Jackson" and used the power of his high office to protect legally elected Republican governments in the South despite commitments allegedly made on his behalf. Instead Hayes turned his back on Republicans who had been responsible for turning the tide in his favor in the hairbreadth presidential election.

Lynch remained politically active on the state level as chairman of the Republican state committee—an assignment he held for eleven years and could have kept longer, had he wished. He, Senator Blanche K. Bruce, and black leader James Hill cooperated to control the state party's machinery, with Lynch and Bruce taking turns as chairman of the state convention and Hill generally serving as floor manager.

The trio almost broke up in 1880 when its members could not agree on whom to support for the party's presidential nomination. Lynch gave way to allow the other two to attend the national convention as delegates when they agreed to back his choice if their own candidate withdrew, and the team held together. Lynch was eager for party harmony. He had decided to try to regain his congressional seat from Chalmers and knew he would need all the support available.

Learning of Lynch's return to the political wars, the *Jackson Clarion* wrote, "The Republicans of the sixth district have nominated Lynch. He was formerly a member and is the ablest man of his race in the South." In the election, Chalmers, who claimed his support among Negroes was growing, was declared the winner by more than three thousand votes.

James Chalmers was seated by the Forty-seventh Congress, but Lynch protested, and the report of the House Elections Committee was in his favor. He was there to present his own case when the fight came up on the House calendar on April 27, 1882. Lynch estimated that an honest count would have given his opponent only about 5,000 of the 21,143 votes polled. He charged that in five counties, 5,000 of his votes had been counted as Chalmers votes. In addition, Lynch said, several thousand Republican votes had been thrown out by the elections commissioners after a hearing about which he had not even been notified—mainly on technicalities such as the failure of clerks to send a list of names with the returns, or in one ward, because the faces of ballots had the "usual and ordinary printers' dashes."

The House did not have to take his word for the kind of tactics used against him. He cited quotes from an interview in the *Cincinnati Enquirer,* in which Chalmers told a reporter: "I think about 5,000 votes for Lynch were thrown out in the district out of 15,000 in all. As self-preservation is the first law of nature, I am in favor of using every means short of violence to preserve intelligent white people of Mississippi in supreme control of political affairs. They are justified in using every means that wit or money, short of open bribery, can procure. If this is Chalmerism, I am proud of it."

Again, as he had so often done before, Lynch called for an end to political fraud in the South and equal protection under the law for every patriotic American. He ended with a quotation from Abraham Lincoln asking for the "considerate judgment of mankind and gracious favor of almighty God" to bring about racial peace and fraternity.

Claiming that he had won in a fair election, Chalmers said some former supporters had deserted Lynch because he had opposed a third term for Grant, a very popular man with blacks in Mississippi. Black and white juries in Mississippi had acquitted all those charged with fraud in Lynch's petition except in one county where the judge said that "a fine of one dollar was sufficient because it was simply a mistake in their judgment of law," Chalmers continued.

The House adjourned on Thursday without a vote. The debate resumed on Friday, and finally on Saturday, there was a vote. The first roll call was on a substitute motion that would have given the seat to no one. It lost 104 to 125 with 62 members abstaining. The committee's resolution was in two parts; it stated that Chalmers was neither elected nor entitled to his seat in the House and that Lynch was. There was a separate vote taken on each part of the proposition. Lynch had enough support to carry both; the last one was by a vote of 124 to 84 with 82 abstentions. He was sworn in, unseating Chalmers, as the Republicans cheered.

By then the first session of the Forty-seventh Congress was half finished. Lynch introduced measures to amend the election laws, to reimburse the depositors of the Freedmen's Savings and Trust Company, to redistrict the Mississippi judiciary, and to clear the way for better rail service in his state.

Having had to fight for a year to win his seat, Lynch had little opportunity to recoup his strength before the 1882 election rolled around. He lost this time by six hundred votes, and returned home to Natchez after Congress adjourned on March 4, 1883. But his political career had not ended.

The next year he finally gave up bachelorhood to marry Ella W. Sommerville. At the behest of Theodore Roosevelt, then in the New York State Assembly, and other party leaders, he ran for the post of temporary chairman of the Republican national convention. He presided for two days before yielding to the permanent chairman, thereby registering another significant first for his race, though Blanche K. Bruce had briefly occupied the chair at an earlier convention.

Lynch led the fight that staved off a move to reduce the size of the Southern delegations in states where the party vote was down because blacks were prevented from voting.

Lynch was a member of the convention committee dispatched from Chicago to Augusta, Maine, to notify James G. Blaine of his nomination. After the ceremonies Blaine took Lynch aside and asked him how things looked in Mississippi.

"I informed him he could easily carry the State by a substantial majority if we could have a fair election and honest count; but that under the existing order of things this would not be possible." Senator Blaine had blocked a Senate investigation of the election of the Mississippi Democrat Senator Lucius Q. C. Lamar. Blaine told Lynch he was sure Lamar would remember that favor and see that the presidential election in Mississippi was fair.

"I know whereof I speak when I say Mr. Lamar would not if he could and could not if he would, secure you a fair count in Mississippi," Lynch replied. The words of the astute Mississippi politician were prophetic. Lamar campaigned hard for the Democrats throughout the state.

Lynch was persuaded to run again for Congress, "although I knew it would be useless for me to do so with any hope of election" against a candidate who was determined to get to Washington by any methods whatsoever.

He worked more strenuously for Blaine than for himself, one of his major problems being to convince outstanding white Southerners to run as Blaine electors. He was elated when Joseph N. Carpenter, a socially prominent Natchez steamboat- and mill-owner, agreed to be on the slate. The joy was short-lived. The newspapers turned their fire on a native Southerner who still dared to associate himself with the party of carpetbaggers and blacks. His business was threatened; his family was snubbed socially; and his children were taunted at school. Reluctantly and sadly he told Lynch he would have to take his name off the ticket. As Lynch knew they would, both Mississippi and the United States went for the Democrat, Grover Cleveland. This time Lynch was defeated by forty-six hundred votes; he appealed to the House and lost.

During Cleveland's first administration, Lynch was at home on his plantation in Mississippi. He remained active in state politics and continued to hold the post of chairman of the Republican state committee. He stayed and plodded on, as one after another of his old friends, black and white, first Bruce and then Ames, became discouraged and moved north.

He was still a national figure in the Republican party. In 1888 he was a member of the Platform and Resolutions Committee. He was the first person to get the chair's attention to move to make the presidential nomination of Benjamin Harrison unanimous. After his election the new Republican President named Lynch fourth auditor of the treasury department.

An interview printed on the front page of the *State Capital* of Springfield, Illinois, on May 28, 1892, demonstrates the Lynch style and his way of dealing with people. Described in the story as "one of the most distinguished leaders of the race and one whose judgment and advice is safe to follow," Lynch obviously succeeded in charming the paper's correspondent.

After Grover Cleveland took the White House away from Benjamin Harrison in 1893, Lynch called on the new secretary of interior, his old political adversary Lucius Lamar; to tender his congratulations. Lamar offered him a job as a special public lands agent at fifteen hundred dollars a year, plus expenses, with the promise of an assignment in the West where he would not, as Lamar put it, be "embarrassed" by racial prejudice.

With gracious thanks, Lynch turned down the appointment. He was proud, he explained, of being a Republican leader in Mississippi even when the party was in eclipse, and he had no desire to move away. He asked Lamar to use his influence to see that some young men for whom he had secured jobs in the pensions bureau were allowed to keep them. The secretary balked in only two cases—one was that of a black physician married to a white woman; the other, that of a white Mississippi lawyer married to a Negro.

As Lynch recalled this incident, Lamar admitted that both men were highly capable, but he said that the people of Mississippi would not countenance any support of mixed marriage. As it turned out, the doctor, on the basis of Lynch's request and Lamar's acquiescence, did retain his job, since the Mississippi papers were not aware of him. The lawyer and his Negro wife left with the change in administration; they later moved to Kansas and prospered. Lynch lost sight of this friend and his family, and assumed they had "been absorbed by the white population as I firmly believe will be true of the great mass of colored Americans."

Lynch also met with President Cleveland, who expressed interest in the country's Negroes and then went on to propose, according to Lynch's account, to foster a division of their votes between the two parties by making sure that qualified blacks received suitable recognition in his administration. He asked Lynch candidly if there had been any problems when he, a Negro man, was put in charge of a federal office with white women employees.

Lynch said that if anyone was ill at ease over working for him, he was unaware of it. The employees gave him the feeling that he enjoyed their respect and goodwill, but he emphasized that their relationship was strictly confined to business. "My contact with the . . . employees was official, not social," he told the Chief Executive. "After office hours they went their way, and I went mine." He lauded Cleveland for his approach and said that if the Democratic party followed his advice, it would free blacks from political bondage and give them a choice at the polls.

Later, Secretary of State Walter Gresham, a friend of long standing, requested Lynch to visit him. He told Lynch that the President had been impressed with him and wanted him to stay on with the treasury department—if Lynch would go on record as saying that he was in sympathy with the main purposes of the Cleveland administration. Secretary Gresham, himself a Republican, urged Lynch to agree; he argued that Cleveland, though nominally a Democrat, was a "better Republican" than Harrison. Lynch said he would be happy to stay, but only if there were no conditions. "The President has no office at his disposal . . . [that] could be a sufficient inducement for me to . . . identify myself with the Democratic party," answered the ever loyal Republican.

Yet he was clearly tiring of the struggle to keep his party alive in the South; 1892 was his last year as party chairman in Mississippi, although he could probably have kept the position if he wished. After his stint as auditor ended in Washington, he returned home and studied law. In 1896 at the age of forty-nine he qualified for the Mississippi bar; he then moved back to Washington and passed the bar examinations there. Appointed major and paymaster of volunteers during the Spanish-American War, he apparently did not practice law at this time. Later he became paymaster in the regular army, first as captain, then as major, with which rank he retired in 1911.

At sixty-three he moved to Chicago and qualified to practice law in Illinois. Being now a widower, he married Mrs. Cora E. Williamson. In 1913 he published a chronicle of the reconstruction period with emphasis on the history he had lived through in Mississippi. The preface to *The Facts of Reconstruction* reveals much about the character of this man of many talents: "Very much, of course, has been written . . . about reconstruction, but most of it is superficial and unreliable; and, besides, nearly all of it has been written in such a style and tone as to make the alleged facts related harmonize with what was believed to be demanded by public sentiment. The author of this work has endeavored to present *facts* as they were and are, rather than as he would like to have them, and to set them down without the slightest regard to their effect upon the public mind, except so far as that mind may be influenced by the truth . . . in language that is moderate and devoid of bitterness, and entirely free from race prejudice. . . . His chief purpose has been to furnish readers and students . . . with a true, candid, impartial statement of material and important facts based upon his own personal knowledge and experience. . . ."

Yet this excellent writer was too polite to tell the whole tragic story of the reconstruction governments—complete with gory details of blood, intimidation, murder, terror. The facts are there, straight and solid, but this aspect of the story Lynch largely omitted.

In one of his last major speeches, he said that the first black congressmen had compiled an honorable record and charged that the facts of history had been perverted by propagandists trying to discredit Negroes through slander. Starting with the administration of William Howard Taft in 1909, the Republicans, he said, had taken a retrogressive position on questions involving the civil and political rights of blacks. Lynch accused Taft of having acquiesced to the virtual nullification of the Fifteenth Amendment, so that states choosing to do so were free to eliminate Negroes as a political factor and those who could vote had only a choice of two evils, Democratic or Republican.

Though an octogenarian, Lynch was still active and living in Chicago in 1929 when Oscar DePriest again broke the Congressional color barrier after twenty-eight all-white years. The forecast for the blacks' return made in 1901 by George H. White of North Carolina, the last Negro congressman, had finally come true. It was an ideal moment to interview Lynch, and the *Chicago Defender* seized it. Negroes needed a man in Congress with the courage to attack not only his political opponents but those within his own party who refused to fight against discriminatory laws, he told the newspaper's woman reporter.

Lynch believed that a Negro representative should expose those who pretend to be the blacks' friend but vote in the opposite direction. Intelligence and ability to hold one's own in the important committees where measures are really put through are far more essential than brilliant oratory, he said.

The ex-Mississippi lawmaker thought DePriest might encounter more opposition in Congress than he had, since there had been considerably more Republicans in the House in reconstruction days.

Lynch—still "tall and lithe at eighty-one"—was obviously proud of having been elected to the House as a qualified Republican and not simply as a Negro. He was enjoying getting the best of insurance companies by living long enough to collect on ten endowment policies.

Lynch remained active for the rest of his life. Much of his time was devoted to writing his autobiography, which was to be titled *Reminiscences of an Active Life*. Shortly after midnight on November 2, 1939, Mrs. Lynch, with a premonition that her husband was not resting well, went in to check on him. On the bed beside him were the manuscript pages of his life story as he had let them fall when he dropped off to sleep. Though ailing and weak for some years, he had only been confined to bed for a couple of weeks. He shifted weakly as his wife came in, lifted his head, then fell back dead on the pillow.

Having lived long past the Biblical allotment, the ninety-two-year-old Mississippi political leader was the last of his congressional contemporaries—white or black.

Robert Brown Elliott/South Carolina

Robert Brown Elliott served twice in Congress, but he made his greatest impact as a South Carolina state official and party leader.

This British-educated Bostonian moved south to work for the *Charleston Leader*, a weekly newspaper, after the Civil War. Of West Indian parentage, he had attended school in Jamaica and in London, and had a working knowledge of several languages acquired through widespread travel.

Elliott, who may have studied law in both England and America, started practicing under the military occupation in South Carolina and continued in the civilian courts when the state reentered the Union. In great demand as an attorney, he amassed one of the best private law libraries in South Carolina.

From its beginning, he was a leader in the state Republican party. He helped to formulate the 1868 state constitution and was one of the party organizers who turned out the necessary votes to get it approved. At the constitutional convention he fought against having former slaveholders paid for their losses. He maintained there never was and never could be any legitimate claim to hold another person as property, and the delegates voted with him, despite insistence by some factions that bona fide contracts were thereby being abrogated.

He pushed for a liberal homestead tax exemption and for elimination of the poll tax, splitting with Joseph Rainey on the latter issue. Elliott's argument was that impoverished blacks, having been cheated out of their wages as slaves, could not afford to pay twenty-five cents, much less a dollar as Rainey suggested. He lost this tussle; the constitution as approved levied a tax of one dollar to help support the public schools.

Elections for a new legislature followed the convention. After turning down a chance to run for the state senate, Elliott was elected to the lower house. He added excitement to the opening of the legisla-

Robert Brown Elliott/South Carolina

ture by giving Franklin Moses, Jr., a well-to-do native white Republican, a close race for the speakership. Elliott lost, but he succeeded in consolidating his position in the party by becoming chairman of the state executive committee. At the close of his term in the legislature, Governor Robert Scott named him assistant adjutant general of the state militia. This group was on constant call as rioting and violence continued to erupt across the state.

Yet there was plenty of gaiety to be found in the free-spending, self-indulgent government set. Columbia, the state capital, was the hub of a relaxed, desegregated social life revolving around Governor Scott and his wife. The gregarious Elliott, a very dark, trim man, who limped slightly from an old Civil War navy wound, was likely to be at these parties. The whites admired his wit and personality, while respecting his intellect and his ability to inspire black audiences by his fiery speeches.

During this period, Elliott was planning his next step up—to Congress. People in his district knew him well from the courts, the legislature, and the militia. With the backing of the party leadership, he gained the Republican nomination in the Third Congressional District, in competition with a Caucasian, S. L. Hoge, in the summer of 1870. In the hard-fought general election J. E. Bacon, the Democratic contender, accused Elliott of having used his position as a state legislator for personal gain. One allegation was that Elliott through his position on the legislature's railroad committee had lined his pockets. He surmounted these undocumented charges and swept the district by a margin of nearly seven thousand votes.

According to opposition newspapers, Elliott was worth a hundred thousand dollars when he went to Congress in March 1871 to take the seat once held by Preston Brooks—the man who had caned Charles Sumner of Massachusetts into insensibility in the Senate chamber before the war. Arriving in Washington as the controversy over the disfranchisement of ex-Confederates was beginning to boil, Elliott opposed a hasty general restoration of political rights, but was willing to consider petitions from individuals who demonstrated a change of heart in their attitude toward the federal government. He introduced such a personal petition for a friend who later became his law partner.

During a debate in the House on March 14 he pointed out that people who were disfranchised had got in that unenviable fix by rushing "madly into rebellion against this, the best Government that exists under heaven." When John Farnsworth of Illinois painted a sad picture of the poor old white man who was barred from officeholding while his lowly, unlettered ex-slave could qualify, Elliott sarcastically noted that the "poor old man" was barred from office for the simple reason that he had once betrayed his oath to uphold the Constitution and now "would only curse the Government" and "murder its loyal adherents" while the ex-slave had put his life on the line to defend the Union.

Elliott maintained that granting general amnesty would be like paying a premium for treason; he said that recalcitrants in the South would take it as a sign of the federal government's weakness and "evidence of the fact that this Congress desires to hand over loyal men of the South to the tender mercies of the rebels who today are murdering and scourging the loyal men of the southern States."

The congressman emphasized he spoke not only for blacks but for his other constituents "whose complexions are like those of [the] gentlemen around me." He pointed out that he came to Congress from a Republican district backed by as large a majority as any man in the House. These voters, he said, expected the government to protect life and property in the South and would not otherwise continue to support the party.

Frederick Douglass' newspaper, the *New National Era*, criticized Elliott for his generalized attack on the former political leaders of the South, but Elliott defended his position. In a letter which ran on the *Era's* front page, he reiterated his conviction that the white leaders, although they had not personally committed any murders, were responsible for them.

In the House he repeatedly demonstrated his debating skill and broad knowledge of constitutional law. During the discussion on April 1 on proposed legislation to curb terrorist groups, he cited detailed testimony from the South Carolina legislature's investigation of harassment and murder during the 1868 election. The Spartanburg Ku Klux Klan, he charged, had forced many county officers to resign; some, he said, had to flee for their lives to the state capital. The intimidation was all very straightforward and candid, with notices posted on county courthouse bulletin boards advising lawfully elected officials to quit their jobs or face the consequences.

Ex-slaves, who charitably refrained from blocking the reentry of former masters into public life, were unchivalrously rewarded by being labeled savages, unfit for and incapable of officeholding. "Pray tell me," Elliott asked, "who is the barbarian here, the murderer or his victim?"

When Democrats argued that the Constitution forbade the federal government to move in to protect the rights of citizens unless asked to do so at the state level, the South Carolina representative disagreed, asserting that the clause calling for a request by the legislature or governor was not intended to inhibit the federal government. As a practical matter, the federal government had to act to quell disorder when state authorities would not or could not, he said. If it did not, the government of the United States might be a "torpid and paralyzed spectator of the oppression of its citizens and the violent . . . overthrow of the [lawful] authorities." State-rights purists, who wanted the United States to stand by and watch its citizens being killed without intervening, reminded him of the Frenchman who refused to save the life of a drowning fellow ship passenger because they hadn't been introduced.

The so-called KKK Act, designed to protect local and state government officials and private citizens from intimidation by disguised bands, was enacted into law on April 20, 1871. Within twelve years the legislation had been voided by the Supreme Court which ruled it was not a function of the federal government to guarantee the safety of its citizens against white-sheeted assassins. Section Two of the law, which made specific reference to disguises, was declared unconstitutional in *United States* v. *Harrison* in 1883 and in *Baldwin* v. *Franks* in 1887.

Elliott also spoke in favor of funds for the aged and infirm in the District of Columbia. The members were haggling over whether such "lazy idlers and vagrants" should have been allowed to settle in the first place in the capital. He replied that the needy, mainly former slaves and war refugees, were destitute "not on account of their own idleness, but by reason of a system of barbarism . . . under which they have been abused, scourged and overworked for the purpose of putting money into the pockets of others."

The South Carolinian defended the Republicans' handling of finances in his war-shattered state, where civil disorders had destroyed the state's credit and kept business away. Not long afterward he was to be embroiled in those very problems in South Carolina. In August 1872, during the summer congressional break, he presided over the state convention and was a prime mover for Franklin Moses, Jr.'s nomination over reformer Daniel Chamberlain for the governorship. The suave, well-dressed Moses was elected governor, although he was accused of gambling, drinking, fast living, and biracial womanizing.

Bribery charges were hurled broadside, and the Moses-Chamberlain rivalry split the party, but Elliott was renominated for the Forty-third Congress. Again he won without difficulty, this time over two Democrats, William McCaw and Samuel McGowan. He returned to Washington for the third session of the Forty-second Congress in December 1872, but soon took leave for a try at a still bigger honor—a seat in the United States Senate.

The state legislature had convened in Columbia to elect a full-term senator to succeed Frederick W. Sawyer, who had been named to an interim term in 1868 when South Carolina was readmitted to the Union. Sawyer was not running for reelection, but the congressman faced two other formidable opponents: John Patterson, president of the Blue Ridge Railroad Company; and Robert Scott, the former governor, whom Elliott had once saved from impeachment. Patterson set up his headquarters in a barn near the state capital. He allegedly admitted pouring out forty thousand dollars to induce legislators to back him, with bribes ranging from fifty dollars to five thousand. Elliott himself was offered ten thousand dollars to withdraw.

Patterson was elected on December 10 by a count of ninety votes with thirty-three for Elliott and seven for Scott. Money was more potent than blood, brotherhood, or racial pride. The legislature that named Patterson was comprised of ninety-six blacks and fifty-nine whites. Elliott, though a man of some means, probably did not think that he had the resources to take on a railroad tycoon in an election contest, and Patterson was accepted by the Senate without a fight.

Already reelected to a second congressional term, Elliott resigned in January 1873 before the completion of his first two years of service. The seat remained vacant for the last two months of the Forty-second Congress while Elliott went home to South Carolina, evidently convinced that he could do more for himself and his party there than in Washington. During this period he may have been trying to line up support to run for the governorship.

By December 1, 1873, when the Forty-third Congress convened, Elliott had decided to return to the House to join the seven-man black bloc and the other Radical Republicans in their drive for civil rights legislation to assure Negroes access to public facilities. Charles Sumner was set to introduce an omnibus civil rights measure as Senate bill number one. It called for a ban on discrimination in public transportation, accommodations, and education.

A dramatic highlight in the House civil rights debate came early in January 1874 when the aging, ailing Alexander Stephens of Georgia was wheeled into place to speak for an hour against the proposal. Not even a decade had passed since he had been vice-president of the Confederacy. Now he was back in the center of government to raise his stirring voice in behalf of white supremacy. Denying racial prejudice, Stephens said that the measure was unconstitutional, that such things should best be left to the states, and that in any event, the blacks of Georgia did not want racially mixed schools.

By the time Stephens had finished, it was late. The House had agreed in advance to hear Elliott speak in rebuttal immediately afterward. Asked if he minded delaying his speech until the following morning, Elliott replied that he would abide by the wishes of the House. Some Negroes objected to the postponement, but the majority of the members voted for adjournment. Forewarned, blacks and whites turned out in force to hear him the next day—January 6.

As the packed galleries listened, Elliott reminded Congressman James Beck of Kentucky that Negroes had never been unconcerned spectators in America's wars and that it was they who had held firm in the battle of New Orleans in 1812 after the white Kentucky reinforcements had fled. Reason and argument, he said, were lost on a man like Beck whose response to the blacks' demand for justice was to intimate that they would next seek legislation punishing white women for racial bias if they dared to refuse to marry Negroes.

Vitriolic opposition to the bill had come from John Harris of Virginia. Harris insisted that not even Abraham Lincoln, the idol of the black masses, had been convinced of the equality of the races. "I say there is not one gentleman upon this floor who can honestly say he really believes that the colored man is his equal," Harris continued. "I can," Alonzo Ransier of South Carolina spoke up. Harris' reply was that he was talking to white men.

Elliott deftly avoided a gutter fight with Harris. "Let him feel a Negro was not only too magnanimous to smite him in his weakness, but even charitable enough to grant him the mercy of his silence" was his reply to the Virginian's racial diatribe and discourtesy to Ransier. The members and the spectators responded with laughter and applause.

After setting forth a carefully drawn argument to show that the proposed measure was constitutional, Elliott emphasized that the constitution of a free government ought always to be construed in favor of human rights. To support this position he quoted Alexander Hamilton, treasury secretary under George Washington: "Is it the interest of the Government to sacrifice individual rights to the preservation of the rights of an artificial being called States? There can be no truer principle than this, that every individual of the community at large has an equal right to the protection of Government. Can this be a free Government if partial distinctions are tolerated or maintained?"

Finally turning his attention to the elderly, crippled Stephens, Elliott said that the Georgian "offers this Government, which he has done his utmost to destroy, a very poor return for its magnanimous treatment" by returning to Congress to spout the obnoxious rejected doctrine of oppression for black Americans. He urged Stephens to catch up with the times and lend his skills to passing laws of which the entire nation could be proud.

74

The *New York Tribune* said the thirty-two-year-old South Carolinian held the galleries spellbound with this speech, which finished with an appeal to the Anglo-Saxons' vaunted sense of fair play. The *Tribune* also praised him for his neat handling of the ungentlemanly gentleman from Virginia who had insulted a black colleague. *The New York Times* was impressed by the beat and cadence of Elliott's speaking style. The *New National Era and Citizen* of Washington thought the entire black race was indebted to South Carolina for sending this powerful, persuasive man to the House where he could appear in person as a refutation of black inferiority.

This was a remarkable response for the press to make to a speech by an obscure House sophomore, but in the ensuing months, Elliott was to be more engrossed with what was going on in his home state than in the national capital. With Negroes playing a larger role there than elsewhere, he felt it was crucial to have an honest, efficient state government. He had supported Governor Franklin Moses, Jr., but he now called for a change in the "character of our administration," whose unsavory reputation was doing irreparable harm to the fight for meaningful civil rights legislation. Elliott said he was merely putting into words what congressional friends, such as Charles Sumner and Benjamin Butler of Massachusetts, were thinking.

When Sumner, the father of the civil rights bill, died, Elliott paid his personal tribute to him on April 14, 1874, in a speech in Boston. Elliott believed that blacks would remember Sumner as the leader who had battered down the walls of their prison house, led them into the sunlight of freedom, and then protected them during reconstruction.

A few months later Elliott again decided to leave Washington to take a personal hand in affairs in South Carolina. He hoped to reverse the tide of public opinion then running against Negro politicians by putting the South Carolina government on an efficient footing. He also wanted to advance his own career. After much soul-searching and carefully prepared groundwork for a return to state office, he announced his resignation from the House for the second time in October 1874. He left Congress before the crucial votes on the Civil Rights Act of 1875. His seat for the rest of the congressional term went to Lewis C. Carpenter, who succeeded him on December 7.

For himself Elliott chose to run for the lower house of the state legislature, and he easily won a seat. The *Charleston News and Courier* continued to be fascinated by the extravagant style in which Elliott and his chic lovely wife, Grace, lived on a salary of six hundred dollars plus a gratuity of a thousand dollars. Their home in a fashionable

75

section of Columbia was in Mrs. Elliott's name, as was other Elliott property in the state capital.

Such publicity did him no harm with the voters or with his peers in the legislature. With C. C. Owen, a white, as his manager, he defeated N. B. Myers, a black, and became Speaker. He wielded his power aggressively for the next two years, clashing frequently with Governor Chamberlain over the handling of the state's finances. There was a bitter hassle over the naming of two widely criticized men to the circuit court by the legislature while the governor was away. Chamberlain charged Elliott with making this move behind his back after promising to stave off action until his return.

Though forced to work together, Elliott and Chamberlain were temperamentally and philosophically incompatible. Historian W. E. B. Du Bois thought Elliott did not trust Chamberlain because of the conservative whites the governor had surrounding him. Certainly Elliott felt the state's chief executive was not giving blacks a proper role in his administration.

They muted their differences in 1876 when Elliott ran for attorney general on the Republican reform ticket with Chamberlain. Elliott's speech at that convention praised the governor's clean-up efforts without actually endorsing him. After a bloody campaign, both parties claimed victory and confusion reigned in South Carolina. Two sets of presidential electoral votes were forwarded to Washington. Two men declared themselves to be governor. Along with the rest of his ticket, Elliott contended he had been elected.

The Republicans succeeded in organizing the state legislature, and again Elliott was a candidate for the United States Senate. On the first ballot he received nineteen votes, but D. T. Corbin, whom the Senate later refused to seat, was elected. Elliott remained as state attorney general until he was forced to give up the office on May 1, 1877—after President Hayes left the Southern wing of his party without federal support.

Elliott defended a number of former South Carolina Republican officeholders brought to trial by the Wade Hampton Democratic administration following its takeover at the state. John W. Cromwell, an early black historian, characterized Elliott's handling of some of those cases before the state supreme court as "models of forensic oratory and legal learning."

The former congressman continued to participate in Republican party activities, but he could not put his heart into such an unrewarding cause. In 1878 he presided over a state convention for the last time. Then he told his friends that it was thankless to dissipate energy and money on state offices, and he resigned. After working briefly as a special treasury agent, he moved to New Orleans and opened a law office there. He missed the stimulus of public life, but there was no place for an outsider in the shrinking Louisiana Republican party.

Malaria ended the life of this hard-driving, talented, controversial politician on August 9, 1884—just two days before his forty-second birthday.

Josiah T. Walls/Florida

When Josiah T. Walls was first elected to Congress in 1870, he had the imposing assignment of representing the entire state of Florida, then entitled to only one member in the House of Representatives.

This bronze native Virginian entered politics with an impressive Civil War record. Though born free on December 30, 1842, in Winchester, Josiah Thomas Walls had been conscripted by the Confederates and forced to serve with an artillery battery until his capture by the Union forces at Yorktown in the spring of 1862. He was taken to Harrisburg, Pennsylvania, where he went to school for a year before joining the Union army, enlisting in a black infantry regiment being organized at Camp William Penn near Philadelphia. Probably because of his previous experience in the Confederate army, he was quickly promoted to corporal, to sergeant, and then to first sergeant.

Walls's regiment took part in the bloody assault on Fort Wagner, South Carolina, in July 1863. This effort to capture the defenses around Charleston was led by the Fifty-fourth Massachusetts Infantry, which suffered heavy casualties. In February and March of the next year, Sergeant Walls's outfit fought in the Florida campaign. General William Birney appointed Walls heavy and light artillery instructor to the troops assigned to the defense of Jacksonville and the St. John's River.

When Walls was discharged with his regiment in 1865, he decided to stay in Florida. Working as a truck farmer and miller, he settled in Alachwa County. He was an excellent farmer, adept at making good use of his land and of the men he hired.

The newcomer joined the burgeoning Republican party and attended the 1867 convention in Tallahassee. One of eighteen black delegates to the state constitutional convention the following year, he was elected to the lower house of the state legislature. He was quick to learn the political ropes, and in 1869, advanced to the state senate, representing the Thirteenth District.

Although Negroes constituted nearly half the population of Florida and about 95 percent of the Republican party, the whites, many of them carpetbagging outsiders, maneuvered themselves into most of the key positions. Finally, blacks snared the nomination to the state's lone seat in the House of Representatives, when Charles M. Hamilton, the incumbent, was persuaded to withdraw in favor of Walls at the 1870 nominating convention in Gainesville. The *Tallahassee Floridian* assessed the nominee as being of above-average intellect despite his limited education. The *Gainesville New Era* praised him for his professionalism, his courtesy, and his efforts to promote peace and harmony in the South.

Election Day was hectic, with precincts throughout the district reporting disturbances. There were organized efforts to keep Negroes from voting. Even getting votes delivered and counted was a hassle. The board of electors threw out votes they believed to be fraudulent in several counties and declared Walls to be the winner. His majority was put at 629 votes out of a total of more than 24,000. Walls went to Washington to take his seat in the House, but Silas Niblack, the Democratic loser, appealed the election decision to Congress.

Florida's first Negro congressman had not been long in the national capital when he introduced two bills: one for land grants to a Florida railroad to secure rail connections with the nearest available harbor serving Cuba and the West Indies, and the other to authorize the secretary of war to buy land adjacent to the United States Army barracks at Barrancas in Florida. He also entered measures to restore voting and officeholding rights to three men. Late in March 1871, Walls, the "sitting member," and Niblack, the man who wanted his place, were both granted an additional sixty days to file more testimony in their dispute over the election.

After the summer recess Walls submitted a measure to reinforce the 1866 Civil Rights Act and to remove legal and political disabilities from all former members of the Confederacy. The *Washington New National Era* praised this move, saying it deserved the support of every Negro in the nation. Many congressmen considered it good strategy to bracket these two items, but the plan backfired as the general amnesty bill went sailing through unsullied while Charles Sumner's civil rights legislation was passed only after many delays and then in an extremely weakened form.

Florida's thirty-year-old congressman was slender, with even features and close-cropped curly hair. He dressed well and favored gay neckties. His first major appearance on the floor came on February 3, 1872, during a debate on a proposed national education fund. Replying to Archibald T. McIntyre of Georgia, who said a federal fund would infringe upon states' rights, Walls cut through to the Southern Democrat's real motive: "We know what the cry about State rights means, and more especially when we hear it produced as an argument against the establishment of a fund for the education of the people. . . . We know that the Democratic party used to argue that to educate the Negro was to set him free, and that to deprive him of all the advantages necessary to enable him to acquire an education was to perpetuate his enslavement. . . .

"Why, sir, so fearful were they that the Negro would become educated, either through his own efforts or by the aid of some poor white person, they enacted laws prohibiting him from being educated even by his own master; and if a poor white person was caught teaching a Negro, he was whipped, or in some States sold or compelled to leave the State; and if by chance a Negro did learn to read, and it was found out, he was whipped every time he was caught with a book, and as many times between as his master pleased."

When McIntyre interrupted to say that his state had just appropriated three hundred thousand dollars for schools that would be open to blacks as well as whites, Walls questioned whether Negroes would be permitted to enjoy their right to education:

"The echo of the past answers no! Not while the Ku Klux Democracy are permitted to burn the school-houses and churches belonging to the colored people of Georgia; not while they shut the doors of the school-houses against the colored children. . . ."

Walls favored a national system of education as the best means of educating black citizens and equipping them to protect their liberties. The federal government, he said, must do the job since the prejudices of ex-slaveholders against education for the Negroes were still too strong to expect Southern states to function effectively in this area.

"Education tends to increase the dignity and self-respect of a people, tends to increase their fitness for society and important stations of trust, tends to elevate, and consequently carries with it a great moral responsibility," Walls stated. People who opposed mass education did so because they knew educated people can not be enslaved, robbed, or made to work for practically nothing.

Supporters of slavery and of states' rights could not be trusted to use federal funds to educate the masses of loyal citizens, black and white, Walls said, explaining: "The Democratic party are opposed to any system that will have the effect of making a majority of the present or rising generation loyal to the Government. It has been admitted by every lover of free government that popular education, or the education of the masses, is necessary to and inseparable from a complete citizenship. . . . Then, let us make provisions for the education of all classes; and if the State governments are unwilling to provide equal facilities for all, then let the national Government take the matter in hand." Congress spent a good deal of time talking about it, but the fund was not appropriated.

Having disposed of thirteen similar cases, the House finally put the Walls-Silas Niblack contest on the calendar for January 29, 1873. George W. McCrary of Iowa explained that the Elections Committee had sifted through stacks of testimony to see if the state board of canvassers had acted properly in throwing out returns from eight counties because of irregularities and declaring Walls the winner by 629 votes.

In one county he said the House committee reinstated 153 votes for Niblack, despite the fact that those ballots had traveled around to various individuals in an envelope addressed to Niblack before finally being delivered late to the state elections board. The committee was not swayed by testimony from scores of intimidated Walls supporters or by the fact that one of Niblack's campaign aides had been convicted of conspiring to keep people away from the polls.

Its recount completed, the Republican-controlled committee reshuffled the figures to drop Walls from a plus 629 to a minus 137, and recommended that he be turned out and Niblack sworn in for the few weeks remaining in the Forty-second Congress.

Before the House voted, George F. Hoar of Massachusetts said that the Niblack challenge could have been thrown out at the outset for having been filed too late. Walls, who had just voted against postponing statehood for Utah and Colorado, said nothing, though he must have still been on the floor. He undoubtedly knew that once his attorney had lost the case with the committee, further talk from him would not affect the House.

No member argued against the report or suggested that a man who all agreed had benefited by intimidation at the polls should not unseat a member on the slim margin of 137 votes. On a voice vote Walls was ejected, and Niblack took the modified oath designed to accommodate pre-Civil War officeholders who had sworn to uphold the Constitution and then broken this trust by fighting for the Confederacy.

Walls, the previous fall, had already been renominated and elected to the new Second District seat by a majority of seventeen hundred votes over Niblack. Early in the Forty-third Congress the congressman tried to block the referral of the civil rights bill to committee. He pointed out that the amnesty legislation on behalf of the former enemies of the Union had not been delayed through referral to committee, and he wondered therefore why a measure in favor of the nation's loyal friends and supporters should be further postponed. He lost this skirmish by a vote of 161 to 70.

He introduced nearly twenty bills: for relief of men serving in the Seminole War, for extension of the limitation on land grants for Brown's Institute, for funds for public buildings in Jacksonville and St. Augustine, for the improvement of the Apalachicola and St. John's rivers and of Pensacola and Key West harbors, for homesteaders in his state, and for private pensions. None of those proposals passed.

He wanted the United States to recognize the belligerent status of Cuba, where he charged the Spaniards, despite their emancipation acts, were still enslaving fifty thousand Negroes. In his public appearances he was an enthusiastic drumbeater for the climate and other natural attractions of his state. In his congressional speeches he frequently called Florida "my own sunny state."

Walls easily won the Republican nomination in 1874, although the Republican governor used his newspaper, the *Florida Union,* to fight Walls even after his selection and tried to split the blacks. He was reelected to Congress over Jesse J. Finley, the Democratic nominee, but this was to be the start of another protracted contest.

When Congress resumed, Walls sought relief for people settling on the public lands in Florida, help for agricultural colleges, and harbor improvements along the coast. In a major speech on March 2, 1875, he surveyed the situation in the South generally, and found the outlook grim: "I reluctantly confess, after so many years of concessions, that unless partisan and sectional feeling shall lose more of its rancor in the future than has been experienced in the past, that unless we shall ere long reach that point in our history when a full comprehension of the true mission of the result of the war will be plain to all public men regardless of party affiliation, Arkansas, Louisiana, Alabama, and Mississippi will not be the only States in this Union in which fundamental law will be disregarded, overthrown, and trampled under foot, and in which a complete reign of terror and anarchy will rule supreme as it does today in Arkansas. But every southern State will follow their example."

The unreconstructed Southerners were quite open about their intentions, Walls said, pointing out that their own newspapers daily repeated that their objective was to get "by the ballot that which we lost by the bayonet." On his desk he had a stack of newspapers from which he quoted to show who was inciting people in the South:

Franklin (Louisiana) *Enterprise*—"They [the blacks] have no record but barbarism and idolatry, nothing since the war but that of error, incapacity, beastliness, voudouism, and crime. Their right to vote is but the result of the war, their exercise of it a monstrous imposition and a vindictive punishment upon us for that ill-advised rebellion. Therefore we are banding together in the White League army. . . . Revengeful means of reconstruction in Louisiana will meet with a terrible retribution."

Natchitoches (Louisiana) *Vindicator*—"The white people intend to carry the State election this fall. . . . We desire your [the Negroes'] cooperation . . . . We propose to do for you more than any party has yet done for you. On the other hand, . . . let it be distinctly remembered that you have had fair warning, that we intend to carry the State of Louisiana in November next, or she will be a military Territory."

Mansfield (Louisiana) *Reporter*—"While the white man's party guarantees the Negro all of his present rights, they do not intend that white carpet-baggers and renegades shall be permitted to organize and prepare the Negroes for the coming campaign. Without the assistance of these villains the Negroes are totally incapable of effectually organizing themselves, and unless they are previously excited and drilled, one half of them will not come to the polls, and a large percent of the remainder will vote the white man's ticket."

Alexandria (Louisiana) *Democrat:* "The people have determined that the Kellogg government has to be gotten rid of, and they will not scruple about the means, as they have done in the past."

Mobile (Alabama) *Register*, reprinting the *Louisville* (Kentucky) *Jeffersonian Democrat*—"The grave question to be settled at much cost is, what is to be done to get rid of the Negro as a voter? Sooner or later, with more or less dispatch, he will be disfranchised and thrust from out our politics. . . . We do not like the predicament. . . . We propose to deal as kindly with him as possible, but to pursue unflinchingly the course which will lead to a peaceful relegation of him back to the cotton and rice fields, minus the ballot. . . ."

Walls wondered how in the face of such facts, reported by the white press, men could stand in Congress and argue that it was blacks who were organizing in opposition to the whites. He said that he would not apologize for the wrongs committed by one or two white Republicans in the South: "I do affirm that the carpet-baggers, assisted by loyal white and black men of the South, have done more to enact laws and to erect public institutions that conform more closely to the genius of our American ideas of civilization, in the short period of six or eight years under Republican administration, than was done by the Democratic slave oligarchy in the South prior to the rebellion."

To further demonstrate what blacks had to put up with from unreconstructed whites, he quoted from the laws enacted in Florida in

November 1865, before the Republicans gained control of the state government. A death penalty was passed for the rape of white women by blacks while white "ruffians" remained free to abuse black women at their pleasure. There were restrictions on intermarriage, with persons of at least one-eighth Negro blood classified as Negroes. Such discriminatory and restrictive laws, typical of those passed all over the South after the war, had naturally made the blacks distrustful of Democrats, the congressman said.

Walls called on Congress to depose the illegal government in Arkansas. "Read the reports of the majority and minority of the committee that was appointed and sent to that State by an order of this House, and you will see that her rightfully elected officers have been forced from the positions to which they were legally elected, none will deny, by force and fraud; her fundamental law disregarded, overthrown, and trampled under foot; murders, assassins and White Leaguers (not Black Leaguers) rule supreme; her rightful governor compelled, with his cabinet, to leave the State; her chief judicial officer outraged and menaced with assassination and ousted from office without cause. And yet it is claimed that Congress should not have taken any action in restoring the legally elected authorities of that State and enforcing the only fundamental law that the State of Arkansas can have a legal claim to, the constitution of 1868."

Reform and regular Republicans had knocked each other out in Arkansas. Augustus H. Garland, onetime Confederate senator, supported by one of the Republican factions, had won the governorship, as the Democrats finally took over the state in 1874 and began to put the brakes on reconstruction reforms.

Walls asked that the federal government intervene to restore general peace to the state, that schools be opened to all, and that Garland be given ten days to retire peacefully home. Congress, however, was unmoved by Walls's plea.

Florida's Second District congressman abstained from the final vote on the Civil Rights Bill on February 5, 1875, because he was unwilling to support what he considered a hopelessly battered and inadequate measure, covering as it did public accommodations and transportation but omitting any reference to schools.

Walls's third term as a congressman began in December 1875. He introduced a number of minor bills early in the session, but he was absorbed in trying to fight off the challenge to his election, and his measures all died in committee. He had been seated with a margin of 371 votes, despite Finley's claim that he had won. Early in 1876, papers on this dispute and seventeen others went to the Elections Committee, and a motion to unseat Walls was tabled.

The fight moved onto the floor on April 18, 1876, with the debate starting right after the Democratic-controlled House had turned down a challenge to Jeremiah Haralson's right to represent Alabama's First Congressional District. In the Walls case, Charles Thompson of Massachusetts said that the committee had reluctantly decided to throw out all the votes in one Columbia County precinct for "gross fraud." Since Walls had received all but 11 of the 599 ballots cast there, subtracting that black precinct would make Finley the winner if the House supported the committee.

The committee decided to take these votes away from Walls because it believed the polls in that precinct had been tampered with by Dr. E. G. Johnson, the Republican candidate for state senator from Columbia County. The case against Dr. Johnson, who won by sixteen votes, was primarily based on the testimony of a campaign associate, who confessed that he had helped Johnson fix the senatorial contest.

No one stated that any of the alleged tampering had been done at the behest of or for the benefit of Walls, who from the beginning had denied any misconduct. A recount in the Columbia County precinct was not possible because the courthouse containing the disputed returns had been destroyed by a fire of suspicious origin. Dr. Johnson was killed before he could answer the charges leveled against him, and the man accused of murdering him was defended by Finley's law firm.

Walls's supporters in the house maintained that the accused Dr. Johnson was guilty only of being a Republican and said that Walls would have had enough votes left to be elected even if specifically challenged ballots were rejected, as the House had done in the past.

Toward the end of the debate, Walls took the floor himself to ask the clerk to read sworn testimony from inspectors of the challenged precinct attesting to the honesty of the election. Walls said he wanted to set the record straight, even though he did not "expect it will do me any good in this House" where he had already encountered difficulty getting the committee to accept his evidence. He surrendered part of his time to Martin Townsend of New York, who summed up how the outnumbered Republicans felt:

"I am also bound to say that the proposition of the majority of the Committee of Elections of this House proposes to turn out a legally-elected member of this House and to put the counsel of the indicted man into the place occupied by the man who has the certificate of election. I believe this is a mere incident of course, but it is an incident very likely to happen to Republicans in many localities in the South."

The key House vote, when it came, was on a resolution declaring that Finley was not elected and that Walls was. The resolution—and Florida's only black congressman—lost on a vote of 84 to 135, with 71 abstentions. Then the majority resolution was agreed to without a division, and Finley was sworn in.

The time had been tightly allocated in this two-day debate, which occupied twenty-two pages in the *Congressional Record,* and not one of the loser's six fellow Negroes was given an opportunity to participate. John R. Lynch, Joseph H. Rainey, John A. Hyman, and Jeremiah Haralson voted for Walls. Robert Smalls, Charles E. Nash, and Walls himself abstained. The resigned tone of Walls's last remarks on the floor made it clear that he knew his cause was lost before the roll call started.

With the party organization aligned against him in 1876, Walls lost the nomination to Horatio Bisbee, who won the November election but was unseated in a House contest. Hoping to use Walls despite the party's shabby treatment of him, the Republican leadership put him on the state legislative slate and the executive committee. Not the sort of person to be anybody's patsy, Walls gave the Republicans no help in the congressional campaign. He won his own election to the state legislature, and he still had enough hope for the party nationally to work to carry the state for Rutherford B. Hayes in the presidential campaign. Florida was one of the disputed states where Negro votes helped to shoehorn Hayes in by a one-vote electoral margin. One would have expected Walls to be rewarded for his part in this victory. If the Hayes administration felt gratitude, it failed to show any. Offered no political appointment, Walls returned to farming after completing his tenure in the state legislature. When frost killed his orange grove and almost ruined him financially, he became farm superintendent at Tallahassee State College, now Florida Agricultural and Mechanical College. He lived on the campus until his death on May 5, 1905, at the age of sixty-two.

Josiah T. Walls was one of the most honest, capable, hardworking, and imaginative men in the House of Representatives during the reconstruction period. Nothing in his conduct merited the fate of being singled out as the only black ever to have been twice unseated by Congress.

Richard H. Cain/South Carolina

"We propose to stay here and work out this problem. We believe that God Almighty has made of one blood all the nations upon the face of the earth. We believe we are made just like white men. . . . Look; I stretch out my arms. See; I have two of them, as you have. Look at your ears; I have two of them. I have two eyes, two nostrils, one mouth, two feet. I stand erect like you. I am clothed with humanity like you. I think, I reason, I talk. . . . Is there any difference between us? Not so far as our manhood is concerned, unless it be in this: that our opinions differ, and mine are a little higher up than yours."

These were the simple powerful words of Richard Harvey Cain, as he addressed the House of Representatives during a civil rights debate on January 24, 1874. As congressman-at-large from South Carolina, Cain was new to Washington, but for years he had been talking in such straightforward terms in the South Carolina legislature and in various Southern and Northern pulpits. He had been equally outspoken in print in the weekly *Missionary Record* which he published.

Though a native of the South, Cain was a newcomer there, having spent most of his pre-Civil War life in the North. The son of a Cherokee Indian mother and an African father, he had been born on April 12, 1825, in Greenbrier County, Virginia. At six he moved with his father to Gallipolis, Ohio, and then on to Portsmouth and Cincinnati. As a youngster he worked on Ohio River steamboats. He probably had little formal education, though he learned how to read through his Sunday school classes at church and studied after work in the evenings.

Religion was to play a crucial role in his life. At sixteen he was converted to the Methodist Episcopal faith in Portsmouth and decided to become a minister. When he was nineteen, he was ordained and was then assigned to various churches in the Midwest. Offended by the segregation in the denomination, he joined the African Methodist Episcopal church and was sent to Muscatine, Iowa, to preach. In 1860 he temporarily gave up the ministry to attend Wilberforce University in Xenia, Ohio, for about a year. Years later, after he was famous, the university awarded him an honorary doctor of divinity degree.

As a student at Wilberforce, he was one of 115 Negroes who went to the governor of Ohio to volunteer for the armed forces only to be told it was a white man's war and that Negroes could have no role in it. He waited, he said in a speech in Congress, until the state of Massachusetts began to recruit blacks for army service and he then answered the call. Cain must not have been inducted, however, as there are no records of his enlistment.

Cain, who wore his hair short with long sideburns, spent most of the Civil War years as a pastor in Brooklyn, New York, having been given the assignment in 1861. He was ordained an elder in the African Methodist Episcopal church in Washington the following year. When the country was reunited in 1865, he was transferred to South Carolina as a pastor and presiding elder. The great task then was to provide direction and counsel to freedmen in starting a new life for themselves. Negroes had not been allowed to operate places of worship freely in much of the South during slavery, so part of his assignment was missionary work, organizing churches in Summerville, Lincolnville, Georgetown, Marion, and Sumter.

South Carolina had reestablished its state government under President Andrew Johnson's plan. An all-white convention comprised of people who had taken the President's oath of amnesty met. James Orr, former speaker of the House and former Confederate senator, was in charge as governor. The new government said it recognized the fact that slavery had been abolished by the United States; it then proceeded to enact a set of black codes remarkably like the discredited body of slave laws.

Late in 1865 Congress began to take over the direction of reconstruction and said it would delay acceptance of the credentials of representatives from such former Confederate states as South Carolina. Military commanders were assigned to handle matters until those states formed governments representing all the males of both races of voting age except those disqualified for their wartime activities. In the interim the governments in these unreconstructed states were provisional and subject to the direct authority of the United States.

Cain's method of advancing reconstruction in his newly adopted state was to plunge into politics. In 1868 he was a delegate to the state constitutional convention. At that meeting he favored a resolution petitioning Congress for a loan of a million dollars from the Freedmen's Bank to purchase land for the poor.

People who did not know Cain from his church or political work were likely to be aware of him through the pages of the liberal Republican weekly, the *Missionary Record*. For seven years he combined the taxing schedule of publishing a newspaper with politics. The top of the paper's front page was decorated with a drawing of two ladies instructing a small class of students. The paper pledged to devote its columns "to the Christian graces, literature, arts, sciences, politics and the progress of civilization." The front page carried the biblical admonition: "Therefore all things whatsoever ye would that men should do to you, do you even so to them." He billed himself in the paper as Richard H. Cain, editor and proprietor. His name continued to appear in the masthead of this paper, an excellent source of news on government and political happenings, after he went to Congress.

In July 1868, the people of Charleston sent him to represent them in the state senate. One of the first measures facing the legislature was the ratification of the Fourteenth Amendment, reconfirming citizenship for the former slaves and establishing a formula for the protection of their rights. Section Two was very explicit. Any state denying the ballot to qualified males would have its representation in Congress reduced "in the proportion which the number of such male citizens shall bear to the whole number of male citizens twenty-one years of age in such State."

Some South Carolina legislators voted against this vital amendment. Cain called for a five-man committee to study whether "the Senators who voted no on ratification of the Fourteenth Amendment have not violated their oaths and committed perjury, and if so, to recommend the course the legislature should adopt to vindicate the purity of its organization."

A vigorous and willing orator, he was much in demand as a campaigner for his party's state and national candidates. In the race of 1870 he emphasized the need for governmental reform in South Carolina. "We could," he said, "favor sending to the legislature honest mechanics and farmers whose minds are not biased by political chicanery; at any rate let us have honest men who are identified with the country's prosperity and the people's interest." After four years as a state senator, Washington beckoned. In 1872 he was successful in a bid for congressman-at-large, running against Lewis Johnson.

Three days after he took his seat on December 4, 1873, he introduced a bill to supplement the 1866 Civil Rights Bill. Throughout his stay in Congress, most of his speeches dealt with this all-consuming issue.

Cain believed that if the last three amendments to the Constitution had invested all Negro men with all the rights of citizenship, that should mean literally "all rights." In a speech on January 10, 1874, he refuted the argument of Robert Vance of North Carolina who claimed that the pending civil rights bill would be detrimental to both races by forcing social equality. Cain said that the bill would merely put the black man on the same footing as every other man and would do nothing whatsoever to alter his social relationships, a matter for every man to decide for himself and quite beyond the province of legislation. He disputed the contention that Negroes already received equal treatment from North Carolina's inns and hotels, eating places and railroads. "Now it may not have come under his observation, but it has under mine, that such really is not the case," he asserted. "And the reason I know and feel it more than he does is because my face is painted black and his is painted white. We, who have the color . . . know and feel all this."

To prove his point the congressman recounted details from his own trip from South Carolina to Washington a few days earlier; public places that were open to serve "hungry men" would not feed him "without trouble or contest" in either Wilmington or Weldon, North Carolina. Cain felt food was not worth drawn revolvers. To prevent a confrontation while traveling by train, he therefore avoided the diner and ordered food brought to his car. Even then the railroad people objected to this service for which he had paid a premium "because they said we were putting on airs."

He disputed the charge that blacks would lose the friendship of Southern whites because of the bill. This certainly would not be the case with the educated, better class of whites. Vance had said that if the law granting equal access to accommodations was passed, some ambitious black man would enter a hotel or a first-class railroad car and thereby create a disturbance. Cain snapped back that if a Negro were granted these rights, there would be nothing ambitious in his enjoying them.

Cain held that mixed classes had proved a success at the University of South Carolina, despite the prejudice of some professors who had quit. This was also true in the North, even in "old Democratic New York" which did not refuse to give blacks their rights. He said that the contributions made by Negroes through two centuries of unpaid toil in the United States entitled them to nondiscrimination now, especially since these rights were theirs through inheritance from God and under the Constitution. He argued forcefully for the jury and education clauses: "I cannot regard that our rights will be secured until the jury-box and school-room, those great palladiums of our liberty, shall have been opened to us. Then we will be willing to take our chances with other men.

"We do not want any discriminations to be made. . . . I do not ask any legislation for the colored people of this country that is not applied to the white people. All that we ask is equal laws, equal legislation, equal rights through the length and breadth of this land."

He agreed with Representative Vance that blacks should not come to Washington begging for their rights: "I want to say that we do not come here begging for our rights. We come here clothed in the garb of American citizenship. We come here demanding our rights in the name of justice." He reminded his fellows that he spoke for more Americans than existed at the time of the "great tea-party" in Boston harbor.

"Inasmuch as we have toiled with you in building up this nation . . . inasmuch as we have together passed through affliction and pestilence, let there be now a fulfillment of the sublime thought of our fathers—let all men enjoy equal liberty and equal rights." As a man who had voted with a "free heart" for general amnesty, he was ready to shake hands over the bloody chasm. But what of the people who still fought against the civil rights bill when amnesty and civil rights should have gone together?

The argument in the House over the civil rights bill resumed on January 24, 1874. Cain's rebuttal this time was directed against still another North Carolina congressman, William Robbins. "The gentleman starts out by saying that if we pass the pending civil rights bill it may indeed seem pleasant to the northern people, but to his section, and to the South, it will be death. I do not think he is correct, for the reason that they have in the South suffered a great many more terrible things than civil rights, and still live. I think if so harmless a measure as the civil rights bill, guaranteeing to every man of the African race equal rights with other men, would bring death to the South, then certainly that noble march of Sherman to the sea would have fixed them long ago." The galleries and the Republicans laughed.

Speaking extemporaneously without notes, he said that the races had lived together in the South before the war without special antagonism although "there might have been some friction in some places and in some cases"; and the laughter increased. The gentleman from North Carolina took great pride in the noble philanthropic efforts made to educate " 'these barbarians' as he terms us," Cain continued, and he asked why was there need for worry about racial antagonisms after such vaunted fruitful Southern education programs.

"The gentleman further states that the Negro race is the world's stage actor—the comic dancer all over the land; that he laughs and he dances," Cain said. "Sir, well he may; there are more reasons for his laughing and dancing now than ever before. There are more substantial reasons why he should be happy now than during all the 200 years prior to this time. Now he dances as an African; then he crouched as a slave." Again the galleries rang with laughter and applause.

He also refuted Robbins' contention that only 1,800 blacks had lost their lives fighting in the Civil War. He figured "the gentleman" must have overlooked who entered Charleston and Richmond first and forgotten battles like Vicksburg, Petersburg, and Fort Pillow. There were an estimated 37,300 Negro casualties in the Union army alone in the Civil War, according to official military records.

Cain said that a people who had been deprived of schooling, for whom education had been a penal offense, could not be upbraided for their ignorance and stupidity. "You robbed us for 200 years," he continued. "During all that time we toiled for you. We have raised your cotton, your rice, your corn. We have attended your wives and your children. We have made wealth for your support and your education, while we were slaves, toiling without pay, without the means of education, and hardly of sustenance." He was particularly incensed by the statement that Negroes had not been educated before in the South because they were not ready. "Not ready, Mr. Speaker; if I had that gentleman upon the floor, with my foot upon his neck, and holding a lash over him, with his hands tied, with him bound hand and foot, would he expect that I should boast over him and tell him, 'You are a coward, you are a traitor because you do not resist me'?"

Nor would he listen in silence to the North Carolinian's declaration that America was a white man's land and government. "I ask in all conscience what becomes of our black men and women and children, to the number of 5,000,000; have we no rights?" As for the issue of social equality, he wanted no more pretense or hypocrisy on that score, though he put it subtly: "We have some objections to social equality ourselves, very grave ones. For even now, though freedom has come, it is a hard matter, a very hard matter, to keep sacredly guarded the precincts of our sacred homes. But I will not dwell upon that. The gentleman knows more about that than I do."

He turned aside Robbins' suggestion that blacks should prepare to migrate to Africa, the West Indies, or some other place outside the United States: "I want to enunciate this doctrine upon this floor—you have brought us here, and here we are going to stay. . . . Our mothers and our fathers and our grandfathers and great-grandfathers have

died here. Here we have sweated. Here we have toiled. Here we have
made this country great and rich . . . It is mean in you now to want
to drive us away, after having taken our toil for 200 years.

"Just think of the magnitude of these gentlemen's hearts. After having taken our toil for 200 years; after having sold our wives and children like so many cattle in the shambles; after having reared the
throne of great king cotton on our labors . . . now we are free they
want us to go away. Shame on you!"

Again the applause exploded.

Cain pointed out that Robbins called the idea of men being created
equal a fallacy propounded by "Thomas Jefferson, that old fool-hardy
man, who announced so many ideas that have been woven into the
woof of the nation. . . . Sir, if he was in error, I accept the error
with pleasure. If he was a foolish man, I would to God that North
Carolina had been baptized in that foolishness about 200 years ago."

Thirteen months later the opposition was still chipping off bits of
the proposed civil rights bill. On February 3, 1875, Cain pooh-poohed
the idea that the law would stir up "bad blood" in the South—
something that had already been done by the forces of terror in their
fight against blacks' voting, holding office, and exercising all their
other rights as citizens.

Cain said that if Congress had boldly passed the bill a year ago the
trouble about schools and social mixing would now be over; as for
bad blood, "The statistics show—I want to illustrate the manner in
which some of the southern people feel about the 'bad blood'—the
statistics show there are 1,728,000 mulattoes in the South. One would
naturally think there was a good deal of 'bad blood' between the two
classes—a great deal of unkind feeling!"

Votes were the issue. Charging that three thousand men, women,
and children had been driven from plantations because they voted
Republican, he continued: "The bad blood of the South comes because the Negroes are Republicans. If they would only cease to be
Republicans and vote the straight-out Democratic ticket there would
be no trouble."

Cain scoffed at the social-equality bugaboo. "Do you suppose I
would introduce into my family a class of white men I see in this
country?" His answer was explicit and personal. "There are men even
who have positions upon this floor, and for whom I have respect, but
. . . I should be careful how I introduced them into my family. I
should be afraid indeed their old habits acquired beyond Mason and
Dixon's line might return."

He indicated a willingness to compromise on the issue of racial integration in schools and cemeteries "for the sake of peace in the Republican ranks." He was a pragmatist and felt it imperative to get the public transportation and accommodations sections of the bill on the books, even if the education clause had to be sacrificed.

"So far as the graveyards are concerned, why, we are not much troubled where we shall be buried," he mused. "We know very well we shall be buried somewhere if we die. We are certain of that; somebody will get us out of the way."

Two days later Cain was among the 162 who voted aye when the roll was called and the House passed at long last the battered civil rights bill.

By now Cain was functioning as a lame duck. He had not been a candidate for reelection in the fall of 1874, since his seat at-large had been abolished for the Forty-fourth Congress. He had, however, been an active campaigner for the Republican reform forces in South Carolina.

His last speech before he left Washington defended South Carolina's reconstruction government and pled for an end to the lawlessness that was keeping the South, with its great climate and natural resources, from agricultural and manufacturing progress. He quoted General Philip Sheridan to the effect that in Louisiana alone since 1866 there had been 2,115 political injuries and 2,144 murders.

"We are bound up together in this country—the two races—no legerdemain can separate us," he said. "I do not care what efforts may be made, we are going to stick right here. Here we began the work, and here we are going to stay and finish it. I rejoice today in this fact, that our Democratic friends cannot succeed without us in the South or our Republican friends either, because we are a part of this nation and you cannot get rid of us. The same principle that gives the Democrat his liberty gives the black man his liberty also; the same principle that guarantees the Republican in his liberties guarantees the black man also in his rights because he is a man. You cannot rub out our manhood by any constitutional enactment or legislation or by any edict of the governor of a State. We will be men still. . . . The colored race must move with you step by step. . . . We are American citizens. . . . Our destiny will be linked with yours in the future."

Two years later he returned to the House, this time as congressman from the Second District. South Carolina's Joseph H. Rainey and Robert Smalls were there also. Cain's seat was contested by Michael O'Connor on the grounds that Cain's election had been falsely certified by a South Carolina secretary of state who was a fugitive from justice. O'Connor also charged that the state board of canvassers, who met secretly to make their official count, were candidates for state office on the Republican ticket with Cain.

When his case came up on October 16, 1877—the second day of the first session—Cain explained that his credentials were from the same secretary of state as those of five men already seated from South Carolina, and if the document was not entirely correct, it was through no fault of his. He asked only that the 15,267 voters who gave him his majority be accorded fair representation in the House. He was seated by a vote of 181 to 89 and sworn in that same day.

In May 1878, O'Connor was still trying to unseat Cain, but the Elections Committee, headed by John Harris of Virginia, unanimously upheld Cain, and the House concurred by voice note. Ex-Congressman John R. Lynch of Mississippi lost an election contest that same day. Cain defended former Governor Daniel Chamberlain for having called out troops to protect the people of South Carolina at election time. He termed it the clear duty of a state executive to protect voters in a time of insurrection, rebellion and violence. He said that there had been only 171 United States soldiers in the counties with the worst disorders and that these had to stand against the membership of seven hundred rifle clubs. He asked that military appropriations not be cut for a growing nation which needed arms to keep the peace domestically and to protect its citizens against Indian uprisings.

His two major bills were both referred to committee. One was a measure to establish a mail and passenger steamship line between United States ports and Liberia—the African country to which some ex-slaves had returned after the war. His other proposal would have provided educational funds from the proceeds of the sale of public lands.

The congressman from South Carolina's Second District called the attention of the House to another deprived group—women. He entered several petitions on behalf of the suffragettes who were demanding the right to vote. He also put in a word for Charleston druggists, asking for a reduction of the "tax on spirits."

In the third session he sought an extension in the jurisdiction of justices of the peace in Washington, restrictions on the sale of policy and lottery tickets in the capital, and better wages for workers in the Washington Freedmen's Hospital. The first of these bills passed the House, but was blocked in the Senate.

Speaking on behalf of a measure for the sale of public lands to raise funds for education, on January 23, 1879, Cain portrayed "vast ignorance" as an evil stalking the land and a major cause of racial prejudice and misunderstanding. This speech was heavily laced with statistics demonstrating that illiteracy made no distinction between the races. The thrust of his speech was that most of those in America who needed more education were of the majority race and that the problem was not a matter of color.

The door was slowly but certainly closing for black officeholders in South Carolina. The Republican party's nominating convention in 1878 selected E. W. M. Mackey, a native white, to run for Cain's seat in the Second District. Some of Cain's critics charged him with having been excessively friendly with whites.

Convinced that politics no longer held any real prospects for him, Cain and his wife, Laura, returned to religious work after he left Congress in March 1879. The African Methodist Episcopal Church appointed him a bishop and assigned him to Louisiana and Texas. In Waco, he helped to organize Paul Quinn College, named in honor of a popular African Methodist bishop, and became its second president. In 1880 he went back to his own post as bishop, presiding over the New York, New Jersey, New England, and Philadelphia territory, until his death in Washington on January 18, 1887, at the age of sixty-one.

The course of his life had taken Cain from deckhand to minister to state senator to newspaper publisher to congressman, and finally back again to the church as bishop.

Richard Cain expected prejudice, but he demanded that the government rise above it and make the law equitable, fair, and non-discriminatory. He had no doubt as to the ability of blacks to compete once the racial strictures were removed. "Place all citizens upon one broad platform," Cain said, "and if the Negro is not qualified to hoe his row in this contest of life, then let him go down. All we ask of this country is to put no barriers between us, to lay no stumbling blocks in our way; to give us freedom to accomplish our destiny. . . ."

Robert C. DeLarge and Alonzo J. Ransier/South Carolina

Many of the first black congressmen were so beset with election challenges they hardly had time to concentrate on their work, but no one had a more star-crossed career in Washington than Robert C. DeLarge.

A farmer with a high school education, he stood out among the Negroes who entered the political arena after the Civil War even in competition with more learned and sophisticated men. Robert Carlos DeLarge came from Aiken, South Carolina, where he had been born into slavery on March 15, 1842. After attending Wood High School, he became an agent in the Freedmen's Bureau and helped to organize the Republican party in South Carolina.

Negroes met in Charleston's Zion Church in November 1865 to map their strategy against the whites' plan to reestablish the state government on a segregated basis. South Carolina blacks asked the United States Senate to reject any state constitution that did not grant voting and officeholding rights to all loyal qualified male citizens without distinction in color. Following similar appeals throughout the South, Congress tightened reconstruction procedures to readmit only representatives from those states that promised to accord full political participation to former male slaves.

DeLarge chaired the platform committee at the Republican state convention in May 1867. He signed an impressive, forward-looking document calling for tax reform, court reorganization, popular election for all offices, welfare assistance, liberal immigration laws, funds for railroads and canals with contracts to be awarded equitably, and a land policy designed to break down the "land monopolies that make the rich richer and the poor poorer and to foster the division and sale of unoccupied land."

It is interesting to note that the courts were restructured during the constitutional convention that followed and that South Carolina's reconstruction legislatures set up a new tax system and authorized funds to rebuild the railroads and finance the sale of some small plots of land to farmers. Other parts of the party's platform also were eventually enacted nationally, but its more visionary provisions have still not come to pass.

Though they had the voting strength to do so, particularly while large numbers of whites remained disfranchised, South Carolina Negroes did not try to freeze out the people who had enslaved them. At least three hundred blacks served in the state legislature between 1868 and 1902. Never a majority in the senate, they controlled the lower house for only five years during reconstruction under the Radical Republicans.

Men of "various colors and mixtures of blood," as W. E. B. Du Bois described them, occupied the offices of speaker of the house, lieutenant governor, secretary of state, and state treasurer. No black sat in the governor's chair, and most of the circuit court posts and local offices were staffed by whites. The black leaders were loyal party men, who wanted to organize the reconstructed government in a workable fashion. They knew they needed the expertise and experience of local whites to succeed, and they worked with missionary zeal to convert capable ex-Confederates to the Republican party.

DeLarge was one of the seventy-six Negroes and forty-eight whites who wrote South Carolina's revised state constitution in 1868. He favored a resolution calling for a three-month moratorium on debts to provide a measure of help for the war-stricken populace. He denied it was class legislation and held up letters from every section of the state "crying out for relief." The convention, however, voted down this suggestion.

He disputed the argument that selling off mortgaged property would benefit the poor by enabling them to buy land. He said neither the needy whites nor the "poorest of the poor"—the freedmen—were in any position to purchase anything. If the farms were sold, he continued, "they will be sold at public sale . . . in immense tracts, just as they are at present. They will pass into the hands of the merciless speculator, who will never allow a poor man to get an inch unless he can draw his life blood from him in return."

After the constitutional convention, DeLarge moved rapidly from one important position to another, going from the lower house of the South Carolina legislature to the office of land commissioner and then to Congress. As land commissioner he inherited a confused financial mess left by his white predecessor, who had been accused of corruption. But DeLarge still managed to get the operation into shape and put some of his own ideas into practice. He was land commissioner when elected to represent the Second Congressional District by less than a thousand votes over Christopher Bowen, an independent Republican, in the fall of 1870. Before the representative-elect left for Washington in March 1871, he reported that nearly two thousand small tracts had been or would soon be taken over by homeowners who would have eight years to pay for them.

DeLarge, a short man with brush sideburns and a receding hairline, was sworn in on opening day despite an election challenge by Bowen. The neophyte congressman had been there only a few days when he tangled with James Blair of Missouri. Assuring Blair he would vote for a bill to lift the political restrictions imposed on prominent ex-Confederates by the Fourteenth Amendment, DeLarge asked Blair in turn to commit himself to support a companion measure to guarantee loyal Southerners federal protection from the Ku Klux Klan and other terrorist groups. Blair was not to be pinned down. While attesting to his willingness to see every Ku Kluxer in the South hanged, he stalled for time to consult his conscience as to the constitutional ramifications.

South Carolina Democrats could not deny that murder and arson were being perpetrated by secret societies in their state, DeLarge said in a speech delivered to the House on April 6, 1871. He blamed both political parties for the lawlessness that had forced the governor to appeal to the President for help in maintaining order in various voting districts. He believed Negroes had erred in placing their trust in ambitious, unscrupulous, white carpetbaggers.

DeLarge explained that he wanted ex-Confederates readmitted to political life to give them a personal reason for supporting the reconstruction government. Pointing out that most of the prewar leaders in his state were still barred from officeholding, he asked "whether it is reasonable to expect that these men should be interested, in any shape or form, in using their influence and best endeavors for the preservation of the public peace, when they have nothing to look for politically in the future?"

DeLarge had no chance to function as a congressman during the second session, which started on December 4, 1871. He was completely occupied in trying to prove his right to keep his seat as papers relating to the contest inundated the House. He took a leave of absence on April 20 to build his case, which had been delayed at his request. Meanwhile, the low-level fighting was weakening his health.

The Forty-second Congress finally took up Bowen's challenge to DeLarge on January 24, 1873, during its lame-duck third session.

George F. Hoar of Massachusetts said the Elections Committee had investigated DeLarge's charge that his counsel had been bribed by Bowen to withhold vital evidence and had found it to be true. Robert Elliott, who had recognized Bowen's and the lawyers' handwritings on a contract, had uncovered the agreement between Bowen and DeLarge's counsel.

Hoar told the House that the bribery charge would have been sufficient grounds for expelling Bowen from Congress had he been seated. He added that Bowen probably could also have been disqualified for having been already sworn in as a South Carolina state legislator and Charleston sheriff. The *New York Globe* commented that Bowen seemed to believe in holding many offices as well as having many wives—a reference to a bigamy charge filed against him.

But the committee had also been impressed by Bowen's counteraccusations of illegal election managers, improperly tallied polls, and ballot-box stuffing. The committee said fraud and irregularities were so rampant on both sides that it was impossible to determine who had been elected, and asked the House to declare the seat vacant for the rest of the term.

As the vote neared, Joseph Rainey explained that DeLarge was ill and had not made arrangements for anyone to speak for him. When Rainey pointed out that the state count showed his South Carolina colleague with a clear majority of the votes cast and asked for a week's postponement to allow DeLarge to be heard, Hoar professed willingness to delay the vote, but the House proceeded to unseat De-Large in a speedy voice vote and left his place vacant.

The House then in effect appropriated funds for a bribe. It voted to pay the contested election expenses of Bowen, who had hired De-Large's lawyer to sabotage DeLarge's career. That minor victory was practically meaningless for Bowen. The investigation had destroyed his chances as well as DeLarge's.

Though a casualty in the political wars, DeLarge, who was married and had a daughter, Victoria, retained his personal popularity in South Carolina, where he had substantial land holdings. After the congressional debacle he was named a magistrate in Charleston.

Robert C. DeLarge occupied the magistrate's post until his death of consumption on February 14, 1874, at the age of thirty-one. The city magistrates' offices closed out of respect to him, and his funeral was crowded with mourners of both races.

DeLarge's successor as congressman from South Carolina's Second District was Alonzo Jacob Ransier, who captured the Republican nomination in the fall of 1872. He had been born free in Charleston on January 3, 1834. Some of his ancestors may have come from Haiti, carrying with them a dash of French blood. He acquired a little education before going to work at sixteen as a shipping clerk for a merchant.

Plunging into public life as soon as the way opened to blacks, he acted as registrar at one of the first post-Civil War elections; he attended a Friends of Equal Rights convention in Charleston in 1865, and was a member of the delegation that was sent to Congress with a petition from that meeting. Chairman of the Republican state central committee for several years, he served as a presidential elector and as a delegate to the 1868 state constitutional convention.

A light-complexioned man with a finely etched profile, Ransier was nominated lieutenant governor by the Republicans on a ticket headed by Robert Scott in July 1870. Ransier's campaign emphasized his reputation for honesty. The Scott slate won, with the Republican candidate for lieutenant governor swamping former Confederate General Matthew Butler by thirty-three thousand votes.

State expenses skyrocketed during this graft- and corruption-riddled administration, but Ransier's name and reputation remained untarnished. Democratic newspapers repeatedly attested to his unshakable integrity. The legislators in the state house applauded his fair rulings and courteous manners as their presiding officer.

The state's first black lieutenant governor maintained a full schedule of speaking engagements and party appearances. In 1871 he headed the Southern States convention in Columbia; the next year he went to Philadelphia as a delegate to the Republican national convention.

Negroes were being courted by supporters of Horace Greeley, who was proposing to run for president as a liberal Republican. Ransier wrote to P. B. S. Pinchback, the Louisiana Republican leader, urging blacks to remain loyal to President Grant and the regular party organization. He said that if Massachusetts Senator Charles Sumner were going outside the party because of his foreign-policy feud with the President, blacks would not follow even him that far. Ransier fought to keep the vote firmly in line for Grant at a black convention in New Orleans in the spring of 1872.

In August the Republicans nominated Ransier for the seat from the Second Congressional District then held by DeLarge. In the election he defeated former Union General William Gurney, an independent Republican, by more than thirteen thousand votes. Bidding farewell to the South Carolina Senate on November 26, 1872, Ransier criticized the state's political parties for splitting on "nearly racial" lines and asked the Republicans, as the majority party, to take the lead in creating a healthier atmosphere.

In Washington, the thirty-nine-year-old congressman introduced a measure to erect public buildings in Beaufort and argued for a "full and complete" civil rights bill. He advocated a six-year presidential term and high tariffs, and opposed wage hikes for federal officials.

Speaking on February 7, 1874, during the debate on the proposed civil rights bill banning discrimination in schools, transportation, theaters, and hotels, he refuted the myth that the great mass of the country's Negroes did not want or need federal help. He said they had been asking for it for years as individuals and groups.

Ransier fought fiercely against sacrificing the education clause—so controversial because of the social issue—to get the rest of the bill through. He was convinced that schooling was the doorway to jobs, to jury service, and the ballot box—and once education was achieved, he expected prejudice to melt like snow under a burning sun.

He said the same people who argued that interracial schools would destroy the public school system had also maintained that freeing the slaves would ruin the South, an apprehension that had proved unfounded. As examples of excellent desegregated colleges and universities, he cited Yale, Harvard, Oberlin, Cornell, and Wilberforce in the North and Berea and Maryville in the South. "Let the doors of the public school-house," he asked, "be thrown open to us alike, sir, if you mean to give these people equal rights at all. . . ."

Ransier warned the Republicans of the power of 840,000 black voters, who had been crucial to Grant's second-term victory. The shortcomings of the hard-pressed reconstruction governments, he said, were no excuse for the denial of equal rights to blacks. He wanted the civil rights bill amended to carry a five thousand dollar fine against racial discrimination on juries. He also proposed to strike the word *white* from all laws, statutes, and ordinances—state, national, and local.

Thanks to Alabama's James Rapier, who yielded some of his time, Ransier argued another round in the civil rights debate on June 9, 1874, a few weeks before Congress recessed for vacation. He presented resolutions from Negroes in Tennessee supporting the bill and said that Virginia's and Tennessee's congressmen added insult to injury when they reported that the blacks in their districts, who had helped to elect them, did not approve of the proposed legislation.

Returning to Charleston after seven months in Washington, Ransier worried over the condition of the government and of the Republican party in South Carolina. While some of the charges of corruption were reckless and exaggerated, he found the situation generally deplorable and feared it would injure his party's national reputation.

Realistically he had to admit that local Republicans were unlikely to satisfy any considerable portion of the Democratic masses in the state no matter how honest, just, and economical their administration. Nevertheless, he urged the state Republicans to clean their own house.

Ransier appealed to each man to act "as if by his individual vote, he could wipe out the odium resting upon our party. . . . Let him feel, black or white, that the country holds him responsible for the shortcomings of his party, and that it demands of him the elevation to public positions of men who are above suspicion. Let each man feel that upon him individually rests the work of reform; let each man feel he is responsible for every dollar of the public money fraudulently used; for every schoolhouse closed against his children; for every dollar of taxation in excess of the reasonable and legitimate expenses of the State; in short, let every man feel that society at large will hold him and the party accountable for every misdeed in the administration of government, and will credit him with every honest effort in the interest of the people and . . . of good government. . . ."

In the summer of 1874, Ransier was in the forefront of efforts to reform the party. His criticism of some of the men still in power, including Governor Franklin J. Moses, Jr., was probably one of the reasons he lost the nomination to Charles Buttz, a white man. A staunch Republican, Ransier supported the ticket, although he said that Buttz had spent four thousand dollars to buy the nomination.

After the election recess, Ransier returned for his final session as the House pushed the civil rights bill forward toward action after months of delay. The key vote came on February 5, 1875. Obviously displeased with the version that omitted education—the heart of the issue in his opinion—Ransier did not vote. Without access to first-class schooling, he saw no chance for blacks to hope to find their way into a proper niche in American life.

Ransier's wife, Louisa, died a few days later, six months after the birth of their eleventh child, Charles Sumner Ransier. His term ended in March, the former congressman was appointed briefly United States internal revenue collector for the second South Carolina district. He appears never to have had a good job thereafter. During his twilight years Alonzo Ransier, the man who had held the highest state executive office of any South Carolina black, worked as a day laborer for the city of Charleston, until his death on August 17, 1882, at the age of forty-eight.

Charles E. Nash and
P. B. S. Pinchback/Louisiana

Louisiana's most fascinating black politician during the reconstruction period, P. B. S. Pinchback, was never permitted to take a seat in Congress although elected to both houses. His "few drops of Negro blood" might never have made such a dramatic difference in his life had he chosen to pass for white, but he was too proud and honest to deny his black ancestry.

His egotistical manner and his refusal to plead for offices he felt he had won did not advance his cause. Nor did his ill-advised decision to go to Washington in 1873 as both a representative-elect and a senator-elect. His House opponent contested and won, and in 1876, after three years of haggling over his case, the Senate also rejected him.

The Louisiana legislature then elected James Lewis, a black who had served as a colonel in the state militia. Obviously convinced he would be treated no better than Pinchback, Lewis did not press the Senate to honor his election, but he too went to live in Washington.

The misfortunes of Pinchback, of Lewis, and of J. Willis Menard, the first Negro elected to but barred by the House of Representatives, leave Charles E. Nash as Louisiana's sole black congressman.

Charles Edmund Nash was born on May 23, 1844, at Opelousas, Louisiana, to a slave family. Before the Civil War he worked as a bricklayer, having attended school briefly. At nineteen he became a private in Company A of the Eighty-Second Regiment of the United States Volunteers. He was promoted to sergeant major with the celebrated Chasseurs D'Afrique and lost a leg fighting at Fort Blakely, Alabama, the last infantry battle of the war. Back in civilian life, he was named night customs inspector in Louisiana in 1865. He apparently held this job when nominated by the Republicans in 1874 to represent the Louisiana Sixth District in the Forty-fourth Congress.

Nash had moved ahead of some very able men to get the party's endorsement. Even during slavery, Louisiana had nearly twenty thousand educated, well-to-do free people of color. The *New Orleans Tribune* was published weekly in French and English from 1864 through part of 1869. The paper appeared briefly in 1865 as the first American Negro daily.

New Orleans had been in federal hands since April 1862. Not long after the Union troops arrived, the state's Republican party was organized by twenty-six men, five of them wealthy Negroes, so light-skinned they were indistinguishable from the white population. Twenty Negroes, only one a former slave, were at the state convention held in New Orleans on September 27, 1865. The legislature voted to restore the prewar constitution over the objections of the provisional governor.

In mid-1866 a preliminary meeting for a constitutional convention disintegrated into a scene of mass murder. Encouraged by the New Orleans mayor and undeterred by the Union general guarding the city, a white mob marched into the meeting and, in the words of W. E. B. Du Bois, "shot down the people who were in the hall." Figures on the number of casualties vary, but there seem to have been at least 38 killed—most of them Negroes—and 148 wounded. Many whites, perhaps forewarned, had stayed away from the meeting. After the shooting was over, General Absalom Baird declared martial law. In this tense atmosphere, 127,639 voters—82,907 of them black—registered.

Unfazed by the violence, forty-nine whites and forty-nine Negroes wrote a new state constitution authorizing schools open to all and universal male suffrage except for disfranchised Confederates. A black man, R. H. Isbell, was temporary Speaker when the new legislature met June 29, 1868. It is estimated that thirty-two nonwhite senators and ninety-five nonwhite representatives sat in the Louisiana legislature during the next eight years. The figure is approximate because racial identification was particularly haphazard in this well-miscegenated state. Other prominent blacks were Oscar J. Dunn, lieutenant governor, and Antoine Dubuclet, treasurer. Dunn, a former slave who had escaped from peonage and bought his freedom, was one of the most promising leaders in the state.

During the 1868 presidential campaign between Ulysses S. Grant and Horatio Seymour armed militarylike groups roamed the state, harassing Republican meetings. People were warned that the Democrats intended to erase the reconstruction changes if they won. The Ku Klux Klan, the Knights of the White Camellia, and the Innocents, an Italian group, did their work well. Grant lost the state by more than a 2–1 margin. Less than three hundred of New Orleans' twenty-one hundred Republicans voted.

The Republican governor, Henry Warmoth, assumed greater powers in an effort to maintain order. The state was heavily in debt, but he believed in well-apportioned graft, and some of the black leaders shared in the handouts. Finally the Negroes, who comprised the bulk of his support, became disgusted. Lieutenant Governor Dunn organized a revolt at the party convention in August 1870. Despite his record, Warmoth was able to get voter approval for a constitutional amendment making him eligible for a second term. There was an open split, with Warmoth leading one faction and Dunn the other. At this juncture Oscar Dunn, the greatest hope for reform, died on November 21, 1871.

In the ensuing years there was the spectacle of two men claiming to be the legal governor and of dual legislatures. Sometimes the situation verged on anarchy, but the Republicans managed to hold onto the reins of government with occasional support from Washington. In 1874 they elected Charles Nash to the House of Representatives. "The Louisiana elections of 1868, 1872, 1874 and 1876," wrote W. E. B. Du Bois, "were of one cloth: intimidation, fraud, open violence and murder, so that there was no real expression of public opinion."

Nash, who had a walrus moustache and a slightly receding hairline, was seated in the House of Representatives along with seven other Negroes. He was named to the Education and Labor Committee. Getting time on the floor was frequently a problem for the first black congressmen; some of their best speeches appeared only in the appendixes of the *Congressional Globe* and *Record*. When Nash asked on May 31, 1876, for ten minutes to speak about a Louisiana election contest, he was offered instead an opportunity to enter his speech in the record. However, he turned this down, saying that he had asked for leave, not to have it printed, but to be heard.

Seven days later he gained the floor to deliver a major speech on political conditions in the South. Nash sharply criticized the Democrats for disparaging all Southern white Republicans, however commendable, and deprecating all black officeholders, however capable. He defended former Confederate General James Longstreet from the sarcastic attack of Jesse Yeates of North Carolina:

"The gentleman admits that General Longstreet performed valiant services for the confederacy, and I will tell him that he had done equal service for the reconstruction of the Federal Union; and I do not understand why he should be specially assaulted for the performance of his duties as a citizen."

The Louisiana congressman charged the Democrats with having

opposed every advance won by the blacks and continuing to oppose their progress even after civil rights and reconstruction measures had been made the law of the land. He praised his own party for such legislative accomplishments as the Fourteenth Amendment, a bulwark, he thought, to the citizenship rights of all Americans for years to come. Nash deplored the efforts of Southern whites to block education for Negroes, pointing out that improved education was vital for all Southerners to protect them against "designing demagogues."

Louisiana's only Negro congressman concluded with a call for brotherhood: "A man with the noblest instincts may succumb to a temporary madness, but he is nevertheless a man, and when the cloud has passed away he is to be restored to a man's loves and rights and privileges. Brother, late our foe in battle but our brother still, this country is our joint inheritance. . . . The glories of our past belong to both of us. . . . We alone by our dissensions can destroy this rich inheritance. Over brothers' graves, let brothers' quarrels die. Let there be peace between us. . . ."

It was then nearly nine thirty at night; the House adjourned as soon as Nash finished. In less than a year the compromise that installed a Republican in the White House in one of the closest presidential contests in history would doom the efforts of Louisiana's white and Negro Republicans to work together in an effective political alliance. Nash himself, though a candidate for reelection, drew little attention from the press during that hotly contested campaign, and he lost the seat to Democrat Edward Robertson by more than five thousand votes.

Nash went home to Louisiana after Congress completed its work on March 3, 1877. In February 1882 he became postmaster of Washington, a Louisiana coastal town, but by May he was ousted from this position as the old power structure began to resume control in the state. Two years later, his wife, the former Martha Ann Wycoff, died at Opelousas. He moved to New Orleans where he married a Frenchwoman, Julia Lucy Montplaisir, in February 1905. Louisiana's only black congressman died there on June 21, 1913, at the age of sixtynine.

The Louisianian who, with any luck, would have preceded Charles E. Nash in Congress was P. B. S. Pinchback. He was the eighth of the ten children of William Pinchback, a white planter of Holmes County, Mississippi, and Eliza Stewart, whose ancestry was African, American Indian, and Caucasian. Major Pinchback had taken the mother of his children to Philadelphia to free her. The couple were returning home to Mississippi when Pinckney Benton Stewart Pinchback was born in Macon, Georgia, on May 10, 1837.

Young P. B. S. and his elder brother Napoleon were sent to Cincinnati to Gilmore High School. After their father's death in the late 1840's, their mother and the other children moved to Cincinnati for safety. Administrators of the estate feared that Pinchback's white relatives, having already robbed his black children of their inheritance, would sell their Negro kinsmen into slavery.

After Napoleon had a nervous collapse, twelve-year-old Pinckney went to work on a riverboat. He started as a cabin boy at eight dollars a month on a Cincinnati-to-Toledo run and moved up to steward on longer hauls on the Missouri and Mississippi rivers. He jumped ship on his twenty-fifth birthday at Yazoo City, Mississippi, and made his way to New Orleans, which the Union forces already controlled.

A few days after his arrival he wounded his brother-in-law in a fight. Tried for assault and attempted murder by a military court, he was sentenced to two years in the workhouse. He was released after a few months to serve with the Corps D'Afrique and given the assignment of recruiting for this elite black infantry outfit.

The second regiment of this corps was ready for combat duty by October 12, 1862. General Benjamin Butler, one of the first Union generals to welcome black troops, put Captain Pinchback in command of Company A. A man who never doubted that he was as good as, if not better than, anyone else, the slender, smartly groomed captain would not tolerate discriminatory treatment of his soldiers. When the army proposed giving second-class pay and assignments to his men, he resigned.

Still eager to make a personal contribution to the war, he mustered another company. Refused the post of commanding officer in this Negro cavalry unit, he again resigned and went to Washington to see President Lincoln and offer to recruit an Ohio and Indiana regiment. The President was assassinated and the war was over before this project could be given approval.

Following a round of speeches to newly freed Negroes in Montgomery, Selma, and Mobile, Alabama, Pinchback returned to New Orleans and organized the Fourth Ward Republican Club. A state committee member, he served as a delegate to the Republican national convention and to the state constitutional convention, where he opposed a 50-50 selection of convention officials on a racial basis and favored a tolerant policy toward political participation by former supporters of the Confederacy. In 1868 he was elected to the state senate.

The erstwhile captain opened a cotton factorage firm—Pinchback and Antoine—but his work in the legislature got most of his attention and enthusiasm. Late in 1870 he started the *New Orleans Louis-*

ianian, first a semiweekly and then a weekly newspaper, which he ran for eleven years.

When Lieutenant Governor Dunn died in November 1871, Governor Warmoth called the senate into special session to elect a president, who would serve as ex officio lieutenant governor. Pinchback was named to this position after a black senator broke a 17–17 tie in Pinchback's favor. It was alleged that the man who switched was promised fifteen thousand dollars by the governor, but when by court order the locked tin box, supposedly containing this money, was opened there was nothing in it. Pinchback's opposition was also charged with buying votes.

The regular session of the Louisiana legislature began in January 1872, but the state senate adjourned from day to day unable to attract a quorum. There was a stalemate in recognizing Pinchback's right to the chair. The statehouse was guarded by militia and police. On January 20, Pinchback got another one-vote majority confirming his election, and business started. Pinchback's ability to bring the senate into line at this crucial moment prolonged the Republicans' tenuous hold on the state of Louisiana for several years.

Pinchback aspired to the governorship that fall and had a chance at the nomination as the party split into two conventions. One nominated him to head the ticket, but for the sake of harmony he chose instead to accept the designation as congressman-at-large on the regular Republican slate with William Kellogg for governor and C. C. Antoine as lieutenant governor in August 1872. This ticket supported Grant's bid for a second term. Pinchback was elected in November, but his fusion opponent filed notice that he would contest.

Because of his role as ex officio lieutenant governor, Pinchback served as acting governor from December 9, 1872, to January 13, 1873, when Warmoth was debarred from his office during impeachment proceedings. The next day the legislature elected Pinchback to the United States Senate. He received twelve votes to nine for the field running against him.

The seats of two Southern senators were among those challenged by the Senate when it convened in special session in March. Two days of deliberation were enough to admit George Spencer of Alabama. Pinchback was kept waiting for two years before he was accorded any serious attention, even though the Louisiana legislature reaffirmed his election.

In the interim the House considered his claim to a seat there at the start of the regular session early in December. Three Louisiana seats were at issue, all with certificates signed by Pinchback himself as acting governor. The two Caucasians were sworn in after a day's delay. The black representative-elect was left dangling until March 26, 1874, when Benjamin Butler of Massachusetts asked that Pinchback's credentials be referred to the Elections Committee, and the House agreed. Entered with the original credentials was a letter from Governor Kellogg, who said the official state records showed that Pinchback had been duly elected.

For the moment, Pinchback preferred the contest to be sidetracked in committee, since this left him free to concentrate on snaring the more desirable Senate seat. James Beck of Kentucky ridiculed him for simultaneously claiming a place in both houses, presumably on the principle that two chances were better than one. "I know," Beck said, "that many rights are accorded to men because of race, color or previous condition, but I never knew that even a Negro could be both a Representative in Congress and a Senator at the same time."

Pinchback, then thirty-six, cut a dashing figure in Washington. According to a reporter from the *New York Commercial Advertiser,* he was the best-dressed Southerner in Congress "since the days when gentlemen were Democrats." Pinchback, who wore a moustache and beard, had brilliant, black, intense eyes and even features. His smile was sardonic, but the reporter found his reserved polite manner and good breeding a contrast to the "Texan and Louisiana Yahoos who shout 'nigger, nigger, nigger' in default of common sense or logic."

The House gave Pinchback a chance to speak for himself on June 8, 1874. He dismissed as absurd the charge that he had maligned its dignity by also applying for a Senate seat, asserting that any other representative would have done the same thing:

"Why, sir, let me ask any Republican member of this House or any Democratic member whether if he had been in my position, elected on the 4th day of November [1872] to the Congress of the United States by a popular vote of his State, and his State had subsequently elected him to the Senate of the United States by what was recognized as the legal Legislature thereof, would he have done otherwise than I did; whether the gentleman would have been so patriotic and considered the dignity of this House so far above that of the Senate to have said 'I will not take the seat in the Senate, I will take the seat in the House?'. . . The rule adopted by all those I am acquainted with has been to take the best office they could obtain. And if I follow in the footsteps of my illustrious predecessors I suppose they must attribute it to the characteristic which they are pleased to ascribe to our race, that of being imitative, and I say I have simply imitated them. Now, sir, I do not believe there is a single member of this

House who situated as I was would have acted in a single particular otherwise than I have done as to this preference."

Pinchback argued that George Sheridan's claim to the disputed House seat was negated by his own credentials—an election certificate from ex-Governor Henry Warmoth dated December 4, 1872, seven days before the votes were officially counted. Pinchback wondered where Warmoth got the extraordinary power to divine a week in advance the exact count of the Sheridan vote.

Pinchback also asked why his signature as acting governor was worthless on his own election certificate when it had been accepted without question to seat four other Louisiana members: "I demand simple justice. I am not here as a beggar. I do not care so far as I am personally concerned whether you give me my seat or not. I will go back to my people and come here again; but I tell you to preserve your own consistency. Do not make fish of me while you have made flesh of everybody else."

When the House adjourned for the summer shortly afterward, the seat of Louisiana's congressman-at-large was still vacant. It stayed that way until March 3, 1875, when by a vote of 121 to 29, Pinchback lost the contest to Sheridan. It wasn't much of a coup for Sheridan since there was no time left to serve. Washington's *New National Era* thought a milder approach on Pinchback's part might have been more successful, but the paper was sure an honest count of the vote would have put him in the House.

A special Senate session of the Forty-fourth Congress followed to look into the question of the legality of the Kellogg government in Louisiana. On the first day of that meeting, Oliver Morton of Indiana, chairman of the Privileges and Elections Committee, asked that Pinchback be seated for the six-year term that should have started March 4, 1873. He stated that the governor and other state officials had certified Pinchback's election. There was a lengthy give-and-take with the opposition charging that the legislature that had elected Pinchback was not a legal body. That short session ended with the Louisiana senator-elect still in suspense.

It was more than a year later when the Senate again took up Morton's motion to seat Pinchback. J. Rodman West of Louisiana, who originally had presented Pinchback's credentials, criticized the Senate for the delay and for not allowing his colleague to appear to speak for himself as had been done previously with other senators-elect.

West said the legality of the government elected in Louisiana on November 4, 1872, had been recognized by the President, by both Houses of Congress, by the courts of Louisiana, and by the people of the state who had approved amendments submitted by that legislature. He said the evidence was all there to show that a legally constituted legislature had legally elected Pinchback to the Senate.

"You are bound," John Logan of Illinois said, "to allow him to take the oath of office, and afterwards, make your inquiries, if any are to be made." The majority went with Justin Morrill of Vermont, who said the Louisiana investigating committee found "organized fraud of the largest dimensions" when looking into the election irregularities of 1872 and that he would not accept the action of the "pretended legislature" though he personally had no prejudice against Negro members of the Senate except in their favor. On March 8, 1876, by a vote of thirty-two to twenty-nine, the Senate ruled Pinchback's election illegal and refused to admit him. He was paid nearly seventeen thousand dollars to cover salary and travel expenses up to that time.

Pinchback went back to New Orleans where his wife, Nina, and their six children were waiting. His money was well invested in stocks and bonds, which provided him an estimated annual income of ten thousand dollars.

Embittered by this dual congressional rebuff and the number of Republicans who had voted against him in the Senate, he switched his support the next year to back Francis R. T. Nicholls, the Democratic candidate for governor. In 1882 he was named customs surveyor for New Orleans. As he approached the mid-century mark, he started studying law, and in the spring of 1886 he was admitted to the bar. Four years later, he moved to Washington, where he died December 21, 1921, at the age of eighty-four.

To the end P. B. S. Pinchback tried to buoy up the spirits of the blacks. He advised them to think for themselves, to defend their rights, and to take courage from the example of the once-enslaved Jews, who by dint of hard work had become princes of commerce and prime ministers of empires.

Thomas E. Miller and
George W. Murray/South Carolina

Thomas E. Miller was the challenger who kept former Congressman Robert Smalls from making a comeback in the Seventh District of South Carolina in 1888. The perky thirty-nine-year-old Beaufort lawyer was only ten years younger than the popular war hero, but he had the advantage of bringing a fresh, undefeated name to the congressional fray. Ironically, when they were no longer rivals, Miller saluted Smalls as "the greatest politician of any one of us."

Thomas Ezekial Miller had been born on June 17, 1849, in Ferrebeeville, South Carolina. Richard Miller and Mary Ferrebee, after whose family the Beaufort County town was named, are given in the records as his parents. For years, however, some of Miller's descendants have been convinced that this free Negro couple were merely his foster parents and that he was the son of a white man and a white girl, whose family would not allow her to keep her baby. It was, these descendants say, a case of reverse passing, a Caucasian living as a Negro. But Miller considered himself to be a Negro, as did his contemporaries, and history has accepted this designation.

Miller went to school first in Charleston and then in Hudson, New York, while working as a newsboy. He attended Lincoln University in Chester County, Pennsylvania, on a scholarship, graduating in 1872. He studied for the bar privately with at least two prominent lawyers and judges. Three years after finishing college, he was admitted to the bar and hung up his shingle in Beaufort.

The first public office that Miller held in Beaufort was as county school commissioner. The people of his district then sent him to the state House of Representatives in 1874 and reelected him twice before he advanced to the state senate. A member of the Republican state executive committee, he was to have run for lieutenant governor in

113

1880, but the Republicans decided not to put up a state ticket that year. As state party chairman in 1884, he stressed the importance of the party's running local and state nominees even if they had to pass the collection plate in churches to finance their campaigns.

His yeoman work with the party helped Miller capture the nomination for Smalls's Seventh Congressional District in the fall of 1888. Smalls had been defeated in 1886, and Miller and his supporters persuaded the ex-congressman not to compete for the nomination. Miller campaigned hard, traveling to Washington to solicit support from national party leaders in his race against William Elliott, the Democrat.

Part of the strategy for nullifying the black vote even in this solid Republican district was a complicated setup, with seven ballot boxes for state offices and two for federal candidates. The *Charleston News and Courier* jokingly urged the whites to capitalize on this by voting early and often. Some may have done precisely that; when the vote was tabulated the white Democrat had carried this heavily black district by thirteen hundred votes. Miller appealed that decision to the House of Representatives, then Republican by a narrow margin.

The House took up the Miller appeal on September 23, 1890, right after seating John Langston of Virginia, one of three Negroes elected to the Fifty-first Congress. Consideration of Miller's case began while most of the Democrats, who had boycotted the Langston debate, were still out of the chamber.

One of the few Democrats present, Charles O'Ferrall of Virginia, kept insisting there was not a quorum. Just as firmly Speaker Thomas Reed said there was, including those not voting. Complaining that Miller had been sprung on them without warning, O'Ferrall asked if the chair refused to hear him. "The chair does. The gentleman is here for delay," Reed answered. An Iowan's request for twenty minutes of debate was turned down. With O'Ferrall still protesting "no quorum," the vote was taken to unseat Elliott, who had been there ten months, and give the post to Miller. Miller won 157 to 1.

As only a week was left before the members recessed to go home to campaign for reelection, Miller had no time to relax and enjoy his victory. He returned to South Carolina and entered a tough three-man contest for the Fifty-second Congress. His opponents were E. M. Brayton, a white Republican, and Elliott, his old Democratic foe. Miller received most of the votes, but Elliott challenged the count. Late in the year he was declared the winner by the South Carolina Supreme Court, which ruled that Miller's ballots were of an illegal size and color.

So it was as a candidate already defeated for reelection that Miller made his first House speech on January 12, 1891. He dismissed Democratic insinuations that the Republicans were biased because they did not reward their black supporters with nominations on the party's presidential ticket. Allotted five of the ninety minutes set aside for debate on a pending measure for federal supervision of federal elections, he said Negroes looked upon holding political office as a precious gift, but there were other considerations even more vital:

"Yes, gentleman, we want office; but the first and dearest rights the Negro of the South wants are the right to pay for his labor, his right of trial by jury, his right to his home, his right to know that the man who lynches him will not the next day be elected by the State to a high and honorable trust; his right to know that murderers shall be convicted and not elected to high office, and sent abroad in the land as grand representatives of the toiling and deserving people."

He called upon Northern representatives to convince the "Chamber over yonder [the Senate] to give us an election law—not a force law —a national law, Mr. Chairman, that will compel the people of the South to register the votes of the Negro and the white man alike, and count them as they are cast, and let the wishes of these people . . . be expressed here by the duly elected Representatives of their States." Such a bill, introduced by Henry Cabot Lodge of Massachusetts, had passed the House, but the legislation was stalled in the Senate.

The measure, which the opposition had cleverly mislabeled "force bill," was still the issue about a month later when Miller told the white Southerners that they had only themselves to blame for the economic retardation of their region:

"It is not the Negro . . . that keeps Northern capital and Western energy from within the borders of the South land, but it is the revolutionary spirit of the white citizens, it is the clannishness of the white citizens, it is the petty prejudices of the white citizens. . . . Caucasian energy and enterprise will seek wealth in any clime, and the color of a man's skin cannot keep them from coming; but men of refinement will not go to a country where the rights of property are not secure; men of religious convictions will not go among a people who, Pharisaical-like, consider themselves the superior of the influx; men of business habits will not go in a country until by the laws of that land investments are secure."

How strange, Miller continued, that the men who were trying to pass a law for the protection of the rights of all American citizens should be charged with breeding sectionalism. He said it was time to stop indulging the South as though it were a wayward child when the record of the last twenty-five years was stained with the blood of blacks and whites who had not been allowed to vote and speak as they pleased even in peacetime for the Republican party.

Twenty-three blacks served in Congress between 1870 and 1935. Before going to Washington, many held key positions in state governments. This composite portrait was prepared by Horace R. Cayton, a Seattle, Washington, newspaper publisher and son-in-law of Sen. Hiram R. Revels, of Mississippi (*right center*), the first Negro to sit in Congress. *Left center* is Blanche K. Bruce, also of Mississippi, the second black senator. (**Schomburg Collection, New York Public Library**)

Joseph H. Rainey, of South Carolina (*second from right*), was the first black to serve in the House of Representatives. Seen with him are, *from left to right:* Sen. Revels; Rep. Benjamin S. Turner, Alabama; Rep. Robert C. DeLarge, South Carolina; Rep. Josiah T. Walls, Florida; Jefferson F. Long, Georgia, and, *far right,* Rep. Robert Brown Elliott, South Carolina. (**Schomburg Collection, New York Public Library**)

Sen. Hiram R. Revels and his family. Mrs. Revels stayed home with their daughters in Holly Springs, Mississippi, when her husband went to Washington in 1870 to serve an abbreviated term in the Senate. (**Schomburg Collection, New York Public Library**)

A Mississippi senator from 1875 to 1881, Blanche K. Bruce later became Register of the United States Treasury. (**Schomburg Collection, New York Public Library**)

John R. Lynch was Speaker of the Mississippi House of Representatives before becoming a member of the United States House of Representatives in 1873. (**New York Public Library**)

Mississippi's senators Blanche K. Bruce (*left*) and Hiram R. Revels (*right*) flank Frederick Douglass, the most famous Negro antislavery leader. They are surrounded by other white and black "heroes of the colored race," including Lincoln, Grant, John Brown, and congressmen Lynch, Smalls, Rainey, and Nash. (**Library of Congress**)

Newspapers praised the dramatic civil rights speech made by Rep. Robert B. Elliott, South Carolina, on Jan. 6, 1874. This is how *Frank Leslie's Illustrated Weekly* covered the address, in which Elliott rebutted the arguments of Alexander Stephens, former vice-president of the Confederacy. (**Library of Congress**)

Rep. Robert Smalls of South Carolina first gained fame in May 1862 when he commandeered the *Planter*, a Confederate steamer on which he was serving as pilot, sailed her past the guns of Fort Sumter (seen in the background in the painting at left), and turned the ship and its cargo over to Union forces. *Below:* engravings of Smalls and the vessel he captured accompanied the report in *Harper's Weekly* about the future congressman's daring feat. (**Negro History Associates; Schomburg Collection, New York Public Library**)

ROBERT SMALLS, CAPTAIN OF THE GUN-BOAT "PLANTER."

THE GUN-BOAT "PLANTER," RUN OUT OF CHARLESTON, S. C., BY ROBERT SMALLS, MAY, 1862.

Besides being the first Negro member of the House of Representatives, Joseph H. Rainey of South Carolina had the longest tenure of any of the early black congressmen. Elected five times, he served several months longer than Robert Smalls. (**Library of Congress**)

Robert C. DeLarge was a South Carolina legislator and a state land commissioner prior to his election to the House of Representatives in 1870. (**Library of Congress**)

Jefferson F. Long of Georgia who served briefly in Congress in 1871, was the first black to make a formal speech in the House. (**Library of Congress**)

Alonzo J. Ransier was lieutenant governor of South Carolina before going to the House of Representatives in 1873. (**Library of Congress**)

Richard H. Cain, a South Carolina newspaper publisher, was elected to the first of two House terms in 1872. Later, he became a college president and a bishop of the African Methodist Episcopal Church. (**New York Public Library**)

Josiah T. Walls represented the entire state of Florida when he entered the House of Representatives in 1871. (**New York Public Library**)

Benjamin S. Turner, elected to the House in 1870, served a single term; previously he had been city councilman of Selma, Alabama. (**Library of Congress**)

John Mercer Langston's first speech in the House, January 16, 1891, as illustrated in the Virginia congressman's autobiography, *From the Virginia Plantation to the National Capitol.*

Pinckney B. S. Pinchback went to Washington in 1873 as both senator-elect and representative-elect, but neither house would seat him. Congress honored certificates of election that he had signed as acting governor of Louisiana for others but not the ones he had signed for himself. (**Schomburg Collection, New York Public Library**)

Henry P. Cheatham of North Carolina as the lone black in the House of Representatives during 1891–93, the second of his two terms, tried to act as spokesman for Negroes throughout the nation. (**Negro History Associates**)

America's blacks lacked representation in Congress from 1901, when North Carolina's George H. White (*above*) left the house, to 1929, when Oscar DePriest (*below, center*) of Illinois began serving the first of three House terms. Here, DePriest is seen with two friends: Louis B. Anderson (*left*) and Dan Jackson. (**New York Public Library,** *Ebony* **Magazine**)

William L. Dawson, a power in Congress, consults with two future Presidents—senators John F. Kennedy and Lyndon B. Johnson, *right*. Dawson represented Illinois' First Congressional District from 1943 until his death in 1970, rising through the ranks to become chairman of the important House Government Operations Committee. (**Jaques Lowe,** *Ebony* **Magazine**)

Above, Adam Clayton Powell, Jr., addresses a New York rally as future President John F. Kennedy and former First Lady, Eleanor Roosevelt, smile their approval. *Below*, Powell and his second wife, singer-pianist Hazel Scott. Though the Harlem congressman's flamboyance irritated some, as chairman of the House Education and Labor Committee, he was directly responsible for enacting some of the most important programs of the Kennedy and Johnson administrations. (**Schomburg Collection, New York Public Library**)

Charles C. Diggs, Jr., has represented a Detroit congressional district since 1955. He and his father, seated in this 1956 photograph, both served in the Michigan senate. (*Ebony Magazine*)

Robert N. C. Nix, lawyer son of a South Carolina college dean, has represented the Second Congressional District in Philadelphia, Pennsylvania, since 1958.

Arthur W. Mitchell, of Illinois, the first black Democratic congressman, receives congratulations from fellow representatives—Raymond S. McKeough, *left,* and Joseph A. Gavagan, *right*—following House passage of an antilynching bill in 1940. The Senate later killed the measure. (**United Press International**)

Augustus F. Hawkins gets a victory hug from his wife, Pegga, after winning election to the House in 1962 from California's Twenty-first District. (**United Press International**)

In 1969, Hawkins (*right*) and Louis Stokes, of Ohio (*center*), as members of the House Education and Labor Committee, inspected a Pennsylvania coal mine. (**United Press International**)

Congressman Stokes held the Bible when his brother, Carl Stokes, whose wife is at his side, was sworn in for a second term as mayor of Cleveland in 1969. (**United Press International**)

William L. Clay with his wife and children (*foreground, left to right*), Vickie, Lacy, and Michelle, just before the St. Louis, Missouri, Democrat was elected to the House in 1968. (*St. Louis Post Dispatch*)

When violence erupted in Detroit's black neighborhoods in 1967, Michigan Rep. John Conyers, Jr., took to the streets with a bullhorn to encourage the crowds to break up and go home. (**Wide World Photos**)

Shirley Chisholm, the first black woman in Congress, represents the Bedford-Stuyvesant section in Brooklyn, New York. She and Rep. Conyers, *below*, were among the black congressmen who appeared before the Senate Judiciary Committee on September 25, 1969, to oppose the nomination of Judge Clement F. Haynsworth to the Supreme Court. (**Wagner International Photos, Inc.; United Press International**)

Edward W. Brooke's family came to the stage to acknowledge the cheers of Massachusetts Republicans just after the party endorsed him to run for the Senate in 1966. With Brooke, then state attorney general, are, *left to right:* his wife, Remigia; his mother, Mrs. Helen Brooke; and his teen-age daughters, Edwina and Remi. (**Wide World Photos**)

Sen. Brooke meets with Secretary of Defense Melvin R. Laird, *center*, and President Richard M. Nixon. Though on cordial terms with the President, Brooke broke party lines to oppose him on many issues. After the Watergate scandal erupted, Brooks was the first Republican senator to call for Nixon's resignation.

Miller was particularly incensed at Georgia Congressman Alfred Colquitt's charge that white men in the South must constantly worry about the chastity of their women. "Great God, is there no limit to the slander and malignant utterances of these self-constituted friends of a toiling, deserving, plodding portion of the American people?" the South Carolina congressman angrily asked. "Stand up and indict a race of males as the invaders of the sanctity of Caucasian home ties, as the brutal destroyer of that in woman which is her very existence. The charge is groundless, mean, slanderous, and most damnably false. . . ."

Miller said there had been no cases of assault or rape by blacks against white women—those "walking emblems of American purity" he called them—in his district since emancipation. In any event, he said, the records of Southern courts would prove that such a charge was usually untrue; generally it was a matter of mutual consent. "Whenever it [a rape charge] is hurled at him [the black man] the crime is laid in a locality where the numbers of the whites and the Negroes are nearly equal, where the whites and the Negroes are equal in morals; and, even after the poor unfortunate victim has been lynched and his spirit gone to the eternal world, letters or verbal admissions coming from the supposed victim of licentious brutality invariably absolve the innocent dead man from the crime charged."

Charging the opposition with having painted a completely false picture of black power during reconstruction, Miller said the truth was it was not Negro domination that was feared but majority rule. As an example of fact-twisting, he quoted a speech from South Carolina's John Hemphill the previous June in which Hemphill had said that he had had to go past the glittering bayonets of a thousand soldiers to vote in 1876, but that he did not mind because every soldier voted Democratic and they had a bigger majority as a result. While Hemphill probably had told the story so often he believed it himself, Miller said people should know that the number of soldiers on duty in Hemphill's county that November was less than seventy-five.

His abbreviated term ended, Miller resumed law practice in the spring of 1891, but he challenged William Elliott's claim to the seat when the new Fifty-second Congress met in December. However, the Democrat was sworn in, and there was no action on the case until February 1893, a month before adjournment, when the Elections Committee rejected Miller's challenge. A minority report favoring the challenger also went into the record; there is no indication that the contest ever reached a House vote. At any rate, it was anticlimactic for Miller, whose hopes for being returned to the Fifty-third Congress had been dashed by the Republicans months earlier when the convention nominated George Washington Murray, a rising black aspirant, to represent the Seventh District.

Miller returned to the South Carolina house of representatives, and in 1895 he attended the state constitutional convention where he and Robert Smalls fought in vain against the adoption of a clause adding a new criterion for voting, which both knew would be used to disfranchise Negroes. The provision, requiring a prospective voter to read and write any section of the state constitution on demand unless he could prove that he had paid taxes on a minimum of three hundred dollars' worth of property, would also be employed as a weapon against poor whites, Miller predicted.

He tangled with Ben Tillman, who had taken time out from the United States Senate, to spearhead the anti-Negro drive. Tillman said blacks had brought this action on themselves by evidencing a total lack of ability when in power in South Carolina.

Miller replied that quite the opposite was true. He said the state's blacks had been largely responsible for the enlightened legislation covering state financing, local government, penal codes, charitable institutions, and most of all, the establishment of a public school system during the reconstruction period. He said these worthwhile measures were a living witness to the black man's fitness to vote and to legislate.

The following year the former congressman helped to establish State Negro College (now South Carolina State College) at Orangeburg, and was appointed its president. During his long tenure there, he used his influence to convince Charleston education officials to hire black teachers for black schools. He resigned the college presidency in 1911 on twenty-four hours' notice at the request of a new governor, whose candidacy Miller had opposed because he thought the man would be unfriendly to Negroes. As long as Miller lived in South Carolina, he slept with a pistol under his pillow for protection, a habit that dated back to his active political days when threats against black politicians were commonplace.

At eighty Miller, who had been living in Philadelphia for several years, felt well enough to address the Association for the Study of Negro Life and History in Washington in February 1930. He talked of how much it had cost him to force the House of Representatives to admit him to the seat to which he had been elected in 1888; he reminisced about the exploits of Robert Smalls in and out of Congress, and he criticized President Rutherford B. Hayes, whose treachery, he said, had practically eliminated the Negro as a political force in the South, though there were a few "flukes of success" afterwards such as Henry Cheatham, John Langston, George White, and himself. He hoped writers, sculptors, and painters would leave behind an accurate record of the contribution of blacks to the building of America.

Miller wrote a book about his own years in public life. Unable to get it published during his lifetime, he reportedly left instructions to have it posthumously privately printed and earmarked funds for that purpose. After his death on April 8, 1938, however, his wishes were not carried out; parts of the manuscript are now in various collections.

"Not having loved the white man less, but having felt the Negro needed me more," the words Thomas E. Miller penned for his epitaph are on his tombstone, and they have perpetuated the mystery surrounding his ancestry.

Miller's successor in Washington—after a two-year lapse—was George W. Murray, the last of South Carolina's eight Negro congressmen. Only four years younger than Miller, Murray was a late bloomer in politics. This erect six-footer was almost forty before he had the chance to run for any office.

George Washington Murray, who was born September 22, 1853 near Rembert in Sumter County to slave parents, apparently had no white blood. The Civil War left him a free but friendless orphan. An industrious, alert, bright child, he fended for himself and somehow acquired enough education to teach. He had never been in a schoolroom until he went there as a teacher.

At twenty-one he qualified through a competitive examination and enrolled at South Carolina University, where he studied for two years until the state's reconstruction government collapsed and the university was resegregated. He then resumed teaching, and for some fourteen years, mixed that profession with farming, acquiring several hundred acres of land. Part of this time he also attended the State Normal Institute at Columbia, where he prepared a number of papers on his teaching technique and philosophy.

In the campaign of 1888 he worked hard for the Republican ticket as Sumter County chairman. Two years later President Benjamin Harrison named him customs inspector for the port of Charleston. He competed with Miller for the congressional nomination that year, but campaigned for Miller when the Republicans chose him.

Murray was determined to push his own candidacy to the limit in 1892. He was pitted against two former black congressmen, Smalls and Miller, as well as a veteran white contender, E. M. Brayton. On the third ballot the teacher-farmer won the Republican nomination. Before the election he stumped every corner of the district and was confident of victory, but the initial count showed him losing to E. W.

Moise, the Democrat. Miller represented Murray before the state board of canvassers and convinced them that he had won by forty votes.

The victory was pleasant news for the country's Negroes who had been disheartened when Henry Cheatham of North Carolina, their last holdout in Congress, was defeated for reelection to the House. Now their hopes in Washington centered on the broad, sinewy shoulders of the man one newspaper labeled "the bold black eagle of Sumter."

Imbued with tremendous drive and wide-ranging interests, he wore modest sideburns, a thick moustache, and his hair slicked straight back. Following his election, he purchased ten thousand acres of South Carolina land, which he subdivided into tracts of twenty-five, fifty, and one hundred acres for resale to Negroes. He patented eight machines for planting, chopping, harvesting, and fertilizing farm crops.

The new congressman called on Grover Cleveland in Washington to inform him that most blacks in the South were worried about what might happen to them under a Democratic President. He told Cleveland there was a wonderful opportunity for him as President to perform a great act of patriotism by showing blacks that a Democratic administration "does not mean special harm to us. Such conviction would crush forever the present formation of the political parties in the South and wipe out political fraud and murders."

Unfortunately, the Democrats chose not to grasp the opportunity. Just a few years earlier Senate Democrats had prevented the Republicans from shoring up the federal laws protecting suffrage. Now the Democrats, in control of both houses of Congress as well as the Presidency, determined to repeal the core of the existing legislation for the enforcement of voting rights.

Obviously nothing was of more concern to the only black left in the national legislature. The strategy of the Democrats was to repeal certain "statutes relative to supervisors of elections and special deputy marshals and other purposes." During the debate on October 2, 1893, Murray said that from personal experience as a supervisor and marshal he knew these men were at the polls only to make sure the elections were properly conducted and not to interfere.

Three days later he ridiculed printed reports that someone was ghostwriting his material for Congress as he again spoke on the need for federal supervision of elections. The South Carolina representative charged that state registration officials had cheated voters in his state out of thirteen registration days at the last election. He said nearly four fifths of the electors had been disfranchised by such tricks while the Southern press spread the canard that Negroes were so pleased with their governments they didn't bother to vote. He quoted statistics to show what a light turnout there had been in South Carolina, Louisiana, and Mississippi compared to Kansas, Minnesota, and California.

"Taxation without representation is tyranny," he reminded his colleagues, had been the battle cry of the American Revolution. What then, he asked, of the South Carolina blacks who paid about one thirteenth of the state's property taxes and were denied the ballot? He called it brazen effrontery to say the federal election laws should be repealed in the interest of white supremacy when the local governments were already in the hands of Caucasians. Large sections of the press always raised the chant of black domination "and we stand helpless and amazed. I declare that the patient, long-suffering, generous black man has never attempted to domineer anywhere in this country. At the very dawn of freedom, when the refusal to act on the part of the master class placed the reins of Government in his hands with only a handful of white men in his party, he gave nearly every position of honor and emolument to them, and there are numerous instances where, when there were not enough white men belonging to his party to fill the offices, he even elected Democrats rather than to appear to dominate the white race."

Obviously sickened by talk of the danger of black control after Negroes had been stripped of almost all participation in their governments, even in areas where they greatly outnumbered whites, he urged blacks to watch the roll call and seek to defeat any man who voted for the bill. This measure passed the House in the first session and later was approved by the Senate and signed into law by President Cleveland in February 1894.

Murray was away much of the second session. The record shows him taking five leaves of absence—three for private business and two for indefinite periods because of illness. He introduced two bills—one to establish normal and industrial schools, and another to exempt the Young Men's Christian Association from taxes. He wanted funds appropriated for a home for aged and needy black people. Proponents of this measure pointed out that the sum amounted to less than sixty cents for each Negro soldier who had served in the Union army during the Civil War.

In the fall of 1894, Murray faced an uphill fight for reelection. The borders of his district had been realigned to eliminate black voters and to include more whites. As a result, by the South Carolina count, Murray lost to Democrat William Elliott by more than seventeen hundred votes. He made plans to appeal this result.

Meanwhile, the third session of the Fifty-third Congress was held from December 1894 to March 1895 without his being in attendance much, if at all. His only entry in the *Congressional Record* for that session was for an indefinite leave of absence for important business. He may have been getting ready to contest Elliott's election.

The Fifty-fourth Congress began its work on December 2, 1895, with Elliott in the seat representing South Carolina's newly drawn First District. The following May, however, the Elections Committee issued a report favoring Murray's appeal, which was supported by petitions from Negroes throughout the nation. The committee found widespread flaunting of the laws in the 1894 election. Polls in three or four precincts, mainly those with large Republican majorities, had not been opened. Blacks were denied registration certificates or given invalid ones, and the conduct of the election boards was irregular. Elliott, the House investigators discovered, had personally "stood like a stone wall between them [blacks] and the ballot box in many instances," and when he challenged, on whatever pretext, their right to vote, they were for the most part turned away.

Though fraud was widespread, the committee focused mainly on Charleston, where there were sufficient grounds to reverse the state's decision in favor of Elliott. There were 1,945 more black than white voters in that city, but Charleston had given Elliott 2,811 votes to 397 for Murray. The committee recommended that all but four of the precincts be thrown out because of the unreliability of the vote. It accepted 217 Murray votes from Haupt Gap in Berkeley County, where when the polls had not been opened by officials who should have done so, citizen volunteers set up the procedure to hold an election in the manner prescribed by law. This, plus the Charleston revisions, was enough to give the seat to Murray by 434 votes, according to the House Elections Committee.

On June 4, 1896, the House voted 153 to 33 to oust Elliott and give the district to Murray. After the roll call vote, he was greeted by applause from the Republicans when he was sworn in by the Speaker. The day after he had been tardily readmitted to their ranks, the members granted him ten-days leave to return home because of illness in the family.

The Republicans in South Carolina held two nominating conventions in 1896. Murray attended the largely Caucasian meeting, but when a white was nominated for the seat in the First District, the Negroes refused to support the ticket, and Murray ran himself. The split ticket, plus the crackdown on black voting, sent Elliott back to the House.

Congress reconvened early in December after the election break, but because of illness Murray was again home in January. When he returned to his House desk, he introduced a federal elections measure designed to repair some of the damage done by the 1894 repeal law. Repeatedly he asked for an investigation of political fraud and intimidation in South Carolina, where he said irregularities were so widespread that the state's electoral vote should be challenged. He also wanted the Cook County, Illinois, political machine scrutinized by the House.

Murray set up a real estate firm in Sumter and failed in his effort to get the House seat back two years later. He was charged with fraud and moved to Chicago in 1905, while his case was pending. The *Chicago Defender* said it was a "political misunderstanding" rather than trouble with the law that drove him North. From his new Illinois base he wrote, lectured, and traveled widely. Among his books, all out of print now, was a volume called *Light in Dark Places.*

By the spring of 1926, the seventy-two-year-old former congressman had not been feeling well for some months. Refusing to go to bed, he stayed up fighting the pain. On April 16 he agreed to the operation his doctors had been suggesting for some time. Five days later, George W. Murray died, leaving behind his wife, Cornelia, and two children. John R. Lynch, the only Negro to represent Mississippi in the House, delivered the eulogy for South Carolina's last black congressman.

Benjamin S. Turner, James T. Rapier, and Jeremiah Haralson/Alabama

James T. Rapier and Jeremiah Haralson, the two most talented black leaders to emerge in Alabama during the reconstruction period, might have lasted longer in politics and been more effective had they curbed their personal rivalries and concentrated on the opposition. The third of Alabama's Negro congressmen, Benjamin S. Turner, was too gentle a man for political infighting even if he had not lived in a state where the Ku Klux Klan thrived.

The Civil War had barely ended when the former slaveowners of Alabama began restoring as much of the prewar racial status quo as possible. By mid-1865 an all-white constitutional convention had been convened under a provisional governor. The legislature grudgingly accepted the Thirteenth Amendment, freeing the slaves, "with the understanding that it does not confer on Congress the power to legislate upon the political status of freedmen in this state."

Black codes, reminiscent of the slave statutes, circumscribed employment, housing, and travel for Negroes. Fearful of backlash from the North, Governor R. M. Patton vetoed much of this legislation, but the laws remaining were of grave concern to blacks, who had no intention of relinquishing without a fight their new civic and political rights. They began to organize locally, and in May 1867 at a convention in Mobile they met to map state strategy.

After Congress took over the reconstruction machinery, 61,295 Negroes and 104,518 whites turned out for the first voter registration. Only 18,533 whites favored holding a constitutional convention. Nonetheless, the convention was held with eighteen blacks among the delegates. This convention went further than Congress in disfranchising men who had fought against the Union during the Civil War. The new constitution, providing for racially mixed schools and full political rights for the former slaves, was ratified early in 1868 with many whites abstaining. By July 13, 1868, Alabama was back in the federal fold.

Nearly one half the state's population were Negroes, and they outnumbered their fellow citizens in the Republican party 90,000 to 10,000. But when the votes of the first election were tallied, blacks had won only twenty-seven of the eight-four seats in the legislature, and none of the state's major executive positions. One of the first actions of this legislature was to restore the political rights to some of the people affected by the strictures in the state constitution—a move supported by the black bloc.

The first ex-slave to forge ahead in national politics in Alabama was Benjamin Sterling Turner who had been in active public life just a few years when he was elected to Congress at the age of forty-five. Born into slavery near Weldon, in Halifax County, North Carolina, on March 17, 1825, he had been taken to Alabama at the age of five. He grew up there without formal schooling, though he surreptitiously obtained a fair education. He probably was not freed until the Emancipation Proclamation.

As a young man in Selma, Turner became well known to whites and Negroes as the owner of a thriving livery stable. For a while he was also a merchant. At forty-two he was named tax collector of Dallas County. Two years later, he became a Selma city councilman, the post he held when he was unanimously nominated by the Republicans to run for the House from the Alabama First Congressional District. He complained of lack of support from carpetbagging whites in his party, but he won handily in the election. He said he sold a horse to finance his campaign.

The Washington correspondent of the *New York Globe* described the new Alabama congressman as a big broad-shouldered man with a large nose and curly hair. The writer gave him credit for having done what a Negro was not supposed to do in his state—become educated. He is "very quiet, seldom seen conversing, always present, never speaks, and among Republican colleagues has a considerable reputation for good sense and political sagacity."

During the first brief session in Washington, which started on March 4, 1871, Turner introduced bills to restore political and legal rights to ex-Confederates generally and to one of his Dallas County constituents specifically.

In the second session his charity was again demonstrated. In a May 30, 1872, speech supporting his bill for a two hundred thousand dollar appropriation to rebuild Selma's public offices, he said that the people there had buried "many of those animosities upon which we hear so many eloquent appeals in this Chamber." In 1865, he continued, two thirds of the city had been reduced to ashes by the United States Army. Churches, schools, manufacturing plants, stores, workshops, public buildings, barns, stock pens, and more than a thousand homes were swept away in flames as "the Government made a display in that unfortunate city of its mighty power and conquered a gallant and high-toned people. They may have sinned wonderfully, but they suffered terribly. War was once the glory of her sons, but they paid the penalty of their offense, and for one, I have no coals of fiery reproach to heap upon them now.

"Rather would I extend the olive branch of peace, and say to them, let the past be forgotten and let us all, from every sun and clime, of every hue and every shade, go to work peacefully to build up the shattered temples of this great and glorious Republic."

Turner, who was accorded no time on the floor for his two major speeches, focused much of his attention on trying to get government action to stimulate the South's economy. He stressed this point in his appeals for a public building program for war-devastated Selma. He returned to it when advocating tax refunds and government loans for the purchase of land.

The Alabama congressman thought the tax of seventy million dollars, which the federal government had collected on cotton from 1866–68, had greatly handicapped the South financially, was unconstitutional, and should be returned. He said that poor Negroes, who worked in the fields, had paid the levy of three cents per pound, and that this imposition had driven foreign customers away and lost the South a quarter of a million dollars when prices plummeted. "But for this tax . . .", he assented, "they [cotton workers] would have been able to purchase one eighth of the land on which the cotton was made."

He asked his fellow representatives from other areas to imagine what would happen to iron, salt, or sugar if the tariff on those items had been replaced by a prohibitory tax. In this same speech, which like the Selma speech was tucked away in the appendix of the *Congressional Record,* he told why he had introduced a bill to authorize federal loans to help poor farmers buy land. He said the newly freed people of his section had "struggled longer and labored harder and have made more of the raw material than any people in the world. . . . They live on little clothing, the poorest food, and in miserable huts."

Turner said that he frequently heard the argument that before the government was generous, it should be just. "Then I call the attention . . . of the House to the fact that we should look to our own interests before we care for those of our neighbors.

"What has been the result of our legislation? We have subsidized for the people of China; we have subsidized for the people of Japan; we have subsidized to feed the wild Indians, roaming over the domains of the West pillaging, robbing and murdering our citizens. These subsidies are sucking vampires upon our people, for not one of those who are benefited by them pay to the United States a single dollar of taxes, while the people in whose behalf I plead pay annually $70,000,000 in taxes to the United States government.

"While we pay gratuitously to Chinese, Japanese, and Indians millions of dollars annually, we hesitate to even lend to the landless but peaceable and industrious citizens of the South $1,000,000 annually to help them aid themselves and at the same time greatly develop the resources of the country. Nor can this loan be attended with the least risk to the Government, for it is secured by the best of security, placing a small portion of the surplus money of the Treasury to profitable use, and at the same time paying the Government large interest."

Turner's bills to revitalize the economy of his state did not pass, and in 1872 he faced his first reelection challenge. The party's nomination was his, but Philip Joseph, another Negro, refused to support him and ran as an independent. As a result, the election went to F. G. Bromberg, who ran as a Democrat and Liberal Republican.

Back for his final session in December, Turner was naturally somewhat dispirited. But he was there with his vote when his Republican mentor, Benjamin Butler, needed it for party-supported reconstruction measures. After the curtain went down on the Forty-second Congress on March 3, 1873, he returned to Selma and took up farming.

As Benjamin Turner left the Washington scene, James T. Rapier arrived to represent Alabama's Second Congressional District. In political life he sought to unite Negroes with poor whites in order to increase their combined influence and improve their financial situation. It is a tactic many people, both black and white, have thought would work in the South, but it has never been fully put to a fair test.

James Thomas Rapier came from a wealthy family. His father, John Rapier, was a white plantation owner, and his mother, Susan, was a free Negro. He was born on November 13, 1837, in Florence, Alabama. He and his three brothers were tutored secretly at home since education for blacks was frowned upon in Alabama. Later, his father sent him to Montreal College in Canada, the University of Glasgow in Scotland, and Franklin College in Nashville, Tennessee. He was an intensely dedicated student, studying long hours.

Rapier taught school for a time in Tennessee, where he spent the Civil War years. He traveled as a correspondent for a Northern newspaper after Union forces captured Nashville. Somewhere along the way he read law and was admitted to the bar, but he never practiced. In 1865 he was a delegate to the Tennessee constitutional convention.

His father's serious illness brought him back to Florence the following year. He went to work on the Rapier land and was soon established as a successful cotton planter. The governor named him a notary public, an assignment of greater significance then than now. He was among the Negro farmers, carriage drivers, and tradesmen who joined white Alabamians in the state capital building at Montgomery in 1867 to write a new constitution under the terms of the Reconstruction Acts.

He enjoyed an official trip across the Atlantic as United States commissioner to the international exposition in Paris in 1867. Afterward, he was Alabama's representative to the Vienna exposition.

As an organizer for the Colored National Labor Union, Rapier, who sported a stylishly trimmed beard, toured the state, lining up workers in the cities and sharecroppers on the farms. He arrived on horseback, his saddlebags packed with books and pamphlets, his full black coat flapping in the breeze. His friends looked after his plantation while he worked for the union by day and attended Republican party organizational meetings by night. An adjunct of the party, the black union, which was formed after a meeting in Washington in 1869, was supported by the predominantly white National Labor Union.

Rapier helped write the state's first Republican platform, which called for free speech, free press, free schools, and equal civil and political rights for all men—regardless of color or previous condition. A labor convention he chaired in the state capital drew a hundred delegates from forty-two counties. Non-blacks, who attended and voted for cooperation between the races for their mutual financial betterment, were later roundly criticized by the white press and in some instances harassed by their more affluent neighbors. A few years afterward, Rapier challenged a black convention to proclaim itself the last of such gatherings. He said he did not want to be considered separate from white people, even for the purpose of deliberation.

Rapier first submitted himself to the electorate as a candidate for the office of secretary of state of Alabama in 1870. He was defeated along with the entire Republican ticket. The next year he was named tax assessor.

Rapier went into newspaper publishing from the labor movement, which was stymied by the South's economic woes. He edited and published the *Montgomery Sentinel* in partnership with a friend, Nathan H. Alexander, who named one of his sons in Rapier's honor.

Their paper crusaded to improve the lines of communication between the races in Alabama.

As secretary of the Alabama Equal Rights League, Rapier arranged for a torchlight parade to celebrate the passage of the Fifteenth Amendment declaring that no United States citizen could be denied the right to vote because of his race or color.

In 1872 a Negro farmer nominated Rapier for Congress at the Republican district convention, and a white man seconded the nomination. He won by a margin of nearly three thousand votes over a former Confederate officer running on the Democratic ticket. Washington's *New National Era* wrote that he had worked steadily and earnestly for the Republican party, despite threats against his life. Ku Kluxers, the paper said, had stripped him of his property and tried to drive him out of Alabama. Another newspaper's charge that he had a prison record was dismissed as emanating from racial hatred. "His character is and has been above reproach," the *Era* assured its readers, but warned them to continue to expect such disparagements from their former oppressors.

In the Forty-third Congress Rapier was one of seven black members. He was named to the Education and Labor Committee, a suitable assignment for one of his background and interests. Like any good freshman congressman, he spent much of his time on the routine concerns of his district, pushing for improved postal and court facilities, for river development and building funds. President Grant signed his proposal making Montgomery a port of delivery on June 20, 1874.

The galleries got their first protracted look at the tall, sparkling-eyed Rapier on June 9, 1874, when he pressed for prompt action on the civil rights bill that had been under consideration for six months. This legislation, banning discrimination in schools, hotels, and public travel conveyances, was encountering tough opposition, especially from House conservatives who feared open education would foster racial amalgamation.

Rapier said that the Negro was in quite a dilemma over the proper approach to this bill "because if he exhibit an earnestness in the matter and express a desire for its immediate passage, straightway he is charged with a desire for social equality, as explained by the demagogue and understood by the ignorant white man. But . . . if he remain silent while the struggle is being carried on around, and for him, he is liable to be charged with a want of interest in a matter that concerns him more than anyone else, which is enough to make his friends desert his cause."

Rapier felt shame for his native land, especially if there were foreigners present "who have been lured to our shore by the popular but untruthful declaration that this land is the asylum of the oppressed." The observant foreigner would learn that in America it was possible for a man to be half free and half slave: "Here he will see a man legislating for a free people, while his own chains of civil slavery hang about him. . . . I am subjected to far more outrages and indignities in coming to and going from this Capitol in discharge of my public duties than any criminal in the country providing he be white. Instead of my position shielding me from insult, it too often invites it."

Rapier said that if he were traveling to Montgomery with a white ex-convict, whatever his crime, the white man would be treated as a gentleman while he would be treated as a convict, kept out of the sleeping car, and "forced into a dirty, rough box [car] with the drunkards, apple sellers, railroad hands, and next to any dead that may be in transit, regardless of how far decomposition may have progressed." Young black women were subjected to the same maltreatment. And "if from any cause we are compelled to lay over, the best bed in the hotel is his [the ex-convict's] if he can pay for it, while I am invariably turned away, hungry and cold, to stand around the railway station until the departure of the next train, it matters not how long, thereby endangering my health, while my life and property are at the mercy of any highwayman who may wish to murder and rob me."

There was not an inn between Washington and Montgomery, a distance of more than a thousand miles, that would accommodate him with a bed or a meal. Noting that in antebellum days any white man denied first-class travel accommodations would have sued and won his case, Rapier said that he was now demanding the same rights for the black man. He looked to the federal government to correct this national grievance because it was to this government that a citizen of the United States owed primary allegiance and from which he should be able to expect protection.

Rapier held that Congress itself was degraded by permitting him to be: "I submit that I am degraded as long as I am denied the public privileges common to other men, and that the members of this House are correspondingly degraded by recognizing my political equality while I occupy such a humiliating position. What a singular attitude for lawmakers of this great nation to assume, rather come down to me than allow me to go up to them.

"Sir, did you ever reflect that this is the only Christian country where poor, finite man is held responsible for the crimes of the infinite God whom you profess to worship? But it is; I am held to answer the crime of color, when I was not consulted in the matter. Had I been consulted, and my future fully described, I think I should have

129

objected to being born in this gospel land. The excuse offered for all this inhuman treatment is that they consider the Negro inferior to the white man, intellectually and morally. This reason might have been offered and probably accepted as truth some years ago, but no one now believes him incapable of a high order of culture, except some one who is himself below the average of mankind in natural endowments. . . . The smaller the caliber of the white man the more frantically has he fought to prevent the intellectual and moral progress of the Negro, for the simple but good reason that he has most to fear from such a result."

Rapier took no comfort from the assurances of Democrats like Congressman James Beck of Kentucky who said they were willing to accord the Negro all the rights they believed belonged to him under the Constitution. The difficulty was that the Democratic platforms in several states indicated that party's unwillingness to admit that full citizenship had been accorded to blacks under the Reconstruction Acts and two post-Civil War Amendments.

Nonetheless, he would take the gentleman at his word. He then asked Beck why, after all those laws, Negroes in Kentucky were still refused the right to testify in court against a white man, why their schoolhouses were burned, their teachers murdered, and the Ku Klux Klan organized to keep them from casting their ballots? Rapier said that professed belief and practice were sadly at variance. He then turned his fire on Alexander Stephens of Georgia because of his earnest opposition to the bill and his "peculiar relations" to the Confederacy (a reference to Stephens' role as vice-president of the secessionist government). Although Stephens states'-rights theory had led to secession and a bloody war "he, Bourbon-like, comes back saying the very same things he used to say, and swearing by the same gods he swore by in other days." By such behavior Stephens stamped himself a living Rip Van Winkle. The states' righters should realize, Rapier continued, that their cause had been lost on the field of battle, that the Stars and Stripes were paramount, and that the pending bill simply gave practical effect to that decision.

He could sympathize with Stephens' difficulties in adjusting, coming from a capital in which blacks had been exposed for sale in the marketplace and no more than three were allowed to gather, to a city where schools had been erected over the slave pens, a fine-looking company of black men such as the Butler Zouaves could be seen parading on any holiday, and Negroes faced him in debate in the House. Stephens' states'-rights ploy was cunning, but if he were sincere about Georgia's willingness to handle the problem, why had he not recommended such a measure to the Georgia legislature?

"Mr. Speaker, nothing short of a complete acknowledgement of my manhood will satisfy me," Rapier asserted. "I have no compromises to make, and shall unwillingly accept any." He had had to go abroad to learn the feelings of a free man and had found that once outside his own country there was no discrimination on shipboard or in hotels: "It was in other countries than my own that I was not a stranger, that I could approach a hotel without fear that the door would be slammed in my face. I feel this humiliation very keenly; it dwarfs my manhood, and certainly it impairs my usefulness as a citizen."

That summer Rapier had little opposition in being renominated by his party, but there was division in the Republican ranks at campaign time, and the Klan was beginning to take its toll. He went down to defeat by an edge of a thousand votes to J. N. Williams, the Democrat candidate. The lame-duck congressman went back to Washington a discouraged man for the short second session, starting in December 1874, and he was to be even more disheartened before his term ended on March 3, 1875.

As the civil rights bill moved toward final action on February 4, 1875, Rapier was given five minutes to answer Alexander White of Alabama, whom he said had misrepresented the sentiments of the people of his state. White had insisted that his opposition to the civil rights measure accurately reflected the opinion of Alabama blacks.

Rapier, though hesitant to prolong the discussion which he thought should have long ago ended, said the last time the black people of Alabama had been heard from on this issue they had endorsed the legislation. He quoted from a statement at a recent Negro meeting: "As citizens of the United States and the State of Alabama, we claim all the civil and political rights and privileges, and immunities secured every citizen by the Constitution of the United States and of the State of Alabama; and we will be satisfied with nothing less."

White had tried to tack an amendment on the bill providing that nothing in the law should be construed as requiring racially mixed public accommodations or schools and that the law should not be enforced against companies offering separate but equal facilities.

Rapier emphasized that he favored the Senate bill as it stood, including the open schools provision: "I have no compromise to offer on this subject; I shall not willingly accept any. After all, this question resolves itself into this: either I am a man or I am not a man. If I am a man, I am entitled to all the rights and privileges and immunities that any other American citizen is entitled to. If I am not a man, then I have no right to vote, I have no right to be here upon this floor."

In the end, despite his call for no compromise, Rapier voted for the only bill the Republicans could get—the anemic version that omitted any mention of open schools. Several white Republican congressmen from Alabama also voted for the bill. Later the Ku Klux Klan there tried to carry off one of these representatives as he was speaking, but his friends rescued him. There was an attempt on Rapier's life, but he was forewarned, and the Ku Kluxers were driven off, some of their number having been, it is said, killed in an exchange of gunfire.

Rapier was out of the new Congress, but another Alabama district had selected a Negro to go to the nation's capital. He was Jeremiah Haralson, a forceful, husky black farmer with a natural political shrewdness. Born April 1, 1846, near Columbus in Muscogee County, Georgia, of slave parents, Haralson, when battling for votes against such light-colored rivals as James T. Rapier, boasted of being a pure-blooded Negro. He had no formal education, but did well with the learning he had been able to pick up for himself. To the *Mobile Register* he was "uncompromising, irritating, bold."

He had been brought to Alabama in 1859 as a slave and remained a slave of John Haralson until emancipation. He was still on the Haralson property as a servant at the end of the war, at which time he could neither read nor write. A letter from the Selma correspondent of the *Washington New National Era and Citizen* in January 22, 1874, gives a hint as to his approach to life once freedom came for him: "No sooner than opportunity offered he applied himself to the study of books and by untiring toil and never-ceasing persever-ance . . . he learned to handle the English language . . . Haralson is a self-made man. . . ."

The contemporary political gossip was that Haralson had accepted money in the 1868 campaign to make speeches for the Democratic presidential ticket of Horatio Seymour and Francis P. Blair, Jr., while actually supporting and working for the Republican standard bearers, Ulysses S. Grant and Schuyler Colfax. According to these reports, Haralson delivered insincere appeals for Seymour, but scored his real points afterward in private conversation with members of the audi-ence and thereby helped carry the state for the Republicans. The *Mobile Register*, in its role as heckler to the Republican party, suggested that Haralson as the most prominent black in Alabama would make a suitable Cabinet officer after Grant won the Presidency.

The details of Haralson's life before he went to Congress are hazy. He was a farmer, and he may have been a minister as well. In 1868 he ran for Congress but was defeated. In 1870 he went to the state house of representatives, having run as an independent against the regular Republican and won by four thousand votes. He chaired the district convention at which Benjamin Turner was nominated for

Congress, and impressed the assemblage with his presiding skill and stirring voice. Two years later, Haralson was elected to represent the Twenty-First District in the state senate.

He tangled with Louisiana's P. B. S. Pinchback at a national Negro meeting in New Orleans in April 1872. The wrangle, which lasted a couple of days, was over a resolution offered by Rapier calling for the convention to repudiate any connection with a splinter movement against President Grant. Haralson favored the resolution; Pinchback opposed it as a slap at Massachusetts Senator Charles Sumner, who had broken with the President over the move to annex Santo Domingo.

A Liberal Republican convention was to be held in May in Cincinnati by the supporters of Horace Greeley for President. With Sumner on their team, the Greeleyites were hotly wooing Southern black Republicans. At that Cincinnati meeting the Liberal Republicans nominated the celebrated newspaper editor, who was also later endorsed by the Democrats in their convention. As a result, Greeley ran as a Democratic Liberal Republican and polled nearly 44 percent of the vote against Grant, the regular Republican.

"I have been a slave all my life and am free on account of the Republican party, and if it comes to an issue, I for one am ready to let Charles Sumner fall and let the Republican party stand," Haralson stated.

"I denounce the Cincinnati convention and go for President Grant. Sumner may have passed the days of usefulness. I do not say he has, but when he goes with the big Dutchman [Frank Blair] over here in Missouri, I will go against him. All Democrats are in favor of the Cincinnati convention and if Sumner is in this conspiracy [against Grant], I am against him.

"I have no ax to grind. I am too poor. Only sorehead Republicans favor the Cincinnati convention and I think there must be some sorehead men here. . . . Some men live too long. Abraham Lincoln was taken just in time. I believe if he had lived any longer we would not have the rights that are ours now. . . . Grant has protected us and he is the only man who will protect us. If he is not elected, we will be worse off than we were before the war. We may all be killed off for what I know."

There were repeated calls for order as Haralson spoke. The next day he softened his position toward Senator Sumner, and he and Pinchback agreed to serve on a committee together. He had not intended to denounce Sumner, Haralson explained, but only to say that if Sumner were leaving the party, the Republicans should let him go, however reluctantly.

Haralson was a loud, abrasive man, but one who obviously could hold his own even with the wily Pinchback. "A ready, shrewd debater, full of wit and sarcasm," was a political reporter's assessment of Haralson. "He is perhaps feared more than any other colored man in the legislature in Alabama." He wore a moustache and a modest beard, and kept his hair close cropped. His gaze was sharp and penetrating.

He entered the race for Congress again in 1874 at the state convention, where he managed to keep the white Republicans in line to support a strong civil rights policy. He won the nomination over two candidates, one of each color. In the general election he defeated Frederick G. Bromberg, a Liberal Republican. Congress convened in December 1875, and he was named to the Committee on Public Expenditures. He introduced six bills, resolutions, and petitions, but delivered no speeches during the session. He sought help for the Medical College of Alabama, the use of the proceeds of the sale of public lands for education and settlement of Civil War claims.

He was dogged, however, by having his election contested. When Bromberg's challenge was first mentioned on the floor on March 23, 1876, indications were that the House would act in favor of "the sitting member." About a month later on April 18, 1876, Congressman John Harris of Virginia called up the case and said the committee held unanimously that Haralson should keep his seat. Since the report was unanimous, he asked that debate be dispensed with, but wanted time himself to give the House and the country the benefit of the committee's report.

"While it retains the sitting member in his seat," he said, "it will show frauds as flagrant and abuses as violent as ever have been committed in this country upon an elective franchise. Moreover, it will show that when two years ago this House was called upon to extend its charitable hand to relieve the sufferings of the colored people of Alabama caused by floods in their rivers, and large quantities of bacon were provided for them, that bacon was taken by the Government officials and used, not in districts where distress existed, but in high lands where the people were prosperous, to influence and control the elective franchise.

"It will be shown, moreover, that the colored voters were intimidated by their own race against voting for the contestant in this case. It will be shown, also, that undue and unwarranted interference on the part of the military to secure the election of the sitting member . . . Notwithstanding [this] the large [2,700] majority . . . could not . . . be legitimately and properly overcome. . . . Having thrown out a large number of votes illegally and improperly cast, they [the committee] still found that the sitting member was entitled to his seat."

Martin Townsend of New York disagreed with this assessment. He said Harris was correct in saying the report was unanimous in favor of Haralson, "but I wish to state to the House and the country that in this case, in my opinion, the committee are unanimous because the perjuries, glaring and flagrant, that were committed by the witnesses who undertook to testify in this case were such as condemned the men that testified, and the witnesses themselves showed that the allegations which they undertook to maintain were impossible; that they could not be true." In his forty-three years as a lawyer, he had never seen "such infamous, such glaring, such self-confuted perjury as was attempted in opposition to the sitting member."

John Caldwell of Alabama said the testimony was fraught with perjury certainly, but the perjurers were the Republican friends of the sitting member. Haralson took no part in this exchange of charges and countercharges. The Democratic House accepted the committee report, and he stayed where he was. A day later Josiah T. Walls of Florida was not so fortunate.

Haralson was criticized for favoring general amnesty, an issue on which he differed with Rapier. He sought to clarify his position in a letter which was published in the *Mobile Register* on January 29, 1876. "Is it not better," he asked, "for us in general, especially in the South, that there be good feeling between white and black? We must drive out these hell hounds and go in for peace between the two races in the South."

His efforts to placate the influential whites in the South did not endear him to the radicals in his party. They looked with disfavor on his friendship with Jefferson Davis, onetime president of the Confederacy, and with white congressmen John Gordon and Lucius Q. C. Lamar. He opposed the use of troops in the South to keep the peace and give protection at the polls in 1876. If the Southern Democratic papers have quoted him accurately, he thought it was bad for his party and that "every blue jacket sent to the South makes Democratic votes." This split within the ranks of the Republican party meant that before many years Haralson and Rapier would join their congressional predecessor, Benjamin Turner, in political retirement.

In 1876 Haralson clashed with Rapier. The state had been redistricted so that the gerrymandered Fourth was the only black Republican district remaining. Both men wanted the Republican nomination for that House seat. Rapier won and picked up the backing of the national and state party, but Haralson decided to run as an independent in the November election. He had the satisfaction of outdrawing his Negro rival at the polls, but the division in the black ranks gave the office to C. M. Shelley, the Democrat.

Rapier, a bachelor, spent his last years as collector of internal revenue for the second district of Alabama. He was holding this position when he died in Montgomery at the age of forty-five on May 31, 1883. Turner, who ended his days as a farmer, died on March 21, 1894, in Selma at the age of sixty-nine. In his later years, he had returned to politics just once, and then only briefly, serving as a delegate to the 1880 Republican national convention in Chicago.

Following his congressional defeat in 1876, Haralson worked as a clerk in the United States Customs House in Baltimore, in the internal revenue department, and in the pension bureau in Washington. He ran for the House of Representatives in 1878 and 1884. When his attempts at a political comeback failed, he moved to Louisiana where he took up farming. In 1904 he worked in Arkansas as a pension agent, before returning to Selma. He next lived in Texas, then traveled on to Oklahoma and to Colorado, where he was a coal miner.

Jeremiah Haralson, the last surviving Alabama black congressman, died about 1916 at seventy near Denver, having reportedly "been killed by wild beasts." The mystery of his death has never been solved, and no death certificate for him is on file in Denver at the Colorado Health Department's Bureau of Vital Statistics.

Divergent types though they were, soft-spoken Benjamin Turner, brash Jeremiah Haralson, and erudite James Rapier had all preached the gospel of racial reconciliation and devoted their time and talents toward that goal.

John Mercer Langston/Virginia

John Mercer Langston sat at his desk arranging the panorama of a full life in his mind. He had found time at last to write his memoirs and was anxious to get his story down as soon as possible.

Doubtless his thoughts flashed back to the Virginia plantation where he had been born on December 14, 1829. Ralph Quarles, the owner, was his father and the only white man living on the large fertile estate, located three miles from Louisa Court House in Louisa County. His mother, Lucy Langston, daughter of an Indian mother and a father of mixed blood, already had three other children by the time John arrived.

Langston remembered her as a "woman of small stature, substantial build, fair looks, easy and natural bearing, even and quiet temper, intelligent and thoughtful, who accepted her lot with becoming resignation, while she always exhibited the deepest affection and earnest solicitude for her children." His parents were not married, but Langston thought they would have been had the law not made it impossible. His mother, who had arrived on the Quarles plantation as guarantee for a loan, had been free for nearly twenty-five years when her last child was born.

Captain Quarles—the title was a carry-over from the Revolutionary War—died late in 1834 at an advanced age, with Lucy and their children by his bedside. She followed him to the grave soon afterward and was buried beside him on the family land. Langston could recall being brought when he was five to see his mother on her deathbed.

Ralph Quarles left all his lands "lying on Hickory Creek and its waters" to his sons and "their heirs forever," as well as his livestock, crops, cash, and bank stock. The property was to be divided among them when the youngest son reached the age of twenty-one. The captain had already provided his only daughter and her husband with a farm.

Quarles also made bequests to white relatives in the hope that they would not try to set aside the will and take his children's inheritance. Langston felt that his father would have left his sons everything except his slaves, whom he would have freed, if he had thought such an arrangement would have been carried out after his death. As matters turned out, the children did receive a share of Quarles's estate, though how much is not precisely clear from the court records; and some of their father's favorite servants were manumitted.

The Langston boys, carrying legal documents to prove they were free, traveled by horse and wagon to Ohio to join William, an older half brother. John went to live with William Gooch, one of the executors of the estate. He stayed with the Gooch family for five years, until they decided to move to Missouri. The Gooches would have taken the youngster with them, except for a court order served en route at the behest of John's brothers, who did not want him transferred to a slave state. Left behind by his foster parents, he lived for a period with another white family before moving to Cincinnati to attend a private school conducted in the Baker Street Baptist Church by two white teachers.

One of Langston's vivid boyhood memories was of the fall of 1840 when a mob of Kentucky whites came over the river into Cincinnati to terrorize Negroes and vandalize an abolitionist newspaper office. Far from intimidating people, this gave the antislavery movement in Ohio a shot of adrenaline. His brother Gideon was among those making the rounds, speaking for the cause.

After two years of school in Cincinnati plus a winter as a pupil of two Oberlin College students in Chillicothe, John entered Oberlin, where his brother Charles had studied earlier. Home for the winter after the fall term, he was hired to teach at a new school eight miles outside the city for ten dollars a month. The job started four weeks before his sixteenth birthday and lasted from November through February. Only one boy in the classroom was smaller than he, but he discovered that firm discipline would keep the bigger youths in line. Parents, who got no help from the government, had to raise the schoolmaster's salary themselves. On paydays his pockets bulged since his salary was paid mainly in coins.

John's brothers, thinking he had had enough education, were considering a trade for him when a note came from one of the Oberlin professors praising John's work there. They decided to send him back to college, though they had their doubts about what good a degree would do a Negro in the slaveholding United States.

His trip back to Oberlin in March gave him his first personal taste of racial discrimination. The stagecoach stopped in Columbus for the night. He was following the other passengers into the hotel when he was told: "We do not entertain niggers. You must find some nigger boarding house." He stood outside in the dark rainy March night while all the luggage except his was carried inside. He would have had to stay there all night except for a black man who noticed his plight and offered him lodging. The next morning the same white man who had kept him out of the hotel barred his entrance to the stagecoach and ordered him to sit outside in the chilly rain with the driver. Langston, who had paid the same fare as everyone else, objected. The other passengers backed him up, and he returned to his seat inside.

He was graduated with honors from Oberlin in August 1849. He had selected his courses with a career in the law in mind. The problem now was to find somewhere for a Negro to study law. Langston was told he could maneuver his way into a New York law school if he were willing to pass as a Frenchman or a Spaniard from the West Indies or Central America. He said he had no intention of pretending to be anything except what he was, a "colored American." In Cincinnati he was refused admittance to a law class taught by a former judge on the grounds that the other "students would not feel at home with him and he would not feel at home with them." He marked time by going back to Oberlin to take a theology course, which included the study of Hebrew, Greek, and Latin. This postgraduate study finished, he stayed on another year at the college, specializing in extemporaneous speaking, already a passion with him.

Once more the search was on for someone with whom to read law. Philemon Bliss of Elyria, Ohio, a lawyer-politician noted for his strong antislavery views, accepted John as a student and as a boarder in his home. Langston's heart was set on the law, but as he worked, he worried about admittance to the bar once he had completed his studies. Bliss advised him to get on with the course and said they would deal with the question of race later, if and when it became a factor. Within two years Bliss decided his pupil was ready for an examination by a committee of lawyers. Langston passed easily. Only one examiner brought up the subject of race; he was mollified when another explained that under Ohio law the twenty-five-year-old candidate for the bar was legally a white man since he looked more white than black. Langston stood up in the back of the room to demonstrate this obvious fact.

Armed with a law certificate dated September 13, 1854, he bought a farm near Lake Erie in Brownhelm, nine miles from Oberlin, and began to practice, with a bootlegger as his first client. By the end of the year his home was a center of community activity. Whites and

Negroes, especially those working for political and social reform, enjoyed his hospitality.

At a political meeting Langston was heckled by a man who accused him of having "learned to walk with white women" at Oberlin. Langston admitted that certainly this was true, and advancing to the edge of the platform, he looked the man in the eye and said: "If you have in your family any good-looking, intelligent, refined sisters, you would do your family a special service by introducing me to them at once." Langston was not one to be told whom he could and could not associate with. He probably would not have gone out of his way to meet anyone's sister though. For some time he had been concentrating on one girl, Caroline Wall, a senior at Oberlin, whom he had known for several years. Their romance had flowered anew after he had become reacquainted with her during a trip South to set up a school in North Carolina. Like Langston's, her parentage was mixed. Her mother was black; her father, Stephen Wall, was a wealthy white North Carolinian who had freed his children and sent them to Ohio to be educated.

Langston and the buxom, dark-haired Miss Wall were married in Oberlin on October 25, 1854. After the wedding they honeymooned in Cleveland and Cincinnati before returning to Brownhelm. The bridegroom was active in the abolitionist movement as a member of the Liberty party. Backed by the party caucus, he was elected township clerk. Some historians believe this to have been the first elective office held by a Negro in the United States. His election brought him an invitation to address the American Anti-Slavery Society in May in New York for a fee of fifty dollars as a part of a banner lineup of speakers, which included the Massachusetts senators Henry Wilson and Charles Sumner.

Langston told the crowd that slavery had deprived everyone in the country—men and women, black and white—of a share of their civil, religious, and political liberty since they were not free to speak their true thoughts respecting the rights of all people under the Constitution.

Langston's practice was going well by the time his first child, Arthur Dessalines, was born on August 3, 1855. The family moved to Oberlin, where he opened a law office on North Main Street. His first clients were practically all whites. Blacks stayed away, Langston thought, because they believed they would fare better if their cases were presented to the all-Caucasian juries by white lawyers. Later he began to attract his share of cases from blacks too as his reputation grew.

By 1857 he was a member of the city council of Oberlin, a post he was to hold for years. He also was on the board of education. A contemporary writer described Oberlin's Negro lawyer, whose practice had expanded to the capital at Columbus, as a man of "medium size and good figure, high and well-formed forehead, eyes full, but not prominent, mild and amiable countenance, modest deportment, strong, musical voice, and wears the air of a gentleman. He is highly respected by men of the legal profession throughout the state." The Langston household was growing. Besides Arthur, the family now included Ralph, Frank, and Nettie.

The quiet of Oberlin was shattered by marauding "Negro-catchers" from Kentucky and other Southern states on the prowl to track down fleeing slaves. There was pay for informers and penalties for those who helped fugitive slaves to escape. Langston's brother Charles was indicted and tried under the Fugitive Slave Law, but he was released by the Ohio courts.

During the Civil War, John Langston helped to sign recruits for the Forty-fourth and Fifty-fifth Massachusetts regiments and later for the Fifth Ohio Regiment, in two instances presenting the regimental colors to the men personally. He spoke in the capitol at Nashville, Tennessee, on January 2, 1865, to celebrate the anniversary of the Emancipation Proclamation. While there, he climbed upon a wagon to thank ten thousand Negro troops for their bravery on the march through Kentucky and Tennessee.

Though effective at convincing other blacks they should fight for their freedom, the thirty-six-year-old recruiter apparently never considered military duty for himself. Like many well-to-do whites, Langston hired a substitute to go to war for him. After the reelection of President Lincoln, Langston went to Washington to confer with the President and his secretary of war on the use of Negro troops. Langston was in Washington when the welcome news was received of Lee's surrender at Appomattox on April 9, 1865, and still there when the "horror of horrors," the assassination of President Lincoln, occurred five days afterward.

Andrew Johnson had not had time to move from his temporary offices in the Treasury Building to the White House before Langston and a black delegation came to see him. Langston had met the new President on earlier speaking trips to Tennessee. After Langston left the capital, he went on a lecture tour of the border states; he spoke to freedmen in the major cities, and frequently appeared before state legislatures. Wherever he went, the newspapers were full of praise.

The *Hannibal Daily Courier* on December 18, 1865, applauded his eloquence: "To the colored men, he said, 'Above all other things, get education! Get money! Get character!' . . . May God speed him [Langston] and bless his noble efforts."

The *St. Louis Missouri Democrat* of January 11, 1866, reported he drew a large segregated audience: "The east half of the hall was exclusively appropriated by the colored people, while the west half was reserved for white persons. . . . [Langston] spoke eloquently and well. His plea in behalf of his race for the simple award of justice and human rights addresses itself with irresistible force to the better judgment of men. Even conservatives, many of whom were present and listened with marked attention, admitted the vanquishing force of his logic, and acknowledged frankly the fairness and justness of his argument."

While in Washington early in 1867, to intercede for a young soldier client in trouble for stealing liquor, Langston qualified to practice before the Supreme Court. He also met General O. O. Howard, head of the Freedmen's Bureau, who in April offered him an appointment as general inspector with the bureau. He was to report to headquarters on the work of the bureau's offices in organizing schools and helping freedmen get a start in their new life.

His old home territory in Louisa Court House, Virginia, was a particularly pleasant stop for the native son returning as an important person. In country style, the oldtimers on the street pointed him out to each other as "Quarles' boy" or "Lucy's son." He visited the graves of his parents and kept up a heavy speaking schedule.

Langston campaigned for Ulysses S. Grant in the presidential race of 1868. In Louisiana he held strategy sessions with state Republican leaders, and in Montgomery, Alabama, he helped to get blacks out to vote for the first time and cast their ballot for the Republican slate. In Georgia, conferring with educational agents of the Freedmen's Bureau, he told a Negro audience that some of them could expect to serve in high national office and was happy to see his prediction soon come true when Jefferson F. Long was sent to the House of Representatives from the Fourth District of Georgia.

A new university, named after General Howard, opened for Negroes in Washington in 1867. Langston set up the law department a year later and eventually became dean of the department. Lecturing in Washington in the spring of 1870, he spoke out against segregation in the churches of the United States. He predicted it would take fifty years to wash away the prejudice brought on by slavery. One step he recommended was striking the word white from the naturalization laws.

His speaking style is well illustrated by a speech he gave in Baltimore on May 19, 1870, in celebration of the passage of the Fifteenth Amendment. He quoted from the Bible, from verses of songs, and led the audience in three cheers for President Grant. He also praised such leaders as Charles Sumner, General Howard, and Postmaster

General John A. J. Creswell for appointing blacks. "When I forget the flaxen hair of these men, I sometimes find myself wondering if they are purely white, if they have not some portion of Negro blood in their composition," he said. Langston's speech seems very florid, pompous, and dated now, but the laughter and applause recorded in newspaper accounts show that he knew how to carry the crowd.

The dean of the law department took over the administration of the university from General Howard, its third president, in December 1873. Almost immediately the meticulous Langston was at odds with the board of trustees over the authority to be accorded him as vice-president. A year later, he submitted his resignation after he found himself competing for the presidency with a field of five, including Frederick Douglass, who was one of the trustees of the university; but the board persuaded Langston to stay on as acting president until the end of the school year. In June 1875, he resigned again at a board meeting which proceeded, against the wishes of the black members, to elect a white president in preference to either Langston or Douglass. Within weeks Langston's resignation as vice-president and dean was accepted, and without any thanks to him for having managed the university efficiently and attracting enough contributions to pull it through a severe financial crisis.

Coincidentally, Langston had been a member of the board of trustees and later of the finance committee of the already floundering Freedmen's Bank, which had made many loans that were defaulted. Rumors of trouble spread, and the situation worsened as panicky depositors began to withdraw their money from the bank. In May 1874, he opposed a move to name Douglass to succeed John W. Alvord as president. Langston thought any change would be ill-advised with the bank already in trouble, and he was sure the newspaperman would be sorry he had taken the job. Yet Langston said he would not vote against Douglass if his friends insisted on pushing him for the post. The forecast turned out to be all too true. Douglass had hardly taken the position before the bank was forced to close its doors in June. He later said that "his friends had married him to a corpse."

Langston had worked for the Republican party since its early postwar years. He began by favoring James G. Blaine of Maine for the presidential nomination in 1876, but campaigned for Rutherford B. Hayes when he received the nomination. After Hayes won, he rewarded Langston in October 1877 by appointing him as minister to Haiti.

The new black representative to the world's oldest black republic was warmly welcomed by the American colony and treated graciously by his predecessor. He found the country invigorating and the people stimulating. He was delighted on one occasion when they greeted him by playing what they believed to be his national anthem, "John Brown's Body." He reorganized the consular service and negotiated with the Haitians for more liberal import regulations on goods brought in on American ships.

As a result of a serious bout of yellow fever in mid-1879, Langston became one of those rare souls who are able to read their own obituaries. Reports reached America that he was dead, and some newspapers printed the story before it could be corrected. He went home to the United States to recuperate that fall and to enroll his son in Oberlin College, but soon returned to his post in Haiti.

Life was not dull in Haiti. During his stay, there was a revolution and an unsuccessful coup d'etat. When the Democrats regained the Presidency with the election of Grover Cleveland, Langston, a Republican appointee, lost his post. His resignation was offered as of January 31, 1885, but he stayed on the job until July 1, when his successor reached Haiti.

In Washington he pressed his claim against the government for nearly eight thousand dollars in back pay. In 1882 the Democratic House had cut his salary to discipline him for having worked for the James A. Garfield-Chester A. Arthur ticket in the presidential campaign two years earlier while he was on the federal payroll as Haitian minister. Congress had not altered the law that fixed the salary but simply appropriated a smaller sum. Langston had not protested at the time, although he believed the action to be illegal. Now he hired a lawyer to fight the case. He won and was awarded the back pay with interest.

His next appointment after Haiti was quite a comedown in salary. He accepted the presidency of the Virginia Normal and Collegiate Institute. Langston said he took the fifteen hundred dollar post at the small Negro state college in Petersburg in order to return to his native state and to help its black citizens. His arrival was celebrated by a banquet attended by black legislators and other state notables. He increased the school's enrollment, and during the summer he ran a teachers' training course.

Most college presidents have their difficulties trying to get along with one board. Former diplomat Langston had to attempt to please two—the state board of education, an all-white group, and the Negro board of visitors—while mediating faculty dissension. Wearied of the struggle, he resigned in 1887, shortly before Christmas.

En route to Salem, Massachusetts, to address an emancipation celebration, Langston was met in Farmville, Virginia, by a committee of citizens, who requested him to stop for a longer meeting on his return to the state early in January. On the second stopover they asked him to run in the next election for the seat from the Fourth Congressional District. He immediately launched a drive for the Republican nomination, taking time out only to attend the national convention.

His principal adversary in Virginia was the leader of his own party —William Mahone, a former Confederate general. Mahone, adamantly opposed to the election of a Negro congressman from Virginia, rammed through a white candidate at the party's district nominating convention, but Langston decided to run anyway as an independent Republican.

Supported by a biracial committee, he campaigned throughout the district, keeping to his schedule despite frequent threats. Some of the hecklers who followed him around were blacks, and contrary to the usual custom in the district, the Democratic candidate refused to appear on the same platform with his opponent.

Republican opposition to Langston was pressed outside the state with an appeal to prominent Negroes to come out against him. Frederick Douglass wrote a letter opposing his candidacy and charging him with making a racial appeal to voters. This letter was distributed throughout the district. To rebut Douglass, Langston brought in stellar names from as far away as Haiti. Bishop James T. Holly of Port-au-Prince called it "treason to the cause of the colored race, for anyone of that race, under any pretext whatsoever, to oppose" Langston's election to Congress.

His enemies said the Virginian was appealing to the "prejudices of the colored people" by asking them to vote for him because of his race and by insisting that because they outnumbered whites in the district 102,071 to 56,194 they certainly should be able to send a qualified black to Congress. The Republican national committee asked him to prove the legality of his nomination. He ignored the request and went on campaigning.

Expecting chicanery at the polls, Langston organized his people in advance to keep watch for irregularities. His supporters were told not only to vote for him but to declare how they voted in a loud voice, so that later there would be evidence available to that effect if needed. When Langston arrived at the polls at about nine o'clock on the morning of November 6, 1888, he found voters moving forward in two lines—one for whites and one for Negroes. The black line was being delayed, so that it would take each Langston backer about three hours to vote, but they were persistent and some 150 people were still queued up at sundown when the polls closed. Langston took their names and addresses. When the count for this particular ward was announced, the Negro contender, who had been considered a shoo-in there, was third.

Edward Venable, the Democrat, was declared the winner by 641 votes—13,298 to 12,657 for Langston. With the Republicans split, the state went Democratic in the presidential election by 1,600 votes. Certain that a fair count would give him the seat, Langston contested the election. He finally found three white lawyers who agreed to take his case for a high fee. It was a grueling affair. One of the leading witnesses for Langston, an election clerk, was arrested on the stand for refusing to testify in the case—a bizarre charge against a man who had just finished answering 316 questions on cross-examination. Another Langston witness was questioned for thirteen days by the House Elections Committee.

To keep his name before the public while he waited, Langston headed a delegation of blacks who visited President-elect Benjamin Harrison on February 18, 1889. He reestablished his contacts with the Republican party in Virginia by working for Mahone for governor that fall. As a result the Republican national committee backed his challenge to Venable in the House.

The Fifty-first Congress had a bumper crop of contested elections. Langston was eighth in a line of seventeen. The longer the delay, the more Langston felt the opposition was solidifying against him. When his case finally reached the House at noon on Tuesday, September 23, 1890, the Democrats sought to block the hearing by boycotting the session.

The galleries of the House of Representatives were packed, and the Republican side of the aisle was fairly well filled, but there was hardly a Democrat to be seen. Speaker Thomas B. Reed, running affairs with a firm hand, brushed aside objections from the few Democrats present who complained of the lack of a quorum. The vote ousting Venable was 151 to 1. Reed then ruled Langston admitted by a voice vote and refused to order a count by roll call. There was prolonged applause from the gallery as the stately, sixty-one-year-old, bearded Virginian moved forward to take the oath.

Only a few days remained before Congress recessed on October 1, and Langston by this time was already busy with his campaign for the Fifty-second Congress. As early as August, black groups in every county of the Fourth District had endorsed him for reelection, but Mahone, instead of getting behind the man who had supported him in 1889, again tried to prevent Langston's nomination. A convention was called despite Mahone, and Langston was nominated. His appeal to Negro voters was strong, but he was less successful this time in attracting white backing. The official count gave the election to James Epes, the Democrat. Langston charged fraud, but decided it was useless to contest the election since the new House had a Democratic majority.

Langston went to Washington for the second session determined to make as much of a record for himself as possible. His first speech came on January 16, 1891, during an appropriations debate, but he chose to range over a wide field. A man with a reputation for talking at length, he began by finding out from the chair that fifty-two minutes had been allotted to him.

In this rambling speech he described voting harassment of whites as well as of blacks in his district and said that the paramount issue was free access to the ballot box: "The question [is] whether every American citizen may wield the ballot in this country freely and according to his own judgment in the interest of the welfare of our common country. It does not matter how black we are; it does not matter how ignorant we are; it does not matter what our race may be; it does not matter whether we were degraded or not. . . ." He charged that the Democrats, when boasting of their plans to carry the 1892 election, no longer made any pretense of using fair means in fighting to keep the Negro down.

The *Cleveland Leader* said that while Langston wandered from the subject under consideration, he was eloquent, effective, and held the attention of the chamber: "There are not five men in the House who can talk as well as Langston. . . . His command of language is masterly. No doubt there are scores of Democrats in that body who would give a year's salary for half as good a gift of oratory."

The next day Langston requested that United States Attorney General William H. H. Miller transmit to the House all communications, orders, directives, and instructions given him by any United States district attorney, marshal, deputy, commissioner, or other officers covering proceedings for suits under the Voting Enforcement Act of May 31, 1870. He asked Attorney General Miller to report back to Congress on the outcome of such litigation. This suggestion was forwarded first to the Judiciary Committee and then adopted by the House, but it had no great impact as far as discrimination at the polls in the South was concerned.

Two days later he introduced a resolution to restrict the vote for federal officials to those citizens who could read and write English and to reduce the representation of each state in Congress in proportion to the number of its male citizens who were not permitted to cast ballots. The second part of his proposal had, of course, been the law of the land for twenty-three years, ever since the ratification of the Fourteenth Amendment. Langston hoped to remind the country of this and to call attention to the fact that this part of the Constitution was being widely flaunted in the South. He entered a measure to set up a national industrial university for blacks. He also wanted national holidays established in honor of Lincoln and Grant. None of these bills was passed. He favored an annual subsidy of five million dollars to make America a sea power, a move he felt would be good for defense and business.

Langston was able to place a number of minor appointees in the government, but he was disappointed that the secretary of the navy held up two appointments he wanted to make to the Annapolis Naval Academy. Langston complained that the man who had held his seat illegally during most of the first session of the Fifty-first Congress had been allowed to name the sons of white Democrats to Annapolis without allowing Negro students of the district to compete in a "fair and scholarly contest" for the places.

In 1892 he was a delegate to the Republican state and national conventions. That fall when the district Republican convention nominated him for the Fifty-third Congress, he declined to run, because he said the party would be more likely to win with a loyal white candidate of name and influence. Langston settled down in a Swiss cottage he had built near Howard University in Washington and started work on his autobiography. The house was surrounded by white birch, sweet gum, spruce, pine, and sycamore trees given him by his old friend Senator Charles Sumner, who also landscaped the grounds. After Congress the Langstons, blessed with a growing number of grandchildren, divided their time between Petersburg and Washington. In the capital they moved in elite circles. A volume of Langston speeches was printed under the title of *Freedom and Citizenship.*

His autobiography, *From the Virginia Plantation to the National Capitol,* was published three years before his death in Washington on November 15, 1897. Hoping it would spark their ambition, John Mercer Langston, then the country's most prominent Negro, dedicated his life story to American youth.

John A. Hyman, James E. O'Hara, and Henry P. Cheatham/North Carolina

John A. Hyman, who was born to slave parents near Warrenton, North Carolina, on July 23, 1840, was the first of four blacks to represent that state's Second Congressional District in Washington.

His early quest for knowledge led to his separation from his family. The overseer found him with friends late one night trying to learn to read from a spelling book. As punishment he was sold to a master in Alabama. There his continuing efforts to educate himself enraged his new owner, and he was again sold. In all he reportedly had eight masters during the years he was a slave. After emancipation, John Adams Hyman returned to Warrenton where he became a successful farmer.

A dapper, rotund man with a small moustache, he attended the North Carolina Equal Rights Convention at Raleigh in September 1865, as well as meetings of the Republican party. Quiet and unassuming, he did not seek the spotlight, though a member of the party's state executive committee, but worked behind the scenes on organizational matters and voter registration. He was one of 15 blacks among the 133 delegates at the North Carolina state constitutional convention of 1868. The liberal body of laws they wrote called for universal male suffrage, a public school system, abolishment of property-holding qualifications for public officials, and state aid to the needy.

The new constitution and the slates for state and national office were submitted to the voters in April. The Ku Klux Klan distributed posters warning Negroes not to vote. On election eve, graves were dug along the roads leading to the polls as a final threat in Warren County. Hyman, who was on the Republican ticket as candidate for the state senate, and the other black leaders convinced people to turn out en masse. The new constitution was approved by twenty thousand votes, and the Republicans won most of the state and congressional offices.

Elected to the state senate, Hyman stayed in the legislature for six tempestuous years. He was a member of the Penitentiary Committee, which was criticized for making questionable land purchases, but there is no evidence that Hyman benefited from these transactions.

The largely white legislature, which included a number of illiterates of both races, was unable to cope with the worsening fiscal crisis. State bonds, voted to the railroads in hopes of improving the economy, merely sank North Carolina further in debt. A governor, who was friendly to the Negroes, was impeached for using the state militia to put down an insurrection. As their woes proliferated, the legislators began breaking up into cliques.

Charges of graft and vote buying were rife. A Conservative-Democratic commission accused twenty Republicans of having accepted $133,746 from lobbyists to vote for railroad financing at a special session of the legislature in 1868. Hyman was charged with having taken a $2,100 bribe. He categorically denied the allegation. He acknowledged that the railroads had contributed to his campaign and that he had borrowed money from a railroad lobbyist, but said he had repaid it.

Throughout his tenure in the state senate, Hyman's eyes were fixed on Congress. He felt that the heavily black Second Congressional District should have a Negro representative, and he himself wanted the position. Defeated in his first try for the nomination, he finally captured the prize in 1874. Opposition newspapers circulated reports that white Republicans planned to bribe Hyman to withdraw from the race. Despite dissension in his party's ranks, he mounted an efficient campaign and swept the election, garnering eighteen thousand votes as opposed to eleven thousand for G. H. Blount, the Conservative-Democrat, and one thousand for Garland White, the independent Republican.

When Congress met late in 1875, Hyman introduced bills to reimburse Jones County, North Carolina, for the destruction of its courthouse by federal troops in the Civil War and to aid the poverty-stricken Cherokee Indians. None of his bills got out of committee. Like so many other reconstruction congressmen, he had to face in the House a challenge to his election. The Elections Committee unanimously declared him entitled to keep his contested seat on August 1, 1876, and the full House agreed. His was one of five cases reported out of committee that day—two from Northern states, and three, including his own and that of John R. Lynch of Mississippi, from those in the South. Before the long session was over, Hyman had to return to North Carolina to seek his party's renomination.

He arrived in Goldsboro two days before the district convention opened there on Wednesday, July 26, 1876. His chief lieutenants—James Harris, a Negro, and Tim Lee, a Caucasian—came in from Raleigh the next morning. The congressman knew he had a stiff fight on his hands to stave off the forces supporting Governor Curtis Brogden. Brogden's people were so sure of themselves that they did not show up in Goldsboro until the night before the meeting, though the governor himself had been there since Monday. Their first move was to set the wheels in motion to throw out the delegates from Hyman's home county in favor of a pro-Brogden slate. "This trick was satisfactorily set up and arranged and after buying up Tim Lee and cursing out Jim Harris," Brogden's top aide confidently retired by midnight, the *Raleigh Sentinel* reported.

The Brogden script was followed to the letter the next day when the convention got under way. W. P. Mabson, a black from Edgecombe County, was prevailed upon to accept the temporary chairmanship. Organizing preliminaries out of the way, the meeting adjourned until late afternoon to allow the committees time to complete their work.

At four o'clock the delegates voted to seat the anti-Hyman delegation from Warren County, and balloting started on the congressional nomination. On the first tally Hyman led a field of seven by three votes. On the ninth and deciding ballot Brogden was chosen with a count of nine, one more vote than was required. No one supported Hyman at the end.

The *Raleigh Sentinel*, a Democratic paper, was so fascinated by the Republican spectacle that it ran three editorials on the nomination fight. The paper charged the Negroes in a district where they had nineteen thousand out of twenty thousand Republican votes with a lack of "manhood" in allowing the state's white leaders to dump a black congressman for a white man who had already grown rich from feeding at the public trough for forty years.

Hyman had been in financial difficulties since his first unsuccessful congressional campaign in 1872, when he mortgaged his farm to help pay his political expenses. The press said he had extravagant tastes and had overdrawn his salary as a representative.

During Hyman's last session in Washington, the shy, retiring congressman, who did not make any speeches or take part in House debates, voted down the line with the Republicans, then the minority party in the House though they still had control of the Senate. At the end of his term on March 3, 1877, he was promised a job with the internal revenue service, but the appointment was never made. Hyman returned to farming and to his grocery and liquor store in Warrenton.

Not long afterward, having been expelled from his church for selling whiskey, Hyman left North Carolina to work first as a post office clerk in Maryland and then with the department of agriculture in Washington. There were brief, condescendingly complimentary obituaries when North Carolina's first Negro congressman died of a paralytic stroke in the nation's capital on September 14, 1891, at the age of fifty-one.

Eight years earlier North Carolina's Second District, which had been in white hands since Hyman finished his term in 1877, had been reclaimed by James E. O'Hara, a black lawyer.

James Edward O'Hara was born in New York City on February 26, 1844. His father was an Irish seaman, and his mother a West Indian. When James was six, the family moved to the West Indies. Although they traveled about considerably among the islands, the boy acquired a good education. Before the end of the Civil War, he went to North Carolina for a visit, and decided to settle there. Though still in his teens, he obtained a job teaching school.

During reconstruction O'Hara became a regular at the freedmen's conventions and Republican party meetings held throughout the state. Energetic and able, he was secretary at several of these meetings and wrote reports on them for the newspapers. He handled the same assignment for the 1868 constitutional convention and used the clerkship as a springboard to the state house of representatives. After studying law in North Carolina and at Howard University in Washington, he passed the North Carolina bar examination in 1873 and began practice in Enfield. He had already been named chairman of the Halifax board of county commissioners, a post he held for four years.

O'Hara's life demonstrates that perseverance is rewarded on occasion. He vied for the Republican party's nomination for the seat from the North Carolina Second Congressional District as early as 1874, but supported John Hyman when the convention chose that Warren County leader. Two years later the white Republicans threw out the delegates from Hyman's home county and gave the spot to the governor.

In 1878, O'Hara was one of many contenders at the Republican district convention. Twenty-eight ballots reduced the field to three names, including his own. The delegates began to shout for O'Hara.

He came forward to acknowledge the cheers, and Craven County changed its vote to put him over the top.

It was a rugged campaign. James Harris also ran as a Republican, splitting the Negro vote. Opponents dredged up some old accusations that had been leveled at O'Hara when he was a delegate to the 1875 constitutional convention. They called him a bigamist, questioned his citizenship, and accused him of "malfeasance in office." O'Hara produced papers to show he had been divorced before remarrying; he said there was no doubt that he was an American citizen, and he denied the unsubstantiated charges made against him as county commissioner.

William Kitchin, the Democrat, was declared the winner by a narrow margin. The *National Republican* in Washington charged the "Democratic canvassing boards in his district with performing every kind of actrocity known to the bull-dozing Democratic politician, even to defying the courts." O'Hara challenged the accuracy of the count, but much of the evidence he needed to support his charges was destroyed when his home burned, and he lost the case in the North Carolina courts and in Congress.

Four more years went by before he won the long-coveted position by a landslide of seventeen thousand votes, after his main opponent withdrew in the waning days of the campaign. During his first few months in the Capitol he was the only black in the Democratic-controlled House. He did not take part in the debate in his first session, which started in December 1883, but he proposed a civil rights constitutional amendment. He believed this was the best way to insure blacks proper treatment in the use of transportation and other public facilities since the 1875 Civil Rights Act had been declared unconstitutional.

Realizing that there was no chance to get his constitutional amendment through, O'Hara in the second session made another thrust against Jim Crow travel. He offered an amendment to the pending interstate commerce commission bill to require that interstate passengers be treated "without discrimination" and assigned accommodations strictly according to the amount paid for them.

Pointing out that Congress had promulgated rules to see that cattle, sheep, and hogs received proper care in transit, he argued that if Congress had the right to regulate the use of freight cars, it had the same authority for passenger cars.

John Reagan of Texas objected to the bill's being broadened to include people, since they had not been considered when the committee shaped the measure. O'Hara called for a vote on his proposal, which passed 134 to 97. It looked like an easy victory until the next day when Charles Crisp of Georgia offered another amendment specifying that "nothing in this act . . . shall . . . prevent any railroad company from providing separate accommodations for white and colored persons."

Robert Smalls of South Carolina, who by this time had joined O'Hara in Congress, hoped the same "good sense" the House had exercised in adopting O'Hara's amendment would be shown in voting down Crisp's proposal. While Negroes were able to travel freely with whites in first-class cars in South Carolina, they were forced into segregated cars when a train crossed the border into Georgia. That, Smalls charged, was why the representative from Georgia had come forward with his revision. Rising to defend his amendment from Crisp's attack, O'Hara regretted that the color question had come into the debate. "I for one, sir," he said, "hold that we are all Americans; that no matter whether a man is white or black, he is an American citizen, and that the aegis of this great Republic should be held over him regardless of his color."

O'Hara said that his proposal was merely intended to make certain that a common man who had paid a first-class fare would get first-class treatment precisely like a person on a higher social level. He added that he simply wanted Congress to give all citizens the same protection already afforded property, animals, and "every other interest."

As a possible compromise, a second amendment, designed to retain discrimination in a somewhat more mannerly, less blatant fashion was offered by William Breckinridge of Arkansas as a substitute for Crisp's proposal. Breckinridge's amendment stated that "nothing in this act shall be construed to deny to railroads the right to provide separate accommodations for passengers as they may deem best for the public comfort and safety. . . ."

Breckinridge, while claiming he did not want O'Hara's rights disturbed under the law, said that railroads must be free "to assort" their passengers into separate but equal facilities for the public convenience and safety. Suppose, for example, people needed to be segregated because of illness or disease, he suggested. He chided O'Hara for interjecting a social consideration into a commercial question and for having come up with a vague provision not clearly applicable to interstate travel.

His voice oozing with sarcasm and humor, Thomas Reed of Maine said he was happy to see the debate lifted from the level of mere politics and color, thanks to Breckinridge. Now that the House was apparently determined to give railroads the legal right of "assorting" their passengers, Reed wanted to know what criteria would be set. Surely the House should go on to write specific regulations.

"Are we to be assorted on the ground of size?" Reed asked. "Am I to be put in one car because of my size and the gentleman from Arkansas into another because of his? . . . Or are we to be assorted on the moustache ground? Are we to be assorted on the question of complexion, or are we to be assorted on a beard basis? . . .

"For my part, I object to having these 'robber barons' overlook and assort us on any whimsical basis they may undertake to set up. Why surely, Mr. Speaker, this House, engaged as it is in putting down discrimination against good men, cannot tolerate . . . an amendment of this character for an instant."

After much parliamentary shilly-shallying, Breckinridge's substitute for Crisp's amendment passed by ten votes. Nathan Goff, Jr., of West Virginia then moved that the clause "provided that no discrimination is made on account of race or color" be inserted. He argued that a bill started as a means of regulating railroads had been twisted into one allowing them to choose between their customers. The chameleon House passed this one by an even larger margin, and the sense of the original O'Hara position was restored. This bill bounced from the House to the Senate during the Forty-eighth Congress, with the Senate-revised version finally bogging down in the House.

The Interstate Commerce Act of February 4, 1887, which was passed by the Forty-ninth Congress, did not mention color, but it forbade the railroads "to make or give any undue or unreasonable preference or advantage to any particular person . . . or to subject any particular persons . . . to any undue or unreasonable prejudice or any disadvantage of any respect whatsoever." Another section stated that if the carriers charged some passengers higher fares than others for like service, they would be guilty of "unjust discrimination." A far cry from what O'Hara had envisioned, this language was evasive enough to allow the railroads to continue segregating passengers, but the act would prove to be a useful legal device for another black counselor-congressman fifty-four years later. Representative Arthur W. Mitchell of Chicago sued under this act in 1937 after he was ejected from his first-class seat and put in a "colored," second-class railroad car while traveling to Arkansas.

The Forty-ninth Congress began its work late in 1885. O'Hara, who had been reelected to a second term by sixty-seven hundred votes, asked the House to launch an immediate investigation of the Carrollton, Mississippi, courthouse murders. The Mississippi governor had refused to act, and a grand jury had failed to indict a group of horsemen who had fired into a peaceful meeting and killed a number of people. The House finished for the day without voting, and when O'Hara pressed his point a few days later, his proposal was referred to the Rules Committee, a gigantic burial ground for bills and resolutions.

In the fall of 1886 O'Hara faced a reelection battle with another black Republican—Israel Abbott—and a Democrat. With the Negro vote divided, his seat went to the Democrat. O'Hara still had one short session to serve, but it was not an eventful period for him. He repeatedly voted to override President Cleveland's veto of pensions for the dependents of veterans. O'Hara thought the President's action a cruel blow to ex-slave mothers who had no resources to fall back on once their sons were dead. He was particularly angered by the President's insinuations that black soldiers had enlisted only for money. O'Hara said it was an insult to brave proud men, some of whom had fought without pay in preference to lowering themselves by taking less than their white comrades received.

His career in Congress ended on March 3, 1887, but he remained active in local politics. Until his death from a stroke on September 15, 1905, James O'Hara practiced law with his son, Raphael, in North Carolina.

Two years after O'Hara lost his seat in the Second Congressional District to a Democrat, it was recaptured by still another black Republican, Henry Plummer Cheatham, who had been register of deeds for Vance County for four years. A pleasant, unassuming man, with even features and a chiseled profile, he had made many friends in that office, both black and white. Self-controlled and conciliatory, he worked quietly for improvement and avoided antagonizing people.

Cheatham was born on December 27, 1857, to a slave who worked as a maid on a plantation near Henderson, North Carolina. He attended public schools and Shaw University in Raleigh, from which he received in 1883 the degree of bachelor of arts. He prepared for the bar but never worked as a lawyer. After graduation he was principal of the state normal school at Plymouth until his election as register of deeds.

In April 1888, Vance County Republicans started the congressional bandwagon for Cheatham while also naming him as a delegate to the party's state convention. He was nominated the following month by a big margin at the district convention.

During the early stages of his campaign, he was subjected to sporadic heckling by supporters of George Allen Mebane, who disputed Cheatham's right to the nomination and still hoped to run himself with the support of the Republican executive committee.

In mid-October Mebane, a Negro, withdrew and asked his backers to support Cheatham for the sake of party unity. The Democrats reportedly spent twenty-five thousand dollars buying four thousand votes, but Cheatham edged past the incumbent, Furnifold Simmons, by a margin of seven hundred votes.

The Fifty-first Congress convened in December 1889 with Cheatham as the only black member. John Mercer Langston of Virginia and Thomas E. Miller of South Carolina faced protracted election contests before being seated on September 23, 1890, a few days before the House recessed.

The new congressman from North Carolina introduced a bill to provide federal assistance to the public schools. He urged the government to reimburse the still not fully compensated depositors of the bankrupt Freedmen's Bank. He asked appropriations for public buildings for his hometown and further compensation for Robert Smalls and the crew of the *Planter*, the ship Smalls had pirated away from the Confederacy during the Civil War. Congress did not act on any of these proposals.

His only speech in the first session opposed a move to tax lard made from cottonseed oil to protect the "pure lard" interest. He split with his party's leaders because he said inexpensive food was of prime concern to his constituents and one home industry should not be favored over another. In the second session he sought unsuccessfully to marshal popular support for his education bill. He introduced a measure to ease a tax revision for tobacco manufacturers and dealers, but it was blocked in the Ways and Means Committee.

Cheatham benefited from a poorly organized opposition in his reelection campaign in 1890. The Democrats had trouble choosing a candidate; when they finally agreed on a standard bearer, he became ill. Cheatham carried the district by twelve hundred votes against a last-minute substitute, James Mewborne.

His second term—this time as the lone congressional spokesman for the nation's blacks throughout the entire two years—was even more frustrating. The men around him showed little support for the most modest Negro demands.

For example, a discussion of an appropriation for an exhibit of Negro art, industry, and agriculture at the 1893 Columbian Exposition in Chicago turned into a hassle over the Republican effort to pass a federal elections inspection law. Democrats warned that "the force bill," as opponents called the fair election measure, would make life even harder for blacks.

When his time came to speak, Cheatham expressed regrets that the boisterous debate had reached such a "hot political phase." He said Negroes did not want their request viewed in that light. "It seems to me," he added sadly, "that whenever the colored people of this country ask for anything, something unfortunate intervenes to hinder their getting what they ask."

Cheatham said all they wanted was an honest exposition of the facts—not available in the census or elsewhere—to demonstrate how far blacks had been able to progress since emancipation.

Asking his colleagues to rise above racial prejudice, to put aside delaying technicalities, and to pass the appropriation, he continued: "We are helpless, so to speak, and we have need of this appropriation. I have said but little this session, I have taken but little of your time."

A Massachusetts congressman advised him to put the request in a bill himself, and "we will vote for it." A few months later Cheatham did introduce a measure to provide funds for a brochure of data on African-American culture for distribution at the Chicago fair, but his suggestion got lost in a welter of arguments over the cost and conduct of the exposition.

Cheatham tried desperately to get information about Negroes and their past before the general public. Besides the World's Fair project, he suggested that a history on the nation's black troops be written and a report be prepared on the Negro in colonial America. He delivered an emotional appeal for legislative safeguards for the small, hard-working farmer. He called for pure food and drug regulations.

Cheatham's try for a third term was complicated by dissension among the Republicans over teaming up with the new Populist party, then a fairly substantial force in North Carolina. He was renominated with smoothness by the district convention, but the party's state convention became embroiled over the Populist issue, and Cheatham, who wanted support from Democrats, Prohibitionists, and the "third party people" as well as Republicans, was caught in the cross-fire. As events developed there was no Populist endorsement for the ticket; the white Republicans, as usual, worked against the black candidate; and the Democrats won by two thousand votes.

Cheatham was away most of the last session of the Fifty-second Congress because of illness. Two years later he attempted to get his old seat back from Frederick Woodard for the Fifty-fourth Congress, but there was a Populist in the race then, too, and this time Cheatham, who received a death threat during the campaign, lost by an even larger margin. He charged widespread fraud and contested the election unsuccessfully.

He was given one more chance against Woodard in 1894, but the Republicans passed him by in favor of George H. White, a black rival the next time the election rolled around.

In 1897 the former congressman moved to Washington to become recorder of deeds for four years before returning to North Carolina, where he raised funds to start a black orphanage at Oxford and became its superintendent. Devoted to his work with the children, he donated half his salary to the home during the depression of the early 1930's, although he had a large family of his own. The main building at that orphanage was made a memorial to him.

Henry Cheatham ran the orphanage until his death on November 29, 1935, at the age of seventy-seven. The newspapers applauded him most for his work as a popular teacher, but he should also be remembered for his attempts to get the facts on Negro contributions to American society into the record.

George H. White/North Carolina

George H. White, whose lineage was a mixture of Negro, Irish, and Indian, was the last former slave to serve in Congress.

Born in Rosindale, North Carolina, on December 18, 1852, he was ten when slavery ended, and he had already started his education with a Caucasian teacher. After emancipation, he attended public school when he could be spared from work in the family farming and cask-making business.

At twenty-one George Henry White pocketed his savings of a thousand dollars and went to Washington to enroll at Howard University. He began by taking a medical course, but did not like it and switched to liberal arts and the law. He financed four years at the university by teaching school during the summers in North Carolina.

Following his graduation in 1877, he taught school in New Bern and Raleigh while reading law with a superior court judge. Within two years he had passed the bar examination and opened a law office in New Bern. He mixed teaching and law practice, but borrowed time from both to take an increasingly active role in Republican party affairs.

In 1880 the voters sent White to the state house of representatives, where he put through several bills of local interest to his constituents, including one to protect Craven County crops from roving cattle and pigs. He worked to get a budgetary appropriation for four Negro normal schools to train teachers, and he was named principal of the New Bern school. His crusade to upgrade the state's school system continued in 1885 in the state senate where he pressed for compulsory attendance regulations, better facilities for black children, reduced administration expenses, and federal aid for education.

The lawyer-teacher edged further up the political ladder in July 1885 by winning the Republican endorsement for solicitor and prosecuting attorney for the Second Judicial District. He carried the general election by two thousand votes over John Collins, the black incumbent, who also ran as a Republican. During two terms as an energetic prosecutor, White maintained residences in both New Bern and Tarboro to cover the territory assigned to him. The *Raleigh Sentinel* said he was a "terror to evildoers" in court. Another Republican newspaper, the *Raleigh Gazette,* rated him as one of the top criminal lawyers in the state when he practiced privately.

The nomination was his for the asking for a third term in 1894, but White, a dynamic speaker, was convinced he had built a sufficient following to send him to Washington. He turned down another four years as prosecutor to vie for his district's seat in the House of Representatives. The principal obstacle in his path was his brother-in-law, former Congressman Henry Cheatham. These would-be candidates were married to sisters—the daughters of State Assemblyman Henry Cherry.

There was a brouhaha over the seating of delegates at the nominating convention at Weldon. Seven men who had been instructed by their counties to vote for White were ejected. After a noisy floor battle, both candidates emerged from the convention claiming to be the nominee. Named to arbitrate this dispute, the Republican congressional committee gave the nod to Cheatham, who lost the election.

Two years later the brothers-in-law clashed again. Strategy as well as personal ambition split these two. Aggressive and demanding, White would tolerate no temporizing on constitutional rights. Diplomatic and conciliatory, Cheatham tried to bring conservatives around to his way of thinking. Again it was a hard-fought contest, but this time White was the nominee. In the November election, he outpolled the combined total of the Democratic and Populist candidates to win this 50 percent Caucasian district by more than thirty-nine hundred votes.

White had gained stature during the summer by taking part in the Republican national convention, which chose William McKinley as its nominee for President. The congressman-elect had not been enthusiastic about the party's choice, because of McKinley's endorsement of the gold monetary standard, but he was happy to see the Republicans back in control of the Presidency.

White, a tall, broad-shouldered, ebony man, was the only Negro member left when the Fifty-fifth Congress began its work on March 15, 1897. The House got its first sample of his relaxed speaking style on March 31, 1897, when he backed the move to enact a high tariff to protect home industries and agriculture. Agreeing with an earlier North Carolina speaker that the list should cover coal, iron, mica, cotton, wool, cattle, and hogs, he pointed out that eastern North Carolinians also wanted the hard-hit lumber industry included. In asking for protection for the American worker from cheap foreign competition, he said he represented nine million blacks, 90 percent of whom were laborers.

He drew laughter with the assertion that the Democrats on occasion had advocated free whiskey, free silver, and in the South, free everything except free ballots and Negroes. During the debate the opposition warned that the Republican party would be swept out of the House if trade barriers were erected. "We will take care of this side of the House," he said. "We have heard of the devil teaching scriptures, but never to save a soul. If we are contented, you ought not to be troubled." Later that year McKinley, who had asked Congress for better protection for American products in his Inaugural Address, signed the Dingley Tariff Act of 1897. This highly protective measure boosted rates to an all-time peak and gave the President authority to work out mutual concessions with other countries.

In another floor speech White enlivened the routine by suggesting that he, as the undisputed black leader, was ready to get together with the members "on the other side" to organize the House to legislate for the entire country. He was a gifted humorist, but as a Southerner with manners, he was not at all amused by some of his Southern colleagues who sprinkled their House speeches with plantation dialect stories about their favorite "darkies."

Absent frequently from Congress during his first two sessions, White was there in January 1898 to deliver a spirited defense of the spoils system. To suggestions that the Republicans were reneging on campaign promises by removing civil service appointees, he said that a party platform, as the Democrats well knew, was like a railroad car platform—"made to get in on, rather than to stand on."

The people of his district, he explained, expected an honest winner to pass along "some emoluments" to his friends, and if he didn't, he would soon be singing "Home, Sweet Home" rather than spending time legislating in Washington. "I proclaim it as my doctrine," he continued, "that to the victor belongs the spoils; or in language a little more primitive, if you please, the ox that pulls the plow ought to have a chance to eat the fodder."

White asked prompt action on a resolution to appropriate a thousand dollars for the family of a Lake City, South Carolina, postmaster, who had been attacked by a band of a hundred armed men. In February the man and his baby son had been killed, his wife and daughter wounded, and their property burned. A Georgia representative objected, and White was refused time to document the atrocity.

When the army was being augmented in preparation for war with

Spain, he vainly tried to open the way for more Negroes to serve. Once again there had been retrogression. Robert Smalls and other congressional pioneers had argued for mixed units; White was merely asking for inclusion of black units in all departments of the army. There were, he said, two Negro regiments in the cavalry and in the infantry, but none in the artillery, and he wanted the army to muster one. He reminded the House that blacks had long since proved their mettle as fighting men. Despite maltreatment, he said, they loved the Union and were eager to share in protecting it as part of their responsibility as citizens, if the whites would only stop being cowards and give them the chance.

The congressman, who had not introduced any significant legislation in his first term, returned to North Carolina in the summer of 1898 to stand for reelection, against two Democrats and a Populist. Addressing the Republican state convention in July, White exhorted blacks to demand their fair share of jobs from their political party. "I am not the only Negro who holds office," he said to wild cheers. "There are others. . . . We don't hold as many as we will. The Democrats talk about the color line and the Negro holding office. I invite the issue."

The campaign proved to be a vicious one. The *Raleigh News and Observer* printed a list of North Carolina's black officials, and the Democrats doubtless gained some support as a result of White's candid call for even more Negro officeholders.

The *Wilmington Record* ran an editorial advising white men to keep a closer eye on their women. In the countryside, the paper said, white women were no more careful in their clandestine meetings with black men than white men with black women. "Meetings of this kind," the editorial continued, "go on for some time until the white woman's infatuation or the man's boldness brings attention to them and the man is lynched for rape. Every Negro lynched is called a 'big burly black brute' when in fact many of these, who have been thus dealt with had white men for their fathers and were not only not 'black and burly' but were sufficiently attractive for white girls of culture and refinement to fall in love with them as is well known to all."

Democratic papers blasted the editorial as a slander on North Carolina's white womanhood. Led by Senator Benjamin Tillman, wearing a gun and a black eye patch, South Carolina Red Shirts came riding into the state. One county registrar, B. B. Steptoe, was driven out of town. Republican leaders, including the governor, spoke of seeking federal protection for the voters, but when Election Day dawned the armed men patrolling some precincts were the self-appointed white supremacy guards. The Negro turnout understandably was reduced, though the *Wilmington Record* had carried an appeal signed by black women asking all black men who weren't "white-livered cowards" to register and vote.

Running as the party of white supremacy, the Democrats swept the state legislature by a two-thirds majority, but enough of George White's Negro and Caucasian constituents came out to vote in the four-man race in the Second District to send him back to the House by a margin of twenty-six hundred ballots.

A few days after the election, a white mob gutted and burned the office of the *Record* and drove the owner out of town. Eleven blacks were killed in a riot that was defended by the *Raleigh News and Observer* as a justified reprisal for the *Record's* editorial slurs against white women. The board of aldermen of Wilmington resigned shortly afterward; the man who had led the mob in destroying the *Record* became mayor. Numerous Negroes and liberal whites were forced to leave the state. White himself soon left also, but only for the trip to Washington for the third session of the Fifty-fifth Congress.

Acutely aware of being the sole representative of his race in Congress, White in his speeches frequently departed from the issue under discussion to call the country's attention to the plight of its black citizens. On January 26, 1899, he charged that Negroes, who had worked for centuries without compensation, were still being denied a chance to compete fairly in American life.

Flaying the Mississippians for their talk of racial supremacy based on fraud, intimidation, carnage, and death, he continued: "Yes, by force of circumstances, we are your inferiors. Give us 240 years the start of you, give us your labor for 240 years without compensation, give us the wealth that the brawny arm of the black man made for you, give us the education that his unpaid labor gave your boys and girls, and we will not be begging, we will not be in a position to be sneered at as aliens or members of an inferior race. . . ."

Expressing his disgust at having to sit in the House and hear blacks vilified as savages and brutes, he again reminded the Southerners that their states were overrepresented in Congress to the extent by which Negroes were deprived of the franchise.

"Our ratio of representation is poor," White continued. "We are taunted with being uppish; we are told to keep still; to keep quiet. How long must we keep quiet? We have kept quiet while numerically and justly we are entitled to fifty-one members of this House; and I am the only one left. We kept quiet when numerically we are entitled to a member of the Supreme Court. We have never had a member, and probably never will; but we have kept quiet. . . . We should have the recognition of a place in the President's Cabinet . . . ."

We are entitled to thirteen United States Senators, according to justice and our numerical strength, but we have not one and possibly never will get another; and yet we keep quiet."

The House and the gallery listened intently as he moved to the climax: "We have kept quiet while hundreds and thousands of our race have been strung up by the neck unjustly by mobs of murderers. If a man commits a crime he will never find an apologist in me because his face is black. He ought to be punished, but he ought to be punished according to the law as administered in a court of justice. But we keep quiet; do not say it, do not talk about it. How long must we keep quiet, constantly sitting down and seeing our rights one by one taken away from us?"

White was determined the historical record would show what he had put up with, not only in Congress, but outside of it where he was considerably abused by the press. On February 5, 1900, during the first session of the Fifty-sixth Congress he asked the clerk to read an insulting editorial about him from the *Raleigh News and Observer.* "It is bad enough that North Carolina should have the only nigger Congressman," the article began. The paper sympathized with the "humiliated" white people of the Second District whose representative had said: "I have investigated the lynchings in the South and find less than fifteen percent of them are due to the crime of rape. And I desire to announce here that if it were not for the assaults of the white men upon the black women, there would be less of the other class." The paper termed White beneath contempt, but indicative of the race problem since he was an educated man. His behavior was cited as proof of the absolute necessity for permanent white rule in the state.

Pointing out that this "vile slanderous" statement had been published just as the state was going into the campaign for a congressional election, White said he wanted it to be fully circulated in order to demonstrate what Southern Negroes had to contend with. He excluded most North Carolinians from his criticism, but noted that unfortunately men of the type who wrote the editorial were in the ascendancy.

He said he had merely told the truth about lynching—that less than 15 percent of the cases did stem from sexual crimes. But, he insisted, he had not justified assaults on white women by black men on the grounds that white men raped black women. He wanted the "white or black brute" who assaulted any woman hanged by the neck, but by court order, not by an infuriated mob.

Early in this Congress, White introduced his most significant piece of legislation—House bill 6963. Based on the Fourteenth Amendment, this measure would have made mob action by lynching, murder, or torture a federal offense and would have punished accessories as well as the principals. White equated lynching with treason and asked the death penalty for it. First of a long series of similar proposals submitted to Congress, his bill was referred to the Judiciary Committee.

White sought to stimulate action on his bill on February 23, 1900, during the debate on a Puerto Rican tariff and other measures affecting territories acquired following the Spanish-American War. He wanted the United States to deal fairly with those multiracial islands, but meanwhile he asked:

"Should not a nation be just to all her citizens, protect them alike in all their rights, on every foot of her soil—in a word show herself capable of governing all within her domain before she undertakes to exercise sovereignty over those in a foreign land . . . ? Or, to be more explicit, should not charity first begin at home?"

White decided not to run in 1900. He had made this decision months before the nominating convention, and he stuck to it. He was convinced he could not win a third term with the white supremacists in control of his state. They had already rammed through a state constitutional amendment designed to keep blacks from voting. Still, White was very much on the minds of the district Democrats, who went out of their way to lambaste him. They vowed to make it forever impossible for another black to represent North Carolina's Second District, which had sent more Negroes to Congress than any other in history.

The *Raleigh News and Observer* ran a cartoon depicting White as a creature with a human head, dragon's spine, and elephant trunk dipping into a container of water. "He doesn't like to let go," ran the caption, "but most people think our Negro congressman has had it [his salary of five thousand dollars] long enough."

White on January 29, 1901, updated Congress and the country on the blacks' contributions to literature, publishing, and the professions. He emphasized that their achievements were made despite job discrimination, Jim Crow, and lynching. He asked the House to act on his antilynching bill, which still languished in committee though petitions supporting it had poured in from all over the country.

Sensing that this might be his last House speech, he bade farewell on "behalf of a heartbroken, bruised, and bleeding, but . . . faithful, industrious, loyal people," who "Phoenix-like" would return to Congress. He offered this suggestion for handling the "so-called" Negro problem: "Treat him as a man; go into his home and learn of his social conditions; learn of his cares, his troubles, and his hopes for the future; gain his confidence; open the doors of industry to him. . . .

Measure the standard of the race by its best material, cease to mould prejudicial and unjustified public sentiment against him. . . ." There was prolonged applause in the House, as was usual for White's hard-hitting, anecdotal speeches, but the sound did not carry enough impact to force action on his bill.

For some time the country's only black congressman had been advising his friends to seek out more congenial climes. Pushed aside himself now after a long public career, he followed his own counsel, and set up a real estate firm in New Jersey, before moving to Philadelphia, where he practiced law until his death on December 28, 1918, at the age of sixty-six.

The demise of George H. White, whom the people of North Carolina elected to four major offices, marked the end of an era. Nearly a generation would go by before blacks would have another representative in the United States Congress.

Oscar DePriest / Illinois

Twenty-eight years passed before Oscar DePriest fulfilled George H. White's prediction and desegregated Congress again.

The son of Alexander and Mary Karsner DePriest, both former slaves, Oscar Stanton DePriest was born March 9, 1871, in Florence, Alabama. His father, a farmer and teamster, was active in the state's new Republican party.

When Oscar was seven, the DePriests moved their large family to Salina, Kansas, but not before the boy had witnessed a black man being dragged from the arms of his weeping wife, shot ten times, and hanged. Oscar DePriest often said he had promised never to move back to Alabama if God would forgive him for having been born there.

After completing a business and bookkeeping course, young Oscar and two white friends ran away to Dayton, Ohio. With his sandy hair, blue eyes, and pale skin, he was indistinguishable from his companions, and he sometimes got into fights with people who insulted Negroes in his presence without realizing he was one.

As a teen-ager he traveled on to Chicago and used painting and plastering as an entrée into the decorating business. Friends said DePriest discovered politics when he and a pal stopped by a Republican party precinct meeting. Everyone else was white, yet before the young man left he had manipulated himself into the job of precinct secretary. He slowly began to build a base in the black community, gaining a reputation as a man who could deliver votes, though he sometimes crisscrossed party lines in bargaining.

For years he was a behind-the-scenes leader helping to put others into office. It was not until 1904 that the Republicans gave him a chance to go before the voters himself as a candidate for Cook County commissioner. He won and served two terms, after which his officeholding career came to a halt until 1915 when he was elected

Chicago's first black alderman. In the city council, DePriest, who by then owned a profitable real estate firm, introduced a civil rights ordinance and battled constantly against job bias.

The man in the street admired the bustling, fiery alderman, but he also had his detractors in the Negro community. Aligned against him were some church leaders, who found him too much at home with gambling and vice interests, and some intellectuals, who looked on him as an opportunistic, what's-in-it-for-me, machine politician of the old school. Indicted and charged with taking a three thousand dollar bribe from a gambling house in his ward, he said the money had been given to him as a campaign contribution. A jury acquitted him, but he did not return to the city council.

The black population in the North expanded sharply during World War I, a period of great business prosperity. With immigration from Europe shut off by the fighting, Northern factories not only welcomed Negro labor from the South, but sent agents into the Mississippi Valley to recruit workers. "While the many were moved by the chance to amass fabulous sums, they all sighed with relief at the thought that they could at last go to a country where they could educate their children, protect their families from insult and enjoy the fruits of their labor," historian Carter Godwin Woodson wrote. "They had pleasant recollections of the days when Negroes wielded political power and the dream of again coming into their own was a strong motive impelling many to leave the South." Between 1910 and 1920 an estimated half-million blacks traveled North in search of a better life. A sizable number of them settled in Chicago and provided a constituency for party leader DePriest.

The turning point in his career came as a result of the death of Martin Madden, the veteran incumbent Republican congressman in the Illinois First District, before the fall elections of 1928. As boss of the third ward, DePriest had supported Madden when other Negroes were insisting that this 60 percent black, lake-shore district should be represented by one of them.

Chicago Mayor William Thompson and former Governor Len Small conferred with ward leaders who were to name the candidate to succeed Madden. DePriest, as one of those party stalwarts, let it be known that he wanted to run and succeeded in getting the endorsement of the Thompson-Small faction of the party. There was a great deal of speculation over how DePriest managed it.

"His detractors have represented Mr. DePriest as practically forcing the Mayor to pay him for certain services involving 'black and tan' resorts, vice-rings, 'protection' collections and other matters in which the two are said to have been associated," George P. Robinson,

Jr. wrote in the *Journal of Negro History* in April 1932. "The exact details of the transactions, if true, will never be known, or, at best, known only by a very few. But it is true that the Mayor practically placed the choice in Mr. DePriest's hands, and that Mr. DePriest named himself as the Thompson-Small candidate for the nomination."

After the nomination, DePriest was indicted by a grand jury for his alleged connections with a vice ring. His supporters said the indictment was a transparent political move intended to intimidate him. He was repeatedly told that the charges, which had been pressed by a state attorney general opposed to the Thompson-DePriest party faction, would be dropped if he pulled out of the race.

The veteran politician, who was the best-known black in Chicago, did not scare easily. Instead he stepped up his campaign to counteract the accusations. With the support of the city Republican machine he won by more than four thousand votes over Harry Baker, the Democrat, and three other candidates. In his victory statement DePriest called his election a triumph for the Negro race.

Illinois thus became the first Northern state to send a black to Congress, though it took a native Southerner to achieve that distinction. DePriest was elected with the grand jury indictment still hanging over his head. The *Chicago Tribune* speculated that the House might exclude him on this account. The charges, however, were dropped the Saturday before the Seventy-first Congress got under way on April 15, 1929, and he was seated without incident.

The Negro's return to Congress was covered in a petty fashion by the white newspapers. Their concern was not what kind of man DePriest was or how well he might succeed in reflecting the sentiments of eleven million black Americans, but the social embarrassment he and Mrs. DePriest would cause in Washington, particularly to the First Lady. Mrs. Herbert Hoover's White House tea welcoming the congressional wives to the capital did not exclude the only black among them—to the dismay of some Southern solons.

"It's all a lot of moonshine for anyone to suggest that a question of social equality was involved in my wife's going to a White House tea," DePriest said, after the papers had overplayed this teapot tempest. "My wife was invited not because Mrs. Hoover thought anything of her personally. She was invited because she happened to be the wife of a member of Congress. That's all there was to that." DePriest blamed the hubbub on prejudiced Southern Democrats, "haters" of the sort who had voted against Al Smith for President because of his religion. The political effect, DePriest said, would be to drive black voters back into the Republican party.

DePriest did not arrive in Washington at a propitious moment. Before the year was out, the stock market crash had plunged the country into the Great Depression. The Hoover administration was all but paralyzed. It was no time for a neophyte congressman to make a legislative record for himself, and DePriest did not. His early speeches exhorted Negroes to stop being backward and to organize for political strength. Pointing out that blacks suffered most from unemployment, he favored a restriction on immigration until every American had a job.

Surviving the Democratic sweep in 1930, DePriest was reelected after a first term in which he had not introduced a single major bill. The *Chicago Bee* credited him with helping to get several Negroes elected to the Illinois state house of representatives.

DePriest threatened to block the organization of the House in December 1931 until he was promised some government action to curb job discrimination against Negroes in the South. The ploy got him a little publicity, but Congress had all it could do just to keep the country financially afloat as unemployment soared at a frightening rate.

Like Hoover, DePriest was such a rock-ribbed Republican that he opposed federal aid to the needy even though there were more than five million men on the streets looking for work. He fought a bill to appropriate twenty-five million dollars for Red Cross-dispensed food and medical relief. No one, he said, could accuse him, a child of the "poorest of the poor," of being unsympathetic to the jobless. He did not, however, want to see a "dole system" set up in America where the tradition was for states and cities to take care of their own down-and-outers.

In demand as a speaker, DePriest kept his engagements in the South despite efforts to frighten him away. Two Protestant churches in Mobile refused to open their doors to allow him to address the National Association for the Advancement of Colored People, but the meeting was held in a Roman Catholic church. He spoke in Miami even though he had been warned his life would be in danger if he came. "Tells Negroes To Use Their Brains" was the headline in the *Pittsburgh Courier* after his appearance in Little Rock, Arkansas.

"He moves straight to his racial objectives with a bluntness and blindness to all other considerations," the *Philadelphia Tribune* said of DePriest. "He appoints Negroes to Annapolis and West Point. He exercises the privileges that go with his high position whether they take him to the Senate chamber, congressional restaurants or a White House reception. He defies Senator [James] Heflin in the Senate, the KKK in Alabama [and] even looks the GOP squarely in the eye and declares he is a Negro before he is a Republican . . . His brusque procedure is very pleasing to the common folk who've been fed platitudes for forty years."

DePriest was reelected to a third term in 1932, again with ease and again over the same white opponent, Harry Baker, in spite of the Democratic landslide, which gave Franklin D. Roosevelt the Presidency, and in spite of charges by a Communist opponent that he had evicted blacks from his Chicago tenements. DePriest sought to amend a Washington school appropriations bill to provide additional land for an overcrowded Negro school. He succeeded in boosting a grant to Howard University for a power plant from $240,000 to $460,000. As a member of the Indian Affairs Committee, he supported assistance to the Ute Indians.

The House restaurant served him with meals, but he continued to have trouble with the treatment of his staff. He argued that his aides, who could never be sure in Washington of decent service in a public restaurant, had more reason to eat in the House dining room than anyone else. Howard University students attempted to desegregate the restaurant. They were called hoodlums by one congressman and accused of "almost precipitating a riot."

If the students had asked him in advance, he would have advised against this impractical move, DePriest admitted later. His disagreement with tactics aside, his stand on the basic issue was well known, however. "If we are good enough to die for this country," he said, "we are good enough to enjoy the privileges of citizenship in this country." His resolution calling for an investigation of the restaurant's treatment of Negroes was finally passed, but blacks had later to retake this territory many times.

Throughout his political career, DePriest was concerned with racial bias in employment. He registered an advance in this area on March 29, 1933, when he added an amendment onto the bill that provided the genesis for the Civilian Conservation Corps. The bill authorized the President to launch programs to conserve and develop the country's natural resources and alleviate unemployment. DePriest's amendment barring discrimination because of race, color, or creed and the employment of incarcerated criminals in the projects, passed the House 179 to 71. The Senate approved the measure with the DePriest insertion intact, and the President signed it two days later. This was the Chicago congressman's most notable legislative victory.

DePriest worried about the inroads Communism was making in America, particularly among some blacks who had become convinced that fair treatment in the courts and elsewhere would never be theirs under capitalism. Addressing the House in early May 1933, he contrasted the courts' handling of the nine Scottsboro, Alabama, boys accused of raping two white girls of dubious reputation with the case of a white naval officer who admittedly had killed a dark-skinned Hawaiian. The naval officer was convicted and given a sentence of an hour. Eight of the Scottsboro nine were convicted and given the death sentence.

"I know the great rank and file of American people are on the square," DePriest said. "But I also know what is everybody's business is nobody's business, and I also know that the great body of Christian America and the great newspapers and periodicals of this country do not universally denounce this crime of injustice meted out to those of my particular group, especially when charged with crimes of that kind. They are convicted before they are tried."

Pointing out that he held no brief for any criminals, he said offenders should be punished by law, not by other standards. He told the House there had been twenty-five blacks lynched in 1930 and warned that no country could keep one tenth of its population down and survive. "If we had a right to exercise our franchise . . . as the constitution provides, I would not be the only Negro on this floor," he asserted.

DuPriest wanted the Fourteenth Amendment revised to assure all citizens equal protection under the law. Under his proposal if the federal courts determined that a defendant could not get a fair trial because of his race or religion, the accused person could ask for a transfer to another jurisdiction. This measure bogged down in the Judiciary Committee.

Although admittedly apprehensive about the potential appeal of Communism to black Americans, DePriest was quick to defend the right of individuals to take unpopular positions. When Dr. Mordecai Johnson, president of Howard University, was accused of making allegedly pro-Communist remarks as quoted in the *Chicago Defender*, DePriest reminded the members of the House that, as they all knew, every man in public life was misquoted occasionally in the press. He personally could attest to this having happened with the *Defender* since it was in his district.

DePriest asked the clerk to read a statement in which Johnson denied being a Communist and in which Johnson said: "On the other hand, I am not in accord with those who believe that the best way to deal with Communism is to persecute those who believe in it. And I am not of the opinion that patriotism requires any thoughtful man to subscribe to the doctrine there is nothing good to be found in the Russian experiment."

Some congressmen were not reassured by the Howard University president's statement. Reminding them that there was the right of free speech in the United States, DePriest said he did not believe that Dr. Johnson, a Baptist minister, was a Communist. However, DePriest agreed with other members that there was cause for concern over possible Communist infiltration into the school system. "Let us know what is going on in our school system," he said. "These long-haired Communist professors are ruining some of our children in many of our institutions."

His resolution calling for an investigation of the spread of Communism went to the Rules Committee where it died. DePriest, as a Red hunter, was a shade ahead of his time. The House Un-American Activities Committee probers did not get standing committee status until 1945.

The Chicago congressman called on the United States to live up to its agreements with the Indian tribes. He reintroduced his measure to provide a thirty dollar monthly pension to a hundred thousand ex-slaves aged seventy-five and older. He figured that if they had been paid for their services during their working years and received the benefit of the amount due them with interest, they would have had eleven billion dollars coming to them. This proposal never reached the floor.

On January 3, 1934, the opening day of the second session of the Seventy-third Congress, DePriest introduced an antilynching bill. His measure defined a mob as three or more unauthorized persons acting in concert to take another's life as punishment for, or to prevent, some actual or supposed offense. The legislation was aimed at those state and local officials who allowed their prisoners to slip through their fingers and fall prey to vigilante justice.

Officials found negligent in such cases by a federal court would be liable to punishment of five years in jail and a five thousand dollar fine—and subject to instant removal from their positions. The county where the lynching occurred would be required to pay ten thousand dollars to the next of kin of the murdered person, unless two counties were involved, in which instance the liability would be shared. Homicide charges against the members of the mob could be brought in federal court if state officials failed "to proceed with due diligence." DePriest's bill was smothered in the Judiciary Committee, and petitions by outsiders like the Illinois General Assembly could not resuscitate it.

Roosevelt's public works and pump-priming proposals were attracting blacks to the Democratic party in increasing numbers. DePriest, who voted with his party against FDR's emergency legislation, which could have helped Chicago's depression-wracked South Side, was defeated in 1934 by Arthur W. Mitchell, an enthusiastic Roosevelt supporter.

The former congressman resumed his real estate business in Chicago and unsuccessfully attempted to regain his House seat from Mitchell two years later. A delegate to the Republican national convention in 1936, he remained influential in his party's political circles. He returned to the city council and led the fight for fair employment standards until he lost his seat in 1947, partly as a result of accusations that he was in league with the Democratic mayor of Chicago.

DePriest, by then in his seventies, was a partner in a real estate firm with his son, Oscar, Jr. Having survived being hit by a bus while crossing the street near his home five months earlier, the North's first black congressman died in Chicago on May 12, 1951, aged eighty of a kidney ailment.

One of the eulogists at DePriest's funeral singled out his efforts to eradicate job discrimination as his chief contribution. "Some day," the minister told the mourners, "you are going to see fair employment practices written into the law of the land and guaranteed by statute. Until that day no brighter torch ever burned along the tortuous path to freedom than that carried by Oscar DePriest."

Arthur W. Mitchell/Illinois

Arthur W. Mitchell had had no experience in public office when in 1934 he became the first black Democrat in Congress.

Like Oscar DePriest, whom he defeated for the Chicago seat, Arthur Wergs Mitchell came from a poor Southern farm family. Born near Lafayette in Chambers County, Alabama, on December 22, 1883, he left home at fourteen to walk sixty-six miles to Tuskegee Institute, where he earned his way through school by working on a farm and as an office boy to Tuskegee's president, Booker T. Washington.

Mitchell stood guard with a rifle one night at Tuskegee when the famous educator had received threats of lynching, because some of his Caucasian neighbors were incensed at the thought of a black man lunching at the White House with President Theodore Roosevelt.

Greatly influenced by the ultraconciliatory views of Washington, Mitchell followed in his professional footsteps and for several years headed Armstrong Agricultural School in West Butler, Alabama. After Mitchell stopped payment on a twenty dollar check in a misrepresented deal, there were rumors of mob action against him, also. He and his wife waited with loaded guns to protect their school, but the crowd dispersed three miles away.

After attending Columbia University in New York briefly and studying law, Mitchell qualified for the bar and started his practice in Washington. Eager for a political career, he moved his law office to Chicago in 1928 and began to work in the Republican party.

Within a few years he had switched from the traditional party for blacks to the Democrats, whose policy toward the unemployed and destitute was more in tune with his own political philosophy. Mitchell first ran for public office in 1934 as a candidate for the Democratic nomination for the Illinois First Congressional District seat, and lost to Harry Baker, the perennial white aspirant. Soon afterward, however, Baker died, and Mitchell, the runner-up in the primary, was named by the ward committeemen to run against the Republican incumbent Oscar DePriest.

The press carried lively accounts of this unprecedented House race between a black Democrat and a black Republican. The forty-nine-year-old lawyer-challenger and the sixty-three-year-old white-haired congressman competed for oratorical honors at nightly meetings throughout the district. When Mitchell challenged DePriest to a series of debates, the Republican's refusal did not arrive for two weeks. "I have this reply from Mr. DePriest," Mitchell told a rally one night. "Dear Mr. Mitchell: I understand that you are a candidate for Congress and, I believe, in my district. . . ." His audience roared. Mitchell said that he felt sorry for his opponent if he had only just made that discovery.

Mitchell protested that DePriest was using his mail-franking privileges illegally to distribute campaign literature. They haggled over whether the city of Chicago was getting a fair share of Public Works Administration funds, each accusing the other of raising this issue for partisan purposes. President Roosevelt's emergency relief measures had revivified the Democratic party and given it new sources of strength. Campaigning as a fervent New Dealer, Mitchell ousted DePriest by more than three thousand votes.

The congressman-elect hoped to win friends for himself and to improve the country's attitude toward blacks by avoiding the "bombast, ballyhoo and noise" of his predecessor. Stressing that nineteen thousand whites had voted for him, he said his first duty was to represent all his constituents. This stance was somewhat disappointing to those who thought that the only black in Congress had the added responsibility of looking out for the interests of all the country's Negroes.

Mitchell had been in Washington less than a month when he fulfilled one of his campaign promises by introducing an antilynching bill. There were thirty-one such measures before the House, and his version was pallid compared to many of the others in terms of penalties and court procedures. The stronger versions were backed by the National Association for the Advancement of Colored People and other civil rights organizations.

Mitchell's racial conservatism set him at odds with many Negro leaders, who would have preferred a less placating representative in the nation's capital. During a furor in the press over whether Mitchell was fulfilling his role as spokesman for a minority group of twelve million Americans, the *St. Louis Argus* chided the *Baltimore Afro-American* and the *Chicago Defender* and his other "clamoring, clawing critics" for tearing him apart before he had had a chance to get settled in the job.

While the criticism raged, the North's second black congressman traveled across the country delivering as many speeches as he could. His first session in the House ended with applause from the *Argus,* a friendly paper, for the bills he had introduced, his liberal voting record on the Roosevelt program, and the Negro judges he had supported.

When Congress resumed on January 3, 1936, Mitchell started a drive against racial bias in the civil service. He suggested that appointments be given to those making the highest test scores, that no photograph be required with an application, and that if sex were a factor in the job decision, it should be specified in advance whether a man or woman was needed. He charged that the ruse of stating that an applicant's sex disqualified him for the position was used as a subterfuge to reject Negro applicants.

His differences with the NAACP were intensifying. Mitchell turned down the request of NAACP executive secretary, Walter White, that he sign a petition to the leaders of the Democratic caucus asking them to shake loose for a floor vote fifteen, substantially identical, antilynching bills. Denying the "wild and false rumors" that he was "not strong for the lynching bill," Mitchell said that he considered his the best of the lot—and it had not been included in White's petition. White, the congressman charged, had been "making a miserable failure" of swaying Congress for fifteen years, and his tactics were now jeopardizing the bill.

Mitchell claimed that an appeal to the Democratic caucus was futile; he said the only way to pry a bill out of committee was through a membership petition signed by 218 representatives. He immodestly claimed that his man-to-man contacts in the House had made at least a hundred converts for antilynching legislation, and he advised White to mobilize Southern Caucasian women to pressure South Carolina Senator James Byrnes into withdrawing his opposition.

The Illinois congressman made one of the seconding speeches for the nomination of Franklin D. Roosevelt at the Democratic national convention that summer and pledged there would be millions of blacks voting for him. Mitchell worked for the national ticket as well as for himself during a busy campaign season. Reelected to the Seventy-fifth ·Congress over DePriest by sixty-seven hundred votes, Mitchell reintroduced his antilynching bill early in 1937.

"Naturally I am more interested in the passing of my own bill, but authorship . . . means little to me compared with the importance of the legislation itself," Mitchell stated. Joseph Gavagan of New York was collecting signatures for a discharge petition to put his much stronger proposal on the Speaker's desk for action. Promising to support whatever measure got on the calendar, Mitchell signed the New Yorker's petition and talked some of his Illinois colleagues into doing so, also.

Still, Mitchell seems to have played into the hands of House conservatives who were maneuvering to prevent the passage of any workable federal antilynching legislation. Hoping to quash Gavagan's proposal, the Judiciary Committee voted out Mitchell's bill, which made no provision for transferring negligent or conspiratorial peace officials and members of the mob to federal jurisdiction. The full House, however, by a margin of better than 2 to 1 declined to consider it.

John M. Robison of Kentucky said that all those who were serious about wanting to stop mob murders, including officials of the NAACP, looked upon Mitchell's bill as a "mere gesture." Mitchell, he reminded the House, had asked only a two- to ten-year sentence for any state or local official who helped a crowd kill his prisoner. Robison said that any official, who did that, would be guilty of the "worst sort" of willful murder and should pay the commensurate penalty, provided by every state in the Union, of death or life imprisonment.

"If the Gavagan bill is passed prosecutions can take place in the Federal courts and G-men can be sent to ferret out those guilty of mob murder," Robison continued.

Gavagan's bill, carrying a maximum sentence of twenty-five years for any official who conspired with a lynching mob, was then forced out of committee, and on April 15—and after a final brief endorsement by Mitchell—the measure overwhelmingly passed the House, only to be blocked in the Senate.

Mitchell was irritated by Negro critics who second-guessed his every move. He said that they either did not understand or deliberately misrepresented his motives. One of the most dramatic disputes came following President Roosevelt's appointment of Senator Hugo L. Black to the Supreme Court. Mitchell thought Black an able and fair man, and supported him even after reporters had ferreted out records of his onetime Ku Klux Klan membership.

Mitchell said that Black was a "genuine, honest-to-goodness New Dealer," who was interested in underprivileged people, and that it made no difference what organizations he might formerly have belonged to. Pointing out that the senator's record as a prosecutor and lawyer in Alabama was a good one, Mitchell predicted he would be a great Supreme Court justice.

"It is no more fair for you to say that because a white man is from the South he is an enemy to the Negro than it is to say because you are a Negro you are worthless as an American citizen," Mitchell told

Black's detractors. "Both statements are viciously false, and no man who wishes to be fair will take either position. . . . Other Congressmen may draw the color line, but I have not done it; and no man, however bitter his criticisms, will cause me to descend from the high stand which I have taken, namely, that of being absolutely fair to all men, paying no attention to their race or their color. . . ." The Senate evidently agreed with Mitchell about Black's credentials: he was confirmed, and turned out to be a very liberal justice on the issue of civil rights.

Mitchell supported Roosevelt's plan to enlarge the Supreme Court to gain approval of his administration's prescriptions for restoring economic health to the nation. The congressman accused the high court of blocking progress whenever the rights of the masses were at issue and said it had struck down every measure passed to help blacks since before the Civil War. The court had, he continued, even subverted the Fourteenth Amendment, which was designed to protect the citizenship of the newly emancipated slaves, by using it solely for the benefit of corporations and property rights.

Running again as a supporter of the President, the Illinois representative was named to a third term in 1938, this time over William L. Dawson, a Chicago alderman. After the election, Mitchell introduced a measure to ban discrimination in interstate travel and resubmitted his bills to curb lynching, to reform the civil service, and to create an industrial commission to look after black affairs. Once more Gavagan's antilynching bill passed the House, but failed in the Senate.

The greatest mass migration in the history of the United States had started as thousands of Negroes left the South in search of better jobs and first-class citizenship. Mitchell recommended a government study of the exodus, which he considered a threat to the country's agriculture. His suggestion followed an exchange of letters with Dr. Kelly Miller, onetime dean of Howard University. Miller was apprehensive about what might happen to a farm-trained Alabama family when transplanted to the unfriendly sidewalks of New York. He wanted "race statesmen" to carry forward Booker T. Washington's advice and persuade blacks to stay down on the farm away from the glitter of city life.

Mitchell paid tribute verbally to his old teacher, but as one who had migrated himself, Mitchell said he knew why so many blacks were moving North. The reasons, he said, were the five thousand lynchings, disfranchisement, injustice in the courts and in the sharecropper system, under which a man could break his back in the fields and be cheated out of his promised percentage of the yield at the end of the year. The northern trek continued with an estimated 1,500,000 Southerners, mostly blacks, crossing the Mason-Dixon line between 1940 and 1950.

Elected to a fourth term over former State Senator William King, Mitchell again offered bills for civil service reform, curbs on lynching, a Negro affairs commission, and desegregated interstate travel. These proposals were submitted on January 3, 1941, the opening day of the Seventy-seventh Congress.

As early as 1919, Mitchell had testified before a House committee asking for legislation against discrimination in interstate transportation. He suggested that the only way to provide equal facilities for all passengers was to allow everyone who paid for them to use the same ones. The chief accomplishment of his fourth congressional term came not in the House but in the Supreme Court in 1941 as the climax to a struggle that started in 1937 when a Rock Island conductor had made him move from his first-class seat into an all-black car as the train crossed the Mississippi River from Tennessee into Arkansas. This was in the days when the railroads provided separate but supposedly equal travel facilities in some parts of the United States.

The Illinois congressman, who had been talking with white friends, objected to being forced into a second-class car, but he moved when the conductor threatened him with arrest, and according to the suit filed later, called Mitchell "vile names too opprobrious and profane, vulgar and filthy to be spread upon the record. . . ." While the white-only, first-class car was modern, air-conditioned, and clean, the Negro car was old, filthy, rundown, and the toilet was out of order. Passengers from the Jim Crow car were not permitted to eat in the diner.

Mitchell filed a complaint with the Interstate Commerce Commission charging the railroads with unjust discrimination, and he asked the Cook County Circuit court for fifty thousand dollars in damages from the Illinois Central and Rock Island railroads and the Pullman Company for "humiliation and inconvenience."

Impressed that the railroads a few months after Mitchell's appeal had replaced the old black-only car by half of a modern, air-conditioned second-class car, with the races separated by a partition, the ICC, which said there was little demand from Negroes for first-class railroad service, rejected Mitchell's appeal. In 1940 all three judges in the Illinois federal district court upheld the commission's position that the ICC had no authority to interfere with the Arkansas law banning whites and blacks riding together on trains.

Mitchell and his lawyer, Richard Westbrooks of Chicago, appealed the ICC ruling to the Supreme Court. On March 13, 1941, the high court unanimously reversed the ruling of the ICC and the district court, and in an opinion written by Chief Justice Charles Evans Hughes, stated that the railroad had violated the Interstate Commerce Act's prohibition against subjecting "any particular person . . . to any undue or reasonable prejudice or disadvantage in any respect whatsoever."

The chief justice said that the equal facilities were to be equal regardless of how few blacks used them and that Congressman Mitchell had a right to travel that particular route with a first-class ticket whenever he wished.

"It's a step in the destruction of Mr. Jim Crow himself," Mitchell told reporters when word of the decision reached him in Chicago. It was a notable case, though segregation was to remain the pattern in transportation for years to come in the South. Eventually the carriers —pushed by the courts—would find the simplest way to make first-class accommodations equal was to allow everyone to use the same cars and dining cars. Still, improvements were tortuously slow, with railroads resisting all along the way and interpreting court orders with a fine-edged legal narrowness. Several years after the Mitchell decision, Elmer W. Henderson, a Negro who had been denied a seat in a diner with plenty of room, sued, and the Supreme Court following the Mitchell precedent ruled in the plaintiff's favor. The Interstate Commerce Commission finally banned segregation in interstate rail transportation in 1955, after the NAACP filed a complaint predicated on the 1954 Supreme Court decision declaring school segregation unconstitutional.

Mitchell, who generally supported labor, sided with Roosevelt in his clash with John L. Lewis, president of the United Mine Workers. Speaking in December 1941, when Europe was already embroiled in World War II and just a few days before Japan attacked Pearl Harbor, he urged Negro miners to stand firmly behind the government during the international crisis, but he also used this opportunity to spotlight racism in the unions by putting into the *Congressional Record* the names of sixteen railroad, airline, and telegraphers' unions whose contracts banned blacks.

Mitchell's bills fared no better in the Seventy-seventh Congress than in the three previous ones. Failure to make legislative headway made a fifth term seem less attractive. His wife's illness may also have entered into his decision not to run for reelection in 1942, as did reports that an alderman was planning to compete against him as a reform candidate in the Democratic primary.

Mitchell waited until December 16, 1942, the last day of the session, to bid good-bye to his friends in the House. He was leaving

Congress voluntarily after eight years, he explained, because he felt he could do better work for "my people and particularly for my beloved Southland than I could do here in Congress."

He was not going to Chicago or to New York but to a new home in Petersburg, Virginia, where his fellow members would be welcomed on visits. "If you see me twenty-four hours from now you will see me in overalls on my own farm," he said. "I go there to dedicate anew my life and every bit of energy I possess to working out better understanding between the two races in the South. . . ." Before he finished, he had been interrupted several times by members who praised him both personally and for his work in Congress.

Mitchell and his wife, Annie, who had worked as an accountant during part of their stay in the capital, moved to their new, fourteen-room, two-storied, white-columned home in Virginia. With the help of a single handyman, Mitchell looked after the twelve acres of fruits and vegetables; he kept the spacious flower garden himself and held open house for the public when the roses were at their loveliest. He returned to Washington now and then to act as an advisor to the defense department.

After the death of his first wife in 1947, he married Clara Smith, a widowed Danville, Virginia, teacher. The retired politician enjoyed being a working farmer. He had a healthy income from the rental of Washington real estate, but he could doubtless have made more money had he chosen to continue his legal practice in Chicago. Occasionally he became involved in political campaigns in Virginia. He supported the Adlai E. Stevenson-John J. Sparkman ticket against Dwight D. Eisenhower and Richard M. Nixon in the 1952 presidential race.

There were twenty-five years of relatively quiet life for Mitchell, before his death at his home in Petersburg on May 9, 1968. Until his more advanced years he traveled in the South for the Southern Regional Council. His personality was ideally suited to this biracial organization, whose headquarters are in Atlanta and whose technique is to tackle the country's race problems unobtrusively.

He was nearly eighty in 1963 when reporters from *Ebony* visited him in his Petersburg home. The erect, white-haired man looked well and vigorous in the pictures taken in his memento-filled study and in his immaculate garden. He thought Congress should be more energetic, but he would not say what specific legislation was needed. "I follow what is going on there," Mitchell said when asked for an assessment, "but I do not feel in a position to comment on any of the Negro congressmen, what they are doing, or what they should do. It would not be fair."

Mitchell's basement study, where he enjoyed relaxing with solitaire, was packed with treasures from his active political days—bound volumes of the *Congressional Record,* copies of his speeches, correspondence, and awards. The material was to be used for the memoirs he planned to write. He kept the court records of his fight with the railroads and the United States government within easy reach. He said the protracted suit had cost him ten thousand dollars, all of it money well spent, but he was unhappy that many lawyers, even black ones, did not appreciate the significance of the case.

Arthur W. Mitchell, a clever lawyer who never graduated from law school, was wistfully hoping in his declining years to be remembered for his personal battle with old Jim Crow.

William L. Dawson/Illinois

William L. Dawson, a hard-working, tough machine politician from Chicago, was the first black to become an accepted leader in the congressional establishment in Washington and in the Democratic party. At the time of his death in November 1970, the veteran party vice-chairman had headed the Government Operations Committee of the House of Representatives for nearly twenty years.

Like his two Negro predecessors from the Illinois First Congressional District, he was a native Southerner. Son of Levi and Rebecca Kendrick Dawson, William Levi Dawson was born on April 26, 1886, in Albany, Georgia, where he received his early education. His father was a barber, and his mother, in Dawson's words, "worked her fingers to the bone" to get the children an education after their father died.

Young Bill Dawson graduated magna cum laude from Fisk University in Nashville in 1909, in spite of having had to work his way through college. He had planned to study medicine, but changed to the law at Kent College in Chicago, hoping to earn money faster to assist his brothers and sisters in their education. One of his brothers later became a physician.

Dawson was studying at Northwestern University Law School in 1917 when the United States entered World War I. He volunteered and served as a first lieutenant with the 365th Infantry in France, where he was wounded in the shoulder and gassed during the Meuse-Argonne campaign.

After the war Dawson resumed his law studies at Northwestern University, waiting on tables to pay his tuition. Admitted to the bar while still a student, he took his oath as an attorney on April 13, 1920, and soon began practicing. He married Nellie Brown, daughter of a Washington minister, on December 20, 1922. They had two children, William L. Dawson, Jr., and Mrs. Barbara Ann Morgan. Throughout her husband's long career, Mrs. Dawson remained behind the scenes, staying for the most part in Chicago instead of going to Washington during congressional sessions.

Dawson entered politics as a precinct aide to Crip Woods, a blind Negro leader of one Republican faction in Chicago's old fourteenth ward, before moving into the second ward. The energetic brown lawyer with the pencil-line moustache was busy in court on weekdays, and on Sundays he was in church joining in the rousing gospel hymns.

In 1928 Dawson was runner-up in the Republican primary to the incumbent from the First Congressional District, Martin Madden, who died not long afterward. As second man in the race, Dawson claimed the right to the nomination, but the election board and the court turned him down. Instead the ward leaders nominated Oscar DePriest, who was Chicago's first black alderman, and he went on to victory in the November election.

In 1932 Dawson was named Republican state committeeman, and the following year he was elected to the Chicago City Council. The Republicans gave him a chance in 1938 to recapture the First Congressional District from Democrat Arthur W. Mitchell, but it was a losing battle with Dawson running on an anti-New Deal platform. A year later he also lost his city council seat to a Democrat; yet interestingly enough, it was this crucial defeat that started him on the pathway to better things.

The Democrats were in the ascendancy, and blacks no longer considered it unthinkable to vote for that party now that it was led by Franklin D. Roosevelt. The shift had been notable in Chicago under Mayor Edward J. Kelly, who talked Dawson into changing parties and established him in the second ward as committeeman with some patronage thrown in as sweetener. "Roosevelt and Kelly made a Democrat out of me" was Dawson's explanation of his political conversion. He credited Roosevelt with saving many people in Chicago's ghetto from starvation during the depression.

In Dawson the Democrats acquired a talented party leader. House by house, he built a smoothly organized machine that was widely copied. By 1942, Mitchell was weary of Congress and ready to retire. Dawson ran for Mitchell's seat in the primary against Earl Dickerson, who had defeated Dawson for the city council. This time the count went to Dawson by a margin of 2 to 1. The shrewd, soft-spoken candidate won the November election over former State Senator William King by three thousand votes. The next year Dawson repaid the man who had ousted him in the city council by backing William Harvey, his secretary, for Dickerson's post. Dickerson ran as an independent, but Harvey was elected alderman.

William L. Dawson/Illinois

In February 1943, Chicago's new congressman made his first speech on the floor of the House, in defense of a longtime friend who had been accused of being a Communist. Dawson also called for a special investigation to see if black Americans could not be put to better use in the armed forces and in defense industries by lifting the barriers of discrimination. He voted against an income tax bill he considered proportionally too high on low incomes. He favored extension of the reciprocal trade agreements, and he appeared before the House Judiciary Committee to testify against the poll tax. He said that this levy deprived more whites than blacks of their franchise. During his first term he took time out from Congress to return to Chicago to campaign for Mayor Kelly's reelection.

Speaking to the 1945 graduating class of Wilberforce University in Ohio, the Illinois congressman urged educated Negroes to become their unlettered, less experienced brothers' keepers. He deplored the bigotry blacks faced in the military and in industry, but he said it would serve no purpose for him to work the graduates into a frenzy of passion over their problems without offering a solution.

While he thought that the treatment of the Negro in "Christian America" was a travesty against justice and fair play, he said that the United States was the best place "in all the world for our people." He urged the young to use courtesy, politeness, and consideration, not switchblade knives, pistols, and blackjacks, as their weapons. He thought white supremacy was fast losing ground and pitied a man if his only claim to superiority "lies in something over which he has no control—the color of his skin."

Dawson headed the Negro division of the Democratic national committee in 1948 and raised substantial contributions for President Harry S. Truman's depleted campaign chest. Dawson's skill in delivering votes doubtless contributed to the 33,600 margin with which Truman carried the state of Illinois over Thomas E. Dewey.

After only six years in office, the Chicago congressman became the first black to serve as the chairman of a regular House committee, when he advanced to the top of the seniority list of the Executive Department Expenditures Committee. Except for the Eighty-third Congress—1953–55—when the Republicans were briefly in control of the House and Dawson dropped down to the position of ranking minority member, he presided over this thirty-five man group for the rest of his tenure.

Later renamed Government Operations, this committee was responsible for reorganizations in the executive branch, for government efficiency at all levels, and for intergovernment relationships between the federal government and such world organizations as the United

Nations. It studied the reports of the comptroller general and weighed all budget and accounting measures except for appropriations.

In the spring of 1951 an effort was being made to turn back the clock on integrating the armed forces. In 1948, President Truman had ordered an end to all-black units by the year 1954, and the program had been speeded up by the Korean War, which was clearly demonstrating that a mixed fighting force was more efficient than segregated outfits.

Dawson, who said he used "speeches only as the artisan does his stone, to build something," took the floor on April 13, 1951, to fight a move to slip a paragraph into the pending selective service act to allow military men freedom of choice in being assigned to black or white units. Recalling his infantry days in World War I, when he led black Americans into battle in Europe, he said: "This mark you see here on my forehead is the result of German mustard gas. This left shoulder of mine is today a slip joint. I cannot raise this left arm any higher than the shoulder unless I lift it with the other hand. That would have been a good joint if hospitalization had been available, and I had not been a Negro American. I served in a segregated outfit as a citizen trying to save this country."

Dawson called for an end to second-class citizenship. "How long, how long my conferees and gentlemen from the South, will you divide us Americans on account of color? Give me the test that you would apply to make anyone a full-fledged American, and by the living God, if it means death itself, I will pay it. But give it to me. . . ."

Dawson found it ironic that some white Americans would deny to their fellow countrymen the dignity they were quite willing to accord foreign officials. "I have sat in the well of this House," he continued, "and I have seen you gentlemen from the South, and rightly so, stand up and applaud members of other races, nonwhite races, who were darker than I am. I have seen you applaud them, yet you will take me, a citizen of the United States, of your own flesh and blood, and brand me with second-class citizenship."

Dawson said that if there was one place in America that should be without segregation, it was the armed services. "I did not make myself black any more than you made yourselves white, and God did not curse me when he made me black any more than he cursed you when he made you white." This forceful speech, which drew warm spontaneous compliments, set the mood for the vote that defeated the segregation provision by a wide margin.

Dawson, in his role as a Chicago party leader, spearheaded the move to dump Mayor Martin Kennelly in favor of Richard J. Daley in

1955. Dawson's four wards gave Daley 40 percent of his winner's margin. In 1960, Mayor Daley named the black congressman to the committee to select primary candidates. The *Chicago Sun-Times* credited him with a good deal of influence in the Illinois state legislature and said he "controlled" three representatives there.

Dawson had national, as well as local, party posts. As vice-chairman of the Democratic national committee, he was one of those selected to second the nomination of John F. Kennedy's running mate, Lyndon B. Johnson, at the party's 1960 convention. Although Johnson, as Senate majority leader, had been largely responsible for the only civil rights legislation to get through Congress in the twentieth century, party liberals were worried about how a Southerner on the ticket might affect the black vote nationally.

At the request of Kennedy's aides, according to the *Chicago Sun-Times,* Dawson wired the Negro delegates at the convention to invite them to a meeting to reassure them about Johnson and his posture on civil rights. Eighty came to meet with Kennedy and Johnson, who gave the blacks his personal commitment to the party's civil rights plank.

It was very late when Dawson made his televised seconding speech for Johnson, endorsing the senator as a man he had known well since they had both been nominated to be secretary to the Democratic congressional committee, a post which went to Dawson. "The question of race, locality, or religion, did not enter his mind then, and it will not enter his mind with the many vexing problems that our beloved country must face now," Dawson said of the man, who as President would push through more civil rights legislation than any Chief Executive in the nation's history.

Kennedy and Johnson narrowly defeated Richard M. Nixon and Henry Cabot Lodge by 118,574 votes with Illinois making a vital contribution to the Democrats' electoral margin. "Who was it that elected John F. Kennedy in Illinois?" Dawson asked a *Chicago News* reporter, and then supplied his own answer. "He carried the state by less than 10,000; my district gave him a margin of 30,000."

In December, President-elect Kennedy informed the press that he had offered the postmaster generalship to Dawson; Kennedy added that the congressman "after some reflection had declined on the grounds that he could best serve his country, his party and Illinois in Congress." Alfred Steinberg in *Sam Johnson's Boy* reported that Johnson had suggested Dawson for the Cabinet post but said Kennedy was against it, because Dawson was "seventy-five, a Negro and inexperienced in the necessary business techniques." Two Kennedy assistants, who wrote about their years with the President, assessed this incident as a bit of prearranged political make-believe. Theodore C. Sorensen considered it an "unsubtle gesture" toward Kennedy supporters who wanted a black in the Cabinet. Arthur Schlesinger, Jr., thought the public announcement was JFK's diplomatic way of avoiding offense to Dawson and Chicago Democratic boss Mayor Daley after the newspapers had printed rumors of the proposed appointment.

Dawson was reelected term after term by two generations of voters with little difficulty, despite opposition from reformers, civil rights activists, and anticrime fighters. "I have been investigated by the FBI, the Treasury and just about every one of the top investigative agencies and they have not found these connections," Dawson said to the *Chicago American* in 1962 in answer to old charges that his organization received payoffs from gambling racketeers. He noted that he had talked to gangsters, trying to get them off his constituents' backs and that he had found some so-called hoodlums more likely to keep their word than some respectable leaders, but he disclaimed any ties with organized crime.

Dawson, who became ill while addressing a political meeting during the 1962 campaign, did his usual good job of avoiding the press. Reporters finally found him at the Bethesda Naval Hospital. Aides denied that he had had a stroke and said he was suffering from exhaustion. Vice-President Johnson visited him in the hospital, and the seventy-six-year-old congressman was still there when his constituents voted to return him to an eleventh term by a margin of nearly 3 to 1. Before the end of the year he was back in Chicago to help reelect Mayor Daley.

In 1964 he was the target of comedian Dick Gregory and other activist leaders in the primary, but he again demolished his Democratic opponent and swamped the Reverend Wilbur Daniel, former Chicago NAACP officer, in the November election. He won the prize with a very modest campaign budget and without making a single speech. As the icing on the election year cake, his district gave President Johnson a margin of 32 to 1 over Senator Barry M. Goldwater, the Republican candidate.

Some black leaders, notably Martin Luther King, Jr., parted with Johnson on foreign policy when as President he began to pour a seemingly endless stream of men and materials into an undeclared war in Vietnam. Not so Dawson, who remained a spirited backer of Johnson's policy in Southeast Asia. In May 1965 the Chicago congressman defended Johnson for protecting the world against the horrors and holocaust of a third world war and used a familiar Johnsonian phrase, "nervous Nellies," to characterize the critics of the war, comparing them to those who failed to see Hitler as a threat in 1938. Dawson endorsed Johnson's decision to send Marines into the Dominican Republic on the grounds that Communists planned to take over that Caribbean island country.

Fred Hubbard, a former YMCA official, who challenged Dawson in the Democratic primary contest in the spring of 1966, was mysteriously wounded early one morning in Chicago. Dawson deplored the shooting and offered a five thousand dollar reward for the capture of the assailant. Visited by King while in the hospital, Hubbard recovered in time to be trounced in the primary.

President Johnson was in Chicago for a speech during this race, and Dawson was among those he invited to fly back to Washington with him. The Reverend E. Franklin Jackson, a Democratic national committeeman from Washington, said it would be a disgrace not to reelect Dawson. "In Congress seniority means more than anything else," Jackson said. "When it comes to the grass-roots floor votes in Congress, Dawson has always had the vote when it counted."

A similar assessment came from Clarence Mitchell, Jr., director of the NAACP's Washington office, who gave Dawson credit for his support of vital New Deal, Fair Deal, New Frontier, and Great Society legislation. Mitchell said the congressman was one of the "faithful who are around when we need them—not just for a record vote but also when the House is meeting as a committee of the whole and sometimes the weak sisters are absent or sneak in a non-recorded vote against us."

As usual, there was no cause to worry about Dawson. David R. Reed, former Drake University basketball star who ran as a Republican, covered the district, calling the congressman an "Uncle Tom" and a Daley machine man, and telling the people they needed a new face in Congress. Dawson mainly dodged reporters, but he paused occasionally to defend his record and his district organization as the best in the nation. He said he did not need publicity because his opponents always twisted his comments. When the votes were tallied in November, the faithful had again voted to send the veteran representative to Washington, 91,000 to 34,000.

Dawson's importance as a man with seniority was apparent as Lyndon Johnson turned to his committee in 1967 in a maneuver to outflank the House Committee of the District of Columbia, which for years had been standing in the way of local government for the citizens of the national capital. Unable to push through home rule, Johnson decided to use his executive authority to revamp the city's government to give local citizens a limited measure of control over their own affairs.

The President said that he would appoint a mayor to replace the three-man commission and a deputy mayor and a nine-man city council to work with him. When Johnson's proposal was submitted in June 1967, it was routed to a subcommittee of Dawson's full committee. After hearings, the subcommittee and the parent committee endorsed Johnson's proposal, but South Carolina's John L. McMillan, chairman of the District of Columbia Committee, tried to torpedo the project. John Blatnik of Minnesota, as chairman of the subcommittee, was given a free hand by Dawson to fight off the McMillan move. The LBJ plan was safely shepherded through the House early in August, and Johnson named a black mayor and five black councilmen to help govern the city of Washington with its 65 percent black population.

After the House Administration Committee slashed his committee budget in 1968 by more than two hundred thousand dollars, Dawson moved to trim expenses by abolishing a watchdog subcommittee on freedom of information. The subcommittee's work had spotlighted black-market corruption and "land reform" graft in Vietnam in a study that the general accounting department called a milestone in congressional sleuthing.

Chairman Dawson was accused of trying to soft-peddle Johnson's war critics, but he stayed out of the papers and fought his battles behind the scenes. In May, Dawson asked for $250,000 more for his committee—or about enough to restore the cut. Two days later, the request was granted. "This is the amount we need to continue without substantial changes in our structure," Dawson said as he quietly scrapped his reorganization plan.

The Republicans ran a thirty-four-year-old schoolteacher, Janet Jennings, against Dawson in the fall of 1968. In ladylike fashion, she promised not to make age an issue, and the eighty-two-year-old incumbent drew more than 84 percent of the vote, having made almost no personal appearances during the campaign.

Age and poor health forced him to be less active in the Ninety-first Congress, where he was the eldest of the ancients presiding over vital committees. The other eight blacks in the House teamed up to fight the Nixon administration on Supreme Court appointments, equal employment policies, and other issues of prime concern to Negroes, but Dawson's name was not on the list when some of their statements were released.

At about the halfway mark of his fourteenth term, William L. Dawson, then the most powerful Negro member of the House of Representatives, announced it was time "to pass on the responsibilities of [his] high office" to a younger man.

His chosen successor was Alderman Ralph H. Metcalfe, who became the fourth black to represent Illinois' First Congressional District. On November 9, 1970, just six days after Metcalfe's election, Dawson died of cancer in a Chicago hospital.

The towering strength of the Negro who served longest in Congress was his adroitness as a politician, who kept voters in line with patronage and small favors. He learned the basics of practical politics and then added new dimensions to the game. In Chicago he helped make Richard Daley mayor. In Washington his recommendation for federal appointments carried great weight with Presidents. Allergic to the limelight, he worked behind the scenes for civil rights legislation and was rarely absent for a crucial vote on that issue. In contrast to Adam Clayton Powell, Jr.'s leaderless Harlem, his South Side was so well under control that Dawson, even though weakened by age and illness, was able to pass his seat in Congress along to his own protégé.

While Dawson was a capable committee chairman, he was criticized by black and white activists alike for not using his investigatory power to strike out against job discrimination by government suppliers and contractors. Yet even some of his critics may begin to miss him when they realize his departure deprived blacks of their only regular standing committee chairman.

Although Dawson was a capable committee chairman, he was criticized by black and white activists alike for not using his investigatory power to strike out against job discrimination by government suppliers and contractors. Yet even some of his critics missed him when they realized that his departure deprived blacks of their only regular standing-committee chairman.

William L. Dawson's accomplishments during a long career in Chicago and Washington proved that talented, ambitious, hard-working blacks can excel in the game of machine politics.

Adam Clayton Powell, Jr./New York

Adam Clayton Powell, Jr., strode into the pulpit of Harlem's Abyssinian Baptist Church in New York City, his black, red-trimmed robe flying open to show the fit, well-tailored figure beneath. He entered with the timing of a Broadway star as the last sounds of the choir's "Shall We Gather at the River" faded into the towering ceiling of the huge Gothic church.

Powell had been preaching for so long in the stone sanctuary built in 1923 by his father that he often drifted through his paces like an actor gone stale in a too familiar part. This Sunday, November 24, 1963, there was nothing perfunctory about the service. Thousands of sorrowful faces turned toward the congressman-minister as he talked quietly about the young President, who had fallen victim to an assassin's bullets in Dallas just two days before. Jack Kennedy, Powell said, had looked more like a college student than a congressman when he arrived in Washington in 1947. Grief, regret, frustration, were clearly reflected in the handsome face and rich voice of Powell as he spoke of his slain friend and political leader.

An aide beckoned to the minister, and he left the pulpit. The music resumed. He returned to announce he had just been informed that the man accused of assassinating the President had himself been murdered in Dallas while being transferred from one jail to another. "There doesn't seem to be anything left to say except let us pray."

In happier times the measure of Powell's influence was reflected when John F. Kennedy and his entourage would arrive in New York City for an election rally. The stage teemed with dignitaries waiting to share the spotlight with the Massachusetts senator who wanted to be President. As the TV cameras zoomed in, one of the first people Kennedy moved forward to greet was New York's only Negro congressman. Powell, who stumped ten states for Kennedy in 1960 and drew 74 percent of the vote in his own Eighteenth Congressional District in New York, made an important contribution to JFK's narrow victory over Republican Richard M. Nixon.

Early in January 1961 some sixteen hundred people, including eleven representatives and two Cabinet members, attended a gala fund-raising dinner at the Abyssinian Baptist Church for the pastor. Greetings came from Mrs. Eleanor Roosevelt, the former First Lady, whom the press had promoted to "first lady of the world." Kennedy sent congratulations to Powell as the new chairman of the House Education and Labor Committee.

"I am what I am because of the Abyssinian Church . . ." Powell said. "The church is my first love. No individual, no honor, no group could ever come between the membership and me." Yet on occasion he had given notice of his resignation. The church, which seats two thousand but had a record membership of thirteen thousand, was a focal point in Powell's life from childhood onward. He was born on November 29, 1908, in New Haven, Connecticut, the same month that his father, Adam Clayton Powell, Sr., a native of Virginia, was called to be pastor of the hundred-year-old church, then in midtown New York on Fortieth Street, between Seventh and Eighth avenues. Adam junior was introduced to the congregation as a six-month-old baby along with his ten-year-old sister, Blanche.

The second Adam Powell was understandably proud of his family. He characterized his father as a radical and prophet, while describing himself as a radical and fighter. The elder Powell, who died in 1953, eight years after his wife, was attracted to the black-and-proud philosophy of Marcus Garvey, who, he said, was the only man he ever knew who made light-complexioned Negroes ashamed of their color. The Powell ancestry is difficult to trace, as is that of most descendants of slaves, but theirs is a well-mixed family. Adam Powell, Jr., spoke in his sermons of his vivid childhood memory of the letter *P* imprinted on the flesh of his grandfather's back where he had been branded as a runaway slave.

Young Powell finished public high school and entered the College of the City of New York. Though he had been a good high school student, he flunked out in his second semester at college. It was the first downward swing for this talented but erratic six-footer. His scholarship improved after a transfer to Colgate University in Hamilton, New York. Here he was "exposed" as a Negro after an all-white fraternity made a routine check of his background, preparatory to initiating him as a member. He was not pledged.

He graduated from Colgate in 1930, having switched from medicine to the ministry, apparently through his father's influence. After graduation he traveled abroad for three months, then returned to

New York where he enrolled as a graduate student at Columbia University. Although only twenty-two, he also became business manager and assistant pastor of his father's church.

Founded in 1808, the Abyssinian Baptist Church had moved uptown to its sprawling new West 138th Street building on June 17, 1923. Powell recalled in a 1969 television interview that he preached his first sermon on Good Friday in 1929. Inspired by a cigarette advertising campaign plastered on billboards across the country, he put this challenge to the congregation: "If you'd walk a mile for a Camel, why not walk down this aisle for God?"

The new minister soon began to make news. In the spring of 1931 he led six thousand demonstrators to City Hall to protest the firing of five Negro doctors from Harlem Hospital. The doctors were reinstated. Two years later, on March 8, he married the dancer Isabel Washington. The bridegroom's father, though reportedly cool to the marriage, officiated at the wedding. Isabel Washington left show business for church work, and Powell adopted her son.

By 1935, the Abyssinian Church's pastor, Reverend Adam Clayton Powell, Sr., who had been successful in real estate as well as the ministry, was talking of retiring. By that year, too, the assistant pastor, Reverend Adam Clayton Powell, Jr., had begun writing "Soap Box," a weekly column published in the New York *Amsterdam News* under his own byline. He used the space to lash out against such men as Father Divine, the black preacher who claimed to be God, and William Randolph Hearst, the white newspaper publisher who sometimes tried to act like God.

The twenty-eight-year-old minister succeeded his seventy-two-year-old father in 1937. Weekday work was making the new pastor famous as he crusaded for a fairer share of available jobs for Negroes. He was among those the city turned to for consultation after the 1935 Harlem riots. He was co-chairman of the Greater New York Unemployment Coordinating Committee, a force to be reckoned with uptown and down. Uptown, the drive was for jobs for Negroes in the stores along 125th Street, the heart of the black business district. Some merchants signed an agreement with the group after a boycott, but this was a battle that had to be fought repeatedly. Threats of picketing put some token blacks on the payrolls of the Consolidated Edison Company and the New York Telephone Company. Pickets in front of the New York World's Fair offices on Fifth Avenue produced some nonjanitorial positions for blacks at the fair.

The most galling sight of all to ghetto residents was the procession of buses passing through Harlem and other Negro neighborhoods with never a black face at the wheel. The few jobs the transportation system had for Negroes were out of sight in garages. After a rally at the Abyssinian Baptist Church in the spring of 1940, they pledged not to ride on those white-chauffeured buses until the company hired at least two hundred black drivers and mechanics. Powell, as the representative of the unemployment committee, signed an agreement guaranteeing the hiring of 210 black drivers and mechanics—and blacks again became passengers.

Having proved himself an effective community leader, Powell decided to run for the city council in 1941 as an independent. He received sixty-four thousand votes, the third highest of six Manhattan winners, and thus became the city's first black councilman. The ambitious, energetic preacher's interests extended far beyond Harlem. He spoke out against the internment of Japanese-Americans during World War II, reasoning that they must have been imprisoned on account of their color since no such fate befell German-Americans or Italian-Americans, though the countries from which they had sprung had started World War II in Europe. He was distressed by color discrimination wherever it cropped up: in the armed services, in war production, and in the city-supported college which had no Negro faculty members. He criticized newspapers for identifying criminals by race, advocated a shorter work week for city employees (then on a six-day schedule), and urged action to find jobs for the city's unemployed.

Whatever the cause, if blacks were involved or if he thought they should be, his voice was likely to be heard. His critics noted that while he talked a great deal, he accomplished nothing concrete in the city council where every Powell-advanced measure was either emasculated or defeated. His explanation was that as a nonpartisan independent he got no cooperation from the party regulars. He did, however, focus on wrongs that needed righting, and eventually many of his suggestions were enacted.

People's Voice, ballyhooed as the biggest Negro tabloid in the world, went on the stands in February 1942 with Powell as editor and writer of the uninhibited "Soap Box" column. He was a sure bet to return to the city council, but Congress became his goal as soon as the reshuffling of congressional boundary lines carved out a district centered in Harlem. He told friends that a black man elected to that House seat could stay there for a lifetime if he wished.

The man who had entered political life as an independent attempted to freeze out effective competition by entering his name in all the major party primaries. This time there was a scramble to get on his bandwagon. His supporters included the New York City Democratic machine, the Republican party, the leftist American Labor party, the Congress of Industrial Organizations, and the tiny Communist party. Powell became the primary choice of the Democrats, the Republicans, and the American Laborites. There was not a ghost of opposition to him in the 1944 general election.

Shortly after this milestone, his wife went to court to sue for a separation. Isabel Washington Powell said that the congressman-elect was infatuated with a woman nightclub entertainer—and it was no secret that she was referring to svelte twenty-three-year-old singer-pianist Hazel Scott. Powell brought a counter-suit, charging that his wife was responsible for their having had no children and that she had objected to his entering politics. Powell married Miss Scott on August 1, 1945, a few days after his divorce from the former dancer became final. Adam Clayton Powell III was born on July 17, 1946. Their only child, whom they called "Skipper," went into broadcasting.

When Powell was sworn in, Mississippi's John Rankin refused to sit beside him. Powell said that the feeling was mutual and asked a House investigation of Rankin as a Fascist. Powell was to clash repeatedly with this Southern Democrat, who peppered his floor speeches with talk about "niggers."

The previously independent politician lined up with the Democrats, the majority party, when the Seventy-ninth Congress was organized in 1945, and was rewarded with a seat on the Education and Labor Committee. Characteristically striking out in all directions, he introduced antilynching and antipoll-tax measures and one of the thirteen fair employment practices bills presented that session. He pushed for an end to segregation in Washington schools, federal buildings, the congressional press section, and wherever else he encountered it.

He complained again that loyal nonwhite Japanese-Americans had been interned, and asserted that United States forces took pride in capturing as few Japanese prisoners as possible. This, he said, was in striking contrast to the handling of white German and Italian prisoners, who were brought to America and given better public transportation and living accommodations than black Americans. Powell was angered that the world heavyweight champion, Joe Louis, was made a sergeant in the army while former titleholders Gene Tunney, Jack Dempsey, and Jimmy Braddock all received officers' commissions.

His first legislative triumph came in February 1946 when he and John Folger of North Carolina collaborated on an amendment that assured free school lunches for black as well as white children. During his second term he offered bills to create a fair employment practices commission, to ban Jim Crow travel, and to curb lynching. He called for restraints on the free-wheeling House Un-American Activities Committee long before it became a fashionable target for liberals. In June 1948 his proposal to allow any person the right to refuse to serve in a segregated military unit was killed by a vote of seven to fifty-four. Powell's first defeat at the polls came in the Republican primary, which he lost by five hundred votes to another minister, but he carried the Democratic and American Labor party primaries and won in the general election.

Much of his energy and drive during his third term went into his fair employment bill to ban racial or religious bias by employers and unions. His measure finally got past the Rules Committee and was approved by the House 240 to 177 on February 23, 1950, but the Senate filibustered it to death. The sense of this legislation, which for years blacks and whites had labored for, eventually became law as a part of the Civil Rights Act of 1964.

Powell began what proved to be the first in a series of battles with the Internal Revenue Service in 1952. The IRS calculated he had underestimated his 1945 tax by $2,740. This claim was settled for $1,190. American folklore has it that once an IRS sleuth sniffs a trail, he keeps coming back to it. Certainly the finances of Powell and his staff were constantly watched and examined.

He was accused of accepting kickbacks from his staff, but nobody took him to court on this charge. His running dispute with the tax department did reach the courts, however. A three-count indictment in 1958 charged that he had underestimated Miss Scott's earnings and filed a false return for her in 1951, and that he had evaded taxes on their joint 1952 return through excessive deductions. In 1951 the Powells paid federal taxes of less than a thousand dollars on their income of seventy thousand dollars; in 1952, he figured they owed about seven hundred dollars on a gross of ninety thousand dollars.

Two of the three counts were dismissed by the judge when the case came to trial in 1960. The government attorney conceded that there was not enough evidence to prosecute the 1952 charge. The second count was dropped after defense attorney Edward Bennett Williams convinced the court that Miss Scott's 1951 income had been overestimated. An all-white jury could not agree on whether Powell was guilty on the remaining count, and the Justice Department decided there was not sufficient grounds to retry the case after the first suit ended in a hung jury. Five years later, Powell's lawyers negotiated an out-of-court settlement with the Internal Revenue Service on federal returns going back to 1949, and the congressman paid back taxes and penalties totaling $27,833.

The Harlem representative will assuredly be remembered in congressional annals for "the Powell amendment," which he attached to numerous bills after the 1954 Supreme Court decision outlawing public school segregation. His rider was designed to make the government color-blind when handing out federal funds. White Northern members of Congress had submitted similar proposals for years, but Powell used the strategy with less restraint.

"Immediately, all of the white press and the white liberals said this [Powell amendment] was against the national interest. . . ," Powell wrote in the September 1963 issue of *Esquire* magazine. "Here and there, an outstanding white person, such as Dr. Buell Gallagher, the president of the College of the City of New York, stood up in favor of the Powell amendment. But even such great liberals as the late Mrs. Eleanor Roosevelt and Mrs. Agnes Meyer [of the *Washington Post*] were against the Powell amendment. For them, the national interest of the United States was schools for children, even if they were segregated in violation of the Supreme Court decision. For me the national interest of the United States was obedience to the law of the land, plus the moral posture of the United States before the world."

In May 1955, Powell almost succeeded in attaching his amendment to a national guard authorization bill, but the Senate knocked it out. Two months later, the House passed his rider to deny federal aid to school construction funds in segregated districts, but the main bill died, and some said Powell had helped to kill it.

President Eisenhower was irritated by the New Yorker's persistence and twice told press conferences he opposed "extraneous" antisegregation riders on major legislation. Some accused Powell of insincerity in tacking on his amendment to so many pieces of legislation, but millions of blacks, who had been waiting a lifetime for full citizenship, saw nothing wrong with making Congress go on record on the issue of bias in public housing, hospital funds, student scholarships, and labor unions. The essence of the Powell amendment was incorporated into the sweeping Civil Rights Act of 1964 as Title Six, covering nondiscrimination in federally assisted programs.

Despite their differences, Powell supported Eisenhower in 1956 against Adlai E. Stevenson. Some people speculated that the Republicans had won Powell's endorsement in exchange for dropping the tax probe. Others believed Stevenson had carelessly offended Powell by not inviting the congressman to accompany him to a street rally in Harlem.

Powell was sufficiently adept at House infighting to keep his twelve years of committee seniority despite his support of the opposition party. Pointing out that the Dixiecrats, who deserted Truman in 1948, had not been disciplined, he defied the Democrats to behave differently toward a black man. This argument, however, did not scare the party regulars in New York City, where Tammany Hall leader Carmine DeSapio announced that the Democrats would not support Congressman Powell for renomination in 1958. The Democratic machine, attempting to purge the man who had been a "traitor" to the party, lined up behind Earl Brown, a Negro city councilman, instead. Powell charged racism; he said the Democrats were trying to block him from the chairmanship of the Education and Labor Committee. Brown was defeated by a margin of 3 to 1 in the primary. With the incumbent on both the Democratic and Republican lines in November, the 1958 election was yet another walkaway. In 1959, Powell was named head of a mining subcommittee and confounded his detractors by turning in a thoroughly sound performance. He also succeeded in repairing his pipelines to Tammany Hall.

Powell's election sweep of 1960 followed upon his second divorce and third marriage. The new Mrs. Powell was Yvette Flores Diago, granddaughter of a former Republican mayor of San Juan, Puerto Rico. He had met the brunette divorcée while campaigning in 1958 for W. Averell Harriman for governor of New York. She had become a worker at a salary of three thousand dollars annually in Powell's congressional office; as Mrs. Powell she was immediately rewarded with a raise of nearly ten thousand dollars.

Powell had the stamina to endure the system, racial insults and all, for eight terms before his turn came in 1961 for a taste of legislative power and glory. As the second-ranking Democrat on the Education and Labor Committee, Powell, who sat next to Chairman Graham Barden, of North Carolina, should have been called on first, according to protocol, during committee discussions and hearings; he should also have been given some of the choice subcommittee assignments. Barden treated his longtime colleague with disdain, did not ask his opinion, and denied him important subcommittee appointments. "I got down on my knees and thanked God" was Powell's reaction to the news of Barden's resignation in 1960.

Powell worked smoothly with the new Kennedy administration and helped put through one of its first major pieces of legislation—the $1.25 minimum wage law. Powell made no effort to attach his amendment to the President's education bill. The New Yorker was an astute, efficient chairman, though, as always, he was inclined to work in spurts. Almost everyone applauded Powell's handling of his biggest House assignment—even the Republican who would have had the job if his party were in control of Congress. He was a sharp contrast to Barden, an obstructionist who had kept civil rights and education legislation bottled up in committee. During Powell's first term as chairman, the committee hammered out eighteen bills which became law. Besides the minimum wage measure, these included a training program for practical nurses, student loans, and the Manpower and Development Training Act.

Chairman Powell remained in the good graces of the Establishment only fleetingly. In the summer of 1962 he went to Europe to gather material on "female labor relations" for his committee. As usual, Europe was besieged with American congressmen, many of them vacationing at government expense under the pretext of conducting "official business." Powell's junket might have gone unnoticed had he not selected as his aides two lovely young ladies. This made the dashing New Yorker much more conspicuous than most of his fellows, who traveled with their own wives or behaved discreetly otherwise. The press naturally was scandalized—or pretended to be scandalized—by his behavior. He was criticized in the Senate, and there was some talk of cutting his committee's budget and depriving him of the usual control committee chairmen have over finances. President Kennedy, however, praised his work, and the voters of his district continued to support him. That fall, he was reelected to Congress for the tenth time with 70 percent of the vote.

Always chided for absenteeism, Powell was never hypocritical enough to hide his boredom with routine committee work or his impatience with the snail's pace of the House of Representatives, but he has defended his record as congressman and chairman. A member should not, he said, be judged for his absentee record in terms of votes cast or quorum calls answered. For example, Senator John Williams of Delaware, who attacked him, had an "almost perfect voting record" in terms of being present, but that record included votes against public housing and all kinds of civil rights amendments. "Which is more important," Powell asked, "a 100 percent record of attendance with no production, or the production of thirty-nine pieces of legislation in eighteen months? The first duty of a chairman is to be a chairman and not a member."

Traditionally, black congressmen have been liberal on rights for women, doubtless understanding how it feels to be a second-class citizen in any respect. In the Eighty-eighth Congress, Powell's committee struck a blow for women with an equal-pay-for-equal-work law. Other measures it shaped included federal aid for higher education facilities, improved vocational training, amendments to the Manpower and Development Training Act; federal assistance to public libraries, and programs for physically handicapped and migrant workers.

Outside Congress the signs were not so good for Powell, who was about to begin a protracted, ill-fated courtroom drama. The congressman did not appear in the New York court in April 1963 to defend himself against the one million dollar libel suit filed by Esther James, a sixty-six-year-old domestic. She had sued after Powell branded her a "bag woman" for the police during a March 6, 1960, telecast in which he appeared as a last-minute substitute in New York for Senator Hubert Humphrey of Minnesota whose plane had been grounded in Washington.

Two gamblers testified that they had made regular payments to Mrs. James for police protection. According to press reports, she swore she was a police informer, but that she had never received money from anyone, either police or gamblers. From the outset, the congressman claimed his television remarks were merely an extension of statements he had previously made on the House floor, where members cannot be sued for libel. He contended that his congressional immunity should apply to the television remarks since the information was substantially the same. Besides, he said, it was his duty to keep his constituents informed.

The jury, which might have been influenced by the fact that the defendant did not show up to speak for himself, upheld Mrs. James, and Powell was ordered to pay $211,500 in damages; on appeal, this sum was later reduced by more than three fourths. Powell refused to pay while the litigation continued, and he ignored repeated summons to appear in court for an examination of his finances. As a result, he was cited for contempt of court late in 1963, and an order was issued for his arrest. For months he visited Harlem only to preach on Sunday, the one day of the week that the order could not be served. Later, after he was convicted of criminal contempt, he became liable to arrest on Sundays, too, and he stopped coming to New York altogether. Friends filled in for him in the church pulpit.

Notwithstanding the worry and distraction of the libel action, Powell continued to work well in Washington with the Southerner, Lyndon B. Johnson, who had succeeded to the Presidency after the assassination of Kennedy. The chairman of the House Education and Labor Committee was handed the first of the seventy-two pens Johnson used to sign the War on Poverty bill in August 1964. This was a token recognition of Powell's indispensable role in passing this measure designed to fight poverty by authorizing the Job Corps, the domestic Peace Corps, and various community action projects.

Powell spoke for Johnson to black audiences outside New York, where he was not subject to arrest, during the 1964 presidential campaign. On one occasion he sardonically told Negroes they should be able to stomach the tall Texan if he could. He had presented the case for Johnson more graciously and accurately in a sermon in mid-1960. Exhorting blacks to give up their prejudices, he said of Johnson, who was then considering running against John F. Kennedy for the presidential nomination, "Lyndon Johnson is the only leader that the U.S. Senate has had in eighty-two years, Republican or Democrat, to effect the passage of a civil rights bill, in 1957 and again in 1960.

"Mark you, Lyndon Johnson brought the 1957 bill to a vote despite the fact that the outstanding presidential candidate, Senator John F. Kennedy of Massachusetts, voted to send that bill back to Mississippi Senator Eastland's committee to be killed.

"Let us not forget when the Southerners issued the manifesto [castigating the Supreme Court for its 1954 school desegregation decision], it was Lyndon Johnson who led the vast majority of the members from Texas away from the Southern Manifesto and refused to sign it, thus proving where he stood."

Powell himself won handily that fall, though unable to campaign in his district because of his legal problems. After Johnson's landslide victory, Powell and his committee helped enact the President's Great Society program. The committee backed laws to provide for school construction in the United States and its territories, aid to the elderly, and an expanded Economic Opportunity Act. On the anniversary of Powell's fifth year as head of the committee, in March 1966, LBJ praised the chairman for his "brilliant record of accomplishment" in "reporting to the Congress on forty-nine pieces of bedrock legislation. And the passage of every one of these bills attests to your ability to get things done."

Powell's court fight with Mrs. James and his trips abroad had received saturation coverage in the press. In August 1966 the House Administration Committee began to look into reports that Mrs. Powell had said someone else was cashing the checks due her as a member of Powell's staff. Years before, Powell had defended putting his wife on the congressional staff payroll, a not uncommon practice in Congress. Though she lived in Puerto Rico, he insisted that from San Juan she could answer correspondence from his Puerto Rican constituents in Harlem.

According to *The New York Times*, Powell "was reported to have acknowledged" depositing his wife's pay checks, but he said he sent her money and paid her bills. For those congressmen who could not abide the Harlem representative anyway, this, in addition to his continual flaunting of the orders of the court in the libel suit, was too much. In September, most of the power of his committee was taken away from him as he lost control of the purse strings.

Powell spent much of this rough period fishing and sunning at his favorite retreat in the Bahamas—the island of Bimini. With him was the ex-beauty queen Corinne Huff, his companion since the early 1960's when she traveled with him to Europe as a committee worker. Meanwhile black leaders—even those who had never gotten along with him personally—came to his defense. They said efforts to take his committee chairmanship away or to unseat him would be viewed as an attack on all Negroes. Still avoiding the city because of his troubles with the law, he scored another impressive reelection victory, this time over three challengers.

In January 1967 the House Democratic caucus voted to depose him as Education and Labor Committee chairman as punishment for having taken private trips at public expense and for his contemptuous behavior toward the New York courts. Supporters of Powell, as well as some others who were not admirers, considered this tough attitude toward him inconsistent in view of Congressional tolerance toward Senator Thomas Dodd of Connecticut, who had been accused of using campaign contributions for his personal expenses without reporting the funds on his income tax form. "Lynching Northern style" is how Powell described the caucus decision.

"There is no one here who does not have a skeleton in his closet," Powell told the House, after it decided to name a special committee to consider his case. "I know and I know them by name. Gentlemen, my conscience is clean. . . . All I hope is that you have a good sleep tonight." After hearings, the committee recommended that Powell be censured, fined, and sent to the bottom of his committee's seniority list. However, the House as a whole went even further, voting on March 1 to exclude him from his seat. Nothing happened on the Dodd case until the newspapers finally shamed the Senate into investigating the matter. Dodd was formally censured but lost no privileges of seniority nor was he fined.

With Powell excluded from the House, New York's Eighteenth Congressional District had a vacancy to fill. A special election was held in April; the winner, with 86 percent of the vote, was Powell. He, however, did not return to the seat, preferring instead to concentrate on the court challenge to his exclusion.

His lawyers cleared away the legal impediments sufficiently for him to return to Harlem on March 24, 1968, to preach for the first time in eighteen months. The congressman came back after his lawyer promised to reinstate his appeal of the criminal contempt citation. Most of his exile had been spent on Bimini, and he soon returned there. In the spring he was ill twice, suffering a "mild seizure" during a speaking appearance at Durham, North Carolina, and undergoing "minor surgery in Miami." He was well enough, however, to deliver a memorial sermon for his father at the Abyssinian Baptist Church early in May.

Powell's critics hoped his woes were catching up with him at the polls. He won the Democratic primary over his former aide John Young by less than two thousand votes—a close race for Powell—but he was not worried. He spent August and September on the lecture circuit in the West and Midwest, reaping high fees and headlines. He did not publicly endorse Vice-President Hubert H. Humphrey when he ran for President in 1968 against Richard M. Nixon, because of Humphrey's support of Johnson's Vietnam policy. The sixty-year-old Powell's principal opponent in the November election was Republican Henry Hall, a free-lance writer. Hall said that Harlem needed a full-time congressman, not an "occasional overnight visitor from Bimini." But "Adam's people," as he often called them, remained loyal, electing him to the Ninety-first Congress by a margin of nearly thirty thousand votes. Convinced that Congress, the courts, and the Internal Revenue Service had treated him unfairly, his constituents did not desert him when his back was to the wall.

Powell was in the House early in January 1969 when Congress was organizing, having by then been elected three times to the seat from which he had been excluded two years earlier. Those who wanted him seated without further to-do and those who wanted him to remain barred compromised; he was fined twenty-five thousand dollars and admitted as a freshman.

His first day back he called for an investigation into the poverty program. Congress, however, was conducting its business at a slow rate, and he spent much time away from Washington. He went fishing in Bimini, and he visited college campuses, where he collected a fee of fifteen hundred to two thousand dollars for a forty-minute lecture. He claimed that he was traveling with "heat men" for protection. Speaking at Buffalo (New York) State College he asked law-and-order advocates to keep their values in proportion. It is not so much "someone snatching a purse, or a rapist, but it is [these] questions: It is who killed Malcolm X, President Kennedy and Senator Robert F. Kennedy? It is who will kill me and who will kill you tonight or tomorrow?"

His tribulations with the alleged "bag woman," who had reportedly collected fifty-six thousand dollars in damages, finally ended when the Appellate Division of the New York State Supreme Court ruled in April 1969 that there had been no grounds for two thirty-day "criminal contempt" sentences and substituted a $250 fine for civil contempt. This happy development for Powell made hardly a ripple in the press.

The best news Powell had had in years came on June 16 when the Supreme Court agreed with his lawyers that the House had violated the Constitution by refusing to seat a duly elected member who met the specified age, residency, and citizenship requirements. It was the first time the high court had ever ruled on the qualifications that Congress could require of its members.

Chief Justice Earl Warren wrote the majority opinion which skirted the matters of color bias, back pay, the twenty-five thousand dollar fine, lost seniority, and committee position. The soon-to-retire Chief Justice noted that the House had in the past barred properly elected members for being polygamists, Socialists, and Confederates, but he said the body had also refused to exclude controversial members on the ground that it lacked the power. While Congress could expel a member by a two-thirds vote, the Constitution did not invest it with a "discretionary power to deny membership by a majority vote."

Powell was uncharacteristically restrained and thoughtful at a Bimini news conference. "I am overwhelmingly grateful with humility that I have been able to fight through to this landmark decision that will be hard to revoke and will be good for 220 million American people," he told reporters. "From now on, America will know the Supreme Court is the place where you can get justice." Later he would decide whether to fight for the restoration of his chairmanship. For the moment he was happy to have been vindicated on the basic issue of his right to his seat.

Charles C. Diggs, Jr., a fellow black congressman from Michigan, introduced a resolution asking the House to restore Powell's seniority and give him his back pay. Powell's lawyers went to court to press his claim for salary and status, which the congressman said he was entitled to because the high court had ruled he never should have been unseated. Complicated by the fact that the offending Congress, the Ninetieth, no longer existed, this legal hassle remained unresolved.

Powell had fought fiercely to get his House seat back, but he was rarely in it. He could be seen more often on college platforms or television shows. "Part-time pay, part-time work," he rationalized. His former companion-in-exile, Miss Huff, married a young Bahamian. The New York *Amsterdam News* said most of what he owned was controlled by Miss Huff.

Like many another in the older generation, he was occasionally harpooned by the college set. Some Fordham University black students walked out in disgust at his lack of dignity, careless speaking style, and evasive flippancy. Before they left, one student forced him into a serious moment with a question on what he was doing in Congress to help blacks: "Congressman Powell, I mean just what are you doing now? My question is not what did you do ten years ago." Powell, suddenly grave and shaken, answered: "Nothing." After a pause he added: "No one can do anything constructive with the Nixon administration and its unholy alliance."

Powell was hospitalized for tests to determine the gravity of a lymph gland disorder late in 1969. Amid reports that he was seriously ill, his doctor said the congressman would resume his regular work schedule. Powell later told House colleagues that though the rumors about his having cancer were true, he would run for a thirteenth term. After campaigning in his usual disorganized, inefficient fashion, he lost the Democratic primary to Assemblyman Charles Rangel by 150 votes in June 1970 and filed to run as an independent, but he did not collect enough signatures to qualify as a candidate.

Weakened by spreading cancer, Powell had been dispirited since losing his chairmanship. Though technically still pastor at the Abyssinian Church, he retreated once more to Bimini. Hemorrhaging from prostate surgery, he was flown from the Bahamas to a Miami hospital. Sustained by life-preserving machines, he lingered for nearly a month before dying on April 4, 1972, at the age of sixty-three. His body was taken to New York to lie in state at the family church; there thousands of obscure and celebrated mourners filed past his casket. A saddened fellow representative, Charles C. Diggs, Jr., eulogized his comrade for the black caucus.

Powell's contribution to American government has not been fully appreciated. The congressman's outrageous life style, his cavalier attitude toward taxes, and his highly publicized court troubles have obscured his achievements as an early civil rights leader and a human rights legislator.

Regrettably, the House shadowed his reputation by an illegal action —refusing to seat him. Eventually the Supreme Court ruled that the House had acted unconstitutionally, but the Court, mindful of the separation of powers, did not consider the question of the restitution of his seniority or the payment of two years' back salary.

Adam Clayton Powell, Jr., shares the credit for statutes mandating color-blind allocation of most federal tax monies, equal employment policies, and equal pay for equal work standards. Enforcement of all these laws unfortunately has been lax since the Nixon Administration.

Few modern congressional chairmen surpassed the record of the playboy-preacher who in a brief period of authority left his imprint on an impressive amount of labor and educational legislation.

Charles C. Diggs, Jr./Michigan

Charles C. Diggs, Jr., a wealthy undertaker and an expert on African affairs, followed William L. Dawson and Adam Clayton Powell, Jr., as the third black to serve as chairman of a standing committee of the House of Representatives.

Since boyhood, Diggs, an only child, had hoped to go into politics like his father, who was a Michigan state senator as well as the owner of a mortuary, insurance, and ambulance service business. Born December 2, 1922, in Detroit to Charles Coles and Mayme Jones Diggs, Charles junior was a star high school debater and won an oratory championship at the University of Michigan, before transferring to Fisk University in Nashville.

Drafted into the Army Air Corps in 1943, he was a second lieutenant at Tuskegee Air Field in Alabama when World War II ended. Returning to civilian life in 1945, he graduated from Wayne State University and went to work in the House of Diggs, one of Michigan's largest funeral homes. Eventually he replaced his father as head of the family enterprise, a post he retained as a congressman.

The elder Diggs, who had first gone to the state senate in 1937, had served fifteen months in prison on two concurrent sentences of from three to five and from four to five years each for "legislative bribe conspiracies" in connection with his vote on a senate bill. Released on parole in March 1950, he was again elected. The Republican-controlled senate challenged the acceptability of Diggs and of another Democrat, Anthony Wilkowski, because of their prison records. It was an odd move; Wilkowski had already been twice reseated since being sentenced for election fraud.

Diggs senior argued his own case before the state senate committee. "It was well known by my constituents I was just out of prison," he said. Since some of those who opposed him were ostensibly worried because as a parolee he would enjoy legislative immunity from arrest during sessions, he offered to waive that right. "This," he charged, "has become a question of discrimination."

When the elder Diggs and Wilkowski were not reseated, Charles junior, then in his first year at the Detroit College of Law, entered the special Democratic primary. The twenty-nine-year-old, tall round-faced Diggs defended his father's record. He appealed to the voters to strike back at the former senator's enemies in Lansing. "Young Diggs Sure of Seat" was the headline after Charles junior won the primary by a vote of seventy-eight hundred to thirty-two hundred; Wilkowski, who vied for renomination from his district, lost. In the November election in the solidly Democratic district, Diggs swamped his Republican opponent, Robert Ward, a court bailiff.

As state senator, Diggs proved to be a self-effacing, soft-spoken, and hard-working supporter of the prolabor administration of Governor G. Mennen Williams. In 1953, Diggs ran for the Detroit city council, but he missed gaining a seat by five thousand votes and stayed on in the state legislature.

Party professionals hooted when on the basis of four years of experience in the state senate, he decided to challenge veteran Congressman George O'Brien in the Democratic primary. Diggs spoke wherever he could get an audience: in churches, union halls, and night clubs. His "Make Democracy Live" stickers were plastered on thousands of cars. Those who missed seeing his billboard or newspaper ads must have heard his radio commercials.

Still, O'Brien was so unimpressed he did not come home to campaign until late summer. As a result the young upstart won the primary in August 1954 by a margin of 2 to 1. The Republicans nominated Landon Knight, thirty-year-old son of John Knight, the publisher of the *Detroit Free Press*, to oppose him. Running on a something-for-all platform designed to appeal to a constituency 55 percent white, Diggs carried the election on November 2, again by 2 to 1.

The *Detroit News* found Michigan's first black congressman-elect "happy but calm" after his election by the biggest majority of any Democrat in the state that year. He hailed his election as a "victory for all the people. . . . This is a great victory for the Democratic party, and it also settles the deeper issues—the racial issue. This is proof that the voters of the Thirteenth District have reached maturity."

"The Battle Hymn of the Republic" poured forth from loudspeakers in the Union Station in Washington as hundreds of well-wishers arrived on the Diggs special from Detroit. In this January pilgrimage were Charles Diggs, Sr., and Congressman Diggs's wife, Juanita, and their three children, Alexis, Denise, and Charles III. The congressman greeted the delegation of friends and supporters with this reminder: "Joyous as the occasion is and important as it is to our race, we must none of us forget for one moment that I am here to represent all of the people of my district." Throughout the campaign, Diggs had stressed this point; now he said the returns demonstrated that he had not been elected by any one group. "What we have done in the Thirteenth District, where there is not a majority of nonwhites, has shown the world the American way of recognizing the essential dignity of all men and . . . of measuring a man on his merits alone."

Diggs joined New York City's Adam Clayton Powell, Jr., and other congressional liberals in seeking to build upon the momentous 1954 Supreme Court decision in the landmark case, *Brown* vs. *Board of Education.* The new Michigan member introduced legislation to establish a civil rights commission, to crack down on job bias, and to lower the voting age to eighteen. His measures were groundwork for the future, though none was passed by the Eighty-fourth Congress.

In September he went to Sumner, Mississippi, to attend the trial of two white men charged with the murder of Emmett Till—the fourteen-year-old boy who on a visit from Chicago, had allegedly whistled at a white woman, and then been killed by her husband and his half-brother. Diggs and the boy's mother, who expected an acquittal but did not want to be in the courtroom to hear it, left before the jury declared the men not guilty. The congressman charged that Tallahatchie County—in which Sumner is situated—did not have a single registered Negro voter although its population was 65 percent black. Mississippi's representation in Congress, he asserted, should be slashed in proportion to its disfranchisement of blacks.

Diggs wrote to President Dwight D. Eisenhower a month later asking him to call a special session of Congress to deal with civil rights. The session, Diggs suggested, should consider legislation to eliminate restrictions on voting in the South; to strengthen the power of the justice department to intervene wherever civil liberties were threatened; to desegregate interstate travel and to end bias in employment. Eisenhower did not grant the request.

The congressman then urged the President to use his State of the Union message to stress the human values at stake in the black man's push for first-class citizenship. Eisenhower in that January 1956 speech hailed the "progress our people have made in the field of civil rights," but he evaded the moral issue and declined to lend his personal support and prestige to help the movement.

Diggs discounted the gloom-and-doom prophecies of some Southerners who said that the Supreme Court's desegregation order would mean the end of public education. He believed federal appropriations should be denied any school that defied the court's order, and he supported Adam Clayton Powell's amendments to cut off funds. In 1956 as a member of the Democratic platform committee he fought vainly for forthright party endorsement of schools open to all. In a speech in Jackson, he said that "integration is as inevitable as the rising sun— even in Mississippi."

Reelected over a Republican, Diggs joined seventy-nine other Democrats in endorsing a far-reaching program for soil conservation, increased social security benefits, school construction, and aid to the United Nations. Since they represented only about a third of the Democrats in the House, the move had little practical effect.

Diggs advanced measures in his third term to help the needy at home and abroad, but Congress did not act on his bills to provide jobs for the unemployed and underemployed in economically depressed areas in the United States or to get surplus food out of American storehouses and into the mouths of the hungry throughout the world. In 1960 he was a member of a group that succeeded in tempering cuts in the Mutual Security Appropriations Bill for military and other aid to friendly countries.

This was the year the congressman, who had been divorced from his first wife, married Anna Johnston, an attorney. Their marriage produced two children but also ended in divorce. Later he married Janet Hall, a State Department officer.

Long before the riot that shook inner-city ghettos across the nation in the mid-1960's, Diggs, a successful businessman himself, called for more participation by blacks in business, particularly in their own communities, to help alleviate unemployment. In 1961 he organized and presided over a National Small Business Conference in Washington, to examine the dilemmas of struggling entrepreneurs and to seek ways to encourage Negro-owned companies. After Detroit's outbreak of burning and looting in 1967, he helped organize the Inner City Business Improvement Forum to assist in developing black businesses.

Diggs has impressively passed his biannual election contests. He defeated five contenders in 1960, and took nearly 86 percent of the vote in 1964, running against Republican and Socialist Worker party candidates. Four years later, the Republicans gave substantial financial and organizational help to a twenty-six-year-old militant, Eugene R. Beauregard, but Diggs was reelected with more than 80 percent of the vote. He won his ninth contest in 1970 over Fred W. Engel, Jr., by a count of 56,400 to 9,000.

With racial unrest growing in their own country, some American

Negroes turned to the newly emerging black republics of Africa as a source of pride in their own heritage. The continent where ancient black civilizations flourished has long been a subject of study for Diggs, first as a member and then as chairman of the Foreign Affairs African Subcommittee. In February 1969, he led a two-man mission to Nigeria for observation of that country's civil war. Their report endorsed America's recognition of the federal military government of Nigeria, and America's refusal to sell arms to either side. A negotiated settlement, they said, should include concessions and guarantees of security to the Ibos and other dissident tribes in Biafra. The United States followed this course until the conflict ended on January 12, 1970, with the surrender of the rebels.

Diggs used his subcommittee to press for a change in U.S. policy toward South Africa. He conducted hearings to show that while this country officially opposed the extreme racism of apartheid and supported the United Nations economic sanctions against South Africa, in reality governmental programs and private business assisted South Africa's economy. He successfully fought the move to authorize South African airline service between Johannesburg and New York.

Diggs, as chairman of a subcommittee of the Committee of the District of Columbia, chiseled away at the rules of that full committee, which functions as the legislative branch of predominantly black Washington. Conservative white Southerners, who show no signs of being moved by worsening crime and poverty in the nation's capital, dominate the parent committee. When social welfare legislation assignments are passed out, Diggs's subcommittee is usually bypassed, despite his repeated protests to the Democratic House leadership.

In 1969, in conjunction with Congressman William Fitts Ryan and Adam Clayton Powell, Jr.—both from New York City—he asked for a six-months suspension of the draft to give Congress an opportunity to reassess American policy in Southeast Asia. The lull, they thought, might help to persuade the Hanoi government that the United States really did want a negotiated settlement of the protracted war in Vietnam. Their resolution lay dormant as the Nixon administration continued military conscription under a lottery system.

Diggs was credited by Powell with helping in the behind-the-scenes maneuvering that readmitted the New Yorker to the House after a two-year lapse. Diggs introduced a resolution to restore Powell's seniority and fifty-five thousand dollars in back salary after the Supreme Court ruled his 1967 exclusion illegal. Diggs asked the House members to look beyond their personal feeling toward Powell and their pique at what many of them considered judicial intrusion into a strictly legislative affair.

"The highest court of our land has spoken decisively, and in my view, correctly," Diggs said in this proposal which took the House leadership by surprise. "The integrity of this body is now spotlighted. If the House follows the suggestions of those who would defy this edict, its reputation as the citadel of law and order and justice will be sorely tarnished." Shying away from further controversy over the Harlem congressman, the House did not consider the resolution.

In January 1971 at the beginning of the Ninety-second Congress, liberal Democrats tried to wrest the chairmanship of the District of Columbia Committee away from John L. McMillan, the South Carolina septuagenarian segregationist who has had more to say about the quality of life for residents of the 71 percent black capital than any other person for more than two decades. The revolt fell short by about thirty votes. Had it been successful, Diggs would have been a leading candidate to succeed McMillan.

The restrained, bespectacled Diggs lacks the charisma of Powell, the astuteness of Dawson, or the drive of Conyers, but Diggs was chosen chairman of the congressional black caucus in 1969 when the number of representatives went up to nine—partly, no doubt, because of his low profile. The caucus soon voted to replace him, first with Louis Stokes of Ohio, and then with Charles Rangel of New York as a step to a more active, visible policy for their expanding group.

Diggs himself was named to a more significant chairmanship in 1973 after McMillan's defeat moved Diggs up to the top of the Democratic seniority list for the District of Columbia Committee. The ranking black congressman has performed cautiously but efficiently as chairman. The self-government measure he guided through Congress permitted the residents of the nation's capital, for the first time in nearly a century, to elect their own mayor and city council, but left the budgetary controls in the hands of Congress.

Charles C. Diggs, Jr., a careful, dependable, second-generation politician, has prospered by lasting long enough to benefit from the congressional seniority system, but he's also capable of surprises—as witness his resignation from the American delegation to the United Nations in protest over this country's "stifling hypocrisy" toward black Africa.

Robert N. C. Nix / Pennsylvania

South Carolina, the state where the Civil War began, has produced more black congressmen than any other state. Robert N. C. Nix, a native of Orangeburg, has been a Pennsylvania representative since 1958 and is the seventh in the South Carolina-born line started a century ago by Joseph H. Rainey.

A successful criminal lawyer, Nix worked his way up through the ranks of the Democratic party. Before going to Congress, he was the perennial committee chairman who helped get out Philadelphia's substantial Negro vote. Suggested as a candidate for judge as early as 1937, he served as special deputy attorney general of Pennsylvania and made several unsuccessful bids for judgeships and the city council before capturing a House seat at the age of fifty-three.

Robert Nelson Cornelius Nix was born August 9, 1905, to Sylvia and Nelson Nix. His father, a former slave, earned a doctor's degree in mathematics and became dean of the faculty at South Carolina State College in Orangeburg. Robert Nix lived with relatives in New York City while attending Townsend Harris Hall High School, then went on to Lincoln University in Chester County, Pennsylvania, where he was captain of the football team as well as an A student. He opened a law office in Philadelphia in 1924, a year after graduating from the University of Pennsylvania Law School. Married to the former Ethel Lanier of Washington, he has one son, Robert Nix, Jr., who was the other Nix in the law firm of Nix and Nix until he resigned in January 1968 to become a Philadelphia judge.

With the backing of Representative William Green, Jr., Philadelphia leader of the Democratic party, the elder Nix ran in a special election to complete the unexpired term of Earl Chudoff in May 1958. He defeated Cecil Moore, a black Republican, by a vote of sixteen thousand to seventy-five hundred, despite the opposition of two influential Democrats—Mayor Richardson Dilworth and Senator Joseph

Clark. Though upset by the behavior of these men whom he had supported for years as a ward boss, Nix won the fall campaign for the regular term by a large margin.

Pennsylvania's lone black representative, a compact man of medium height, joined William L. Dawson, Adam Clayton Powell, Jr., and Charles C. Diggs, Jr., in Washington in June. He worked quietly as a member of the large contingent of liberal Democrats from Pennsylvania. This group meets frequently at breakfast or lunch to exchange views and to decide how to use their numbers to the greatest effect. Nix's early bills dealing with discrimination in the armed forces, hunger in underdeveloped countries, and unemployment in America were buried in committees, the usual fate of freshman-authored measures, but the voters liked him well enough to reelect him by an imposing sixty thousand majority.

By the time he ran for his third complete term, in 1962, the congressman had mended his political fences so well that he and Senator Clark, who had originally opposed him, campaigned for each other. Nix's reapportioned district retained only three of its old wards. His opponent, Arthur Thomas, a lawyer, said the issues were "bossism and not enough civil rights legislation by Bob Nix." Thomas told the voters that if they wanted to rid the city of graft and corruption, they would have to free Philadelphia from the clutches of the Democratic "bosses" and allow the two-party system to function. "Bob Nix," Thomas charged, "votes the way Bill Green tells him to vote."

Nix refused to talk about his opponent or reply directly to his accusations. Instead, he dwelt on the advances Negroes had made under the administration of John F. Kennedy, which he said had received his vote 98 percent of the time. The congressman was worried about unemployment—particularly of poorly educated blacks. "This is the richest and most technically advanced country in the world," he said. "Every citizen should enjoy the opportunity to make a living consistent with his abilities and skills." The people that fall gave him a mandate of 2 to 1 over Thomas.

In the new Congress, Nix introduced a bill to reduce any state's representation in the House in the same proportion to which qualified adults were not allowed to vote. The Judiciary Committee blocked this effort to enforce the Fourteenth Amendment.

As the day drew near for Martin Luther King, Jr.'s civil rights march on Washington in the summer of 1963, Congress, the President, and the capital police became increasingly jittery. They feared the gathering of two hundred thousand freedom marchers might turn into a riot, with resultant loss of life and property. To reassure his colleagues in the House, Nix reminded them that the demonstration was completely in the American tradition. The first such mass appeal was staged in Philadelphia in 1783, he said, by several hundred Revolutionary War veterans, seeking long overdue military pay. The response of Congress then had been to lock its doors for protection. Other predecessors of Dr. King's marchers had included the jobless petitioning for work, women seeking the ballot, and blacks pressing for first-class citizenship. In each case, Nix continued, critics had predicted violence and lawlessness, and had frequently sought to link the protest to Communism. Apprehensions continued, but many congressmen stayed around to talk with the marchers, who turned out to be peaceful and disciplined, though determined to turn the country around in its treatment of blacks.

"Ladies and gentlemen of the House of Representatives, I appeal to you to examine your attitudes toward the August 28 march in terms of the total cause of which that event is only a symbol. I urge you to take into consideration the fact that all men's civil and personal rights are of paramount importance at present; that they are not . . . subject to being rationed at the will of some so-called master group. I ask you to accept the inevitable; not because it is inevitable . . . but because it is right and no other course will protect the Negro or the Nation's future."

Nix's rivals could not fault him for lack of legislative action on civil rights in 1964. He went home to campaign that year after helping to pass a measure covering access to public accommodations, school desegregation, allocation of federal funds, and job bias. It was a joyful election year for Democrats, and Lyndon B. Johnson's landslide election boosted Nix to victory by a vote of 125,000 to 30,000.

Johnson's drive to extend full citizenship rights to blacks continued in the Eighty-ninth Congress, with voting as a priority item. During the House debate, Nix refuted the arguments of South Carolinians who insisted that their state already had a free and open voting registration process. This was a myth, said Nix, citing the use of literacy tests (in a state where 61 percent of blacks over twenty-five were school dropouts), short registration hours, and intimidation to reduce Negro registration in South Carolina. The Voting Rights Act of 1965 suspended literacy tests and other restrictive devices and provided federal examiners to supervise registrations and elections in states with a history of disfranchising minority-group citizens.

Nix faced a more serious challenge than usual at the polls in 1966, but a primary bout with three aspirants left him unscathed. Then came reports that the Republicans were prepared to spend half a million dollars to beat him; his was one of the one hundred districts pinpointed for capture. Big names, including Senate Minority Leader

Everett Dirksen of Illinois, lined up behind his opponent, attorney Herbert Cain, Jr. The congressional boundaries had been redrawn again, with some wealthy white neighborhoods added to the Nix territory. Cain's attack focused on the incumbent's "nonvoting" record on such matters as a proposed investigation of the Ku Klux Klan. Nix had answered only 60 percent of the roll calls that term, but his winning margin for reelection was a healthy twenty-five thousand.

Summing up his congressional accomplishments on November 19, 1966, in the first of a series of byline columns in the *Philadelphia Tribune*, the country's oldest continuously published Negro newspaper, Nix said he had sponsored legislation in a variety of areas ranging from urban renewal and mass transportation to disarmament and food for underdeveloped areas. He had backed Medicare, aid to education, and public works. According to the *Tribune*, Nix had supported the liberal position 100 percent of the time in the Eighty-ninth Congress.

Nix was touched, albeit faintly, by the hint of scandal in the spring of 1967. A survey in the *Philadelphia Bulletin* reported that nearly 10 percent of the House members had hired their own kin. Among the congressional relatives on the payroll was Robert Nix, Jr., an employee in his father's office for two and one-half years, during which time he had had eight raises in pay, bringing his salary up to twenty thousand dollars a year. Philadelphia reporters who tried to query young Nix about what he did to earn his salary as a congressional staffer found the well-to-do lawyer too busy in court to be interviewed.

Congress had started its session in 1967 by depriving Powell of first his committee chairmanship and then his House seat. Nix battled behind the scenes for his colleague but did not take part in the floor debate. Later, Nix advanced an interesting theory as to why the House had barred the New Yorker: "I think many of the people opposed to Adam are opposed to Adam's morals, and these moral people are really just upset because they see Adam surrounded by all those beautiful women and they wish they were there," Nix was quoted in the *Bulletin*. "It is absolutely true that they hate somebody who has what they'd like to have and can't."

The Pennsylvania representative said congressmen had been inundated with mail from irate citizens demanding that Powell be thrown out; "vitriolic, denunciatory" news reports casting Powell "as the sole iconoclast in an otherwise stable Congress" had brought on the outcry, Nix charged. By July, Nix thought public opinion had shifted; he asked Congress to admit it had never given the New Yorker a fair hearing and to correct the error.

The man who had expressed confidence in the Freedom Marchers a few years earlier was apprehensive himself that the Poor People's Campaign of the Southern Christian Leadership Conference might spark violence. In mid-1968 he advised the Reverend Ralph Abernathy, who had assumed the SCLC presidency after Dr. Martin Luther King's murder on April 4, 1968, to dismantle Resurrection City, which had been set up on public grounds in Washington, and leave only a small group behind to lobby for the organization's food and jobs program. Abernathy replied that the poor people would not leave until Nix and other congressmen like him got the message and did something for them. However, the demonstration ended shortly afterward on assurances from the agriculture department and other agencies that improvements would be forthcoming.

The sixty-three-year-old Nix had no primary opposition for his sixth full term in 1968. His Republican challenger, Herbert McMaster, a thirty-five-year-old Korean War veteran and a state tax supervisor, started door-to-door canvassing in May. Busy in Washington, Nix did not get into the field until late October.

McMaster attacked his opponent for missing Monday and Friday roll-call votes. The Republican hopeful also said his private surveys showed only 11 percent of those in the district knew who their congressman was and that this was a clear indication that Nix was out of touch with his constituents—an allegation that Nix ridiculed. He was in his main Philadelphia office every Saturday morning with more than a hundred people waiting to see him, the congressman replied, and on other days his two district offices were staffed with aides who knew the community and its problems. The Nix strategy functioned as smoothly as usual in November, when he drew a hundred thousand votes to forty-two thousand for McMaster.

The Postal Operations subcommittee he has headed since 1967 held hearings in 1969 and 1970 on bills to prohibit the mailing of unsolicited credit cards. Nix wanted Congress to regulate the indiscriminate distribution of the cards, which he said was contributing to inflation, lining the pockets of mailbox thieves, and inducing people to live beyond their means at 18 percent interest. He was appalled when Federal Reserve Board Chairman William McChesney Martin defended the practice as a profitable way for banks to obtain new customers. Nix asked why the same board that hiked interest rates to halt inflation also fought for credit cards to stimulate impulse buying when credit already was overextended to 1929 levels. His committee reported out a bill limiting the postal distribution of unsolicited cards to registered mail, but Congress passed a stronger measure banning the mailing of such cards to nonsubscribers "except in response to a request or application" and the President signed it into law.

Nix's workload increased in the Ninety-first Congress when he was given a second subcommittee chairmanship, covering foreign economic policy, and was named to a select crime committee. He endorsed the crime committee's report calling for a relaxation of the laws against marijuana smoking while studies were being made to find out whether the teen-agers' favorite relaxant was more harmful than their fathers' cocktails. He backed legislation to set production quotas and tighten distribution controls on amphetamines in an effort to limit the use of the so-called pep pills to the treatment of illness. A comprehensive drug-abuse law finally was enacted in October 1970. It lowered the first-offense penalty for the possession of marijuana or other drugs, if acquired illegally, to a maximum of one year, while stiffening the punishment for peddlers. No curbs were placed on the manufacture of amphetamines.

Nix was named to his ninth term in November 1974 over Republican James W. Woods, Jr., by a count of 75,000 to 26,300. The deaths of Dawson and Powell had placed him second in seniority among the black congressmen.

An energetic subcommittee chairman, Nix lost one chairmanship when the House began to divide the committee assignments more equitably. He retained the international economic policy post and mounted a schedule of wide-ranging investigations into the operations of multi-national corporations. The committee considered whether giant concerns were taking sorely needed jobs out of America, whether the conglomerates were avoiding taxes, and whether their payment of illegal bribes to foreign government officials was escalating the arms race.

The Nix hearings in 1975 revealed that the Internal Revenue Service was delving into reports that 111 American companies had illegally deducted as business expenses domestic political contributions and/or bribes paid overseas to obtain contracts. Nix urged the IRS to crack down and to make sure the companies were assessed for their fair share of taxes.

Nix's probe, held contemporaneously with a similar one in the Senate, also dramatized the prevalence of bribes, kickbacks, and payoffs in foreign trade. Significantly, a press release from Lockheed Aircraft Corporation acknowledging their payment or commitments to pay more than $200,000,000 in five years to consultants on foreign accounts came a day after Nix wrote the Department of Defense asking for declassification of a list of sample fees given to foreign agents by American companies.

In the post-Watergate era, with Congress and the public having been made more conscious of questions of morality in politics and business, Robert N. C. Nix, the dedicated, publicity-shy Philadelphia lawyer-congressman, and his subcommittee had found an issue that put them in the news for a brief period.

Augustus F. Hawkins/California

A diligent congressional champion for equal rights for women and minorities, Augustus F. Hawkins, first won the seat for California's Twenty-first District in 1962 with a smashing victory—70,500 to 12,000—over his Republican opponent. Before going to the House, the light-complexioned native of the state of Louisiana had represented a highly cosmopolitan assortment of Orientals, Mexican-Americans, blacks, and whites in the California state assembly for twenty-eight years.

Augustus Freeman Hawkins was born on August 31, 1907, in Shreveport, Louisiana, to Nyanza and Hattie Freeman Hawkins. His English-born paternal grandfather was an African explorer. Gus, the youngest of five children, was ten by the time Nyanza Hawkins sold his pharmacy business and moved to Los Angeles. The boy worked as a soda jerk in a drugstore and as a part-time postal clerk while attending high school. He graduated in 1931 from the University of California at Los Angeles with an A.B. degree in economics.

Among his classmates was Ralph Bunche, later undersecretary for Special Political Affairs at the United Nations. At UCLA, Hawkins had a work scholarship as janitor in the girls' gym—a much sought-after assignment for any young man with a well-developed sense of girl-watching, while Bunche had to content himself with sizing up professors as he helped to clean the administration building. Hawkins teased his friend Bunche about those days, suggesting that had their roles been reversed, Bunche might have become the politician and he, Hawkins, the diplomat.

Hawkins had to abandon his plan to be a civil engineer after graduation because his family's finances were depleted by the depression. Instead, he went into business for himself while attending the University of Southern California's Institute of Government. His first venture, a partnership in the automobile appliance field, quickly failed. He and his brother Edward then set up a real estate agency. This was more successful, but he already was leaning toward politics, his preferred vocation.

Inspired by the gubernatorial candidacy of Upton Sinclair and his "end poverty in California" theme, Hawkins worked hard in the writer's unsuccessful campaign. The results were more to his liking when he assisted in getting out the vote for a victorious Franklin D. Roosevelt in the 1932 presidential election.

Convinced he was well enough known to attract some votes himself, Hawkins ran for the California state assembly seat from the Sixty-second District in 1934. He won over Frederick Roberts, a Negro Republican, who had been in office for sixteen years. This, Hawkins told the voters, was too long. During the race Hawkins said that if he were elected, he would see that the street-car fare was cut from ten to five cents, a pledge he could not deliver. Instead of dropping, the fare rose. "This," he said later, "taught me a valuable lesson—never be irresponsible with campaign promises."

Loren Miller, publisher of the *California Eagle,* called the five-foot-five, newly elected assemblyman a "political accident." He said Hawkins had slipped into the legislature by default because Roberts had carelessly neglected to crossfile—that is, to try for the primary backing of both major parties—thereby leaving the Democratic nomination to Hawkins. There was nothing accidental about what followed. Hawkins settled in at the capitol at Sacramento and chalked up a longevity record far greater than that of the man he had ousted. The Democrat kept his assembly seat for nearly three decades, before leaving for Washington. One of the powers in the state capital, he was known as "unofficial dean" of the assembly.

Besides serving on the joint committee on legislative organization, he chaired committees for unemployment, labor and capital, public utilities, and rules. Working without bombast or publicity, he wrote laws covering job training, day-care centers for farm workers, workmen's compensation for maids and housekeepers, fair housing, and slum clearance. Hundreds of California statutes bear his name as author or coauthor. One of the peaks of his career came in 1959 when the legislature finally passed California's Fair Employment Practices Act, a measure he had been trying to push through since 1954.

His wife was an invaluable assistant. He met Pegga Adeline Smith, a Marysville, California, ranch girl, who wanted to be a singer, while he was a novice lawmaker. The romance started slowly. It was three years before the erect, brown-eyed realtor and legislator asked her to go out with him, and a year of dating before, as Mrs. Hawkins put it, "one day, in his unique, matter-of-fact way, he just asked me to live with him—very legitimately, of course." They were married in 1941.

Mrs. Hawkins, who died in August 1966, was "fascinated" by politics and attended the legislature's sessions regularly. She steadfastly defended her husband's profession from people who considered politics disreputable and politicians selfish manipulators out to enrich themselves. "When Gus entered politics," she said, "he only made a hundred dollars a month. It took wealthy or very dedicated people, and Gus was never wealthy. Besides, no man can hold office unless the people want him there." Mrs. Hawkins was a key member of her husband's precinct team. "When people congratulate me on my husband's political victories," she told an *Ebony* magazine reporter, "I congratulate them for having picked such a good candidate. Gus is a heck of a good politician. He has a very astute mind."

After losing the 1962 congressional election to Hawkins, his Republican opponent charged that the California Democratic party leaders had shunted Hawkins to Washington in order to keep a Negro out of the Speaker's seat in Sacramento. The mild-mannered congressman-elect was not ruffled by this accusation. "I ran for Congress because many of the issues with which I am deeply concerned, such as Medicare and low-cost housing, transcend to the national level. I felt that as a congressman I could do a more effective job than in the assembly."

A shoeshine man in his district predicted as Hawkins left for Washington: "He won't be popping off much like [Adam] Powell, but you can bet your boots that Gus will deliver the goods." The prediction proved accurate. Hawkins works quietly and deliberately, and generally shuns publicity. When the congressional schedule allows, he relaxes by fishing or doing odd jobs around the house and yard. He is an avid Los Angeles Dodgers fan and tries to catch at least one home game each baseball season. He reads constantly to keep up on political developments.

Though not given to banging his own drum, the Los Angeles representative is anything but silent on issues that concern him. He has blasted the country's emphasis on military supremacy. He has told educators they must be doing something radically wrong, judging by the products they are turning out. He has lashed out at those who balance budgets by increasing the taxes of the poor and middle classes instead of reforming the tax system. He has spoken for what he calls the "silent minority," black soldiers fighting in a Vietnam war for the freedoms denied them at home. This nondramatic man constantly warns that there will be more riots unless the inhabitants of the ghettos are helped out of the poverty in which they are trapped. And if more riots come, he says that the blame will rest with the legislators and other decision-makers who have ignored the plight of poor people in a rich country.

Hawkins, whose district includes Watts, the black ghetto which exploded in an orgy of burning and looting in 1965, informed Senate investigators two years later that conditions in the area had worsened, not improved, since the riot. He said that programs set up under the Economic Opportunity Act had been delayed by squabbling among public officials and had then been taken over by the city of Los Angeles, with no provisions made for real community participation on the part of the poor.

"Let us face head-on the fact that sporadic violence in our slum ghettos can be expected for at least another decade for we are limited in providing solutions by the economic and ideological limits fixed by those jealous of giving up power or spending money on such intangibles as race relations, preventive programs and a better society," Hawkins warned the Senate Manpower and Poverty Subcommittee at its hearings on Los Angeles on May 12, 1967.

"It is not that we lack the capacity to avoid a decade of disorders but the will—the will to redirect such institutions as our schools, to provide saturation programs to overcome long-existing deficiencies, and to admit the disadvantaged into the mainstreams of American society. Many public agencies don't even want the poor involved in community action for their own benefit out of insatiable fear the poor may gain power to change conditions, including perhaps some public officials.

"The threat of violence can become worse or the outlook can be greatly ameliorated. And we should not blame the victims of poverty if those who control the choice make the wrong decisions."

Hawkins said the situation was bound to deteriorate if Congress permitted the poverty programs to be turned over to states and local communities without adequate safeguards for constitutional rights, the achievement of stated national objectives, and meaningful participation by the poor. Such federal programs as urban renewal, he charged, had already been subverted and used against the disadvantaged.

An extremely articulate man, who usually speaks from notes rather than from complete, prepared texts, Hawkins described some of the errors that blacks should guard against in an address to a dental group in July 1967: "With little support in fact we throw superlatives around like beer cans at a boilermaker's picnic. To us our hero is the greatest; someone else proudly boasts of having or being the only Negro in some office, job or achievement; another so-and-so takes all the credit because he is loudest and after a time we believe him.

"Actually what we have is a handful of responsible leaders and organizations struggling desperately to carry the load of 20,000,000 people as against a conglomeration of publicity seekers."

As an example of one of those carrying the load, he cited Clarence Mitchell, Jr., director of the Washington office of the National Association for the Advancement of Colored People, who managed to accomplish a great deal with a limited budget and staff.

Hawkins thought "it is our fault" for placing more value on dramatics and senseless action than on stability, character, and clarity of objectives. He asked: "How many of you who resent whites telling 'darky' stories laugh at Negroes who make anti-Semitic cracks about 'those Jews'?

"And how many of you, when some rip-snorting crank talks about killing 'whitey' smile with a sense of smug revenge or indifference," not mindful of what this does to the emotionally-charged black or white person?

Hawkins criticized Negroes with status and houses in fancy neighborhoods for not being sufficiently concerned about the struggle of the masses still bogged down in poverty during a time of unprecedented prosperity for the nation. Unless the trend was reversed, he feared the unemployment rate for nonwhites might be five times that of the country as a whole by 1975, with blacks relegated to the sidelines as were the American Indians and Japanese-Americans in earlier years.

"The political power in this nation resides heavily in about ninety Southern congressmen whose votes swing back and forth between the Democratic and Republican parties. These congressmen seldom represent the true interests of their districts not only in race relations but on such matters as foreign affairs, urban and farm problems, poverty and industrial relations. If anyone should vote for an anti-poverty program, it should be these congressmen from Alabama, Mississippi, etc., for they represent the poorest of the poor as well as the states with the least ability to provide schools and job opportunities."

Hawkins thought blacks, properly organized and aroused, could offset these nonrepresentative representatives, but he emphasized that this was something they would have to do themselves. "While disfranchisement is a barrier to this potential in many areas of the country, (and even this is changing) it is also true that our own apathy prevents a forceful exercise of our political strength. Several million Negroes are either unregistered or fail to vote in such places as New York, Philadelphia, Los Angeles, Cleveland, Oakland, and as a result, instead of at least twenty-five Negroes in Congress, we have only five, an average of one for each decade in this century."

The political punch of blacks should not be confined to electing other Negroes to office, "as desirable as this may be, or to an exclusive Negro bloc," but used effectively to bring about essential reforms in a pluralistic society. "The issues of our times do not necessarily separate neatly into black versus white. There is not a solidarity among whites anymore than Negroes constitute an unwavering phalanx."

Hawkins suggested in a House speech in April 1969 that one had only to look critically at the defense department to understand the frustrations of much of the populace. "Our men fight and die for the preservation of . . . 'liberty and the pursuit of happiness.' Yet these are denied in too many instances. . . . How can there be acceptance of the stated objectives of our national policy if the Department of Defense, without good reason, grants contracts to textile mills which violate the Federal law pertaining to civil rights—the right to equal opportunity in employment? This action, the flouting of equal employment laws and regulations, demonstrates that 'race relations' has low priority among the considerations which lead to policy in defense matters."

The California congressman asked for a change in the philosophy of the department "which spends most of our money but provides the least evidence that it has a social responsibility." He wrote Defense Secretary Melvin R. Laird requesting an up-to-date count on the number of Negro civilians in policy-making jobs in his department. Hawkins later reported that there were only three blacks in 523 supergrade positions at the Pentagon, and they were not in decision-making areas.

Hawkins did make headlines in July 1970 after he and William R. Anderson, a Tennessee representative, protested the "savage mistreatment" of the men, women, and children they had found hidden away in "tiger-cage" cells in a secret section of the Con Son prison in South Vietnam. They released their own illustrated minority report after the House select committee issued what Hawkins called a "whitewash" and "snowjob" account of the trip, which ignored the horrors he, Anderson, and a committee aide, Thomas R. Harkin, had discovered on their own.

The two congressmen asked President Nixon to demand immediate corrective action from the South Vietnam government. Within a week *The New York Times* said that more than five hundred Con Son prisoners had been flown on American military planes to Saigon for release. Shortly afterward, the South Vietnam government announced it had suspended the use of the small concrete disciplinary cells while they were being "overhauled to provide adequate hygienic facilities."

Third ranking in length of service among the black members, Hawkins cosponsored and guided numerous laws through Congress during twelve years on the Education and Labor Committee. As chairman of its equal opportunity subcommittee, he coauthored the Legal Services

Act to provide legal assistance for the poor and the Juvenile Justice and Delinquency Prevention Act of 1974. Although teen-agers now account for 45 percent of serious crime in America, this national program to halt the rise of youth violence has not been implemented by the Ford Administration.

His subcommittee held hearings to pressure government and industry to live up to the racial and sexual antibias strictures of the 1964 Civil Rights Act and subsequent equal employment opportunity laws. Results have been mixed; the agencies charged with enforcement have been lax.

Hawkins publicized the backlog of 100,000 complaints piled up at the Equal Employment Opportunity Commission and supported class action job discrimination complaints against the United States Civil Service Commission. His concern mounted in 1975 when a severe recession and rising unemployment "practically wiped out the gains of the past few years as minorities and women bore a disproportionate burden of unemployment."

Augustus Hawkins, a tireless worker himself, is convinced that solving the country's economic dilemma is the only way to deal with the problems of blacks. His primary goal for the future is passage of his full employment bill guaranteeing a useful job to every American who wants to work. His nonutopian proposal, which the Library of Congress estimated could be launched for $8.1 billion, has top priority on the legislative agenda of the congressional black caucus.

Edward W. Brooke/Massachusetts

Hiram R. Revels was seated by the United States Senate in February 1870 after days of legislative stalling. Blanche K. Bruce was accepted in 1875 with no racial unpleasantness but with no prospects for tenure. Edward W. Brooke, the third black senator, and the first to be elected directly by the people rather than by a legislature, was sworn in routinely ninety-two years later, and his chances for survival were strictly up to him.

This self-possessed six-footer blended in immediately with other liberal-moderate Republicans. From the outset he said that he did not intend to be a national black leader but to concentrate on his job as a Massachusetts senator. The skilled, cautious legislator apparently does not think of himself in racial terms and prefers that others do not. He sympathized with John F. Kennedy for being stereotyped as the first Roman Catholic President. When Brooke wearied of talk of the numerous firsts he had achieved for his race, he reminded people he was also a Protestant who had won in a Catholic state and a Republican who had triumphed in a Democratic one.

The boy who would grow up to be the first black senator since reconstruction was born on October 26, 1919, in Washington, D.C., to Edward William and Helen Seldon Brooke. His parents named him Edward William after his father and grandfather, but the senator omits the third when signing his name. His father was a lawyer with the Veterans Administration for fifty years. The family frequently vacationed in Virginia, where the first Edward Brooke's father had been a slave. His grandparents told Edward III that he was descended from Thomas Jefferson, third President of the United States, and related to Rupert Brooke, the British poet.

Young Ed Brooke attended Dunbar High School and received his bachelor of science degree from Howard University, his father's alma mater, in 1941. Hours after the Japanese attacked Pearl Harbor on

December 7 of that same year, ROTC-trained Second Lieutenant Brooke was called to active duty. Assigned to the all-Negro 366th Infantry Regiment, he served in Italy. Part of his work was behind the enemy lines as liaison officer with the Italian partisans. With his dark curly hair and light skin, Brooke, who had learned Italian in a hurry, masqueraded as a native of the country under the code name of Captain Carlo.

Brooke and his men served in the Apennine Mountains as a part of General Mark Clark's Fifth Army. They undoubtedly heard the widely circulated rumors that black units were not performing effectively in combat. "We were fighting hard and fighting well," Brooke recalled in his book *The Challenge of Change*. "Our morale was high in spite of heavy casualties. And yet there was an undercurrent of resentment in the regiment. . . . In a hundred subtle and not-so-subtle ways, we were treated as second-class soldiers.

"Our soldiers (first class by any definition) asked, 'Why are *we* fighting this war? It's supposed to be a war against Nazism—against racism and for democracy. Well, what about *us?* Why are black men fighting a white man's war? What's all this double talk about democracy?'" Brooke told his men to fight on until the war was over and then to challenge racial injustices at home.

After Germany surrendered on May 7, 1945, Brooke had free time as he waited to be sent back to America. While relaxing on a beach near Naples, he introduced himself to the prettiest girl in sight— Remigia Ferrari Scacco, daughter of a Genoese paper manufacturer. They had only a few dates before he returned home, but she took the captain home to meet her parents, and he had already decided that Remigia was the girl he wanted to marry.

In the army Brooke had benefited from on-the-job training as a lawyer after he was assigned to defend GIs in court-martial cases. This experience stimulated him to choose the law as his profession. Following his discharge, he studied at Boston University Law School where he was an editor of the *Law Review* and earned his master's degree. He kept in touch by mail with Miss Ferrari Scacco; after two years, she came to America, and they were married.

The neophyte lawyer was beginning to build up his private practice in 1950 when he and two friends from his army days decided that he should run for the state legislature. He cross-filed for nomination by both major parties and was selected by the Republicans, but he lost the general election—as he did a second bid for the legislature two years later.

Mrs. Brooke was not happy when her husband ran for the Massachusetts house of representatives. They were starting to raise a family, and like most women, she preferred a husband who could be at home in the evening. Two rebuffs by the voters and his wife's lack of enthusiasm for public life kept him from reentering the fray until 1960 when they agreed he would stand for Massachusetts secretary of state against the Democrat, Kevin White. Though there was nothing overtly racial about the campaign, one of the themes used by the Democrats—"Vote White"—was subject to dual interpretation. Brooke lost for the third time, but the margin of his defeat was such—less than 112,000 votes—that the Republicans considered it a victory of sorts since he had managed to poll a million votes against a powerful Democratic surge inspired by John F. Kennedy's candidacy for President.

Governor John Volpe named Brooke to head the Boston Finance Commission. As chairman of this hitherto docile watchdog agency, he uncovered irregularities in the city's building, real estate, and fire departments, and as a result, some heads rolled. He so impressed the voters that on his fourth try for elective office in 1962 they chose him as state attorney general; this time, he won by nearly 260,000 votes.

Prosecutor Brooke compiled a solid record as he followed through on the investigative work of the Massachusetts Crime Commission. He secured grand jury indictments against scores of politicians, private citizens, and corporations for charges ranging from conflict of interest to bribery and perjury.

In the fall of 1964, Brooke received national attention when he delivered a seconding speech for Governor William Scranton of Pennsylvania at the Republican national convention in Los Angeles. Barry Goldwater, the conservative Arizona senator, not Scranton, was the delegates' choice for President. Up for reelection as attorney general, Brooke refused to endorse Goldwater. Democrats throughout the state crossed the line to vote for Brooke, who retained his position by nearly 800,000 votes, while Goldwater lost Massachusetts by 1,200,000. This was, in the words of a Brooke brochure, "the largest plurality achieved by any Republican in the United States in 1964 and by any Republican in the history of Massachusetts." And it had happened in a state where less than 3 percent of the population was black.

Landslide notwithstanding, reporters still pestered the attorney general with questions about whether he had been handicapped by his race. "I certainly wouldn't say it had been a hindrance," he told *U.S. News & World Report* in February 1965. "I would like to believe that it balanced out, though I have no figures to prove it. But my vote crosses party lines, it crosses racial lines and it crosses religious lines. . . . Actually, it could have been a help, rather than a hindrance. What is that quotation? 'The pursuit of the difficult makes men strong.'"

Negro activists were not pleased when the highest black office-holder in Massachusetts called a student strike against school desegregation illegal. "I am not a civil rights leader, and I don't profess to be," he explained in the same interview when criticized for his lack of personal involvement in the mushrooming civil rights movement. "I don't think all Negroes should or can be civil rights leaders. I recognize Dr. Martin Luther King [Jr.], Roy Wilkins, Whitney Young [Jr.], James Farmer . . . as the civil rights leaders. . . . I am a lawyer and . . . the attorney general of Massachusetts. I can't serve just the Negro cause. I've got to serve all the people of Massachusetts."

In 1965 veteran Massachusetts Senator Leverett Saltonstall took a step few men take willingly—he announced his retirement. Brooke won the backing of the state Republican convention against a young conservative. In the general election he faced former Democratic governor Endicott Peabody, an old-line Bostonian with a good civil rights record.

The ingratiating, articulate Brooke, a fine campaigner himself, had some help from Saltonstall and from Mrs. Brooke, who, to her husband's delight, turned out to be a "natural" once she conquered her initial shyness. Teen-age daughters, Edwina and Remi, also joined in their father's campaign.

Meanwhile, the popular Senator Edward Kennedy made the rounds with Peabody. Brooke changed his dark, well-fitted suits three times a day, keeping fastidiously neat on his hand-shaking tours. "You can vote proudly for Brooke, a creative Republican," his posters proclaimed. The creative Republican stood between the doves and hawks on the Vietnam War. He endorsed the goals of the civil rights movement. He supported open housing and interim school busing. He decried white and black extremists. The Brooke campaign rolled to a victory by 438,712 votes on November 2, 1966.

On the night of his greatest election triumph, Brooke said "the people of Massachusetts judge you on your worth alone. The people of this state have answered all the George Rockwells [head of the American Nazi party] and all those who would divide us." He promised "to merit the faith" shown "in me as a man."

After a vacation in the Virgin Islands, the senator-elect left Mrs. Brooke and their daughters temporarily behind in their ten-room house in Newton. He would commute between Washington, where his mother, a widow of two years, lived and his home base in the Boston suburb where the girls attended school.

Shortly after Brooke arrived in the capital, some members of the

National Association for the Advancement of Colored People walked out on a Washington reception in his honor, criticizing him for not having gone to the aid of Adam Clayton Powell, Jr., then about to be excluded from the House of Representatives. Brooke side-stepped that hassle, limiting himself to a criticism of House Minority Leader Gerald Ford for needlessly involving the Republicans in "the Democrats' mess."

Charles Percy of Illinois and Brooke were assigned to the Banking and Currency and Aeronautical and Space Science committees, and Brooke won seniority with the toss of a coin in both cases. The Senate began with a hassle over procedure. Brooke lined up with the liberals on January 24 when he voted to stop an eight-day filibuster and clear the way for consideration of proposals to modify the Senate rule requiring a two-thirds majority to cut off debate. He was one of fifty-three voting for cloture, but it was not enough, and Senate Rule 22 remained intact.

America was wracked by a succession of ghetto riots in the long hot summer of 1967. Roxbury, where Brooke lived during his early years in Boston, was the scene of one of the first outbreaks. Eruptions that followed in July in Newark and Detroit were even more violent as blacks released their pent-up fury against discrimination, deprivation, and the police in an orgy of arson and looting. It was as though thousands of people were having a simultaneous nervous breakdown. More than eighty people, nearly all of them Negroes, were killed before the big-city concrete jungles settled back to their normal state of hopeless lethargy.

Brooke and ten others were appointed by President Johnson to investigate the disturbances and see what could be done to avoid recurrences. After inspecting the devastation and talking with hundreds of people, the President's Commission on Civil Disorders issued a report warning that America was splitting into separate black and white societies. The government was asked to move promptly to provide jobs, welfare reforms, and better schools and housing, all on a color-blind basis. Johnson, who had supported the aspirations of the black and the poor in the past, was a lame-duck President by the time the report came out, and he was more engrossed in the Vietnam War than in breathing fresh life into his languishing Great Society programs. Brooke and the other commission members were disheartened at the administration's failure to implement their suggestions.

Brooke was instrumental in getting one of the Commission's recommendations enacted when the Senate resumed work early in 1968. Up for consideration was a House-approved measure to protect blacks and civil rights workers from harassment. Aware that this was the only civil rights bill with a chance of passage in the Ninetieth Congress, Brooke and Senator Walter Mondale, a Montana Democrat, asked that it be broadened to cover housing bias. Early in February they introduced an amendment making it illegal to refuse to rent or sell a house or an apartment to anyone because of his race, color, religion, or national origin. Their proposal covered most of the country's housing.

Aided by other liberals, Brooke and Mondale kept their rider alive through weeks of filibustering. Johnson had asked the Senate to approve open housing, but the Senate leaders did not want it attached to the over-all rights bill. Efforts to round up the two-thirds margin necessary to close off debate failed.

A break came when the Senate Republican Leader, Everett Dirksen of Illinois, agreed to vote for cloture. Vietnam War veterans, who impressed Dirksen with the argument that they should be able to live where they chose at home after fighting for somebody else's freedom abroad, reportedly helped to change Dirksen's mind about cutting off debate, and a compromise was worked out.

Still, the maneuvering was far from over. Supporters of a crackdown on housing bias had to fight off a number of crippling amendments, including one that would have made the law applicable only to black veterans, their families and relatives. Brooke said "no Negro worth his salt wanted that kind of bill" and added that surely the Senate did not intend to tell blacks that the only way they could avoid discrimination was to join the army. Cloture was voted on the fourth try on March 4. That roadblock past, the 1968 Civil Rights Bill, including the compromise Dirksen-labeled amendment, covering about 80 percent of the country's housing, was approved by the Senate and the House by wide margins.

Brooke campaigned for Richard M. Nixon in 1968 and was among those who could get in for occasional meetings with him after he became a somewhat inaccessible President in 1969. The senator asked Nixon to capitalize on his opportunity as head of a new administration to resume strategic arms limitations talks with the Russians before the two super powers became hopelessly locked in a self-perpetuating contest to outproduce each other in multiple-headed rockets. The talks eventually got underway in 1970, but not before Nixon had rammed through Congress a bill authorizing deployment of the Safeguard Anti-Ballistic Missile system, thereby speeding up the arms race.

Brooke and Nixon again clashed on the President's choice for a Supreme Court vacancy. First to blast the nomination of Judge Clement F. Haynsworth, Jr., of South Carolina were the black members of the

House, who had no vote on the confirmation but who worked to influence those who did. Brooke fired the initial volley in the Senate fight to keep the United States Court of Appeals, Fourth Circuit, judge off the high bench a few days later when he told the press that he had written the President asking him to withdraw the nomination.

"If there is a consensus in the Senate at the moment, I think it is the view that Judge Haynsworth is not the distinguished jurist whom the country expected to be nominated . . . ," Brooke wrote Nixon. The senator warned that there would be a bitter floor fight. The judge had been criticized for not disqualifying himself in cases where he had a financial interest. Union leaders accused him of antilabor bias. NAACP Executive Director Roy Wilkins said Haynsworth had used his position to try to slow the progress of desegregation to an "eyedropper" speed.

Brooke thought Nixon might lose in a floor confrontation and asked him to spare Republican senators who opposed Haynsworth because of his questionable ethics and weak civil rights record the embarrassment of a conflict between their principles and their sense of obligation to the President. Instead of withdrawing the name, Nixon brought the pressures of his office to bear against wavering senators. When the vote came on November 21, 1969, the count was not even close; Haynsworth was rejected fifty-five to forty-five, with seventeen Republicans, including the party's Senate leaders, voting against the nominee. Not in forty years had a President suffered such a rebuff.

The Senate had to wait until January to learn Nixon's second choice—Judge G. Harrold Carswell of the United States Court of Appeals for the Fifth Circuit. The Florida justice was such an obscure figure that almost no one had heard of him, but it was soon evident that there was more to be known about Carswell than Attorney General John F. Mitchell, who recommended him to the President, had found out.

Reporters unearthed a 1948 speech in which Carswell had proclaimed himself a white supremacist forever. The judge answered that if he had ever felt like that he did so no longer. Yet more recently he had helped to circumvent the law by incorporating a private golf club in Tallahassee to exclude Negroes. Law professors and students documented his undistinguished record on the bench, but the American Bar Association pronounced him acceptable although higher courts had found it necessary to reverse an unusually large percentage of his decisions. Weary of fighting over an empty seat on the court, the Senate was reluctant to deny the President a second time. It began to look as though Carswell might just make it in spite of the objections.

Only seventeen senators, including Republican Charles Goodell of New York, had publicly expressed their opposition to the President's nominee. Weeks went by without any word from Brooke. Finally on February 25 the Massachusetts senator began a brief speech to a nearly empty Senate chamber with the words: "I will vote against confirmation of Judge Carswell." Brooke said a careful study of Carswell's career had convinced him that the Florida judge still harbored the "racist views" he had expressed in that long-ago speech, notwithstanding his repudiation of those sentiments in testimony during the Senate Judiciary Committee hearings on his nomination. Brooke charged Carswell with cavalierly turning down habeas-corpus petitions and with habitually antagonizing civil rights lawyers without provocation. The senator was particularly distressed by Carswell's decisions in school desegregation cases, some of which—had they not been reversed on appeal—would have postponed compliance with the 1954 Supreme Court ruling until the mid-1970's.

After this speech the resistance to Carswell solidified. Democratic Senator Birch Bayh of Indiana, who had directd the floor fight against Haynsworth, and Brooke joined forces to try to line up enough senators to keep Nixon's second choice off the Supreme Court. Supported by civil rights and labor organizations, they kept the issue alive in the newspapers and on television with carefully timed announcements as they picked up additional anti-Carswell votes.

On April 6, 1970, there was an unsuccessful attempt to sidetrack the nominee by recommitting his name to the Judiciary Committee for further study—a move which, while killing the nomination, would have spared senators another direct collision with the President. Aware that some senators, who considered Carswell unqualified for the Supreme Court thought it cowardly to turn him down on a technicality, Brooke and Bayh had been concentrating on the vote on the nomination itself, which was set for two days later.

April 8 arrived with the outcome still unpredictable. Two hours before the vote Brooke heard that Nixon aides had informed other Republican holdouts that Margaret Chase Smith of Maine had agreed to support the President. Brooke relayed this information to her before she reached the Senate chamber. A very independent-minded senator, she was, as Brooke expected she would be, incensed at this report since she had assured him she was not going to tell anyone how she would vote in advance. He rushed back to the floor to report that Carswell's backers did not yet have the Senate's only distaff member in their camp.

Vice-President Spiro Agnew was in the chair, hoping to use his vote to break a possible tie and give the victory to the President.

Tension was great in the packed chamber as the roll call began. Marlow Cook of Kentucky, who had been among the uncommitted, answered with a loud no. There were signs of surprise as Arkansas' J. William Fulbright, a conservative on everything relating to race, answered with a soft no. When her turn came, Mrs. Smith's even softer no was applauded by the gallery.

The cheers that greeted Agnew's announcement that Carswell had been rejected fifty-one to forty-five continued as Bayh pushed across the crowded aisle to congratulate Brooke, whose final tally showed thirteen Republican votes against the President's nominee. TV men were outside the chamber, waiting to interview Brooke and Bayh. At a news conference an obviously furious Nixon berated those who had again blocked his man from the court for their "hypocrisy." He said he had concluded he could not get confirmation on any Southerner who believed in the "strict construction of the Constitution" and that he would turn elsewhere for his next candidate.

Brooke found it "incredible" that the President would make such a "mistaken and unfortunate statement." He said those who opposed Carswell, "including many distinguished members from the South," would support a Southerner who shared Nixon's views on the interpretation of the Constitution if the man was qualified to serve on the high court bench. There was no chance to see if Brooke was right. A few weeks later, the President turned to the Midwest for his third nominee, Federal Judge Harry Blackmun of the Eighth Circuit Court of Appeals, who was unanimously confirmed by the Senate.

Despite their differences over court appointees, the missiles race, the Vietnam War, and Nixon's "cold, calculated political" decision to slow down integration, Brooke, the only black Republican in Congress, pragmatically kept up his contacts with the Chief Executive, who considered the senator a shrewd political tactician.

Convinced that Nixon was so deeply implicated in the Watergate cover-up that only a miracle could save his Presidency, Brooke became the first Republican senator to call for the President's resignation. First on national television and then to his face, Brooke asked the President to step down rather than put the country through the trauma of impeachment. Nixon refused to take the "coward's way out" then, but did resign nine months later.

Edward W. Brooke, re-elected by a landslide in 1972, has continued to work for liberal economic measures and for a "sane" military policy, while astutely neutralizing anti-busing amendments and protecting landmark civil rights legislation from erosion in floor debates in the Senate.

John Conyers, Jr./Michigan

John Conyers, Jr., heralded by some observers as a likely successor to Adam Clayton Powell, Jr., as a congressional spokesman for the black community, has aspired instead to a broader role, having run for speaker of the House of Representatives to protest the "stagnant" Democratic leadership. Comparisons with Powell have continued because neither congressman submitted easily to the strictures of the Establishment though both understood them thoroughly.

Conyers first saw Powell at a political meeting in Detroit when his father took him to a rally to hear the fiery Harlem congressman speak. By the time the Michigan youngster grew up and went to Congress himself in 1965, Powell, then a twenty-year veteran in the House of Representatives, was at the peak of his power as head of the Education and Labor Committee.

Before his election to the House, Conyers had been best known outside of Michigan as a defense lawyer for Mississippians accused of voter-registration irregularities. Born on May 16, 1929, in Detroit, he grew up in a strong trade-union family. An international representative on the board of the United Automobile Workers, his father worked on a Chrysler Corporation assembly line. After completing high school, young John obtained a job in the Lincoln car factory, where he was named education director of UAW Local 900. He earned extra money by playing the cornet in a dance band.

At twenty-one he entered Wayne State University, but soon had to leave for the army when his National Guard unit was called to active duty in August 1950. Commissioned a second lieutenant in the corps of engineers following his graduation from officer candidate school, he served four years, including twelve months of combat in the Korean War.

His military stint finished, he returned to Wayne State University and received his law degree in 1958. While practicing law as a senior partner with Conyers, Bell and Townsend, he also was legislative assistant to Congressman John Dingell, Jr., of Michigan's Fifteenth District and general counsel for the Detroit Trade Union Leadership Council. In 1961 he was appointed a referee for the Michigan Workmen's Compensation Department.

He resigned that post to run for Congress, entering a crowded Democratic primary in August 1964. Most labor and black leaders backed Richard Austin, a prosperous accountant, over the thirty-five-year-old, low-pressure lawyer, but Conyers had the advantage of having worked in part of the redrawn First District for his former boss, Congressman Dingell. Beyond that, his main assets were his father, a battalion of women volunteers, and his own self-confidence. He squeaked in by a margin of 45 votes. The general election was a pleasant contrast; Conyers won over Republican Robert Blackwell by a margin of about 113,000 votes.

The Washington career of the five-foot-ten, well-dressed bachelor began auspiciously when he secured a seat on the Judiciary Committee despite intensive competition. The National Association for the Advancement of Colored People and other lobbyists argued it was time that a committee presiding over human rights legislation had a black member and backed Conyers for the assignment.

Congress had already given Lyndon B. Johnson his blank check for war in Vietnam in the form of the August 1964 Gulf of Tonkin Resolution allowing the President "to take all necessary measures" to prevent further aggression in Southeast Asia. Warning that the country was dissipating its strength in the Indochina conflict, the new representative began to battle for peace. One of his early House speeches favored a $55,000,000 outlay for an arms control and disarmament agency. In May 1965, he announced that he could not support Johnson's request for an additional $700,000,000 for Vietnam because he thought the war was a mistake. There were only six other negative votes in the House, where the war hawks predominated. Twice in 1966 he was one of three members who dared say no to the President's request for still more billions to feed a seemingly insatiable military machine.

Conyers was equally adamant in his domestic positions. Three of the black members voted for the battered remains of an open-housing proposal in 1966 as a last resort, but Conyers, who had introduced his own, stronger amendment, did not. This was lost motion since the civil rights package of 1966 died in the Senate, but it was indicative of how Michigan's second Negro congressman would conduct himself as a legislator.

Running on his record of cosponsorship of such laws as the Voting

Rights Act of 1965, Medicare, and the cold war GI bill providing educational and vocational training and housing assistance for veterans of the post-Korean War period, he was reelected in 1966 with 84 percent of the vote, the fourth highest margin of any congressman. In the Ninetieth Congress he reintroduced legislation for home rule for the District of Columbia, abolition of the House Un-American Activities Committee, and truth-in-lending controls. None of these measures passed.

Conyers' second term began in January 1967. The newly convened House faced the dilemma of deciding what to do about Adam Powell, who had been accused of misusing congressional funds and ignoring the courts' orders in a New York libel case. Conyers was the lone black on the nine-man committee named to investigate the charges, and he was the only Negro who spoke on the House floor in support of the Harlem representative's right to his seat.

The group's report recommended that Powell be seated, fined forty thousand dollars, and deprived of his seniority, though Conyers said he personally felt any punishment beyond censure was improper since there was no precedent for other sanctions. It was a mistake, Conyers asserted, to view Powell's failure to explain his actions to the House select committee on the advice of his counsel as a sign of disrespect to the House.

After the full House bypassed the committee's recommendation and refused to admit Powell, Conyers told a teamsters' meeting that Congress had torn a page out of the Constitution for all men of color and labor when it closed the door to the man who had helped shape every piece of labor legislation in the last five years.

During this term Conyers was a key man in staving off legislation that could have delayed court-ordered "one man, one vote" congressional redistricting in many states until 1972. He fought the move first in the House, which voted to allow population variances of up to 30 percent in congressional districts for the next two elections; then, on the fringes of the Senate, where Edward Kennedy of Massachusetts and Howard Baker of Tennessee lowered the figure to 10 percent, and finally in the protracted discussions of the Senate-House conference committee until there was nothing left in the bill as passed to circumvent the Supreme Court's redistricting formula.

"In every other aspect of American life Negro ghettos are treated as totally separate," Conyers told Morgan State College students in Baltimore in 1967. "But when it comes to drawing political boundaries, Negro ghettos are suddenly paired with white suburbs to keep Negroes in a minority in every district . . . [and] to insure that only in the smallest number of districts are Negroes a really significant political factor."

In Congress and out, Conyers preached the gospel of the power of coalition. He reminded audiences that poor whites and blacks both needed jobs, housing, and better education; that Negroes, Mexican-Americans, Puerto Ricans, and Indians were underrepresented not only in Washington but in state capitals; that the unemployed and the elderly were alike in having to struggle for the bare essentials, and that civil rights workers and peace activists could agree that the billions of dollars going into Vietnam were badly needed in America.

As the Poor People's Campaign was being readied in early 1968, Martin Luther King, Jr., said the passage of Conyers' full opportunity act would meet their demands. That ambitious bill, to be funded at $30,000,000,000 annually, provided for family allowances, minimum wage hikes, educational aid proportional to the need, and jobs for all, with people to be trained to fill essential functions in medicine, education, and conservation.

After Dr. King's assassination his followers marched to Washington without him. Conyers escorted three hundred of them into the House galleries, but their presence was not enough to stir what Conyers has called the "most reactionary branch of the government" to action on his sweeping program. The measure the congressman cosponsored to protect civil rights workers and blacks from violence did pass, however, along with the strongest open housing statute in the nation's history.

Conyers tried to organize blacks to pressure the Democratic party to fashion a presidential slate and platform to appeal to minorities and antiwar groups. His influence on the tightly controlled national convention was nil. Neither he nor any of the other doves could convince Hubert Humphrey, the nominee, to repudiate Johnson's Southeast Asia policy and come out strongly in favor of peace. With no place else to turn, Conyers finally endorsed the party's choice, and along with most blacks, voted for him.

Once again in January 1969 the House had to decide how to greet Powell, who by then had been reelected to his old seat three times. On the eve of his own third term, Conyers wired all the members asking them to join him in seating Powell on opening day. He repeated his appeal during the debate preceding the compromise agreement to fine and accept Powell without restoring his seniority. No thanks were forthcoming from the New Yorker, who reportedly had called Conyers a "black Judas" for serving on the 1967 disciplinary committee. Jealous of his prerogative as the former spokesman for his bloc, Powell saluted Robert N. C. Nix and Charles C. Diggs, Jr., for their behind-the-scenes help, but told reporters that as far as he knew, Conyers had just come into the fight "in the last few days."

Still, Conyers, Powell, and other blacks collaborated on a proposal to amend the law "to make the selective service boards reflect the ethnic and economic nature of the areas" they served. Conyers reintroduced his full opportunity act as a tribute to Dr. King, with more than twenty cosponsors, and proposed that the murdered civil rights leader's birthday be proclaimed a national holiday. Measures like these were doomed in the Ninety-first Congress, which even had trouble getting essential housekeeping bills passed.

Conyers joined Louis Stokes of Ohio and William Clay of Missouri in House speeches to dramatize their apprehension over the impact of the Nixon policies on the black community. Emphasizing the President's failure to fulfill his campaign promise to end the war, Conyers charged that the President was not proving his belief in freedom and democracy to black America or to the world by continuing to support a "foreign government [Vietnamese] which has shown little or no interest in freedom, justice, or democracy." At home, he said, the urban crisis and the race problem had yet to command the attention of the administration and added: "Any hope of reporting to black America that this Federal government will move with more commitment or more speed to overcome the inequality in this country is rapidly fading: and this point of view, I am sorry to note, is increasingly being shown across the country."

Black leaders in the fall of 1969 were determined that Clement F. Haynsworth, Jr., would not serve on the Supreme Court. As spokesman for the Negro House members, Conyers asked the Senate Judiciary Committee to reject the Nixon nominee because of his past record of "infidelity to the principles of racial equality."

The Michigan representative played a crucial role in organizing the opposition to the Haynsworth nomination. On September 30, Conyers, Clay, Stokes, and Diggs met with Senator Edward Brooke, the only Negro in a position to vote on the nomination; the next day, Brooke wrote the President asking him to withdraw the judge's name. By then Conyers and the others had visited Senate Republican leaders Hugh Scott of Pennsylvania and Robert Griffin of Michigan to ask them to oppose Haynsworth.

Except for Griffin, there might have been no vacancy. He had led the Senate attack on Abe Fortas, who resigned from the bench after having been charged with impropriety for accepting a consultancy fee from a foundation supported by a financier then serving a jail sentence for stock manipulation. Now, ironically, the man nominated by the President to succeed Fortas was being criticized for failing to disqualify himself in cases where he had a personal interest.

Conyers spent hours on the phone briefing Michigan businessmen, churchmen, Jewish leaders, and party figures on the Haynsworth case. He asked them to contact Griffin and urge him to vote against the nomination. The congressman generated the same kind of pressure in Pennsylvania with calls and wires to black newspaper publishers and lawyers. Scott, a candidate for reelection in 1970, was well aware that his last margin of victory over a conservative Democrat had come from Negro votes. It was a severe blow to Haynsworth when these two ranking Republican senators told the President they could not support his choice. In the final vote the nomination failed by ten votes.

While liberals blocked the appointment of Haynsworth and a second Southern judge, G. Harrold Carswell, to the Supreme Court, they were unable to shift the government's best energies from war to peace, though Conyers was looking to young people of both races to speed up this process. Win or lose, Conyers, who heads a Judiciary subcommittee on crime, is a tireless fighter. In May 1972 he originated a resolution calling for the impeachment of Nixon for illegally continuing an undeclared war in Vietnam and killing hundreds of thousands of innocent civilians. Widely publicized, his proposal was cosponsored by two white and five black representatives.

Two years later Michigan's bachelor congressman shuttled back and forth behind the scenes in the Judiciary committee working with the unconvinced Democrats and the wavering Republicans to shape an impeachment article that would pass the committee overwhelmingly. On television Conyers told his audience that he favored impeachment for many reasons beyond the Watergate scandal—attempted bribery of a federal judge, tax evasion, illegal impoundment of $40 billion in funds for duly authorized programs.

A Conyers resolution demanded a full House probe into President Gerald Ford's hasty pardon of his predecessor. Instead of digging, the subcommittee accepted Ford's explanation of "no deal, period." The Democratic leadership once more had given in to the Republicans, Conyers said, and the House had performed a little charade that amounted to a cover-up of its own.

John Conyers, Jr., has continued to be re-elected by wide margins while his reputation as a battler for the downtrodden has been enhanced. He has challenged the "horse and buggy economics" of the Ford Administration, the lackluster performance of the House leadership, and the failure of the Ninety-fourth Congress itself to take affirmative political and economic action after an impressive beginning.

Louis Stokes/Ohio

At the height of the national jubilation over the first manned landing on the moon by Apollo 11 astronauts in July 1969, Louis Stokes cautioned that America's claim to greatness would rest more on earthly accomplishments than space spectaculars.

The tall, slender Ohio representative contrasted the space triumph, achieved at a cost of some twenty-five billion dollars, with the "joblessness, homelessness, poverty, ignorance, blight, pollution, racism, discrimination, and a myriad of unsolved domestic problems, which make life on earth miserable for many Americans."

Admitting he himself had been exhilarated while watching the moon walk on television, the older brother of Mayor Carl Stokes of Cleveland told the House of Representatives: "Today is a good day for us to reexamine our national priorities, to evaluate the posture of the President of the United States and the goals which he has set for people here on earth. . . . How, Mr. Speaker, for instance does this Nation justify sending a man to the moon while we are still studying hunger . . . ?" It was difficult to explain, Louis Stokes said, why, in a country which had sent a man to the moon, some Americans were without shoes, a place to live, a chance for an education—or even decent air to breathe.

Stokes's words were perfectly consistent with his actions. Earlier he had voted against the nearly four billion dollar annual appropriation for the National Aeronautics and Space Administration, believing that the money might be better spent for schools, medical research, and welfare.

Stokes, a man who knows from personal experience how hard many ordinary taxpayers have to work to raise those dollars for space, had not run for office previously when he was elected to the House from Ohio's Twenty-first Congressional District in November 1968. After finishing high school in Cleveland in 1943, he went into the United

States Army where he served three years as a personnel specialist during World War II. Back in civilian life he worked in the Cleveland offices of the Treasury Department and Veterans Administration while studying at Western Reserve University on the GI bill at night. Later he was a full-time student at Cleveland-Marshall Law School, from which he received a law degree in 1953. He practiced law in Cleveland, part of the time in partnership with his brother, Carl. When named to Congress, he was a member of the firm of Stokes, Character, Terry and Perry.

Many congressmen continue their law practice while serving in Congress, which frequently results in a booming business for their associates from companies and individuals eager to be represented by a firm with a congressman's name on the door. Stokes said that this would not be the case with him. "I am associated with the Cleveland law firm only in the sense I still am clearing up a few cases on which I was working before I entered the congressional race," he explained.

The Supreme Court of the United States laid the foundation for Stokes's election in February 1964 by ruling that House districts had to be as nearly equal numerically as possible. The effect of this decision and subsequent ones amplifying it was to give city dwellers a more equitable share of congressional seats, since urban areas had generally been short-changed in the past and rural areas overrepresented. In order to conform to the court's rulings, many states throughout the nation had to reapportion their congressional districts, and politicians at the state level naturally vied to draw the new district lines in ways that would favor their own parties. In Ohio, while redistricting the state in 1965, the legislature gerrymandered Cleveland in a manner that dissipated the group voting strength of the city's black residents.

Backed by the National Association for the Advancement of Colored People, which was protesting inequitable districts in the state of Ohio, Charles Lucas, a real estate agent and veteran Republican leader, went to court to battle this case of gerrymandering, with Louis Stokes as his attorney. Lucas and Stokes won on an appeal to the Supreme Court.

Buoyed by this victory and heartened no doubt by the public response to his brother, who in a matter of months had gained national attention as the first black mayor of a major city, Stokes decided to bid for the Twenty-first District seat. The white incumbent was shifting from this now 65 percent black district to the adjoining Twenty-second to challenge an aging Republican representative there. Stokes won the Democratic primary over thirteen other contenders in May 1968. Ironically his Republican opponent in the general election was

Lucas, with whom he had collaborated to force a revision of the district's boundaries.

With his brother so much in the news, Louis Stokes's first problem was to get across to the voters who the other Stokes was. He had the advantage of his solid reputation as a trial lawyer who had devoted much of his life to defending the poor, frequently without pay. In recognition of his labors in that field, he had received the distinguished service award of the Cleveland branch of the NAACP and a certificate of appreciation from the United States Civil Rights Commission.

He had handled antidiscrimination lawsuits for the NAACP and represented people arrested during desegregation sit-ins, marches, and demonstrations. His clients ranged from black militant nationalists to ordinary poor people in trouble with the law. One of his crusades was against Ohio's "stop and frisk" law, which hit hardest at the young Negro standing on the street corner with no place else to go. The law allowed the police to search anyone they pleased, merely because a person looked suspicious and even though no crime had been committed in the vicinity.

The energetic counselor also found time to lecture at colleges, law schools, and bar association meetings. He became an expert on constitutional and criminal law. In 1966 he wrote a volume, *Criminal Law,* which was published by the Cuyahoga County Bar Association. His bar association work established his reputation with the leaders of the community, while his courtroom activity made him known to the general public. He chaired the Cleveland NAACP's legal redress committee for six years. He headed the criminal courts committee of the Cuyahoga County Bar Association from 1964 to 1968. He was chairman of the committee on criminal justice of the Ohio State Bar Association.

His college background and his work with the bar associations gave him entrée to predominantly white suburbia during the campaign for his congressional seat. Blacks could identify with him on all levels. Like so many people in the ghetto slums of his district, he had to scrounge for subsistence in a fatherless household during his early years. His Georgia-born mother had gone to work as a domestic to support her boys after their father, Charles Stokes, a laundry worker, died when Louis was three. As a youngster he shined shoes, sold newspapers, worked in a whipped-cream factory, and clerked in a store. He told voters he could well understand "black militancy and the desire to destroy a society oblivious to black people's problems." At the same time, he warned the impatient young that taking to the streets with guns was no solution.

Backed by progressives and young people, Stokes won over Lucas, eighty-six thousand to thirty-one thousand. Cleveland's new representative, a gracious, relaxed man, moved into a Washington apartment. He received assignments on the Internal Security and Education and Labor committees. His wife, the former Jeanette (Jay) Francis, who had worked for the Cleveland school board before their marriage, remained in Cleveland temporarily so that Shelley, Louis, Angela, and Lorene would not have to change schools in midyear.

Stokes, a pragmatist, soon learned that he could get along in Congress even with segregationist Southerners by recognizing their legislative abilities and demanding the same respect from them. He tangled frequently on the Internal Security Committee with Albert Watson, the South Carolina Republican, but Watson commended the Ohioan for his legal skill and bantered with him after their clashes.

Stokes had not wished for appointment to the famous, Communist-hunting security group. In his campaign, in fact, he had advocated the abolition of the House Un-American Activities Committee—as it was then called—and once in Congress he not only voted against appropriating funds for the group's work, but introduced a bill to put an end to its existence.

Having lost that skirmish, Stokes used his influence to try to shift the committee's emphasis. "Instead of concentrating on repressive laws against the students, perhaps we should concentrate on the problems of society," he suggested during a hearing on the role of the Students for a Democratic Society in fomenting campus disorders. If the committee were redirected, Stokes said, it could become a "forum for bridging gaps between young and old, black and white, the haves and have nots. If the committee constructively employs its power to investigate and intervene, we could find out why there are so many dissidents."

The Ohio congressman offered legislation dealing with workmen's compensation, railroad passenger service, small business construction, and vocational education. With Representatives Shirley Chisholm, John Conyers, Jr., Charles C. Diggs, Jr., Augustus F. Hawkins, and others he cosponsored a bill to promote population control by making family-planning services available to all the people who wanted them. A similar measure was enacted.

He cooperated with the other black representatives on many issues they considered of special importance. They protested the nomination of Judge Clement F. Haynsworth, Jr., to the Supreme Court, the ousting of Equal Employment Opportunity Commission Chairman Clifford L. Alexander, Jr., who resigned after Senate Minority Leader Everett Dirksen threatened to get him fired, and the awarding of government contracts to companies that would not hire blacks.

In mid-1969, Stokes, John Conyers, Jr., of Michigan, and William L.

Clay of Missouri, one after the other, arose in the House to tell the country of their dismay over Nixon's "lack of sensitivity" toward the needs of the black and the poor. Strokes enumerated these failings of the Nixon administration: the absence of nonwhites in the Cabinet; the easing of school desegregation guidelines; budget cuts in education; failure to fight against the slashes in the low-income housing programs, and unwavering devotion to military spending.

He criticized Attorney General John F. Mitchell for trying to weaken the Voting Rights Act of 1965. The Ohio congressman offered a point-by-point refutation of Mitchell's arguments against the flat extension of the law, which provided federal supervision of registration and elections in states or counties requiring literacy tests or similar prerequisites and with less than 50 percent of their adult population registered or voting in the 1964 presidential election.

Stokes ridiculed the contention that the act, which had opened the polls to thousands of Southern blacks for the first time, was unfair to the South. The law theoretically covered all jurisdictions, he explained, but it had the greatest impact in those areas where people had not been allowed to vote. Beyond that, he said, most laws enacted by Congress could be termed regional, for example, oil depletion allowances, import controls, and cotton subsidies. "There is nothing whatsoever wrong with this," he added, "because obviously any problem should and can be solved where, and only where, it exists."

"The [Nixon] administration's final reason for not recommending extension, that the need for the law has ceased to exist, would be a persuasive one if it were only true. Unhappily, it is not. While we all share the Attorney General's enthusiasm about the 800,000 Negroes registered to vote in the seven States to which the law has primarily applied, it nevertheless seems a bit naïve to stop the investigation at the statistical level and not explore the substance of what is currently happening in the South."

To document what was still going on, he referred the House to a United States Civil Rights Commission report on Mississippi city elections in May 1969. "Many did not register because of bombing threats," Stokes said. "Others could not because of intentionally shortened registration hours or deceptive practices which gave the voters the impression they were registering when they were not. Many potential black candidates were purposely given false information on how to file.

"On election day, black poll watchers were not allowed near the polling places, the token number of black election officials was not permitted to assist the blind or the handicapped, and white officials attempted to influence illiterates not to vote for black candidates. In one town, an armed deputy harassed black citizens until many gave up without voting."

The report was issued, Stokes stressed, just ten days before Attorney General Mitchell appeared before the House Judiciary Committee and "indicated all was now well [with voting] in the Southland." While it was possible that the attorney general had not done his homework, Stokes felt this more likely was another rebate by Nixon to Senator Strom Thurmond of South Carolina and "other participants in the southern strategy." Stokes continued: "If the latter is the case, and it indeed appears so, then the President has intentionally aligned himself with the forces of reaction and bigotry, and deserves the shame of all his countrymen who sincerely believe in the concept of equal rights for all Americans."

Liberals in the House were five votes short on December 11, 1969, when they tried to stave off Nixon's weak substitute and extend the 1965 law. The Senate later renewed and broadened the 1965 civil rights act and added a provision lowering the voting age to eighteen. This version passed the House in mid-1970, and the President signed it despite his reservations about the constitutionality of the teen-age ballot clause.

Stokes was elected to succeed Charles C. Diggs, Jr., as chairman of the congressional black caucus in 1972, after the newer representatives had demanded it take a more forceful stand on issues of concern to minorities. Stokes gave the thirteen-person group more drive and direction and better financing through a successful $100 a plate dinner supported by major corporations. He insisted the caucus's aims be set forth concisely so that people who expect "many things of us that are not in our jurisdiction" will not be disappointed.

Stokes served a second term as chairman, then was succeeded in January 1974 by Charles B. Rangel of New York. It is perhaps not surprising that the strong, highly individualistic members of the caucus have yet to rally around any leader long enough to build him or her up as a national black spokesperson with ready access to the media.

Stokes was returned to Congress by nearly 46,000 votes in 1974 after successfully amending the Education Appropriations Law to add $487,500,000 to cover a range of programs from general aid to public schools to special projects for handicapped children. Although very active in Democratic politics in his home city, he misses the support of former mayor Carl Stokes, who wearied of political infighting and left Cleveland to become a television newsman in New York.

Louis Stokes, a member of the Appropriations and Budget committees, has continued to work and vote for liberal causes, but he's still waiting for the Federal Government to recognize the gravity of the plight of the increasingly black inner cities of America and to use its resources to attack their monumental problems.

William L. Clay/Missouri

The nine black members of the House of Representatives wrote President Richard M. Nixon in February 1970 asking to meet with him in order to discuss the deep and dangerous alienation of the country's twenty-five million Negroes. Two months later a staff aide replied to say the President had not been able to clear time in his schedule for such a meeting.

America heard about Nixon's snub from William L. Clay in a House speech. Charles C. Diggs, Jr., of Michigan, chairman of the black caucus, had received the White House letter, but it was the freshman from Missouri who spoke out in May to "make known at this time our outright disgust with the President's policies and his refusal to give us an audience. . . ."

"There is no question about where Mr. Nixon has placed his priorities," Clay declared. "He has traveled more than 35,000 miles in foreign countries. He has entertained hundreds of foreign dignitaries but refuses to meet with the elected representatives of the black 'nation' within this country."

While he was too busy to confer with them, the congressman said the Chief Executive had found time for meetings with eleven veteran and patriotic groups, association executives, the head nurse of a Vietnamese children's hospital—and for many cocktail parties and state dinners.

To Clay it was "pathetic" that the well-traveled President "had not seen the suffering and deprivation" in Watts, Hough, Harlem, Fillmore, and the other United States ghettos. He charged that the President's failure to give priority to such domestic concerns as poverty, housing, and unemployment "testify to his apathy not only toward black people—but toward all poor Americans who since January, 1969, have truly known what it means to be 'forgotten.'"

Clay is well qualified to discuss life in an American ghetto, having grown up in one. He was born April 30, 1931, in the crowded St. Louis First Congressional District which he now represents in the House. Irvin and Luella Clay and their nine children lived in a tenement with no indoor plumbing and no hot water. Until his retirement, Irvin Clay was an acetylene-torch operator.

Young Bill started to work at thirteen as a janitor in a clothing store. Taught to sew by his sister, he was promoted to tailor and then to salesman at the age of eighteen. His savings put him through St. Louis University in 1953 with a major in history and political science. He was one of four blacks in a class of eleven hundred.

Drafted the day after graduation, he was stationed at Fort McClellan, near Anniston, Alabama. Though it was several years after President Harry S. Truman's executive order banning segregation on military installations, Clay ran right into Jim Crow. When black soldiers tried to beat the muggy heat with a swim, they were told that the two pools were reserved for National Guard training units. Yet white regular army personnel on the base regularly used them.

On Thursday nights the noncommissioned officers' club was off limits for Negroes while whites danced with members of the women's club of Anniston. Worse still, all the post barber shops were segregated. On Saturdays a black barber was imported from Anniston to give the blacks haircuts.

Clay organized black soldiers into a protest group. Nearly three months went by with many of them refusing to have their hair cut. Singling Clay out as the instigator of the trouble, the colonel threatened to discipline him and then gave him a direct order to get a haircut. "I didn't refuse the order, I merely refused to have a haircut on Saturdays," Clay explained. "I went to the barber shop Monday through Friday each day. The colonel, after about a week of this, was more adamant about his intention to court-martial me. At this point I decided to give real grounds for such action."

So Clay, accompanied by his wife, their children, and some of the children's friends "crashed the gates of the all-white swimming pool and went swimming." Other soldiers blocked the doors of the NCO club and the black press picked up the story. The army abruptly shipped Clay to another camp, but the protests continued until most of the racial barriers at Fort McClellan came down.

After finishing his military hitch, Clay moved restlessly from job to job for several years. He tried aeronautical chart-making, bus driving, real estate, and insurance. Participation in the St. Louis civil rights campaigns of the Congress of Racial Equality gave him an opportunity to get into Democratic politics.

At twenty-eight he defeated the veteran white Democratic incumbent and another challenger to become alderman of the largely black twenty-sixth ward. Not long afterward, he and two friends were arrested when they insisted on eating at a Howard Johnson's restaurant in St. Louis. The judge dismissed the case on the ground that the city could not use police powers to enforce segregation. Clay cosponsored the St. Louis ordinance which now makes it illegal to refuse to serve blacks in restaurants, theaters, or other public places.

During this period, the tall, dark alderman, who also was business representative for the Municipal Employees Union, marched on civil rights picket lines. "An Anatomy of Economic Murder" was the title he gave his report on employment bias in five hundred businesses in St. Louis. This statistical study provided effective ammunition for campaigns to open up jobs for blacks in public utilities, garages, aircraft plants, bakeries, breweries, and banks.

Clay was imprisoned in 1963 for demonstrating against the hiring policies of the Jefferson Bank and Trust Company of St. Louis. He and thirteen others were charged with contempt of court for violating an order against interfering with the bank's business. One of three leaders sentenced to jail, he served 112 days of a 270-day term and paid $1,000 in fines and $105 in court costs before being paroled. However, the financial institutions got the message. The number of blacks in nonmenial jobs in St. Louis banks went from sixteen to seven hundred in five years.

"I think things were accomplished that far outweighed the 112 days spent in jail," he said. "That demonstration just might be the reason the city hasn't burned. It shook a lot of industries up and they went out and began looking for Negro workers."

Alderman Clay simplified job hunting for poorly educated whites and blacks with a fair employment ordinance forbidding the use of testing procedures, arrest records, diploma requirements, or length of unemployment to bar otherwise qualified applicants. The mayor vetoed his measure to prohibit the release of arrest records for people who were not convicted as charged, but the board of aldermen overrode the veto. Still in effect, the law has not been tested in the courts.

Elected to a second term as alderman in 1963, Clay resigned that same year to run for the politically more worthwhile job of ward committeeman. In this influential local party position, which he held when named to Congress, he unfailingly brought out the voters for the Democrats.

In February 1966, he became the education coordinator of the Steamfitters Union Local 562, then an all-white union. He told critics he was not ashamed to be associated with a progressive union that had won many fringe benefits for its workers. Clay used his position, which paid him a salary of fifteen thousand dollars annually, to open the field to Negro apprentices, trainees, journeymen, and college students in summer programs. Within three years there were thirty black steamfitters working in the St. Louis area at wages of thirteen thousand dollars and up.

Court-ordered redistricting paved the road to Congress for Clay by reshaping the First District to incorporate nearly all of St. Louis' 250,000 Negroes. Frank Karsten, who had represented the district, chose retirement when his territory became 55 percent black. "Clay for Congress" stickers appeared the day after the incumbent announced his decision. On August 6, 1968, Clay won a five-way primary contest, beating runner-up Milton Carpenter by sixty-five hundred votes.

By October, the unpretentious, gregarious Democrat looked like a winner over Curtis Crawford, a Republican lawyer, who called for "law and order" and less federal spending—a platform with scant appeal for slum dwellers. Clay advocated a crackdown on police brutality, welfare reforms, better schools and housing, and more jobs for blacks. He accused his opponent of offering a program suitable for any white racist. Clay promised to represent all the people of his district, but he emphasized that action to assure minorities just treatment was of paramount concern. He defeated Curtis by nearly thirty-five thousand votes. Clay brought his wife, Carol, and three children, Vickie, Michelle, and Lacey, to Washington in 1969 and later the family moved into a house in Silver Spring, Maryland.

Assigned to the Education and Labor Committee, Clay introduced a measure to boost the minimum hourly wage to two dollars and co-sponsored a bill to strengthen the fair employment provisions of the 1964 Civil Rights Act. These two bills were among the thousands the Ninety-first Congress did not act upon—to nobody's surprise. A bigger disappointment for him came late in 1970 when Nixon vetoed the $9,500,000,000 manpower training bill that the Missouri congressman had cosponsored and helped put together in the Education and Labor Committee.

During his first term Clay pressured the administration to enforce the existing civil rights statutes. "Over and over I have heard that this government is a government of laws and not of men," he said at Texas Southern University in Houston in May 1969. "If this is so, why is it that the law against inciting to riot is being strictly enforced but attempts to enforce the law against discrimination in employment is called harassment?"

Blacks and young people in general, he said, were well aware of the true facts. "The black man," he continued, "has been told to obey the law, but not to expect equal rights under the law. The student has been taught to respect the truth of democracy and the rights of man —but not to question war or discrimination or poverty or hunger. If there is truly an alliance of black people and youth today—it is obvious why. They share an equal disgust for the double standard and hypocrisy which exist."

He and the other black representatives protested when Clifford L. Alexander, Jr., was forced out as chairman of the Equal Employment Opportunity Commission. Clay was even more disturbed after Alexander's successor, William Brown III, also a Negro, proposed to discontinue public hearings, which had been one of the agency's strongest weapons.

Clay said that the question of whether industries were living up to their commitment to the law in their employment policies was the public's business. "It is . . . ," he pointed out, "a public law, which passed the Congress in 1964—not a private law. . . . Closet equal employment hearings in darkness, and Senators [Everett] Dirksen and [Strom] Thurmond will effectively manipulate the machinery to prevent compliance with the law. Chairman Brown won't live long enough to see compliance under those circumstances."

Clay asked the Justice and Labor departments to investigate the "racist record" of the International Association of Bridge, Structural and Ornamental Iron Workers Union, whose national membership was less than half of 1 percent black or Mexican-American. The union's policies, he charged, were in "gross violation" of Title Seven of the 1964 Civil Rights Act which forbade unions or employers to discriminate against people because of race or religion. The congressman accused John Lyons, president of the union, of using the pejorative "nigger" during a civil rights conference. Lyons' response was that he had made a "freudian" slip of the tongue. Clay's complaint against the iron workers' almost-white union brought no action from the executive branch of the government.

In July 1969 Clay joined with Ohio's Louis Stokes and Michigan's John Conyers, Jr., in House speeches analyzing the record of the Nixon administration. Clay criticized the Republican President for weakening the school desegregation guidelines, for cutting back the Job Corps programs, for failing to meet the country's housing needs, and for reducing the education and poverty budgets.

Clay feared that blacks and white liberals could hope for little more than a holding action until there was a change in Washington. "We have," he said, "a government which upholds its responsibility for common defense and ignores its responsibility for justice and domestic tranquility. Nothing short of individual concern and involvement and awareness can prevent a total repression of minorities." He documented where the money was going—$1,000,000,000 spent annually in fiscal 1968 to pay farmers not to grow crops, while Americans suffered from hunger, and $80,000,000,000 for defense compared with $3,200,000,000 for health, education, and welfare combined.

Clay was particularly distressed to see the United States pouring its resources into a Southeast Asia war that many black Americans and other nonwhites throughout the world considered to be "racist." While the United States fought in Vietnam ostensibly to prevent the spread of international Communism, the Missouri congressman pointed out that Americans were being told it was in their best interest to coexist with the "chief architect" of that international conspiracy. The government was dividing the Communists into good and bad ones. "It may just be coincidental that all the bad Communists are peoples of color—Chinese, Cubans, Vietnamese, Koreans," he said in a November 1969 House speech. "If in truth it is coincidence, I contend it is racist coincidence. . . ."

Although relieved after the public and Congress finally forced Ford to halt the Vietnam War, Clay was distressed that, even in peacetime, insatiable military demands continued to get priority over the human needs of America's deteriorating, nearly bankrupt cities.

In 1975 his worries took a more personal turn as he became entangled in three major investigations. Clay, who had been re-elected to his fourth term by a comfortable majority, denied accusations that he had padded his congressional office payroll, evaded taxes, or been involved in illicit drug trafficking. The Justice Department found no cause for action against him on the drug charges, and he filed a $12,000,000 damage suit against the *St. Louis Globe-Democrat*, which broke the story about his alleged meeting with illegal narcotics marketers. Probes into his office payroll and tax returns continued.

Within the congressional black caucus Clay has concentrated on the media's coverage of the black community and minority employment in broadcasting and publishing. His hearings produced witnesses who charged that the white-controlled news media "grossly excluded, distorted, and exploited" black news and the black movement. Clay struck hard at publicly owned television, attacking it for discriminating against minorities and women in jobs, programming, and top management.

William Clay, one-time union official and now Missouri's only black congressman, heads the Post Office subcommittee on employee political rights and intergovernmental programs. Under his direction the subcommittee has proposed measures to grant public employees stronger collective bargaining rights and to amend the Hatch Act to allow government workers to participate voluntarily in politics on their own time but to resist involuntary party activities forced on them by superiors.

Shirley Chisholm/New York

Shirley Chisholm, the sixty-sixth of her sex to sit in the House of Representatives, became an overnight celebrity as the first black congresswoman. Daughter of a Barbadian seamstress and a Guyanese factory worker, this former schoolteacher blossomed in the warm glow of flash bulbs and television lights.

A woman who wanted to compete for a high political office was likely to be told to stay in her place. Never one to be deterred by such admonitions, Mrs. Chisholm won her seat from New York's Twelfth Congressional District in competition with one of the best known blacks in America, James Farmer, erstwhile director of the Congress of Racial Equality.

Mrs. Chisholm's impact in Washington came as no surprise to anyone who knew of her previously. Hard-working, opinionated, resourceful—and anything but modest—she has not advanced in a white man's world by worrying about rules or traditions. The five-foot-four, dark dynamo has boundless energy and does not mind using it to get what she wants.

Brooklyn's lady congressman immediately was besieged by broadcasting and newspaper reporters. A few months and hundreds of interviews later, she threatened to call a halt to the flurry of publicity, but she continued to be very much in evidence in newspapers and magazines as well as on radio and TV. She made countless speeches, accepted innumerable awards, conducted a weekly radio program over WLIB in New York, and still managed to fulfill her basic responsibility—attendance to official congressional and committee business on Capitol Hill.

Mrs. Chisholm was born Shirley St. Hill on November 30, 1924, in Brooklyn's Bedford-Stuyvesant, New York City's second most infamous ghetto and the heart of her present congressional district. Being a native of the area was a tremendous plus for her in the race against

255

armer, who was celebrated for his freedom bus rides and other civil rights work. "Mr. Farmer and I agreed on practically everything," she said. "But the main issue was that the people considered him a carpetbagger. Since he lived in Manhattan, it would have made more sense for him to run in Harlem."

When she was three, Shirley and her sisters were taken to Barbados to live with their grandmother. Surrounded by six cousins and an aunt and uncle, the St. Hill girls had little chance to be homesick for Brooklyn or their mother and father. The parents stayed behind to earn and save as much money as possible for their children's education.

In 1934 Shirley and her sisters returned to Brooklyn to live with their parents. The depression cut into their father's hours at the burlap factory, and Mrs. St. Hill got a job as a domestic. The girls found it hard to adjust to a bitterly cold, cramped apartment after years of running free on a sunny Barbados farm. Changing schools was difficult for Shirley, but special coaching in American history and geography soon enabled her to catch up with her class.

An exceptionally adept high school student, she graduated from Brooklyn College on a scholarship and earned her master's degree in education at Columbia University. She was a nursery-school teacher and director of a child-care center before joining New York's Day Care Division as an educational consultant in 1959. Community activities gradually led her into Democratic politics as a clubhouse worker. Her husband, Conrad Chisholm, a private investigator who later went to work for New York City in the Medicaid Claims section, often accompanied her to meetings. A compactly built, easy-going West Indian, he has said he is quite willing to work behind the scenes and let his wife be "the star in our family."

Life as an elected official did not begin for Mrs. Chisholm until the age of forty. Bedford-Stuyvesant sent her to the state assembly in Albany in 1964, where she was the second black woman member and the first to represent Brooklyn. From the start, she was a political maverick, coming out against the election of Stanley Steingut, the Brooklyn Democratic boss, as state assembly speaker in her initial assembly speech. During the next four years Mrs. Chisholm, who had to stand for reelection sooner than usual because of reapportionment, was named to her seat three times.

She helped get three substantial measures through the state legislature—day-care centers, unemployment insurance for domestic workers, and the SEEK college students program. SEEK, which stands for Search for Elevation, Education, and Knowledge, finds places in colleges for talented underprivileged boys and girls, who

256

may not meet the traditional entrance requirements. She wants this program adopted nationally.

The Supreme Court reapportionment decision of 1964 made possible the election of the country's first black congresswoman. The court held that congressional districts should be carved out to contain about the same number of voters. The New York legislature after lengthy procrastination moved to correct the inequities in some districts including central Brooklyn early in 1968. The revamped Twelfth Congressional District, 70 percent black and the remainder mostly Puerto Rican, Jewish, and Italian, was the result. Mrs. Chisholm announced her candidacy as soon as the district lines were drawn.

"Everybody felt so sorry for me," she said. "I had to give up my [assembly] seat to run for Congress and that was a safe thing." Her primary opponents, former State Senator William Thompson and Dolly Robinson, previously a special assistant to the director of the women's bureau of the labor department, had backing from some of the party leaders. Mrs. Chisholm was supported by the Unity Democratic Club and hundreds of volunteers. The driving, intense, sedately dressed educator won by 788 votes in a district where registered women voters outnumbered men.

There was little time for jubilation. The pressure was on for the November election contest against James Farmer, who had entered the race on the Liberal ticket and later gained the Republican nomination, also. A tumor operation put Mrs. Chisholm out of action for three weeks in July, but she was cheered by her selection as Democratic national committeewoman. She went back to her packed schedule as soon as the doctor would allow, speaking at innumerable gatherings and shaking thousands of hands. She lost seventeen pounds, but she won the race by a margin of 2½ to 1.

The rule about speaking only when spoken to applies to new representatives as well as to children. The House was just getting started on organizational matters when Mrs. Chisholm confounded the leadership by refusing to accept quietly and uncomplainingly a committee assignment she considered nothing short of ridiculous. This member from a slum district of the nation's largest city was named to the Agricultural Committee's subcommittee on forestry and rural villages.

Betty Smith's *A Tree Grows in Brooklyn* had enjoyed global popularity, but Mrs. Chisholm immediately made it clear she did not want anyone to have the misconception that hers was a district where the big concern was agriculture, or any sort of growing things except maybe kids. "Apparently all they know here in Washington about

Brooklyn is that a tree grew there," she stated. "I can think of no other reason for assigning me to the House Agriculture Committee. . . .

"It seems to me that it is time for the House of Representatives to pay attention to other considerations than its petrified, sanctified system of seniority, which is apparently the only basis for making most of its decisions," Mrs. Chisholm said in a statement issued to the press after the closed Democratic caucus.

"There are only nine black members of the House. Even though this is the largest number since Reconstruction, it is far too few to fairly represent black Americans. The House leadership has a moral duty to somewhat right the balance by putting the nine members it has in positions where they can work effectively to help this nation meet its critical problems of racism, deprivation and urban decay."

Much to the dismay of the traditionalists, who thought the upstart New Yorker was undermining the system, the House leadership did find another spot for Mrs. Chisholm—on the Veterans Affairs Committee. Education and Labor was what she longed for, but Veterans Affairs was an improvement over forestry. She had set the posture she was to follow in the House as a woman of drive and determination who would not be ignored.

Hale Boggs, the majority whip in the House, saluted her on WNBC-TV, New York, as "the only person in my knowledge to have defeated the [House Democratic] Committee on Committees. I think it impressed everybody in the House that here was . . . a Negro woman, the first ever elected in history, who was able to take on the Speaker, the Majority Leader, the Majority Whip and everybody— and beat them."

Perhaps more than anything Mrs. Chisholm longs to change the seniority system of Congress, which, she said, had locked the control of the nation's destiny in the hands of fifteen men, selected not for capabilities, intellect, or ability, but for longevity. She charged Congress with neglecting the planet earth while authorizing exorbitant military and space ventures. The fault, she feels, lies primarily with those "old men from the Southern oligarchy."

The Brooklyn member warned in her first House speech in March 1969 that she would vote against every defense bill "until the time comes when our values and priorities have been turned right side up again." The priorities she had in mind were the basics for the country's disadvantaged people: jobs, housing, education, child care, and medicine. Much of the legislation she has cosponsored covers these general areas, where Congress made few advances during her first term.

Mrs. Chisholm is not one of those past-thirty politicians who suffers from the generation gap. Her understanding of America's strangely-attired, long-haired, restless collegians came through clearly in a speech at Notre Dame University in South Bend, Indiana, in March 1969. She thought the campus disorders symptomatic of the grievous ills and decadent values in modern society. She said it was not surprising that university trustees were out of touch. She described the average trustee as a fifty-plus, white, Protestant businessman, who was probably also a conservative and obviously not the sort to give students or progressive faculty members a voice in running the university. Stifling campus dissent, she said, would only swell the protest ranks: the answer was to make the universities fulfill their responsibilities to urban society.

As a former educator herself, she has been a tireless booster for education. On her radio program, she advised children to mix play and study. She told them fun alone was not enough to get them by economically in modern life and "only weaklings give up in the face of obstacles."

Mrs. Chisholm also advocated strong laws to protect consumers and favored the creation of a Cabinet-level post to handle consumer affairs. "Let's take a look at ourselves and try to analyze our superficial values," she said in an Ohio University speech about advertising and the way it has turned Americans into "passive consumers. . . .

"For hundreds of years now, black people in America have been spending huge sums of their scarce money on hair straighteners and skin lighteners. Women of all colors have been agonizing daily in uncomfortable corsets, and nightly in head-piercing hair rollers and ghastly face creams. Today men buy fake sideburns so that they can look dashing at parties while remaining straight at their offices.

"Why do we alter ourselves, torture ourselves, to look as much like everyone else as possible? It is because we have adopted the Miss America or the Pepsi generation or the Bacardi rum image as our standard of beauty. As we are constantly inundated by advertising for products designed to make us conform to these commercial images, we begin to incorporate these values as our own. We say subconsciously, 'I don't want to be me, because me doesn't look like what I am told is beautiful. Instead let me recreate myself in the image of a nameless, personless Fun Boy or Girl.' That means consuming all the thousands of products absolutely essential to become that new, vacant self. Without the products, we cannot achieve the new identity."

While working diligently in Washington, Mrs. Chisholm made frequent trips back to New York, where she was becoming increasingly influential in city and state politics. She campaigned energetically for

259

John V. Lindsay's reelection in 1969 and was one of those the New York City mayor, supported by Democrats and Liberals after the Republicans refused to nominate him, thanked in his November victory speech. Yet not long afterward, she sharply criticized the city's police department for allegedly taking bribes to protect numbers racketeers, drug pushers, and prostitutes.

Her interests are legion, and the demands for her attention insatiable, but she is especially moved by the plight of two groups—women with unwanted pregnancies and young men forced to fight a Southeast Asia war many of them consider cruel and senseless. As honorary president of the National Association for the Repeal of Abortion Laws, she launched a national campaign for a number of test suits designed to give pregnant women the right to decide whether they wish to have the baby.

"If we are going to wipe out the horror of the present system, where an estimated million women a year are forced into the abortion underworld," she said, "we must guarantee that abortion becomes a medical decision between a woman and her physician." The New York state legislature agreed that times were changing and passed a bill legalizing abortions in 1970.

In her efforts to protect thousands of unwillingly drafted, Vietnam-bound young men, the childless congresswoman blasted the Nixon draft reform as a hoax. She voted against the administration-backed lottery bill, which she said was designed to appease the violent dissenters among the middle-class youths. "A democracy that depends on conscription of often unwilling citizens is not a democracy at all," she said in calling for a switch from conscription to an all-volunteer army. "Even worse, when a country preys on its politically weakest element—nonvoting youth—it is nothing more than an elitist jungle where only the strong and the lucky can survive."

Being a woman, Mrs. Chisholm often says, has been more of a handicap to her in her career than being black. Yet two years in Congress have established her as a person to be reckoned with, not only in New York City, where she has been called in to talk to rioting prisoners, but also in the state, where she and other liberals are trying to revitalize the Democratic party, and throughout the country, where she is one of the Establishment figures still listened to by the disenchanted young.

Mrs. Chisholm did not advance her own or her party's fortunes by running for the Democratic Presidential nomination in 1972. Rife with funding irregularities for several Democratic candidates as well as for the Republican, Richard M. Nixon, this campaign left her fashionable skirts splattered with mud.

The General Accounting Office charged the Chisholm campaign

organization with failing to keep proper records on contributions and to file required reports. GAO said her campaign committee received $686 in illegal corporate contributions and reported a $6,000 debit when it had a cash balance of $18,000.

Upset by newspaper headlines she considered unwarranted for a $99,000 campaign, Mrs. Chisholm explained that the audit was made before all bills were paid. Record-keeping irregularities she attributed to a small, nonprofessional staff. Revealing she made $30,000 from lectures and book royalties in addition to her $42,000 salary, she denied the press's inference that she might have used campaign funds to buy clothes or her Virgin Islands home.

"I never will forget what Adam Powell said to me," she told *Jet* magazine. "He described me as not being a quiet and gentle sort of politician, but a fighter, a rock-the-boat type of individual who they'll eventually get. I laughed at what Adam said. But now I know what he meant." No charges were brought against Mrs. Chisholm; the Justice Department said in 1974 that proper records had since been submitted and there was no evidence to substantiate the other accusations.

Mrs. Chisholm has had the satisfaction of achieving some priority goals. She fought with the women's and population control groups for every woman's inherent right to decide whether to bear children. The missionary work of the feminists brought about the liberalization of the New York State abortion law. Even more significant was the Supreme Court decision of 1973 that held abortion during the early months of pregnancy to be a matter for a woman and her doctor to decide, though some states continue to make this operation difficult to obtain, especially for women on welfare.

Mrs. Chisholm is an articulate member of the liberal block, which helped force the Republican Administration ultimately to end the war in Vietnam and the Democratic House leadership to modify the seniority system sufficiently to unseat some veteran chairmen and to spread the subcommittee chairmanships more widely. As chairwoman of the Education and Labor subcommittee on elementary, secondary, and vocational education, she has held hearings to prod the bureaucrats to curb sex and racial bias, particularly in vocational schools. She worked to extend the $2.20 minimum wage to cover domestics, who handle housekeeping chores.

Shirley Chisholm, bright, volatile, resourceful, has her district so well under control that the Republicans virtually concede the contest. Matured by the unpleasantness of her 1972 Presidential race, America's first black congresswoman occupies a unique niche in history. Unless she joins the discouraged governmental dropouts, her political story is far from finished.

George Collins advanced through the ranks of city government in Chicago to give Illinois its second black-represented congressional district in 1970.

Ronald V. Dellums, representative from California's Eighth District (formerly the Seventh) since 1971, pushed for a thorough probe of the Central Intelligence Agency as a member of a select House committee. (**Lance D. Weaver**)

Ralph Metcalfe, successor to William L. Dawson in the First Illinois District, has feuded with Chicago boss Mayor Richard J. Daley over police brutality and inefficiency.

Parren J. Mitchell, professor turned congressman, represents the increasingly black city of Baltimore, Maryland. He was one of six Negro freshmen in the 92nd Congress. (**Joseph Daniel Clipper**)

Charles B. Rangel defeated the charismatic Adam Clayton Powell, Jr., in a Democratic primary in 1970 to take over the New York district which is centered around Harlem. (**Dev O'Neill**)

Walter E. Fauntroy, non-voting delegate from the District of Columbia since 1971, was the fourth black minister elected to Congress. (**Chase Studios Ltd.**)

Yvonne B. Burke of California, who presided over the national Democratic convention in 1968, is the first woman elected by her colleagues to head the congressional black caucus.

Cardiss Collins followed her late husband, George Collins, in the Seventh Illinois District. She won the post in her first try for public office in mid-1973. (**Bonner & Bonner**)

Barbara Jordan, the first black member from Texas, helped force Richard Nixon from the presidency with her work on the House Judiciary Committee.

Andrew Young, a minister and former aide to Martin Luther King, Jr., went to the House in 1973 nearly a century after his Georgia predecessor had been forced out of public life. (**Dev O'Neill**)

Harold E. Ford, sent to the House in 1975 by Memphis voters, has two brothers in Tennessee State Legislature, one of whom holds his old seat there. (**Dev O'Neill**)

Ralph H. Metcalfe/Illinois
George Collins/Illinois
Charles B. Rangel/New York
Ronald V. Dellums/California

The civil rights movement inspired by Martin Luther King, Jr., the Voting Rights Act of 1965, and court-ordered redistricting have cleared the way for the election of a steadily rising number of black Americans to the House of Representatives. Between 1971 and 1975, black congressmen were seated for the first time ever from Maryland, Tennessee, and the District of Columbia; for the first time since Reconstruction from Georgia, and from California and Illinois to represent additional districts.

Four of these male newcomers were from the North or the West— Ralph H. Metcalfe and George Collins of Illinois, Charles B. Rangel of New York, and Ronald V. Dellums of California. The third black to represent the First District of Illinois since Oscar DePriest redesegregated Congress in 1929, Ralph Metcalfe, a world champion sprinter, opted for moderation during fifteen years on the Chicago city council but has become more militant, impatient, outspoken, and demanding since going to the House.

Elected in 1970 to succeed William L. Dawson, the tall, gray-haired, moustachioed Metcalfe soon amassed enough seniority to head the Merchant Marine and Fisheries subcommittee on the Panama Canal, a post with potential importance, considering the mounting controversy over America's control of this busy waterway. More significantly, he was named by Speaker Carl Albert to represent the congressional black caucus on the revitalized Democratic Steering and Policy Committee in 1975 after it assumed responsibility for making House committee assignments.

A native Southerner, like all his Negro predecessors from the district, Metcalfe retains a touch of Georgia in his voice, having been born in Atlanta on May 29, 1910, to Major Clarence and Mayme Attaway Metcalfe. The Metcalfes soon moved to Chicago, where Ralph's father was employed in the stockyards and his mother made clothes at home to earn extra money to support their three children.

Ralph went to work at the age of seven, pumping water to steam the machines in a pressing shop, cleaning the store, and delivering clothes. Later he shined shoes, washed cars, delivered groceries. He was given permission to skip school on Fridays so that he could manage a fish market while his Jewish employer prepared for the Sabbath.

At the age of fifteen he started competing seriously in track events, and within four years he became national interscholastic sprinting champion. A B student despite his grueling work, study, and track schedule, he graduated from Marquette University in 1936 as class president.

Chancellor Adolf Hitler walked out in disgust after Jesse Owens, a non-Aryan, black American won the 100-meter dash at the 1936 Olympics in Berlin; split seconds behind him was Metcalfe. These two champions also helped the United States capture the 400-meter relay race.

Back from Europe with two more medals to add to his collection, Metcalfe taught political science and coached the track team at Xavier University in New Orleans, then took a leave to earn a master's degree in physical education at the University of Southern California. During World War II he served in Louisiana as a first lieutenant with the Army Transportation Corps. He returned to Chicago to become civil rights director for the Human Rights Commission and to marry Madelynne (Fay) Young. Named to the Illinois State Athletic Commission, he used his influence to break the racial barriers for qualified referees, timekeepers, and stadium physicians.

Metcalfe was past forty when in 1952 he won his first elective position, third ward Democratic committeeman. Within three years he had picked up enough public support to unseat the Reverend Archibald Carey on the Chicago City Council.

Accustomed to the discipline of athletics, Metcalfe cooperated with the regular Chicago Democratic organization and generally stayed in line on its decisions. Black reporters faulted him for supporting Mayor Richard Daley even when the Democratic boss cold-shouldered Martin Luther King's jobs demonstrations in Chicago. Still, Metcalfe was following a winning game plan—in an arena where no one disputed Daley's control. In 1969, Metcalfe advanced to president pro tempore of the City Council, a post analogous to vice mayor.

Congressman Dawson, forced into retirement by age and illness, backed Metcalfe in a primary race against A. A. Rayner, an alderman-undertaker. Campaigning on his City Council record with the assistance of the Daley machine, Metcalfe piled up a plurality of 28,400 votes. In the general election he breezed past the Republican candidate, schoolteacher Janet Jennings, by 84,000 votes.

Assigned to the Interstate and Foreign Commerce Committee, the neophyte congressman made his biggest impact as an investigator and a critic of the Chicago police department. Metcalfe, who lives near the Chicago ghetto of his childhood, was disturbed by the increase in street, person-against-person crime, on the one hand, and the incidence of police harassment of law-abiding citizens on the other. He blasted the police department and called on Daley to act promptly to correct the situation.

Getting no satisfaction, he held ad hoc hearings to collect testimony from victims of alleged police maltreatment. For example, a seventy-year-old dentist, after suffering a stroke, was arrested as a drunk and held without medical attention until it was too late to save his life. Metcalfe formed the Concerned Citizens for Police Reform to negotiate their demands with the city. Metcalfe has charged that Daley reneged on promises to appoint a negotiating team to discuss the black community's grievances.

Nonetheless, some of the Concerned Citizens' recommendations have been put into effect. A Civil Service Commission–administered psychological testing program was set up to weed out undesirables before they get on the police force. The Special Police Operations Group— commonly called the "task force"—was instructed not to disregard the citizens' civil rights when chasing down law breakers in the high crime areas. The minimum height for police officers was cut to five feet six, a boon for women and Spanish-Americans who want to be cops.

Voters supported the congressman's fight for better police service for ghetto neighborhoods, and some activists who once considered him too conservative, were transformed into Metcalfe boosters. The people have reelected him by increasingly large margins. He won by 91 percent in 1972 and by 95 percent in 1974, in each case, against weak Republican opposition.

Metcalfe intensified his battle to reform the Chicago police after newspaper stories revealed that the department's intelligence division spied on local community leaders, elected officials (including Metcalfe), teachers, and newspaper reporters and, in his words, "thousands of Chicagoans whose only crime was to get on the mailing list of any one of dozens of local organizations." A General Accounting Office study ordered by the representative found that the undercover division had spent $10,000,000 in two years, much of it coming from federal funds earmarked for other purposes. Metcalfe called for an end to the diversion of monies from their authorized purpose to illegal spying on opponents and critics of the city administration.

Those unfairly accused of crimes may be aided by the Speedy Trial Act of 1974. This is similar to a measure introduced earlier by Metcalfe to require federal criminal cases to be tried within ninety days. His bill banning the manufacture and sale of handguns except for official use, many people believe, would decrease murder in the big cities, but neither Democratic congresses nor Republican Presidents have been willing to stand up against the gun lobby and support such a curb.

Metcalfe has cosponsored several health laws and has made creative use of ad hoc hearings and the General Accounting Office services to expose bureaucratic shortcomings in this and other areas. Alabama public health clinics stopped using venereal disease victims as guinea pigs to test syphilis drugs after the congressman's hearings revealed that four hundred patients, apparently without their knowledge, had been allowed to go untreated by the clinics' doctors.

Citing General Accounting data as proof, Metcalfe has charged the Health, Education and Welfare Department with failing to enforce compliance with legislation designed to provide preventive medical care for needy children; the Federal Aviation Administration with ignoring the recommendations of the National Transportation Safety Board, and the Federal Bureau of Prisons with isolating inmates for up to three years while "inhuman" mind control techniques were employed to reshape their behavior patterns.

Ralph H. Metcalfe, a loyal party leader, who came up through the ranks and waited in the wings for decades before moving onto the national scene, has capitalized on his House seat to strike out fearlessly against powerful targets, with results that could drastically affect his own political future.

A Metcalfe colleague among the Chicago Democratic regulars, George Collins also used the City Council as a stepping stone to the House of Representatives. A freshman in the Ninety-second Congress in 1971, along with Metcalfe and four other blacks, Collins gained a few days' seniority on his fellow newcomers when he was sworn in for an unexpired term in the Ninety-first Congress.

Collins was born on March 5, 1925, in Chicago. He attended public schools there. The youngster sold newspapers and worked in a drugstore, where he caught the eye of the "most popular man around," Eddie Brown, the local Democratic precinct captain. After finishing

Waller High School in 1943, he served for three years with the Army Engineers Corps in the South Pacific during World War II. Back in civilian life, he tried real estate briefly and then resumed his education, to receive a business law degree from Northwestern University in 1957. A year after graduation, while working as a clerk in the municipal court, he married Cardiss Robertson, a secretary.

Already the personable Collins was on his way in politics; like his idol, Eddie Brown, he had been named a precinct captain on Chicago's West Side. Friends and hard work moved him along from court clerk to Cook County deputy sheriff to alderman's secretary.

The turning point for Collins came in 1963 when he was chosen twenty-fourth ward committeeman; he was then working as administrative assistant to a health commissioner. This put him in line to run to represent the ward in the city council after veteran alderman Benjamin Lewis was shot down on the street in Chicago gangland fashion. Collins bested four rivals who hoped to succeed the flamboyant politician, reportedly slain for asking for a bigger cut from the gambling rackets.

In the council, Collins was viewed as a Daley man who worked with the mayor through the system to get what he could for the black inner city, where he and his family had learned first hand in the 1930's how difficult it was to survive during a depression. Collins was constantly on call to his constituents as alderman, just as he had been as a precinct captain.

Following the death of Representative Daniel J. Ronan in August 1969, Alderman Collins decided to compete for the Sixth Congressional District seat. With Daley's support, he won the Democratic nomination by 80 percent. In the general election in November 1970, voters pulled the lever twice—first to signal their choice for Ronan's unexpired term and then to name his successor to the Ninety-second Congress. Collins received more than 68,000 votes to about 54,000 for Republican Alex Zabrosky, a steel salesman, in each instance.

In Congress, Collins said his aim was to be of service "in any way" possible to the voters. He kept his district office open six days a week and tried to get back to Chicago every weekend. He spent hours listening to people who lined up to see him about their troubles with poor housing, unemployment, and the spreading drug traffic.

On the floor of the House, Collins supported President Nixon's revenue-sharing program as a move in the right direction, though far from adequate to meet the expenses of the hard-pressed states and cities with mounting welfare loads. He also backed Nixon's family assistance plan for a $2,400 guaranteed annual income for a family of four because it was the only proposal of its kind with a chance of passing. Weakened by lack of White House support, this innovative, though miserly, measure died.

Collins appealed to the Federal Housing Administration and to the Housing and Urban Development Department to protect the public from unscrupulous realtors and speculators. He charged the FHA with underwriting mortgages for the poor without properly inspecting the properties involved. In his district numerous unsophisticated buyers had been cheated by realtors.

The freshman member of the Government Operations and Public Works committees defended the seniority system because, he said, he'd like to stay around long enough to benefit from it. The smiling, round-faced representative told interviewers he personally had not experienced racial bias in the House; he felt his race could be an "advantage in Congress. People go out of their way to prove that because I'm black they don't want to hold me back."

When Vice President Agnew sarcastically contrasted strong African leaders with their grumbling black counterparts in America, Collins advised him to take off his rose-colored glasses and look at the condition of the poor and the blacks. Then, Collins said, Agnew could see for himself what black American leaders were complaining about—poor housing, joblessness, inadequate education, all contributing to the sharp rise of crime in urban America.

Collins walked a diplomatic line between Daley and Metcalfe after Metcalfe's crusade against police brutality strained the Metcalfe-Daley relationship to the breaking point. Collins agreed that the charges were serious, but he deplored the personal nature of the controversy between his two longtime associates.

Trouble loomed for Collins in 1972 when the Sixth District was redrawn to increase its white composition, while many of his supporters were assigned to the Seventh District, held by Frank Annunzio. Daley reportedly offered Collins his choice of jobs in the city administration if he would not challenge Annunzio.

Proving himself no Daley toady, Collins refused. A confrontation was avoided when Annunzio ran in the Eleventh. Nominated in the revamped Seventh, Collins defeated Thomas Lenta, the Republican, by 83 percent.

Looking forward happily to a second term, Collins embarked for Chicago on a rainy, foggy night—December 8, 1972. He was hurrying back to plan the annual Christmas party for the district children. While approaching the airport, his plane crashed without warning into a residential section and burst into flames. The forty-seven-year-old congressman was killed along with forty-four others, including Mrs. E. Howard Hunt, wife of one of the Watergate conspirators, who died carrying $10,000 in cash. Speculation followed that this was part of the "hush money" paid to the burglars, but her husband denied that the bills were linked to Watergate.

White and black associates eulogized Collins at his funeral. Metcalfe stressed his work on the council, where Collins could always be depended upon to support worthwhile legislation. Parren J. Mitchell of Maryland said that Congress would miss his "quiet, dogged determination." John Conyers, Jr., of Michigan said that Collins had been a "real comer" in the House. Daley mourned his loss of a friend and the country's loss of a great leader.

A military honor guard saluted the casket at the gravesite in recognition of the congressman's World War II service. Then came the too familiar sight of a folded American flag being handed to a veiled, sad-eyed widow, Cardiss Collins, who sat next to their only child, thirteen-year-old Kevin.

Like many nineteenth-century black congressmen, George Collins, a man of patience, thoughtfulness, and promise, had served too fleetingly in the House to make a lasting imprint.

A Collins contemporary, Charles B. Rangel was a little-known assemblyman when the New York City voters chose him in 1970 to replace the fiery, bombastic Adam Clayton Powell, Jr., as representative for one of the country's toughest, most economically depressed, districts. In Powell's heyday, Harlem, the heart of the district, was the cultural and entertainment capital of black America. By the 1970's many of its riot-scarred streets had been taken over by dope peddlers and addicts.

Powell's careless disregard of the basics of smart politics cleared an opening for Rangel's election by this liberal biracial constituency. The veteran congressman had not built a solid organization or a capable staff that could be relied upon to handle essential details after he himself became ill and discouraged.

Some Powell admirers thought his past contributions entitled him to die in office. Charles B. Rangel indicated that while he had nothing personal against Powell, he believed that New York's Eighteenth Congressional District was entitled to a working congressman who would attend House sessions regularly.

One of three children of separated parents, Rangel was born June 11, 1930, in Harlem. The youngsters lived with their mother, Blanche Horton Rangel, and with her father, Charles Horton. Rangel's mother worked in a garment factory; more often than not, his father—Ralph Rangel—was unemployed.

Young Charley dropped out of De Witt Clinton High School, fearing he couldn't compete. But the teen-ager didn't admit this; he said he was quitting to work in the garment district to aid his family. The congressman, who has fought fiercely to force the Federal Government to crack down on illicit drug traffic, says he is thankful that heroin was not so accessible in his boyhood, for peer pressure might have tempted him to experiment with the lethal white powder.

With no decent job in sight, Rangel became a soldier in 1948. He was wounded during the Korean conflict while leading forty men from behind enemy lines back to their unit. Mustered out in 1952 as a bronze-star–decorated staff sergeant, he finished high school and attended New York University on the GI bill. A dean's list student, he still found time to work as an unpaid volunteer in the district attorney's office. Rangel received his law degree from St. John's University in 1960.

After being appointed assistant United States attorney for the New York southern district, he celebrated by inviting judges, attorneys, and other courthouse regulars to a luncheon party honoring his cherished grandfather, whom many of them knew as a longtime elevator operator.

Rangel left this position in a few years to become counsel to the speaker of the New York State Assembly. Elected to the assembly in 1966, he worked to decentralize the school system of New York for greater community control and to get additional funding for Harlem Hospital. He wrote the police department's fourth platoon bill, which rescheduled tour duties to put more officers on New York City's streets during high crime hours.

A defeat in the Democratic primary race for the New York City council presidency in 1969 taught Rangel how it felt to lose an election. Despite this rebuff at the polls, Manhattan Borough President Percy Sutton chose the short, curly-haired assemblyman to give the already groggy Adam Powell a knockout blow. Former baseball star Jackie Robinson helped Rangel win the Republican nomination in Powell's district. Then, backed by Sutton, who blamed Powell for keeping him out of elective office for years, Rangel mounted a well-planned drive for the Democratic nomination in 1970.

Powell still was spending much of his time at Bimini in the Caribbean even though the House finally had readmitted him a year earlier. In March 1967 his colleagues had excluded him from his seat in the Ninetieth Congress for his alleged misuse of public funds and for his failure to purge himself of contempt of court charges growing out of a New York libel suit brought against him by an elderly widow whom he accused of being a "bag woman" for the police.

On the lecture circuit and on television, the ailing minister-congressman bragged that the House was getting its money's worth from him since a disciplinary fine was being taken out of his paycheck. In campaigning, Rangel did not attack Powell directly but talked about what an active representative could do for the people. Rangel edged Harlem's former hero in the primary by 150 votes and went on to defeat Liberal city councilman Charles Taylor by 46,400 votes in the general election.

The new congressman soon fell into one of his predecessor's less admirable habits. The New York *Post* rated him the "top truant" in the House, saying he had been absent from the session about one third of the time during his first months in office. Rangel says this story was unfairly slanted, that he was spending these months setting up an efficient district organization. However, after this publicity, he answered more roll calls.

Since his election, Rangel has concentrated on shaking the country out of its complacent acceptance of an estimated 600,000 heroin addicts as an insolvable problem. He charged New York City police with corruption and said they shared responsibility for open street-corner sales of a variety of illicit drugs to people of all ages. He urged Congress and the White House to stop drug shipments before they reached the United States. He used extensive publicity as a weapon in an attempt to mobilize worldwide public opinion against the drug-supplying nations.

In September 1971, President Nixon phoned Rangel, then the secretary of the black caucus, informing him that Turkey, which furnished an estimated 80 percent of America's heroin supply, had agreed to cut down on the production of opium poppies. Later it was revealed that American taxpayers were sending Turkey about $35,700,000 annually, part of it to go to ease the pain of the opium cutback for the farmers.

Keeping the pressure on, Rangel began introducing amendments to use foreign economic and military aid as an inducement to stop the shipment of unlawful drugs to America. In February 1972 a Rangel amendment to the Foreign Assistance Act of 1971 empowered the President to suspend economic and military assistance to any country if he determined that its government had failed to take adequate steps to keep illegal narcotic drugs produced, processed, or transported there, from entering the United States. Rangel attached a similar rider to funding legislation for the Asian Development Bank, the Inter-American Development Bank, and the International Development Association.

Since he defeated Powell, Rangel has not had to worry about re-election. Since 1972 he has run on the Democratic, Republican, and Liberal party lines against poorly financed, obscure, fringe-party rivals. His strength was not diluted by his assignment to the revamped Nineteenth District, which retains most of his old territory.

Rangel lives near his boyhood neighborhood in Harlem with his wife, Anna, and their two children. He has upgraded his committee assignments from Public Works to Judiciary to Ways and Means. The sixteen-member unofficial congressional black caucus named him its third chairman in 1974.

His most dramatic House assignment came as a member of the Judiciary Committee during the impeachment hearings brought against Richard Nixon. Rangel had advocated impeachment of the Watergate-implicated Chief Executive long before the committee began considering the case against him in January 1974. Six months later, Judiciary's nationally televised hearings were drawing huge audiences as sentiment mounted for a vote against Nixon for interfering with the official investigation of the break-in at the National Democratic Committee headquarters. The tide had started to turn strongly against Nixon despite his repeated denial of involvement in the Watergate cover-up. Some committee members spoke of the sorrow of the occasion as they set forth their positions in the controversy.

Not so Rangel, who told the television audience he considered it a bright, not a dark day in history, which proved that no man, however high his office, was above the law. Rangel presented evidence to document the charge that Nixon had passed along information received from Assistant Attorney General Henry Petersen about the grand jury deliberations to persons implicated in the case, notably the President's two chief assistants, John Ehrlichman and H. R. Haldeman. Because Nixon had not lived up to his oath of office as President, Rangel said, he would fulfill his own oath by voting for impeachment.

Rangel was revolted when Nixon's chosen successor, Gerald Ford, who, as Vice President–designate, had indicated he would let the court process run its course in the Watergate investigation, instead preempted the prosecutors and pardoned Nixon before any of the complaints made against him could be tried. "While it is constitutionally possible," Rangel said, "it is immoral to give a blanket pardon to someone who has not even admitted guilt. What it does mean is that the President of the United States can be charged with criminal conduct, resign, and look forward to being pardoned."

In contrast to Nixon, who kept the black caucus waiting for more than a year before conferring with it, Ford set up a date shortly after assuming the Presidency. The blacks asked the new President to act on unemployment, to grant amnesty to the men who had followed their convictions and refused to serve in Vietnam, to cut back on military spending, and to concentrate on domestic needs. Although Ford has been friendlier and more accessible to the black caucus members, legislatively his takeover has made little difference to them. He has vetoed bill after bill that might have benefited inflation-plagued jobless Americans—millions of whom are black.

Neither Ford nor Nixon made use of Rangel's military aid cutoff amendments as a weapon to fight the drug traffic, and hard drugs have continued—after a brief period of scarcity brought on by a temporary reduction in the Turkish acreage—to pour into New York and other major ports. While Ford did not accede to pleas for action to stop the resumption of the poppy crop in Turkey, Congress, with the support of the black caucus, clamped a ban on the sale of arms to Turkey in February 1975. This was in response to Turkey's illegal use of American military supplies to invade the island of Cyprus and had no effect on the opium controversy. Congress, in October, eased the embargo and enacted a Rangel-sponsored amendment asking Ford to initiate talks with Turkey to cut off the supply of illegal opium to America and to report to Congress within 160 days on the discussions.

Rangel and the black caucus were criticized by some observers for rejecting Representative Fortney Stark, a white California Democrat, for membership; he had asked to collaborate with them on common problems in their multiracial districts. Rangel said Stark was not turned down because he was white but because the black caucus, like the Democratic and Republican caucuses, couldn't admit an "outsider." Carl Rowan, a well-known black columnist, called this reasoning comparable to that of South Carolina whites who for years used grandfather clauses to keep blacks out of the Democratic party.

Blessed with a safe district, Charles B. Rangel gained enough visibility during two years as chairman of the black caucus to enable him to advance within the Democratic party council in New York as well as in Congress. Unhappily, despite some victories, his on-going campaign against the drug pushers and suppliers has yet to produce lasting improvement either nationally or in his own district.

Unlike Rangel, California's second black congressman, Ronald V. Dellums, has always faced serious opposition when running for Congress, though he wins by comfortable margins. Even after nearly three terms, this maverick representative seems surprised to be in politics and unsure of Congress as a place to accomplish what he wants to do with his life.

Tall, tan, with a Fu Manchu moustache and a moderate Afro with graying sideburns, he is in some respects the most radical of the black representatives. Whether peace-crusading actress Jane Fonda needs Washington facilities for a press conference or the Oglala Sioux Indians are looking for support, Dellums usually is the person to whom the nonconformists turn.

Understanding other people's frustrations comes naturally to this sensitive legislator who not so long ago was a psychiatric social worker. He still looks sad as he recalls a "paranoid" client who said, "I don't need talking, man, I need a job." There was no place Dellums could send him except on a futile round from one agency to another.

Born November 24, 1936, to Willa Terry Dellums, a government clerk-typist, and Vernie Dellums, a Pullman porter, Dellums grew up in West Oakland, California. His parents, from the South, though not college-educated themselves, were determined their son would go to a university. Grades were no hassle for him until he failed to make the high school varsity baseball team because the coach didn't want a "black prima donna pitcher." After that Ron lost interest in his studies.

Having graduated with marks too low for the hoped-for scholarship to the University of Southern California, Dellums entered San Francisco Community College. Feeling "terrible" because he had lost the scholarship and his mother was "sacrificing" to send him to college, he signed on with the Marine Corps for two years, knowing that the GI bill would help him finance his studies later.

With assistance from the bill and earnings from outside jobs, he graduated from San Francisco State College in 1960 and received his master's degree in social welfare from the University of California at Berkeley two years later. Finishing his education was complicated by a broken teen-age marriage, which had produced two children.

Following graduation, Dellums worked in the mental hygiene department at Berkeley and used this as a springboard to move on to progressively better administrative posts in a variety of anti-poverty programs. The news from northern California during this period was dominated by stories of war protests, student demonstrations, and rumors about the Black Panther party. Widely known in the community as a passionate spokesman for peace, Dellums was invited to a meeting where a coalition slate for the Berkeley city council would be selected. When his turn came, he spoke fervently about why he did not want to be a politician who would have to make white speeches to white people, black speeches to black people, and liberal speeches to liberals, but he agreed to accept the group's endorsement as a black unity candidate when offered a chance to run on his own terms. He was elected in 1967.

They called him the radical-in-residence on the council, where he practiced a new style of progressive-left politics. He spoke on behalf of blacks, women, students, and anti-war protestors. Queried by reporters about his absence at council meetings, he replied he had to work for a living. Dellums said he fulfilled his responsibilities on the council, even though his job as a senior consultant with Social Dynamics, a private manpower firm, required him to travel.

In 1970 he challenged liberal six-termer Jeffrey Cohelan for the Democratic nomination for the Seventh District seat in the House of Representatives. Dellums said Cohelan was out of step with his constituents both on the Vietnam War issue and on domestic matters. Some observers thought Dellums' loud, militant supporters would alienate the more conventional voters, but he won with nearly 55 percent of the vote.

Hoping to defeat this outspoken anti-war candidate, the Republicans boosted their advertising budget and sent in Vice President Spiro Agnew and other big guns to help elect John Healy, a twenty-five-year-old Vietnam veteran. Healy attacked Dellums' attendance record in the city council and his association with the Black Panthers and other "lunatic left wing" friends. Healy also accused Dellums of making racist appeals of the sort that would have branded him, Healy, a Ku Kluxer had he used the same approach with white voters.

Agnew labeled Dellums a "radical extremist." Mrs. Martin Luther King, Jr., who campaigned for him, said that if Dellums was an extremist, she was too. Dellums didn't shrink from the radical label—he has always been candid about believing in the need for basic shifts in America's priorities—but with a well-advertised drive, he defeated Healy 88,800 to 63,800.

Even with substantial contributions from unions, California's new representative arrived in Washington with a campaign debt of at least $20,000. Gradually he whittled away at it with contributions from supporters and fund-raising events. He earned about $20,000 on the lecture circuit and used part of that money to buy office equipment and other supplies not covered in his expenses.

Fashion reporters in the capital soon dubbed the modishly attired Dellums one of the best-dressed men in Congress. The House assigned him to the District of Columbia Committee. He had a personal stake in the District, since he and his second wife, Leola (Roscoe) Higgs, and their three children had moved to Washington.

Dellums has held a series of ad hoc hearings—some under the auspices of the congressional black caucus—to deal with issues he believes to be inadequately treated by the regular House committees. He has explored subjects ranging from war crimes committed in Indochina by the United States, to racism in the military, to "lawlessness" within the Federal Government.

Until the American forces were finally brought home from Indochina in 1974, the Vietnam War was a burning issue with Dellums. Early in 1971 he had fought for a House resolution asking for withdrawal of all American troops from Southeast Asia by the end of the year; to his dismay the House passed a substitute proposal calling for a pullout by the end of 1972. This, Dellums complained, strengthened Nixon's hand and gave him authority to continue militarily at will for two more years.

Dellums is disturbed by the congressional subservience to the military, which demands billions for "unnecessary wars" while life-supporting projects go begging. He wonders if Congress, an "expedient place full of professional politicians," is capable of solving the human problems in an America run by an "imperial President."

On May 5, 1971, during the climaxing confrontation of a peace offensive held in Washington against the war in Vietnam, Dellums, along with two other black congressmen, Charles B. Rangel of New York and Parren J. Mitchell of Maryland, and Bella Abzug of New York, met with demonstrators on the Capitol steps. As Dellums spoke, the police plowed into the crowd and arrested about 1,300 of the mostly young protestors. Outraged, the representatives worked throughout the night to get as many people as possible released.

An estimated 14,000 demonstrators had been detained in the Washington Coliseum and the Robert F. Kennedy Stadium during several days of protests staged in a concerted effort to bring the government to a halt as means of forcing Nixon to end the war in Southeast Asia. Later the President praised the metropolitan police for their handling of the tense situation and minimized the constitutional issues involved in these mass arrests.

Dellums disagreed and decided to bring a class action suit in federal court on behalf of himself and the demonstrators. In January 1975 the American Civil Liberties Union won the case of *Dellums vs. [James M.] Powell*, head of the capital police at the time of the arrests. A racially and sexually mixed jury in the United States District Court for the District of Columbia awarded nearly $12,000,000 in damages— one of the largest awards ever made in a civil liberties suit. Demonstrators, who had been arrested on the Capitol steps, were granted about $10,000 each for violation of their First Amendment rights, for unreasonable arrest, and for cruel and unusual punishment, the size of the awards varying depending on the length of time each person was confined.

Though not arrested himself, Dellums was granted $7,500 for interference with his right to free speech when the police took his audience away. However, no money has yet been paid to Dellums or his fellow plaintiffs, pending the outcome of a Justice Department appeal of the decision. Thousands of demonstrators arrested elsewhere during the May Day protests presumably could sue individually for similar damages if they wish, but class action damage suits for protestors at the Justice Department and other targets were not accepted.

The California congressman continually blasts "governmental lawlessness." During a 1972 black caucus hearing, he called current and past public officials as witnesses to document his charges that the Nixon Administration and federal agencies were refusing to implement the laws passed by Congress. He accused the Justice Department, the Civil Service Commission, the Agriculture Department, and the Health, Education and Welfare Department with failure to comply with statutes enacted to protect minorities and with policies set by Congress to aid the poor. Dellums insists that a law passed by Congress and signed by the President ought not to be ignored by bureaucrats being paid to implement it.

One example of bureaucratic lawlessness offered at a Dellums hearing came from Jack Anderson. The columnist produced a list of 5,000 black citizens who had been kept under surveillance by the Federal Bureau of Investigation. The *Washington Post* hailed Dellums for these productive investigations. Dellums was shining light into dark crevices in Washington that would be more fully explored later in the Watergate hearings and in congressional probes into the FBI and the Central Intelligence Agency.

Dellums, who says it is difficult to support a young family on a congressman's salary, has had to campaign aggressively and spend substantial sums to hold his seat. He won re-election the first time by 56 percent against Republican and American Labor party opponents. His margin over Jack Redden, the Republican contender, was 27,600 votes in 1974.

Many of his early legislative proposals were written to stop the "insane" Vietnam War. He cosponsored numerous other measures that passed—including limited self-government for the District of Columbia, repeal of legislation authorizing detention camps for use against Americans in national emergencies, and a cutback on funds for South Korea. Most of his priority proposals are too controversial for the current Congress. He's planting seeds for the future with bills like the World Peace Tax Fund, to be comprised of money withheld, for diversion to peaceful purposes, by taxpayers protesting the country's huge military budgets.

A member of the Armed Services Committee, Dellums in 1975 joined the freshman rebels in ousting Pentagon booster F. Edward Hebert from the chairmanship. This change became less significant as the Democratic majority in Congress continued to vote even larger outlays for the military in peace than in war. Dellums has worked painstakingly, but so far unsuccessfully, to get a bill through Congress to save some money by cutting down on America's overseas troop deployment.

As a member of the House Select Intelligence Committee, Dellums gave strong support to Chairman Otis Pike in probing the effectiveness as well as the illegalities of the Central Intelligence Agency. Appearing before the group, William E. Colby, the CIA director, remained true to the agency's tight-lip policy and refused to tell the American public how much they were paying to finance authorized and some admittedly illegal intelligence programs. Dellums, a sharp questioner, asked the somber-faced director of the agency charged with plotting murder and assassination abroad and widespread spying on Americans at home: "What makes you the person who decided he can play God?"

When a CIA analyst revealed that false data designed to mislead the general public also had put the United States high command off guard during the 1968 Tet offensive in Vietnam, Dellums's questioning disclosed that thousands of Americans had died as a result. Dellums and Pike were themselves threatened with assassination after the press identified a CIA agent who later was murdered in Greece.

These four junior black congressmen from the North or the West —Ronald V. Dellums, Ralph H. Metcalfe, Charles B. Rangel, and the late George Collins—have represented a variety of positions in the political spectrum. Yet each has concentrated on concerns imperative for every citizen: full employment, improved health services, and equal job opportunities. Like Martin Luther King, Jr., in the final months of his movement, perhaps most of all they seek to correct the imbalance between military and nonmilitary spending and to free billions of dollars to meet the essential domestic needs of America.

Dellums, Metcalfe, and Rangel would wage their wars domestically against organized crime, the debilitating drug traffic, the military-industrial complex, unemployment, infringement on personal liberties, and the forces at home which would ignore the principle that democratic government should be responsive to the governed.

Yvonne Brathwaite Burke/California
Cardiss Collins/Illinois
Barbara Jordan/Texas

Yvonne Brathwaite Burke of California, Cardiss Collins of Illinois, and Barbara Jordan of Texas, though strikingly different in appearance and personality, are generally in agreement on vital social and economic issues. The first black women elected to Congress from their states,˳they have brought a fresh viewpoint to the House of Representatives, where their visibility is magnified by the scarcity of women. Together with the veteran Shirley Chisholm of New York, they comprise nearly one fourth of the total female membership of the Ninety-fourth Congress.

Mrs. Burke, who has a flawless complexion and a heart-shaped face, initially attracted national attention when, as cochairwoman, she presided over the 1972 Democratic convention in Miami. Beautiful, confident, expressing herself with fluency and charm, she became a television celebrity, soon to be in demand for speaking engagements across the country.

Born Yvonne Watson in Los Angeles on October 5, 1932, she grew up in a section so depressing that on Sunday outings her family visited nicer neighborhoods "like Watts." James Watson, her father, worked at the Metro-Goldwyn-Mayer film studios as a janitor and was named president of the Hollywood local of the Service Employees International Union. Lola Moore Watson, her mother, was a real estate agent.

When Yvonne's teachers said she needed more competitive stimuli, her parents enrolled her in a school for exceptional children at the University of Southern California. The only black child there, she was taunted by some of her classmates. Nevertheless, she did well in her studies, and by junior high school had decided to become a lawyer.

Serving as vice-president of the Los Angeles Manual Arts High School student body and appearances in state oratorical contests gave the popular Yvonne valuable platform experience.

Granted a scholarship by her father's union, she graduated from the University of California at Los Angeles and studied law at USC, paying her way with earnings from jobs at swimming pools, libraries, and a garment factory. Barred from the university's legal sorority, she and two Jewish students formed a new sorority, one without religious or racial barriers.

Following her admission to the California bar in 1956, she entered private practice. A year later she married Louis Brathwaite, a mathematician. During ten years as an attorney, she handled many civil rights cases and acted as a police commission hearing officer, a deputy corporation commissioner, and a staff lawyer to the McCone Commission, which investigated the Watts riots of 1965 and recommended measures to prevent similar civil disorders in the future.

Mrs. Brathwaite, by then divorced, entered the political arena in 1964 as a volunteer worker for the Johnson-Humphrey Presidential ticket. Two years later, with backing from friends and her father's union, she easily defeated six white men to win a seat in the California assembly.

During three terms, she put through measures to protect the jobs of debt-ridden workers whose wages had been garnisheed, to provide major medical insurance coverage for infants, and to ensure relocation for home owners and tenants uprooted by government action. Other legislation championed by the assemblywoman, who headed the Urban Development and Housing Committee, set standards for board and care facilities, including halfway centers for former mental patients.

When she launched her candidacy for the Thirty-seventh Congressional District seat in Los Angeles, she received valuable support from Coretta King, the widow of Martin Luther King, Jr., and Gloria Steinem, the feminist leader, who campaigned for Mrs. Brathwaite in the race against Billy Mills, a popular city councilman. Student volunteers also contributed to her 54 percent victory over Mills and a field of lesser candidates. Two weeks later, in June 1972, she married William Burke, a business consultant and a former aide to Mills. Mills, a childhood friend of Mrs. Burke, pledged to support her in the general election.

As a presiding officer at the Democratic convention in July, she neatly avoided parliamentary pitfalls and kept the proceedings moving. Mrs. Chisholm had put herself forward as a Presidential candidate around whom minorities and women could unite to bargain at the convention. The ploy failed. Her exercise in futility contrasted sharply with Mrs. Burke's effective, businesslike performance on the podium.

Back in California, Mrs. Burke overcame the confusion arising from being listed on the general election ballot as Brathwaite because her second marriage came too late for a change to be made. It didn't matter. The voters had seen her on television; most of them knew who she was. Her Republican opponent, Gregg Tria, a conservative of Filipino-Greek ancestry, concentrated on the school busing controversy, while she toured black and white neighborhoods discussing jobs, housing, and health. She won 73 percent of the 168,600 votes cast in a Presidential landslide year for the Republicans.

The first woman member from California in twenty years, Mrs. Burke was sworn in by the House in January 1973 with two other black newcomers and assigned to the Public Works and Interior and Insular Affairs committees.

In short order, she made her presence felt in Congress. After the House Armed Services Committee decided that disorders on the U.S.S. *Kitty Hawk* and the U.S.S. *Constellation* did not stem from racial discrimination, she and Ronald V. Dellums of California launched a more comprehensive investigation. The report of the new inquiry cited evidence that both black and white servicemen were losing faith in the fairness of the military's racial policies. She also joined forces with Dellums and Parren J. Mitchell of Maryland, urging the House to start impeachment proceedings against President Richard Nixon for continuing an undeclared war in Southeast Asia.

In the fall of 1973, Mrs. Burke gave birth to a daughter, appropriately named Autumn. The only congresswoman to have a baby while in office was asked by a network television interviewer if her daughter would be a member of Congress too when she grew up. "No," was the prompt answer. "She's going to be President."

Other good news for Mrs. Burke was the passage of the Alaskan Pipeline bill carrying an equal opportunity amendment she had co-sponsored to ban discrimination for any activity connected with the construction and operation of the project. But her campaign newsletter stressed matters closer to home. She reminded her constituents that she had voted and worked to pass social security and minimum wage increases, private pension reforms, and key sections of the Elementary and Secondary School Act. Redistricting gave her the new Twenty-eighth District with more blue collar suburbanites and fewer inner city blacks. Nonetheless, in the 1974 election, she defeated Thomas Neddy, the Republican, by more than 4 to 1.

The House shifted Mrs. Burke to the Appropriations Committee, where she became an outspoken critic of the Ford Administration.

Ford's program to solve the energy shortage by raising oil prices would, she charged, place a serious handicap on low-income workers without noticeably affecting the well-to-do.

She was appalled when Ford rushed to subsidize jobs and housing for Vietnamese refugees after he had turned a deaf ear to pleas from millions of unemployed Americans, including Vietnam veterans. Pointing out that 8,000 black soldiers had come home from Indochina in metal boxes and that their families had paid taxes to send $150 billion to General Nguyen Van Thieu, she questioned Ford's concern for Americans. "Does," she asked, "the President rate commitment to a foreign military dictator who resigned with a final volley of curses at America more valid than our own constitution and the black citizens of this country?"

A dedicated protagonist for the Equal Rights Amendment barring sexual discrimination under federal law, she sponsored legislation for staggered hours for part-time civil service jobs to accommodate young mothers and for job training and other assistance for "displaced homemakers"—that is, women who once ran households without compensation as dependents of other family members but who, because of divorce or other reasons, are no longer supported by their families.

Mrs. Burke achieved one of her legislative goals when Congress authorized a National Center for the Prevention and Control of Rape in the omnibus health services bill which passed over Ford's veto in July 1975. She urged congressional action after a survey revealed that in Los Angeles alone some woman is raped every four hours and that these victims, of all ages, colors, and economic conditions, frequently are subjected to humiliation and indignities at the hands of the authorities.

In her public appearances Mrs. Burke deplores the lack of sufficient feminine representation in all levels of government, including Congress, where she wants blacks and women on all major committees. More women, she argues, will make government and politics more credible. For example, the country could have been spared the agony of Watergate if California voters had seen through the false Communist charges candidate Richard Nixon leveled against Helen Gahagan Douglas in 1950 and had sent her, not him, to the Senate.

Yvonne Burke sees her own long-term future not in the House but in California politics. When her daughter reaches school age, Mrs. Burke will, she says, seek a suitable elective post in her home state. Until then, she intends to stay in Congress. Her position in Washington was enhanced in January 1976 by her election as the first chairwoman of the congressional black caucus.

While Mrs. Burke came up through the ranks in elective office,

Cardiss Collins, the newest black congresswoman, is one of thirty-one women who were initially elected or appointed to Congress to complete the unexpired terms of their late husbands. Like George Collins, she won her seat in Chicago's Seventh District in June 1973 with the backing of the city's well-oiled Democratic machine.

Mrs. Collins was born on September 24, 1931, in St. Louis, to Finley and Rosia Cardiss Robertson. Her mother was a nurse, and her father worked as a laborer. She graduated from commerce high school in Detroit, where her family moved when she was ten. She attended Northwestern University in Chicago but left to take a stenographic job with the Illinois labor department. Later, with additional training, she was promoted to accountant.

After her marriage to Collins in 1958, she became an active partner in his political career. While continuing to work as a state tax auditor, she managed their household, looked after their only son, Kevin, and served as twenty-fourth ward committeewoman. She helped plan and execute all her husband's campaigns—from committeeman to congressman.

Then, a month after his re-election in 1972, the congressman was killed in a plane crash along with forty-four others, including Mrs. E. Howard Hunt, wife of one of the Watergate burglars. Despite rumors of possible sabotage, Mrs. Collins does not want a further investigation. She believes her husband's death to have been an accident.

With the assistance of the late congressman's friends and Mayor Richard Daley's organization, Mrs. Collins campaigned tirelessly for the crucial April 17 primary contest. When the returns were in, she had captured 85 percent of the vote against former State Representative Otis Collins (no relation to her husband's family), and Milton Gardner, a Columbia University law student, both blacks. The special election in June was even more of a runaway; Mrs. Collins, the regular Democrats' choice, received 34,000 votes to 1,400 for Lar Daly, whom viewers have frequently seen on television wearing red, white, and blue and demanding equal time as a Presidential aspirant. Mrs. Collins was re-elected for a full term in 1974 with 63,900 votes to 8,800 for Donald Metzger, the Republican.

In Congress, her prime aim, in her words, has been to seek "to provide better living and working conditions for the people of the Seventh District and other low and moderate income people throughout the country." The Chicago representative serves on the Government Operations and International Relations committees. In addition, as one of three at-large majority whips, she must round up the members for the Democratic leadership when the bell rings for a vote, a first for a black woman. However, the *Congressional Quarterly* showed her to be the top truant in the Illinois House delegation during the first half of 1975.

Mrs. Collins feels compelled to visit her district nearly every weekend to keep in touch with the voters. She favors a four-year House term to free representatives from the necessity for constant campaigning and to give them more time for their legislative duties.

She crusades for women's issues, many of them long neglected or slighted by men. The Illinois congresswoman introduced a bill to bring the cost of postmastectomy breast prosthesis under Medicare for patients who couldn't afford to pay; she argued that remolding the chest of a cancer victim was not merely a cosmetic operation—but comparable to an artifical limb, which serves a psychological, protective, and functional purpose. In January 1975 she happily told the House it would not be necessary for her to reintroduce the measure because the Social Security Administration finally had relented and revised its regulations to cover this plastic surgery operation. Now she's working to get Pap tests for uterine and cervix cancer included under Medicare-paid services. Women too poor to afford this regular medical checkup, she points out, may discover they have cancer too late to halt its spread. Cancer accounts for one out of every six deaths in America.

Mrs. Collins has collaborated with the other three black congresswomen on demands for clear, consistent Health, Education and Welfare guidelines for sterilization and for federal curbs on the use of dangerous birth control drugs whose side effects have included sterility. After widespread publicity about the young Relf sisters in Alabama, who were allegedly sterilized without their knowledge in a public health clinic, HEW tightened its restrictions, but the controversy over sterilization, particularly for minors and incompetents, seems certain to drag on for years. Mrs. Collins favors a ban on the sterilization of minors.

Mrs. Collins appeals to black women to take the lead in melding the forces of the black-led civil rights movement and women's liberation. Negro women, she suggests, can serve as a bridge between the two groups, thereby helping to overcome the white and black males' fear of the aggressive, insistent feminists. That she does well with men was evidenced by her election as secretary of the congressional black caucus in January 1976.

Illinois' first black congresswoman, who will continue to introduce measures to benefit the aged, the sick, the jobless, and the poor as long as her constituents reelect her, is encouraged by the prospects for still further gains for black politicians if they can attract more grass roots support from the country's biggest minority. She is not, however, optimistic about the never-ending fight for racial harmony and equality. "While Northern whites would support integration in the South during the 50's and the 60's," says Cardiss Collins, "they're opposing it [in the 70's] in their own backyard."

One of the most powerful voices for racial justice belongs to Barbara Jordan, a national figure since she presented her powerful arguments for impeachment as the House Judiciary Committee moved inexorably toward a televised vote against President Nixon in 1974. This woman, who mesmerizes audiences with her erudition, enunciation, and sincerity, was born on February 21, 1936, to Benjamin and Arlyne Patton Jordan.

The Reverend Benjamin Jordan, in a not unusual circumstance for Baptist ministers, could not support his family on his pastor's salary—he doubled as a warehouse assistant. Young Barbara and her two sisters sang gospel hymns in their father's church and tried to please him by bringing home report cards with as many A's as possible.

Determined "to be somebody," Barbara chose law as a career while in the tenth grade, after learning to her amazement that a woman could be an attorney. Her inspiration came from Edith Sampson, guest speaker at Houston's Phyllis Wheatley High School, a lawyer who later became a Chicago judge.

Barbara finished high school with honors, then entered Texas State University. She rose to stardom on an outstanding debate team. After graduation in 1956, she entered Boston University Law School as the only woman in a class of 128, and received her bachelor of laws degree three years later.

Having qualified for the bar, she set up her practice of law in the family dining room. Even after she opened an outside office with a partner, the returns from domestic relations, real estate, and probate cases weren't enough for her to contribute much to the family income, so she also worked as an administrative assistant to County Judge William Elliott.

She plunged into Democratic politics in 1960 as a volunteer for the Kennedy-Johnson Presidential ticket. One speech at a church rally proved she was a spellbinder. Encouraged by the response, she borrowed the $500 filing fee and ran for the Texas State House of Representatives in 1962. She lost, but 46,000 people had voted for her, so she decided to keep trying. After a second unsuccessful race for the lower house, she was elected to the Texas senate in 1966 by a margin of 2 to 1 over J. C. Whitfield, a former state representative.

Her reaction to a reporter's question typifies her down-to-earth approach to politics and government service. Was she nervous about being the lone female and black in a legislature teeming with racists and sexists? "You must understand," she replied, "I have a tremendous amount of faith in my own capacity. I know how to read and write and think, so I have no fear."

The first black state senator in Texas since 1882 prepared for Austin by becoming an expert on the convoluted rules of the legislature. She staved off a restrictive voter registration law that would have hit hardest at Mexican-Americans and blacks; she crusaded against job discrimination in the private and public sectors. As chairwoman of the Labor and Management Relations Committee, she showed how, in the words of a Texas reporter, to keep a committee "rolling like General Patton."

Miss Jordan wrote laws to improve workmen's compensation, to create a Texas Fair Employment Practices Commission, and to set a minimum wage for "the really poor people, laundry workers, domestics, [and] farm workers."

Originally against her, the Houston papers soon began to praise "our Senator Jordan." President Lyndon Johnson invited the tall (5 feet 8 inches), hefty, short-haired Miss Jordan to White House receptions and lauded her talents. She reciprocated as a delegate to the 1968 Democratic national convention, where she used her considerable skill to keep the Texas group on record in support of Johnson's Vietnam War. She was cool toward that doomed conflict personally, but loyalty—she liked Johnson—and pragmatism—she knew he could help her career—kept her on the LBJ team.

In 1971, State Senator Jordan served as vice chairwoman of a Texas congressional redistricting committee, which carved out a new 42 percent black district in her home city. When she announced for that Eighteenth District seat, State Representative Curtis Graves, her chief primary rival, charged she had sacrificed the "safe" black Texas senate seat for a chance to go to Washington, and there hasn't been a black senator in Austin since. He also accused her of being too close to the white establishment and to the oil interests, which traditionally suppressed minorities and the poor.

Miss Jordan later told a *Wall Street Journal* reporter that she had tried to keep her old senate seat black after the senatorial districts were redrawn. During her first congressional campaign, she talked about the many laws she had put on the books as a senator. She won 80 percent of the votes cast in the May 1972 primary in a contest with Graves and two other men. The general election was also a romp. She received 85,600 votes; Paul Merritt, a Republican design engineer, 19,300.

No one was more pleased with this coup than her old friend Lyndon Johnson, who by then was living in retirement in Texas, having been driven from the White House by vehement protests against the war

in Vietnam. Johnson coaxed his friends in the House to put his protégé
on the Judiciary Committee. The former President, who may be remembered most favorably as a civil rights leader, died a few months
later, on January 22, 1973. Texas's first black representative eulogized
him in her maiden speech in the House.

Miss Jordan prepared for Washington as thoroughly as she had for
Austin. "If you're going to play the game," she told an *Ebony* reporter,
"you'd better know every rule." She attended sessions, followed debates closely, and during her first term voted 96 percent of the time.

Washington kibitzers soon found she wasn't much interested in
social small talk. Calling it hard work to stand around drinking and
chatting with strangers, she avoided cocktail parties. She did not try
to ingratiate herself with people, and reporters sometimes found her
unnerving. In a cartoon layout for a celebrity party, *Esquire* magazine
captioned her caricature: "She'll scare the bejesus out of you. Move
on."

The novice Judiciary Committee member participated in confirmation hearings for two vice presidents and the impeachment hearings
for one President. She voted against Vice Presidential confirmation for
Gerald Ford, whom she felt had never displayed the leadership
qualities required to be President, especially in such complex, demanding times. And she voted for Nelson Rockefeller for Vice President because she believed his priorities were right and he had been able to
attract talented people to government service. Ford's House record of
insensitivity toward minority problems and his efforts to weaken civil
rights legislation, including the 1970 Voting Rights Act, also disturbed
her. Far from holding this against her, after he became President, Ford
put her on the first congressional mission he dispatched to China.

Ford, like everyone else, had been impressed by her performance
on television during the impeachment hearings. When Peter Rodino,
the silver-haired, soft-spoken Judiciary chairman, recognized the
"gentlelady" from Texas, she began solemnly, alternately reading or
talking from notes on her desk. " 'We the people' is a very eloquent
beginning," she told the millions watching on July 25, 1974. "But when
the Constitution of the United States was completed on the seventh of
September in 1787, I was not included in that 'We, the people.' I felt
for many years that George Washington and Alexander Hamilton just
left me out by mistake, but through the process of amendment, interpretation, and court decision, I have finally been included in 'We the
people.' "

Having established her equity in the Constitution, she pledged to
protect it. "My faith in the Constitution is whole, it is complete, it is

total," she said. "I am not going to sit here and be an idle spectator to the diminution, the subversion, the destruction of the Constitution."

She charged that Nixon knew money collected for his Presidential campaign was used to pay off the men who broke into offices of the Democratic National Committee, and "beginning shortly after the Watergate break-in and continuing to the present time, the President has engaged in a series of public statements and actions designed to thwart a lawful investigation by government prosecutors."

To buttress her argument, she quoted from the Federalist Papers, James Madison, past court decisions, and the records of the South Carolina constitutional radification convention. If Nixon had new evidence that would exonerate him, as his defenders claimed, "the committee subpoena is outstanding, and if the President wants to supply that material, the committee sits here," she asserted.

Miss Jordan reportedly was equally effective in the closed sessions, helping to keep the focus on whether Nixon was guilty of the type of offenses the founders envisioned as "high crimes and misdemeanors" at the time they wrote the impeachment clause into the Constitution. When die-hard Nixon apologists complained he had not been given due process, she answered he had had due process, tripled and quadrupled.

Yet after the committee voted 21 to 7 to recommend impeachment on Article I, and the end of Nixon's Presidency was clearly in sight, she took no pleasure in his downfall. "I don't want to talk to anybody," she told reporters who rushed up to her after the vote.

Her fall report to Texas covered not Nixon's forced resignation but the congresswoman's legislative record. Prominent mention went to her amendment to the extension of the safe streets, anticrime bill, requiring that this $850,000,000 program be administered so that its benefits would be fairly distributed "regardless of race, color, national origins or sex." She included a clause specifying that funded programs be evaluated as to whether they do in fact reduce crime. Unfortunately, enforcement of this amendment has not been effective.

After the impeachment hearings, requests poured in for Miss Jordan to lecture and to appear at fund-raising affairs for the Democratic party and black organizations. Stumping for other candidates but campaigning little for herself, she was re-elected in 1974 over Republican Robbins Mitchell by more than 80 percent of a modest vote.

If Nixon's disgrace enhanced her reputation and stepped up demands for speaking dates, the downfall of Ways and Means Chairman Wilbur Mills augmented her prestige and influence. In December 1974 the Democrats rearranged the lines of authority in the House after Mills was replaced as chairman because of his drunken escapades with a dancer. The Policy and Steering Committee was given the task of parceling out committee assignments (subject to the approval of the Democratic caucus), an important chore that had been handled by Ways and Means since 1911. Speaker Carl Albert named Miss Jordan to the Policy and Steering Committee and to its task force to make up an action agenda for the Ninety-fourth Congress.

Although that agenda was largely demolished by a succession of Presidential vetoes, she did help to broaden the voting rights act to cover Texas; this landmark legislation was extended to 1982. Mexican-Americans and other "language minorities" are now encompassed in the protective guarantees that have dramatically boosted black registration in the seven Southern states where the 1965 Voting Rights Act has had the greatest impact. Her bill outlawing state "fair trade" measures that had been passed to maintain manufacturers' minimum prices on products like major appliances became effective in March 1976.

Miss Jordan is in the inner circle, not only in Congress but in the Democratic party nationally as a committeewoman, and statewide as Texas vice-chairwoman. She defended the legislative record of the Ninety-fourth Congress during a 1975 fund-raising telethon. Then she asked the question on everybody's mind: "Why aren't we [the Congress] getting more done?"

Congress had been busy, she said, fighting off administration attacks on increased Social Security payments, battling an "energy program" that was nothing but gas rationing by price, and redesigning the tax cut bill so that the largest rebates didn't go to the upper income set.

Quoting a favorite Democrat, Harry Truman, Congresswoman Jordan said that Congress has to devote so much effort to stopping the Republicans from "turning the clock back, that we're still having to run twice as fast just to stay even."

Barbara Jordan has the keen mind, driving ambition, and political skill for substantial achievements. Being a woman and black has not handicapped her or Yvonne Brathwaite Burke or Cardiss Collins. These congresswomen all have capitalized on assets that would have been detriments earlier in this nation's history.

Parren J. Mitchell/Maryland
Walter E. Fauntroy/District of Columbia
Andrew Young/Georgia
Harold E. Ford/Tennessee

The South, which gave America its first Negro congressmen after the Civil War, has been slower than the rest of the country to elect black national legislators in more recent times. Parren J. Mitchell of Maryland was chosen as the first twentieth-century member from below the Mason-Dixon line in 1970. Several months thereafter came Walter E. Fauntroy of the District of Columbia. In 1972, after a lapse of more than a century, Andrew Young was elected Georgia's second black representative. Harold E. Ford of Tennessee entered the House of Representatives in January 1975—the sole black newcomer in the Ninety-fourth Congress.

Parren Mitchell, a slight, deceptively mild-looking, former college professor, comes from a celebrated Baltimore activist family. His brother, Clarence Mitchell, Jr., lobbied so long and effectively in Washington for the National Association for the Advancement of Colored People that the press dubbed him the 101st senator. The congressman's nephew, Clarence Mitchell III, a Maryland state senator, supports his uncle as a political leader in a city with many customs carried over from the antebellum South.

The boy who grew up to be Maryland's first black congressman was born on April 29, 1922, in Baltimore, to Clarence and Elsie Davis Mitchell. The father supported his ten children by waiting on tables in a downtown hotel. Young Parren joined his big brothers in picketing department stores to force them to employ blacks.

After the United States entered World War II, he fought in Italy as the captain of a Ninety-second Division infantry company during the Apennines campaign. Wounded in action, he still carries several fragments of German shrapnel in his knee. Back home in Maryland, Mitchell worked nights at the social security office while attending Morgan State College during the day. Following his graduation in 1950 at the age of twenty-eight, he sued to force the University of Maryland to admit him as its first black graduate student. While earning his master's degree in sociology, he worked as a junior analyst with the Commerce Department, then as a Baltimore probation officer.

Subsequently he moved restlessly from job to job, mixing day and night, salaried and volunteer work, and sometimes holding two positions simultaneously. He taught sociology at Morgan State for several years while continuing to counsel ex-convicts as a probation officer, an experience that had a profound effect on him and made him exceptionally sensitive to the problems of people in trouble with the law. He completed the required university credits for a doctorate but never wrote his thesis.

In May 1963, Mitchell was named executive secretary of the Maryland Commission on Interracial Problems and Relations; in this role, he administered Maryland's Fair Employment Practices Law and other state antidiscriminatory legislation. He left to lead Baltimore's war on poverty as executive director of the Community Action Agency.

He moved ambitiously into politics in 1968, challenging Representative Samuel Friedel in the Democratic primary for the Seventh District seat in Congress. Losing by 5,000 votes, the number polled by the third candidate, Mitchell then returned to Morgan State to teach sociology and to direct the Urban Studies Institute, and Friedel easily defeated Republican Arthur Downs in the general election.

He filed against Friedel again in the primary two years later. Carl Friedler, a white state senator, and Walter Dixon, an elderly black former city councilman, also vied for the post. Mitchell ran an intense campaign, blanketing the district with in-person meetings and with hundreds of student volunteers from Morgan who rang doorbells as they canvassed for him. They attacked the incumbent for his failure to get things done in Congress, his liberal voting record notwithstanding. Mitchell hit hard on the waste and cruelty of the Vietnam War and promised voters aggressive representation in Washington if he was elected.

The city famed for its rows of red brick houses with white steps had been badly scarred physically and emotionally by the riots that followed the assassination of Martin Luther King, Jr., in 1968. Remembering the burning and looting by young blacks, Baltimoreans, black and white alike, were edgy and apprehensive about the possibility of racial disorders when primary day dawned on September 15, 1970.

Many polling places opened late; some locations were changed without prior notice. There was a shortage of voting machines, and many of the ones that were at the polling places broke down. Blacks in some areas ran a gauntlet of insults in order to vote. When the returns came in, the race was too close to call.

The next day Friedel announced he had won by 182 votes. Not so, said Mitchell, claiming to be the victor by a 466 margin. A United States Civil Rights Commission panel listened to accounts of widespread harassment of black voters and recommended that another primary be held to decide the issue. Finally, on September 29, the Batimore Board of Elections Supervisors declared Mitchell the winner by thirty-eight votes. Friedel said illegalities had defeated him and he would appeal to the House. He changed his mind, however; it was too near the general election for a primary rerun.

With so little time left, Mitchell stepped up the pace against Republican Peter Parker, a lawyer and an enthusiastic supporter of President Richard Nixon, then very popular in Maryland. Mitchell's headquarters were bombed and set on fire (luckily no one was hurt). Mayor Tommy D'Alesandro, Jr., a Mitchell backer, deplored the violence and pleaded for calm. Parker labeled Mitchell a racist and said his funds came from the Black Panthers. Mitchell spent about $53,000 in a well-organized, smartly advertised drive. Face-to-face debates with his opponent won some undecided voters. Running ahead in Jewish neighborhoods as well as in black communities, he took the general election 60,300 to 42,500.

In Washington, Mitchell joined the growing number of disillusioned liberals who had found that Congress wasn't moving fast enough to bring relief to the festering ailments of urban America. He complained that the Federal Government was subsidizing airlines, farmers, oil companies, and insurance firms while doing little to launch blacks into the mainstream of the free enterprise system. His hearings, under the auspices of the congressional black caucus, dramatically pointed up the difficulties of getting financial support for black-owned businesses.

"I urge black Americans to recognize the essential linkage between political power and economic power," the congressman warned the United Mortgage Bankers of America. "They are inextricably tied together. If we elect black candidates who must turn solely and exclusively to the white community for campaign funds, no matter how strong that black man may be, sooner or later he is forced to begin to compromise against his people."

When Ralph Nader's interviewers talked with Mitchell in 1972, they found him disillusioned about what a representative with low seniority could accomplish legislatively. "The reality is that bills I introduced are not going to get anywhere—the bills of any liberal member don't move," he said. Some of his stillborn measures would have speeded the end of the Vietnam War, created a cabinet-status agency for minority-owned enterprises, and tightened consumer protection for everyone.

Like many black congressmen, Mitchell is out in front on the women's issues. Congress, he believes, would be stronger with representation more proportional to the makeup of the population, ethnically, racially, and sexually.

Mitchell, who wears a modest moustache and a natural hair-style, commutes daily to Capitol Hill from his bachelor apartment in his district. His name is in the Baltimore phone book, and he sometimes answers his home phone and doorbell himself. A very important person in an increasingly black city, Mitchell jousts with other black and white Democratic leaders for control of Baltimore.

In Congress he is known for his caustic, sometimes cutting, no-holds-barred speeches. He is proud of having led a walkout from a tense meeting with Spiro Agnew in 1968 after the then governor of Maryland unjustly blamed black leaders for allowing the riots to break out in Baltimore.

When the congressional black caucus finally got in to see President Nixon, Mitchell warned the Chief Executive that the black community would not be blackjacked into silence or lulled into apathy. The government, he asserted, would ignore this smoldering powder keg at its own peril.

During one of many interminable House debates on the school busing issue, the Maryland congressman lashed out at his colleagues as hypocrites, bigots, and racists. " 'My country 'tis of thee/Sweet land of bigotry,' " he quoted a young man from his district. "There are blacks tonight whom you forced to say. 'We want no more of America because America has lied to us.' You're asking too much of us blacks to accept the kind of insult you're heaping on us tonight." Still, the 1972 proposed ban on court-ordered, long-distance busing for school integration passed the House; later, it was defeated in the Senate.

Loud, early, and often, Mitchell called for the impeachment of Nixon. In April 1974 at Johns Hopkins University he complained that America was still being tortured by the presence of a "disgusting, duplicitous, disgraced President" even after his associates had been driven out by their wrongdoings. No one was surprised when Mitchell's name turned up on Nixon's "enemies list."

More startling was a grand jury revelation of a secret file kept by the Baltimore police. Mitchell, one of those spied upon, damned this as a "Watergate-type operation against black people and white social activists" and demanded that it cease. The Nixon–John Mitchell Justice Department, he said, had set back the cause of civil liberties and bred the kind of disdain for the poor and blacks that now was being practiced at state and local levels.

As proof, he cited the failure of the government to protect students at Kent State University and Jackson State College or to bring their murderers to justice. Lawmen called in to restore order during demonstrations on the campuses of these educational institutions in May 1970 killed unarmed students, some of whom reportedly had not even been taking part in the protests. Mitchell also expressed skepticism about the handling of the murder investigations of Chicago Black Panther Fred Hampton, allegedly shot in the back by police while sleeping, and Martin Luther King, Jr., gunned down on a Memphis motel balcony in 1967, supposedly by a lone assassin, who later sought a new trial after having pleaded guilty without benefit of a public hearing.

Parren J. Mitchell, Baltimore's candid, tough-talking black congressman, who was reelected by a comfortable edge in 1974 after a close primary race, fights for black business, equal access to housing, lower mortgage rates, public service jobs for the unemployed, and an end to American support of the African nations that still exploit their black citizens.

On March 23, 1971, three months after Maryland sent Mitchell to Congress, Walter E. Fauntroy, a Baptist minister and former King associate, was elected to serve as nonvoting delegate to the House of Representatives from the 72 percent black District of Columbia. Legislation readmitting a representative from the nation's capital after the lapse of nearly one hundred years, permitted him to vote in committee but not on the floor.

Walter E. Fauntroy was born February 6, 1933, to William and Ethel Vine Fauntroy in the Shaw ghetto of Washington. His father worked for forty-five years as a clerk in the United States patent office. A good student, Fauntroy graduated from Dunbar High School in 1951 and enrolled at the Virginia Union University, paying his expenses with outside jobs and with help from the New Bethel Baptist Church in Washington. In 1958 he received a bachelor of divinity degree from Yale University Divinity School. Within a year he had been named pastor at New Bethel.

During the 1960's he mixed preaching and civil rights movement activities with community and governmental jobs. As Washington director of King's Southern Christian Leadership Conference, Fauntroy was on-the-scene coordinator for the 1963 march on Washington for jobs and freedom. He helped set up the Selma to Montgomery march against discrimination and segregation in Alabama two years later. He was vice chairman of the White House conference called to lay the foundation for legislation guaranteeing the rights demanded by blacks. Fauntroy, a short, curly-haired man with a pencil-thin moustache, was appointed by President Lyndon Johnson to serve as vice chairman of the Washington City Council in 1967, but he resigned to direct an urban renewal project in his old neighborhood.

In the primary race for the House seat last held by Norton P. Chapman in 1873, Fauntroy stressed his activist, militant role in the civil rights movement. Despite the position's lack of power, seven Democrats filed in the primary. His most formidable opponents were Channing Phillips, a minister and Democratic national committeeman, and Joseph Yeldell, chairman of the Metropolitan Area Transit Authority, who ran with the backing of the appointed mayor, Walter Washington.

A clergymen-for-Fauntroy committee was organized to get out the vote for him. His supporters laid special emphasis on his experience as a civil rights lobbyist during the Kennedy-Johnson era and his association with King, whose widow participated in the campaign. Spending considerably less than his chief rivals, Fauntroy captured 44 percent of the vote to 31 percent for Yeldell and 22 percent for Phillips. Having avoided a runoff by four percentage points, he faced another crowded field for the general election in March 1971. The denim-dressed candidate moderated his tone and campaigned in a more subdued manner as a front-runner against John Nevius, a white Republican attorney, and several other white and black minor-party aspirants. Fauntroy won by nearly 40,000 votes, although Nevius outspent him by an estimated $40,000.

The demands from his overcrowded, poverty-stricken, crime-harried, slum-ridden district are staggering. On Capitol Hill and in his district office, he is besieged by requests for assistance on everything from garbage pickups to better police and fire protection. He handles some of the "casework" himself and keeps his constituents informed with regular radio and television programs. He also continues as pastor of the New Bethel Baptist church, with the help of an assistant minister. He loves to sing and has recorded hymns and pop songs for Stax Records; the proceeds are shared by his church and the Dr. Martin Luther King Jr. Center for Social Change.

In Congress, Fauntroy boosted the funding for the District of Columbia by arguing that it shouldn't be compared with cities, which benefit from shared revenues from a state or county. He helped stave off a sales tax hike on food. He cosponsored the measure that gave

Washington its first rent controls since World War II. He also worked with other minority representatives to shape legislation to provide funds for the prevention and treatment of sickle cell anemia, a disease of substantial proportions among the country's 22,700,000 black citizens.

In 1972, Fauntroy ran as a favorite son in the Presidential primary in order to control Washington's delegation to the Democratic convention. He won by 70 percent and, at the same time, was renominated for Congress. He joined Louis Stokes of Ohio, then the black caucus chairman, and William Clay of Missouri in organizing Negro delegates at the Miami convention as a block to bargain with Presidential candidate George McGovern. They promised enough votes to put him over on the first ballot in exchange for a commitment for substantial black representation throughout the executive and judicial branches should he win. Fauntroy's cadenced seconding speech at the convention introduced the "Come home, America" theme for McGovern's acceptance address. This politicking came to naught; McGovern was pulverized at the polls by Nixon.

Yet Fauntroy delivered Washington to McGovern and won his own congressional race by a 55,000 margin over Dr. William Chin-Lee, a Republican. In conceding, Chin-Lee pledged to support Fauntroy's crusade for true home rule for the nation's capital.

Charles C. Diggs, Jr., the veteran Michigan congressman, then in line to chair the District of Columbia Committee, said he would not rush the legislation; the issue needed careful study. Fauntroy and Ronald V. Dellums of California pressed for action. Late in 1973 a compromise home rule bill passed and was signed by Nixon, allowing Washington residents to elect their city council and mayor. Congress retained a veto over finances and kept the strings on other matters as well.

Diggs maneuvered adroitly to send the measure to the floor in a form that would pass and was understandably proud of his handiwork. Fauntroy took his share of the bows too, but he would have preferred a stronger bill. Though friendly with Chairman Diggs, Fauntroy tangles with him politically. Fauntroy had to appeal to the House Democratic Committee on Committees to establish the seniority status that put him in line for his current chairmanship of the District of Columbia government operations subcommittee. Earlier Diggs had turned down the nonvoting representative's request for seniority ranking on legislative committees.

The *Washington Post* speculated that Fauntroy might run for mayor against Mayor Washington. When the congressman didn't, reporters theorized it was because a campaign budget of $200,000 to $300,000 was hard to raise. Fauntroy, however, said Congress was a better place for him to tackle national problems.

Having assisted in getting Washington a degree of local self-govern- ment, Fauntroy is now working for statehood for his constituents. The District of Columbia, as he keeps reminding the rest of the country, has 760,000 residents and outnumbers the seven least populous states, all of which can speak through two votes in the Senate and one or more in the House, while the delegate from Washington has no vote in Con- gress. He wants legislation to share the fruits of the American Revolu- tion—voting representation—with Washington citizens. Anything less, he insists, is a "mockery of the democratic process."

Walter E. Fauntroy devotes himself as enthusiastically to politics as he does to preaching. He hasn't said if he'll be satisfied with a House seat, or if he'll run for the Senate, if and when the District of Columbia becomes the fifty-first state.

While Fauntroy's activities have been centered mainly in Washing- ton, the sixth black minister to serve in Congress has been influential on a wider scale. Andrew Young attracted national attention as an aide to Martin Luther King, Jr., during the struggle for civil rights in the deep South; some saw him as a possible successor to the martyred crusader.

Andrew Young (he could add a "Jr." if he wished) was born on March 12, 1932, in New Orleans, the son of Andrew Young, a dentist, and Daisy Fuller Young, a public school teacher. He prepared for the ministry at Dillard University in New Orleans, Howard University in Washington, and the Hartford (Connecticut) Theological Seminary. After receiving his bachelor of divinity degree in 1955, he was ordained by the United Church of Christ.

Young preached in Marion, Alabama, and Thomasville and Beachton, Georgia, before becoming the director of youth activities for the National Council of Churches in New York City. Inspired by King's dynamism and dedication, and eager for a chance to return South, he joined the staff of the Southern Christian Leadership Conference in Atlanta in 1961 and worked his way up to the post of executive director. Young's special talents were resolving behind-the-scenes dis- putes, setting up voter registration drives, and mapping plans for future legislation. He also walked in the freedom marches and demon- strations against segregation and discrimination.

In July 1963, after Birmingham police arrested King and a top assistant, the Reverend Ralph Abernathy, Young led the agitated demonstrators into a nearby church for prayer and new instructions. His calm and assured manner averted a possible panic. The marchers returned to the streets to confront Public Safety Commissioner Eugene (Bull) Connor and his police. Television newscasts of the demonstrators—men, women and children—being knocked to the ground by blasts of water from fire hoses and being set upon by police dogs and nightstick-swinging cops outraged millions of American viewers, who until then had not been committed to the civil rights movement.

Young credits the SCLC-sparked movement with giving black people a sense of their worth as "children of God who mean something in this society." More pragmatically, the biracial, nonviolent demonstrations by thousands of neatly dressed, well-mannered citizens created the climate for the sweeping Civil Rights Act of 1964 and the Voting Rights Act of 1965, both of which Young, as an advisor, helped to draft.

Following King's assassination in 1968, Young served as executive vice-president of SCLC. His cool head and skillful diplomacy aided in keeping the tensions at the Poor Peoples' Resurrection City encampment in Washington from exploding after it became clear that no significant action would be taken on unemployment or other grievances. He then left SCLC to return to preaching and lecturing.

SCLC's headquarters city, Atlanta, has been praised for showing that improved racial relations can be reflected in the business and cultural life of a city. Young contributed to the bustling city's vitality as chairman of the Community Relations Commission.

Atlanta's Democrats chose him in 1970 as their candidate for the Fifth Congressional District seat. Despite good publicity, he lost to the Republican incumbent, Fletcher Thompson, by 20,000 votes at a time when a GOP President was helping his party recapture much of the South.

Two years later, after redistricting made Atlanta's Fifth District 44 percent black, Thompson chose to run for the United States Senate instead of the House. Once more nominated by the Democrats, Young faced Rodney Cooke, a white Republican who had President Nixon's support. Backed by youthful white and black campaigners, Young, an attractive man with a pleasant smile, shook as many hands as possible and promised to concentrate on getting things done for Atlanta when he went to Washington.

Cooke attempted to tie him so closely to George McGovern's coattails that Young would be swept away by a Nixon landslide. Young talked issues, defended his party's Presidential nominee, called for biracial cooperation, and drew 72,200 votes to 64,400 for Cook. As the incumbent in 1974, he polled more than twice as many votes as Wyman Lowe, the Republican standard bearer.

At the outset as a member of the Banking and Currency Committee, Young concentrated on constituent services. Despite northward migration, the South still is home for millions of blacks and poor whites who feel alienated from their own conservative congressmen. Many of these people bring their problems to Young. His wife, Jean Childs Young, a public-school teacher, and their four children, live in Atlanta. Their father preaches frequently in various churches and sees them on weekends.

Georgia's black congressman appealed to Nixon to stop bombing Indochina and divert the daily cost of $3,100,000 to programs that would serve human needs and economic development. Higher minimum wages, increased social security payments, reformation of the House seniority system, and more public committee sessions were legislative advances in which Young played a role.

Young's amendment to the National Mass Transportation Assistance Act of 1974 provided for the involvement of private citizens in developing areas surrounding bus and subway stations and corridors. Funds were to be made available for neighborhood groups to join with banks in building senior citizen housing, shops, and community centers adjacent to new stations.

He split with the rest of the black caucus to vote for the confirmation of Gerald Ford as Vice President, "casting a vote of faith and hope that he will be a uniting and stabilizing force in a nation beset by division and crisis." Young cited Biblical chapter and verse to prove that a person "can overcome past parochial views and develop a broader perspective which takes into account the interests of all the people."

The representative has been caught up in the busing controversy that repolarized several big cities. He opposed the massive transport of school children in Atlanta, but he also opposed any law or constitutional amendment that would circumscribe busing as a tool of integration. Busing for racial balance, he feels, is working in many areas, including Atlanta, where there is limited implementation.

Young, who demonstrated to spur Congress to pass the Voting Rights Acts of 1965, opened debate on behalf of the Rules Committee in 1975 on the bill to extend the law another ten years and expand it to cover some language minorities. When an opponent of the measure complained that one had to live under the act to know how it felt, Young assured the congressman, "It surely feels wonderful."

Pointing out that twelve of his friends had been killed in the initial struggle to get the law enacted, he said extension was required because there were still 2,500,000 unregistered blacks. The law, he said, had created a new spirit of democratic participation and racial progress in the South and enabled it to move ahead of trouble spots like Boston and Detroit. The right to call on federal examiners, he noted, had not been abused. Supervisors had been sent in to protect minority voters in only 60 of the 553 eligible Southern counties. The mere threat of federal inspection had caused many local registrars to abide by the law and register blacks. The Senate limited the extension to seven years, but the act was renewed and expanded.

Andrew Young, whose black Georgia predecessor had been forced out of politics by prejudice and violence more than a century ago, preaches the gospel of tolerance, consideration, and common sense. "What we must do," he says, "is deracialize our problems. Blacks and whites face the same problems. What the black folks suffer today, whites will tomorrow." Most Americans, he maintains, are people of goodwill and look with hope for someone to ease the tensions.

Thirteen years junior to Andrew Young, Harold E. Ford of Tennessee, the newest black congressman, took his Memphis district away from Daniel Kuykendall, a bitter-end supporter of Richard Nixon. Calling the Republican incumbent "the worst congressman in the United States" and playing up his close association with the Watergate-plagued Chief Executive, Ford was elected in a close race in 1974.

The tall, slender, light-complexioned Democratic candidate managed to establish his own identity despite his youth and the militant image of his brother, John, a state senator. Born on May 20, 1945, in Memphis, Harold E. Ford, the ninth of Newton and Vera Ford's fifteen children, received a Bachelor of Business Administration degree at Tennessee State University in 1967, then attended graduate school briefly before leaving to specialize in mortuary science at John Gupton College. After completing this course, he managed N. J. Ford & Sons, a highly successful funeral home established by his father.

Newton Ford campaigned unsuccessfully for the state legislature in 1964. Six years later his son, who had gotten his first political experience as an aide to his father, won a seat in the Tennessee General Assembly. Harold Ford served two terms and became majority whip and chairman of a select committee formed to investigate utility firms that refused to serve poor and/or black customers.

His legislative record won him the Democratic nomination for the Eighth District by 27,000 votes over five contenders. The entire Ford clan, including brothers and sisters living in Los Angeles, Detroit, and New York, flew to Memphis to lend a hand in the general election campaign. Ford charged Kuykendall, his Republican opponent, with representing special interest groups and rubber-stamping Nixon policies while ignoring the vital human needs of a district that includes the entire city of Memphis. Ford campaigned tirelessly, talking about jobs and the spiraling cost of living and emphasizing his accomplishments in the general assembly. He warned the election commission he would guard against trickery at the polls and during the tallying of votes.

Joint appearances with his Republican rival before the Junior Chamber of Commerce disintegrated into "shouting matches." Ford agreed to meet Kuykendall in a televised debate, but Kuykendall refused. Well-publicized telephone calls to Kuykendall from the beleaguered President, who was about to leave Washington in disgrace as a result of the Watergate scandal, lessened the odds for a Republican victory.

Nonetheless, early returns from the polls convinced radio and television pundits that Kuykendall would be reelected, though Ford was at that point ahead in actual votes by his count. He and his aides hurried to the election commission office in search of a possible explanation. He waited for ninety minutes until the results from the 216 polling places were in. A routine check found that the votes from six precincts were missing.

Meanwhile, broadcast stations, analyzing returns supplied by the Junior Chamber of Commerce and Data Communications Corporation, gave Kuykendall the lead by several thousand votes. At one juncture Ford charged that the returns from the unaccounted-for six precincts had been thrown into garbage cans and discarded.

Shortly after 11 P.M. the Shelby County Election Commission declared Ford the victor by the slight edge of 744 votes. After the missing votes had been found, Ford attributed his "garbage can" outburst to fatigue, anxiety, and suspicion. "Kuykendall's bad record of not serving the human needs was what beat the man," Ford told reporters. Congratulatory calls came from Senator Robert Byrd of West Virginia and National Democratic Committee Chairman Robert Strauss—they had campaigned for him earlier. They also passed along congratulations to Ford's older brothers, John, on his election to the state senate, and Emmitt on being named to fill Harold's statehouse seat.

Harold Ford was indebted to both blacks and whites for his victory. Blacks had voted for him solidly, but without white support he would not have won. Tennessee's first black congressman called for a balanced budget, a strong national defense posture but without a blank check for the military, an end to the use of taxpayers' dollars to buy the friendship of foreign governments, and a cut in national welfare expenditures. Unpopular actions would have to be taken, he stressed, "to get the economy back in shape."

He cited spiraling unemployment, escalating interest rates, tight money, high food prices, and the rising cost of gasoline, as the key problems. He advocated price controls on the giant oil and utility monopolies. He questioned whether there had been a real shortage of gas at the time of the 1974 energy crunch.

Ford opposed massive school-busing for pupil balance but stood behind the "law of the land" as set down in the Supreme Court's ruling: The bus is an acceptable tool for integration. His assessment of the voters' most pressing dilemma: making a decent living in the face of raging inflation.

The neophyte member of the Banking, Currency and Housing, and Veterans' Affairs committees returns to Memphis to spend weekends with his wife, Dorothy Bowles Ford, and their three sons, and to attend community functions. His integrated staff set up town meetings throughout the city as a platform for the congressman to report to his constituents. He has worked for all sections of Memphis in Washington and has gone out of his way to build support among whites.

Ford is aggressive, energetic, and budget-conscious. In the spring of 1975 he introduced a limousine limitation act to cut the number of government-owned executive cars from eight hundred to twenty-seven. Taxpayers, he charged, spend $13,000,000 a year in drivers' salaries alone to chauffeur federal executives, who repay the citizens by cutting food stamp, school lunch, and social security outlays.

"Perhaps if we asked these civil servants to spend more time living like the average citizens we would find them a bit more sympathetic to the nation's needs," Ford said in introducing his bill. Cited as examples of executives in need of object lessons: a former secretary of Housing and Urban Development who had made $60,000 a year and fought for his free limousine as head of HUD, even while ordering a moratorium on new housing for the poor, and Veterans Administration officials who insisted there were funds for their fleet of cars but no monies to air-condition six VA hospitals. This suggestion makes Tennessee's new congressman sound akin to the black Populists who served in Congress after the Civil War, but Ford is also extremely practical and obviously a fast-study at political ladder climbing.

When a fellow Tennessean resigned from the House to run for mayor of Nashville in the fall of 1975, Ford, a mere freshman and one of the youngest members of Congress, was named to succeed him on the prestigious Ways and Means Committee. Ford noted proudly that his membership on the committee continued a Tennessee tradition started in the Fourth Congress by Andrew Jackson.

Harold E. Ford, Parren J. Mitchell, Walter E. Fauntroy, and Andrew Young, though Democrats, operate in Congress in a style reminiscent of their nineteenth-century Radical Republican predecessors, and they confront many of the same ingrained, albeit more subtly evidenced, racial prejudices.

The battle for access to transportation, public facilities, and the voting booth has been won, but contemporary black representatives still hear acrimonious bickering over integrated schools, open housing, and job discrimination of the sort that prompted Congressman Richard H. Cain of South Carolina to tell the House in 1874: "We do not come here begging for our rights. We come here clothed in the garb of American citizenship. We come here demanding our rights in the name of Justice."

Epilogue

The eighteen black men and women currently in Congress, speaking as they often do for the country's white and black poor, unemployed, sick, and elderly, demonstrate what might be possible in the national legislature if it were a truly accurate reflection of America's multi-faceted population.

The contemporary black representatives are no more monolithic than their white counterparts. They range from radical-progressives, as personified by Ronald V. Dellums of California, and John Conyers, Jr., of Michigan; to such liberals as Barbara Jordan of Texas, and Louis Stokes of Ohio; to moderates in the style of Charles C. Diggs, Jr., of Michigan, the senior black in the House of Representatives, and Andrew Young of Georgia, the first black elected from the deep South since the Reconstruction. While they naturally represent their own district's particular interests, including business concerns, especially when employment is at stake, they wage their most heart-felt campaigns on behalf of human needs and individual rights.

The forty-one black men and four women who have served in Congress since blacks were first allowed to participate in national government have greatly enriched America's past by their talents, personalities, ideas, and accomplishments. Collectively, their record is an inspiring example of what can be achieved despite impediments and difficulties. This was particularly true for the nineteenth-centruy congressmen, thirteen of whom were just a few years removed from slavery when they went into public life.

In 1870, when Hiram R. Revels of Mississippi became a member of the United States Senate, the country was wracked by bitterness and turmoil in the aftermath of the Civil War. Still, the outlook for the future was promising. For a few fleeting months of high, unfettered hopes, Revels had a psychological advantage over modern, sophisticated black congressmen, who know from painful experience and past history that racial progress in America often means four steps forward followed by two steps backward.

Throughout the South in the 1870's blacks held offices as aldermen, sheriffs, judges, state legislators, district attorneys, and lieutenant governors. Revels himself seemed to be living proof that the war had substantially advanced the cause of human rights. Surely the Senate's acceptance of the black Mississippian showed that the Federal Government could be relied upon to force reluctant states, South or North, to treat Negroes like other citizens. Surely the well-publicized response to Revels as a senator and an orator would clear the way for more civilized acceptance of all blacks.

Unhappily, the aspirations of the Reconstruction era were not fulfilled. Revels and the blacks who followed him into Congress never had sufficient power to prevent the nullification of the postwar civil rights statutes or the Fourteenth and Fifteenth amendments. Rarely did the early black members of Congress enjoy the mere luxury of being able to concentrate exclusively on the legislative job at hand. The simplest daily routines—traveling back and forth between their homes and Washington, or finding living accommodations in the capital—were struggles in a Jim Crow society.

Campaigning was hazardous when armed Red Shirts and Ku Kluxers patrolled the polls to defeat Negroes and white liberals in the South. Black politicians and their white colleagues were killed, and their murderers went unpunished.

Protracted election challenges in the House of Representatives drained the limited resources of men who had spent most of their lives working without pay. Elections were contested much more frequently during this period than they are today, and whites as well as blacks lost their seats, but these delaying tactics were especially damaging for men who had been elected to the lower house. The brevity of the two-year term there has frequently been criticized by political scientists on the ground that a newcomer barely gets accustomed to his duties before another election rolls around. This truism was demonstrated to the point of absurdity in the cases of some of these representatives who were literally kept out of their seats by election challenges until the next Congress was under way. Further, some duly elected blacks were never seated at all.

Even black representatives who were repeatedly reelected, such as the able, resourceful Robert Smalls of South Carolina, lacked the committee chairmanships or other power bases from which to bargain for their legislative proposals. Logically, as spokesmen for biracial constituencies that were important to the Republican party, they should have had political leverage. Nonetheless, the national Republican administration would not stand behind the Fourteenth Amendment when Revels warned that the Reconstruction would collapse in Georgia if that state was not barred from Congress until the blacks were allowed to vote and hold office without intimidation.

By 1876 it was obvious the Republicans could not retain the White House without Negro support. Yet Revels' black successor, Senator Blanche K. Bruce, and his white Republican allies were no more successful at saving the Reconstruction government in Mississippi than Revels had been in the case of Georgia, whose state government had been recaptured by white supremacists despite Revels' warnings of what this would mean for racial relations and human rights. A special Senate investigating committee concluded that terror had been used to elect Democrats to state office in 1875 and recommended that Mississippi be deprived of its congressional delegation. When neither the President nor Congress challenged the results of that election, Bruce and Representative John R. Lynch realized that their party was doomed in Mississippi. Still, the loyal black Southern Republicans helped elect Rutherford B. Hayes to the Presidency in 1876. Hayes "rewarded" them by withdrawing the last vestiges of military protection from the South, leaving the well-armed white supremacists free to carry out their announced threat to drive blacks out of public life.

All the while, black congressmen, through their speeches in Washington and at home, were compiling a chilling chronological account of the atrocities perpetrated against blacks in the United States since the Civil War. In debates Robert B. Elliott was masterly, as were Richard H. Cain, Josiah T. Walls, and James T. Rapier. Though they lacked the influence to get most of their bills passed, these early black congressmen set visionary goals for the future with their proposals for aid to education, tax relief for the war-torn South, fair treatment for Indians as well as blacks, women's suffrage, economic protection for small farmers, and anti-lynching laws.

Their philosophies varied, but not one of the legislators believed in separatism. To them, common sense dictated that blacks and whites must cooperate if the nation was to achieve its highest potential. They kept reminding the majority race that the Constitution required that each person receive "equal protection of the laws," and they demanded that the nation make good on its written promises to all its citizens.

George H. White, a brilliant lawyer whom North Carolina elected to four major offices, completed the line of nineteenth-century black congressmen. Aware that much of the South, including his own state, was disenfranchising blacks, he sat through scathing racial insults during two terms in Washington before quitting politics in 1901 to move North. Neither his debating skill nor his fresh wit had been enough to move the minds or hearts of his white colleagues in the House who seemed to take fiendish pleasure in defeating the lone black congressman's proposals, however modest and worthwhile.

Blacks made their congressional comeback in Chicago, where Ralph H. Metcalfe, a crusader for improved police services, now represents the First District, which has been in black hands since 1929. The third black to hold the seat, William L. Dawson, an old-style party politician, represented this district for nearly thirty years and used his influence—usually behind the scenes—to fight bias in government and in the military.

Just the opposite technique was employed by Adam Clayton Powell, Jr., a Dawson contemporary, who loudly blasted discrimination wherever he found it. As chairman of the House Education and Labor Committee, Powell left his personal stamp on scores of bills covering nurses' training programs, education for the handicapped, higher minimum wages, equal pay for women, and the ambitious War on Poverty programs. Two principles for which he battled aggressively for years—fair employment and a flat ban on the allocation of most federal funds to segregated activities of any sort—were embodied in the 1964 Civil Rights Act. Scrupulous adherence to those two provisions of the act would result in an overnight improvement in the racial climate of the United States because of the Federal Government's involvement as an employer, a customer, or an underwriter in so many aspects of national life.

Edward W. Brooke, the only black senator in modern times and the sole Republican among the current group of black legislators, pushed through an open housing law in 1968. This legislation covers most of the country's living facilities, but once again the results have been disappointing because of lack of compliance. In the Senate he staves off amendments that would set back school integration and weaken equal employment policies. He usually can be depended upon to oppose appointees who are insensitive to civil liberties.

Sparked by John Conyers, Jr., in the House and Brooke in the Senate, the blacks worked effectively to pressure the Senate to reject two of Richard Nixon's Supreme Court nominees because of their support of segregation. Clement F. Haynsworth, Jr., and G. Harrold Carswell were barred from the Court, but the black and white liberal opposition folded when Nixon nominated William H. Rehnquist, a man with an even more suspect record on matters of concern to minorities.

As their numbers increased in the House, the blacks in 1969 established the congressional black caucus to work on common goals with black elected officials throughout the country. Charles C. Diggs, Jr., the senior in legislative experience, served as their first chairman.

More significantly, in 1973 he became the third black to head a permanent standing committee in the House. Under his direction the District of Columbia Committee shaped a bill giving the residents of the predominantly black nation's capital the right to elect their own mayor and city council.

By then the chairmanship of the black caucus had shifted to Louis Stokes of Ohio. During two terms in the post, he expanded the use of ad hoc hearings to spotlight injustices. Charles B. Rangel of New York succeeded Stokes as chairman in 1974 and in turn was followed by Yvonne Burke of California in 1976 after his House committee assignments became more demanding.

Members of the caucus frequently vote together, as they did to cut off military aid to Turkey, hoping to keep opium out of America. They have worked to influence the State Department to evolve a more coherent, enlightened policy toward the developing countries in Africa. They push constantly for legislation to put the unemployed back to work.

However, the black caucus is too small numerically and too diversified in its membership to have any significant clout in a Congress with weak party discipline. On the national scene they must compete with a growing number of state and city black elected officials for public attention. Further, as Barbara Jordan of Texas has pointed out, the successful black members of Congress must get into the mainstream. So there is no true "leader" of the caucus.

The leading black in Congress is whoever has had the most propitious platform lately—whether it's Yvonne Burke, working to make the black caucus more effective, Barabara Jordan at the impeachment hearings, John Conyers, Jr., pushing for gun controls, or Ronald V. Dellums jousting with the director of the Central Intelligence Agency.

All the black contemporaries in the House and Senate agree that with the racial minorities ghettoized in America's inner cities, blacks should have more equitable representation in Congress. Bringing this about is one of the prime goals of the blacks who are already there.

Chronology

Name	State	Term of Office	U.S. Congress
Sen. Hiram R. Revels	Miss.	Feb. 25, 1870– Mar. 3, 1871	41st
Rep. Joseph H. Rainey	S.C.	Dec. 12, 1870– Mar. 3, 1879	41st–45th
Rep. Jefferson F. Long	Ga.	Jan. 16, 1871– Mar. 3, 1871	41st
Rep. Robert C. DeLarge	S.C.	Mar. 4, 1871– Jan. 24, 1873 [1]	42d
Rep. Robert B. Elliott	S.C.	Mar. 4, 1871– January 1873 [2] Dec. 1, 1873– Nov. 1, 1874 [3]	42d 43d
Rep. Benjamin S. Turner	Ala.	Mar. 4, 1871– Mar. 3, 1873	42d
Rep. Josiah T. Walls	Fla.	Mar. 4, 1871– Jan. 29, 1873 [1] Dec. 1, 1873– Mar. 3, 1875 Dec. 6, 1875– Apr. 19, 1876 [1]	42d 43d 44th
Rep. Richard H. Cain	S.C.	Dec. 1, 1873– Mar. 3, 1875 Oct. 15, 1877– Mar. 3, 1879	43d 45th
Rep. John R. Lynch	Miss.	Dec. 1, 1873– Mar. 3, 1877 Apr. 29, 1882– Mar. 3, 1883	43d–44th 47th

[1] Unseated by contested election
[2] Resigned exact date not in record
[3] Resigned

Name	State	Term of Office	U.S. Congress
Rep. Alonzo J. Ransier	S.C.	Dec. 1, 1873– Mar. 3, 1875	43d
Rep. James T. Rapier	Ala.	Dec. 1, 1873– Mar. 3, 1875	43d
Sen. Blanché K. Bruce	Miss.	Mar. 5, 1875– Mar. 3, 1881	44th–46th
Rep. Jeremiah Haralson	Ala.	Dec. 6, 1875– Mar. 3, 1877	44th
Rep. John A. Hyman	N.C.	Dec. 6, 1875– Mar. 3, 1877	44th
Rep. Charles E. Nash	La.	Dec. 6, 1875– Mar. 3, 1877	44th
Rep. Robert Smalls	S.C.	Dec. 6, 1875– Mar. 3, 1879	44th–45th
		July 19, 1882– Mar. 3, 1883	47th
		Mar. 31, 1884– Mar. 3, 1887	48th–49th
Rep. James E. O'Hara	N.C.	Dec. 3, 1883– Mar. 3, 1887	48th–49th
Rep. Henry P. Cheatham	N.C.	Dec. 2, 1889– Mar. 3, 1893	51st–52d
Rep. John Mercer Langston	Va.	Sept. 23, 1890– Mar. 3, 1891	51st
Rep. Thomas E. Miller	S.C.	Sept. 24, 1890– Mar. 3, 1891	51st
Rep. George W. Murray	S.C.	Aug. 7, 1893– Mar. 3, 1895	53rd
		June 4, 1896– Mar. 3, 1897	54th
Rep. George H. White	N.C.	Mar. 15, 1897– Mar. 3, 1901	55th–56th
Rep. Oscar DePriest	Ill.	Apr. 15, 1929– Jan. 2, 1935	71st–73d
Rep. Arthur W. Mitchell	Ill.	Jan. 3, 1935– Jan. 2, 1943	74th–77th
Rep. William L. Dawson	Ill.	Jan. 6, 1943– Nov. 9, 1970 [4]	78th–91st
Rep. Adam Clayton Powell, Jr.[5]	N.Y.	Jan. 3, 1945– Jan. 2, 1967	79th–89th
		Jan. 3, 1969– Jan. 2, 1971	91st
Rep. Charles C. Diggs, Jr.	Mich.	Jan. 5, 1955–	84th–
Rep. Robert N. C. Nix	Pa.	June 4, 1958–	85th–
Rep. Augustus F. Hawkins	Calif.	Jan. 9, 1963–	88th–
Rep. John Conyers, Jr.	Mich.	Jan. 4, 1965–	89th–
Sen. Edward W. Brooke	Mass.	Jan. 10, 1967–	90th–

[4] Died
[5] Also elected to 90th Congress, which refused to seat him

Name	State	Term of Office	U.S. Congress
Rep. Shirley Chisholm	N.Y.	Jan. 3, 1969–	91st–
Rep. William L. Clay	Mo.	Jan. 3, 1969–	91st–
Rep. George W. Collins	Ill.	Dec. 8, 1972[4]	91st–
Rep. Louis Stokes	Ohio	Jan. 3, 1969–	91st–
Rep. Ronald V. Dellums	Calif.	Jan. 21, 1971–	92nd–
Rep. Ralph H. Metcalfe	Ill.	Jan. 21, 1971–	92nd–
Rep. Parren J. Mitchell	Md.	Jan. 21, 1971–	92nd–
Rep. Charles B. Rangel	N.Y.	Jan. 21, 1971–	92nd–
Rep. Walter E. Fauntroy	D.C.	April 19, 1971 [6]	92nd–
Rep. Yvonne B. Burke	Calif.	Jan. 3, 1973–	93rd–
Rep. Candiss Collins	Ill.	June 5, 1973–	93rd–
Rep. Barbara Jordan	Tex.	Jan. 3, 1973–	93rd–
Rep. Andrew Young	Ga.	Jan. 3, 1973–	93rd–
Rep. Harold E. Ford	Tenn.	Jan. 3, 1975–	94th–

[6] Nonvoting representative

Bibliography

Ames, Blanche Ames, *Adelbert Ames, 1825–1933*, New York, Argosy-Antiquarian, Ltd., 1964.

Aptheker, Herbert [ed.], *A Documentary History of the Negro People in the United States*, Volume II, New York, The Citadel Press, 1968.

——, *Nat Turner's Slave Rebellion*, New York, Grove Press, Inc., 1968.

——, *To Be Free*, New York, International Publishers Co., 1968.

Barnes, William Horatio, *History of Congress: The Forty-first Congress of the United States 1869–71*, New York, Washington, W. H. Barnes & Co., 1872.

——, *The American Government*, Volume I, New York, Nelson & Phillips, 1873.

——, *The American Government: Biographies of Members of the House of Representatives of the Forty-third Congress*, Volumes II, III, New York, Nelson & Phillips, 1874.

——, *The Forty-second Congress of the United States 1871–73*, Volumes I, II, Washington, W. H. Barnes & Co., 1872.

Bennett, Lerone, Jr., *Before the Mayflower: A History of the Negro in America 1619–1964*, Baltimore, Penguin Books, 1968.

——, *Black Power U.S.A.—The Human Side of Reconstruction, 1967–77*, Chicago, Johnson Publishing Company, Inc., 1967.

Billington, Ray Allen [ed.], *The Journal of Charlotte Forten: A Free Negro in the Slave Era*, New York, Collier Books, 1967.

Blaine, James G., *Twenty Years of Congress*, Volumes I, II, Norwich, Connecticut, The Henry Bill Publishing Company, 1884, 1886.

Blaustein, Albert P., and Zangrando, Robert L., *Civil Rights and the American Negro*, New York, Washington Square Press, 1968.

Bowers, Claude G., *The Tragic Era*, Boston, Houghton Mifflin Company, 1962.

Brawley, Benjamin, *A Social History of the American Negro*, New York, Macmillan Company, 1921; New York, London, Johnson Reprint Corporation, 1968.

——, *Negro Builders and Heroes*, Chapel Hill, North Carolina, University of North Carolina Press, 1937.

Brooke, Edward W., *The Challenge of Change: Crisis in Our Two-Party System*, Boston, Toronto, Little, Brown & Co., 1966.

Bryant, Dr. Lawrence C. [ed.], *Negro Lawmakers in the South Carolina Legislature 1868–1902*, Orangeburg, South Carolina, School of Graduate Studies, South Carolina State College, 1968.

———[ed.], *Negro Legislators in South Carolina 1868–1902,* Orangeburg, South Carolina, School of Graduate Studies, South Carolina State College, 1967.

Chamberlin, Hope, *A Minority of Members—Women in the U.S. Congress,* New York, Praeger Publishers, 1973.

Chapman, Gil & Ann, *Adam Clayton Powell: Saint or Sinner?* San Diego, California, Publishers Export Co., 1967.

Chisholm, Shirley, *Unbought and Unbossed,* Boston, Houghton Mifflin Company, 1970.

Clayton, Edward T., *The Negro Politician,* Chicago, Johnson Publishing Company, 1964.

Congressional Index, Ninety-first Congress, New York, Chicago, Washington, Commerce Clearing House Inc. 1969–1970.

Congressional Quarterly Almanac, Washington, Congressional Quarterly Inc., 1945–1974.

Congressional Quarterly Weekly Report, Washington, Congressional Quarterly Inc., 1960–1976.

Cowley, Charles, *The Romance of History in "The Black County" and the Romance of War in the Career of General Robert Smalls,* Lowell, Massachusetts, published by author, 1882.

Cromwell, John W., *The Negro in American History,* Washington, The American Negro Academy, 1914; New York, Johnson Reprint Corporation, 1968.

Daniels, Josephus, *Editor in Politics,* Chapel Hill, North Carolina, University of North Carolina Press, 1941.

Dann, Martin E. [ed.], *The Black Press (1827–1890),* New York, G. P. Putnam's Sons, 1971.

Dictionary of American Biography, New York, Charles Scribner's Sons, 1928.

Dionisopoulos, P. A., *Rebellion, Racism, and Representation—The Adam Clayton Powell Case and Its Antecedents,* Dekalb, Illinois, Northern Illinois University Press, 1970.

Du Bois, W. E. Burghardt, *Black Reconstruction in America,* Cleveland, New York, World Publishing Company, 1964.

Elmore, Joseph Elliot, *North Carolina Negro Congressmen, 1875–1901,* Chapel Hill, North Carolina, University of North Carolina [thesis], 1964.

Franklin, John Hope, *From Slavery to Freedom: A History of Negro Americans,* New York, Vintage Books, 1969.

———, *Reconstruction After the Civil War,* Chicago, London, University of Chicago Press, 1961.

Fulks, Bryan, *Black Struggle—A History of the Negro in America,* New York, Delacorte Press, 1969.

Garner, James Wilford, *Reconstruction in Mississippi,* Baton Rouge, Louisiana, Louisiana State University Press, 1968.

Greenberg, Jack, *Race Relations and American Law,* New York, Columbia University Press, 1959.

Hamilton, J. G. de Roulhac, *Reconstruction in North Carolina,* Gloucester, Massachusetts, Peter Smith, 1964.

Hickey, Neil, and Edwin, Ed, *Adam Clayton Powell and the Politics of*

Race, New York, Fleet Publishing Corporation, 1965.

Hinds, Asher C., *Hinds' Precedents of the House of Representatives of the United States*, Volume II, Washington, Government Printing Office, 1907.

Hughes, Langston, and Meltzer, Milton, *A Pictorial History of the Negro in America*, New York, Crown Publishers Inc., 1956.

Langston, John Mercer, *From the Virginia Plantation to the National Capitol*, Hartford, Connecticut, American Publishing Company, 1894; New York, London, Johnson Reprint Corporation, 1968.

Lawson, Elizabeth, *The Gentleman from Mississippi: Our First Negro Senator, Hiram R. Revels*, New York, published by author, 1960.

Lewis, Claude, *Adam Clayton Powell*, New York, Fawcett Publications Inc., 1964.

Lincoln, C. Eric, *The Negro Pilgrimage in America*, New York, Toronto, London, Bantam Books, 1967.

Logan, Rayford W., *Howard University: The First One Hundred Years, 1867–1967*, New York, New York University Press, 1967.

Lonn, Ella, *Reconstruction in Louisiana After 1868*, Gloucester, Massachusetts, Peter Smith, 1967.

Lynch, John R., *The Facts of Reconstruction*, New York, Neale Publishing Company, 1913.

——, *Some Historical Errors of James Ford Rhodes*, Boston, New York, The Cornhill Publishing Company, 1922.

McPherson, James M., *The Negro's Civil War*, New York, Vintage Books, 1967.

Meltzer, Milton [ed.], *In Their Own Words*, New York, Thomas Y. Crowell Company, 1964.

Metcalf, George R., *Black Profiles*, New York, McGraw-Hill Book Company, 1970.

Morton, Richard Lee, *The Negro in Virginia Politics*, Charlottesville, University of Virginia, 1919.

Muelder, Hermann R., *Fighters for Freedom*, New York, Columbia University Press, 1959.

National Cyclopaedia of American Biography, New York, James T. White & Company, 1892.

Nordholt, J. W. Schulte, *The People That Walk in Darkness*, New York, Ballantine Books, 1960.

Oberholtzer, Ellis Paxson, *A History of the United States since the Civil War*, Volume II, New York, Macmillan, 1922.

Owen, Thomas McAdory, *History of Alabama and Dictionary of Alabama Biography*, Chicago, The S. J. Clarke Publishing Company, 1921.

Patrick, Rembert W., *The Reconstruction of the Nation*, New York, Oxford University Press, 1967.

Pearson, Drew, and Anderson, Jack, *The Case Against Congress*, New York, Pocket Books, 1969.

Pike, James S., *The Prostrate State: South Carolina Under Negro Government*, New York, D. Appleton & Company, 1874.

Ploski, Harry A. and Brown, Roscoe C., Jr. [eds.], *The Negro Almanac*, New York, Bellwether Publishing Company, 1967.

Powell, Adam Clayton, Jr., *Adam by Adam*, New York, The Dial Press, 1971.

——, *Keep the Faith Baby!* New York, Trident Press, 1967.

——, *Marching Blacks*, New York, Dial Press, 1945.

Quarles, Benjamin, *The Negro in the Making of America*, New York, Collier Books, 1968.

Ralph Nader Congress Project—Citizens Look at Congress, Washington, Grossman Publishers, 1972.

Reynolds, John S., *Reconstruction in South Carolina, 1865–1877*, Columbia, South Carolina, The State Co., 1905.

Rhodes, James Ford, *History of the United States from the Compromise of 1850 to the Final Restoration of Home Rule at the South in 1877*, Volume VI, New York, Macmillan Company, 1906.

Richardson, Joe M., *The Negro in the Reconstruction of Florida, 1865–77*, Tallahassee, Florida, Florida State University Studies [thesis], 1964.

Rose, Willie Lee, *Rehearsal for Reconstruction*, New York, Vintage Books, 1967.

Schlesinger, Arthur M., Jr., *A Thousand Days: John F. Kennedy in the White House*, Boston, Houghton Mifflin Company, 1965.

Shenton, James P., ed. with an introduction by, *The Reconstruction, A Documentary History of the South After the War: 1865–1877*, New York, G. P. Putnam's Sons, 1963.

Simkins, Francis Butler, *The South Old and New*, New York, Alfred A. Knopf, 1951.

—— and Woody, Robert Hilliard, *South Carolina During Reconstruction*, Chapel Hill, North Carolina, University of North Carolina Press, 1932.

Simmons, William J., *Men of Mark*, Cleveland, Rewell Publishing Company, 1891.

Smith, Arthur J., *The Negro in the Political Classics of the American Government*, Washington, published by author, 1937.

Smith, Samuel Denny, *The Negro in Congress, 1870–1901*, Port Washington, New York, Kennikat Press, 1966, reprint.

Sorensen, Theodore C., *Kennedy*, New York, Harper & Row, 1965.

Stampp, Kenneth M., *The Era of Reconstruction 1865–1877*, New York, Vintage Books, 1967.

Steinberg, Alfred, *Sam Johnson's Boy*, New York, Macmillan Company, 1968.

Sterling, Dorothy, *Captain of the Planter*, Garden City, New York, Doubleday & Company, 1958.

Sterling, Philip, and Logan, Rayford, *Four Took Freedom*, Garden City, New York, Doubleday & Company, 1967.

Storey, Moorfield, *Charles Sumner*, New York, Russell & Russell, 1970.

Taylor, Alrutheus Ambush, *The Negro in South Carolina During the Reconstruction*, Washington, D. C., The Association for the Study of Negro Life and History, 1924.

——, *The Negro in the Reconstruction of Virginia*, Washington, The Association for the Study of Negro Life and History, 1926.

Tindall, George Brown, *South Carolina Negroes 1877–1900*, Columbia, South Carolina, University of South Carolina Press, 1952.

United States Congress, *Biographical Directory of the American Congress*, Washington, United States Government Printing Office, 1961.

——, *Congressional Directory*, Forty-first through Ninety-fourth Congress, Washington, United States Government Printing Office, 1869–1975.

————, *Congressional Globe*, Forty-first and Forty-second Congresses, Washington, Office of Congressional Globe, 1869–1873.

————, *Congressional Record*, Washington, United States Government Printing Office, 1873–1976.

Welles, Gideon, *The Diary of Gideon Welles*, Volumes I, II, Boston and New York, Houghton Mifflin Company, 1911.

Wheeler, Gerald E., *Hiram Rhoades Revels: Negro Educator and Statesman*, Berkeley, California, University of California [thesis], 1949.

Williams, Alfred B., *Hampton and His Red Shirts*, Charleston, South Carolina, Walker, Evans & Cogswell Company, 1935.

Woodson, Carter G., *The Negro in Our History*, Washington, The Associated Publishers Inc., 1922.

Wright, Nathan, Jr. [ed.], *What Black Politicians Are Saying*, New York, Hawthorn Books, Inc., 1972.

Index

Index